The Puritan Ideology of Mobility

The Puritan Ideology of Mobility

Corporatism, the Politics of Place and the Founding of New England Towns before 1650

Scott McDermott

ANTHEM PRESS

Anthem Press
An imprint of Wimbledon Publishing Company
www.anthempress.com

This edition first published in UK and USA 2025
by ANTHEM PRESS
75–76 Blackfriars Road, London SE1 8HA, UK
or PO Box 9779, London SW19 7ZG, UK
and
244 Madison Ave #116, New York, NY 10016, USA

First published in the UK and USA by Anthem Press in 2022

Copyright © Scott McDermott 2025

The author asserts the moral right to be identified as the author of this work.

All rights reserved. Without limiting the rights under copyright reserved above, no part of this publication may be reproduced, stored or introduced into a retrieval system, or transmitted, in any form or by any means (electronic, mechanical, photocopying, recording or otherwise), without the prior written permission of both the copyright owner and the above publisher of this book.

British Library Cataloguing-in-Publication Data
A catalogue record for this book is available from the British Library.

Library of Congress Control Number: 2024943621

ISBN-13: 978-1-83999-376-3 (Pbk)
ISBN-10: 1-83999-376-6 (Pbk)

Cover Image: Cookmaid with Still Life of Vegetables and Fruit, c.1620–5 by Sir Nathaniel Bacon 1585–1627, Photo by Tate Gallery, London

This title is also available as an e-book.

For
Prof. Michal Jan Rozbicki
(1946–2019)
Mentor and friend

"goe whare you will, god he will find you out."
—the mother of John Dane of Ipswich to her son[1]

---

1. John Dane, *A Declaration of Remarkable Providences in the Course of My Life* (Boston, MA: Samuel G. Drake, 1854), 8, in Google Books.

CONTENTS

List of Figures   ix

Preface: Protestant Scholasticism and Puritan Ideology   xi

Acknowledgments   xxiii

A Note on Dates   xxv

Chapter One   Puritans and Society in the Stour Valley   1

Chapter Two   The Puritan Ideology of Mobility   33

Chapter Three   Land Distribution in Colonial Ipswich   53

Chapter Four   Town-Founding in Essex County: The Communities around Ipswich   79

Epilogue: The Future of Corporatism and the Ideology of Mobility in America   97

Notes   105

Works Cited   149

Index   175

FIGURES

1	Ramist table from John Yates, *Modell of Divinitie* (1622)	xiv
2	John Rogers of Dedham	15
3	Richard Rogers	16
4	Frontispiece to Francis Bacon, *Instauratio Magna*, 1620 edition	43
5	Detail of 1637 Petition to the Governor and Council of Massachusetts	56
6	Deed of farm called Argilla in Ipswich from John Winthrop Jr., to Samuel Symonds, Februrary 8, 1637/38	56
7	Section of letter from Samuel Symonds to John Winthrop Jr., 1647	69
8	Boundaries of Essex County towns in 1643, when Haverhill became part of Norfolk County	83
9	Detail of Plan of Rowley surveyed by Joseph Chapin	85
10	Nathaniel Ward's "spirit and people" letter to John Winthrop Jr., 1635	90
11	Part of the chart listing each householder's proportional share of Haverhill's second division of "plow land" in 1652	95

PREFACE
Protestant Scholasticism and Puritan Ideology

"So, what possible relevance do you think the Puritans could really have for today's student?"

I instantly knew I was not going to get the job at the major Catholic, Jesuit university my interviewer represented. I don't know why I was so taken aback. As David D. Hall put it, "Too many people in the United States have come under the sway of Arthur Miller's *The Crucible* and Nathaniel Hawthorne's *The Scarlet Letter*," and that includes academics.[1] Nor was this scholar the first whose supposedly brash, iconoclastic, plain-spoken attitude barely concealed the various ideologies which captivate contemporary academia.

I'm grateful in hindsight, however, that this attack surfaced so that I knew in future encounters to address the issue, even when more polite scholars let it remain unspoken. On this particular occasion I tried to make a joke of it, stammering something about how John Winthrop's flagship in the 1630 Great Migration, the *Arbella*, carried 3,500 gallons of water and 10,000 gallons of beer.[2] In a more recent interview, I brought up the question myself, asking how anyone could question whether the Puritans, with their mania for social regulation, would appeal to students in the era of Bernie Sanders.

Teachers must be "presentist" to some extent, trying to relate past events to contemporary issues, but I hope in this work of scholarship I can bypass our current ideologies as I try to explain why Puritan ideology interests me. The original research question that took me to graduate school has not changed: how did medieval political ideas, including natural law, natural rights, popular sovereignty, corporatism (the image of society as a body politic), the Aristotelian concept of natural sociability, the right of resistance and moral economy, as well as the primacy of the common good ("general welfare") in politics, find their way into American political culture? The largely unspoken, unexamined consensus of mainstream academics has been that they arrived by way of Enlightenment thinkers, but these notions seemed to me too deeply ingrained in American life to have appeared so late in the formation of colonial communities. I had already been exploring Catholic vectors of influence on the founding of the United States, especially Charles Carroll of Carrollton, the only Catholic signer of the Declaration of Independence, but I found few additional leads.

Then I took a course on Britain under the early Stuarts and came across John Neville Figgis's comment, in *The Divine Right of Kings*, that "the Presbyterian and the

Papal theories of politics have common elements." That led me to King James I's famous remark, "Jesuits are nothing but Puritan–Papists."[3]

So I began to wonder whether the New England Puritans might somehow have transported these originally Catholic political precepts across the Atlantic, perhaps stowed away in the hold along with the beer, since of course the Puritans would never have acknowledged their debt to medieval scholasticism. I soon became aware of the tradition of Protestant scholasticism in the Reformed universities of Britain, especially Cambridge, and on the continent during the early modern period.

Needless to say, the theology curriculum in Protestant universities changed drastically after the Reformation, but theology was an exclusively graduate course that began only after the aspirant to a bachelor of divinity (DB) degree had already taken both his BA and his MA. The course of study for the latter two degrees—the arts curriculum—rested throughout the seventeenth century on the medieval *trivium* (grammar, rhetoric and logic), the *quadrivium* (arithmetic, geometry, music and astronomy), and the "three philosophies" (ethics or moral philosophy, metaphysics and natural philosophy).[4] DB degrees were rare and the degree was not required for ordination; the doctor of divinity (DD) degree was bestowed even less frequently and seems to have functioned as a "lifetime achievement" award for noted theologians. The vast majority of Puritan ministers and parish lecturers entered their calling equipped only with one or both of the arts degrees; they were formed by the arts curriculum, in the great tradition of the medieval university. As William T. Costello put it, "By 1600, of course, the Reformation was a fact in England, but the trouble between the London court and the Pope [...] seemed not to disturb the philosophical and literary traditions which lay outside the fields of dogma and canon law."[5] Politics were studied under the rubric of moral philosophy or ethics.

As my research progressed, I became increasingly convinced that Protestant scholasticism provided one "missing link" between medieval thought and American political culture, and I explored this connection in a published article and in my dissertation.[6] However, this approach seems to conflict with a significant body of scholarship that has emphasized the influence of the new humanistic learning on English political thought during the early modern period.[7] A debate has ensued as to whether the reformed English universities were predominantly "scholastic" or "humanistic." Costello found in favor of scholasticism, not only in logic but also in ethics, which was "perhaps, the most carefully prepared dish in the curriculum, whether as served up by such Catholic commentators as Victoria, Lessius, De Lugo, Suarez and Dominicus Soto, or such Protestant Aristotelians as Melanchthon or Grotius."[8] Emphasizing the humanism of the universities, however, Margo Todd condemned Costello's "notion that Aristotelian logic is inherently a scholastic enterprise" as "absurd."[9] More recently, scholars have played down the contradiction between scholasticism and humanism. In his history of the Reformation, Diarmaid MacCulloch pointed out that humanists did not know they were practicing humanism, since the term was not coined until the early nineteenth century. Presumably humanists would have just seen themselves as academics; "far from being 'New Learning,'" MacCulloch writes, humanism "represented a refocusing of old learning." Humanists gave new importance to fields like rhetoric, as well as history and ethics, while emphasizing literacy in Greek; but this did not, of course, necessarily mean the banishment of the Aristotelian scholasticism pioneered by Thomas Aquinas. In the political field, many humanist ideas had deep roots in medieval scholarship.[10]

Turning to the curriculum of the Reformed British university for insight, we find that few documents remain from the early modern period that shed light on what tutors actually taught their students. Fortunately for our purposes, the most important surviving evidence comes from Emmanuel College, the alma mater of Nathaniel Ward (author of Massachusetts' first law code, the 1641 Body of Liberties) and of several other leaders who will be considered in this book. Emmanuel was staunchly Puritan, as a 1603 document concerning "The publick disorders as touching Church Causes in Emmanuell Colledge in Cambridge" attested. "In Eman: Coll:," the author complained, "they receive the Holy Sacrament, sittinge upon Forms about the Communion Table, & doe pull the Loafe one from the other, after the Minister hath begon. And soe the Cupp, one drinking as it were to another, like Good Fellows."[11]

Like many Tudor gentlemen, sixteenth-century academic foundations often profited from the destruction of the religious orders in England, and Emmanuel College was no exception. Sir Walter Mildmay, who served as chancellor of the Exchequer under Elizabeth, bought the old Dominican friary in Cambridge as the nucleus for Emmanuel in 1583.[12] The first Master of Emmanuel was Laurence Chaderton, an ex-Catholic and fellow of Christ's College where he tutored the great Puritan scholar William Perkins.[13]

Under Chaderton, according to a recent history of Emmanuel College, the structure of the curriculum "remained formally scholastic, and the systematic ordering of knowledge invented by Aristotle still reigned supreme."[14] In 1588, the Master and fellows of Emmanuel adopted a series of orders that summed up the experiences of four years of successful operation. The Orders extended to matters great, like the provision for a regular "conference" for the sharing of faith and spiritual insight among the student body, and small, such as the bounty of twopence offered to anyone who caught another student "making water" in an inappropriate place. They provided that in order to prepare for lectures, the students should have read through "Ramus Logick Aristotles Organon Ethicks Politiques and Physiques: and if they can or will they may read Phrigius his naturall Philosophie."[15]

Clearly, the study of Aristotle was alive and well at Emmanuel's "nursery of Puritanism," with not only his *Organon*, the medieval compendium of Aristotelian logic, as required reading, but also the *Nicomachean Ethics* and *Politics* in moral philosophy. Apparently, however, the new logic of Petrus Ramus (1515–1572) also received favor at Emmanuel. To what extent did Ramism vitiate the dominance of Aristotelianism in the college? Ramus, a French Huguenot murdered in the St. Bartholomew's Day Massacre, replaced medieval scientific logic with a merely probable logic based on the categories of "invention" and "disposition" imported from rhetoric. Walter Ong argued that whereas medieval scholasticism had sought truth through oral, Socratic dialogue, Ramus's method of finding truth was essentially didactic. "Inventing" or discovering the truth meant locating it spatially within the schema of all known truths, categorizing it in relation to other truths. Ong linked this spatializing of truth to the onset of printing.[16] An unmistakable sign of Ramist influence on a text is the presence of a table like the one John Yates used to distribute and classify the fundamentals of Christian faith in his 1622 *Modell of Divinitie* (Figure 1).

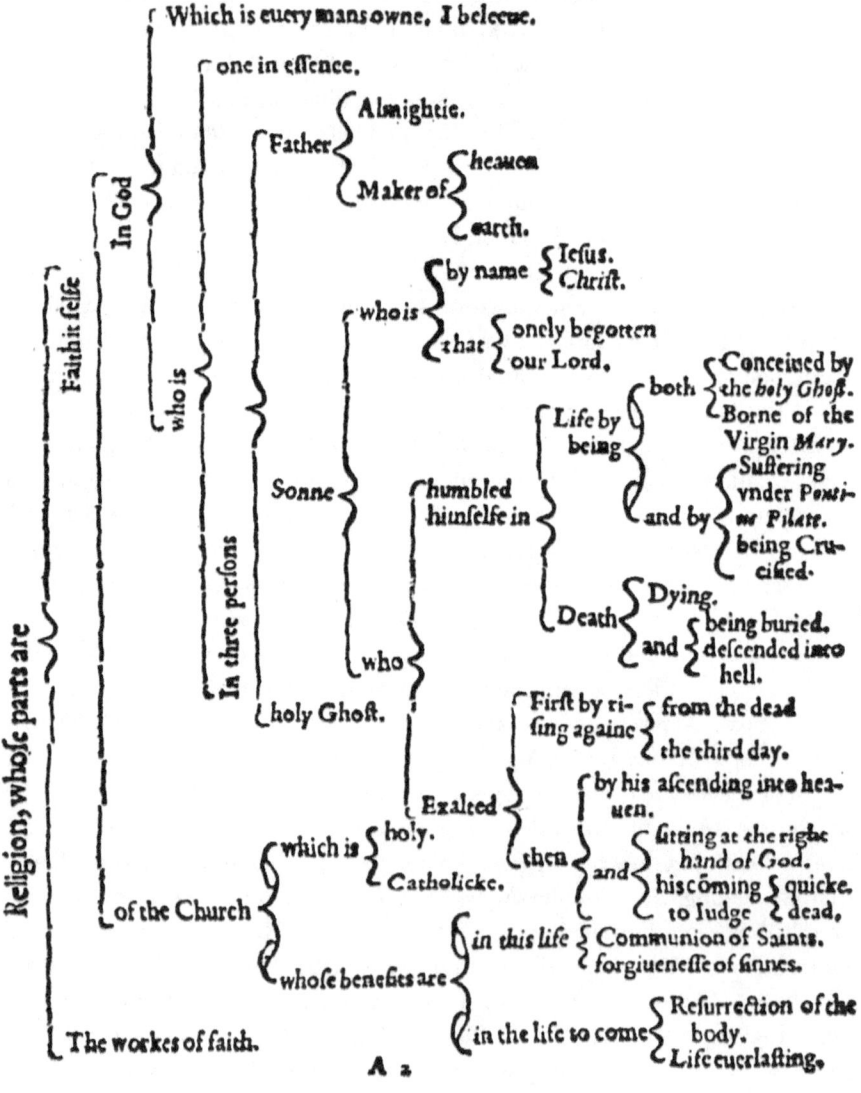

Figure 1 Ramist table from John Yates, *Modell of Divinitie* (1622)

PREFACE   xv

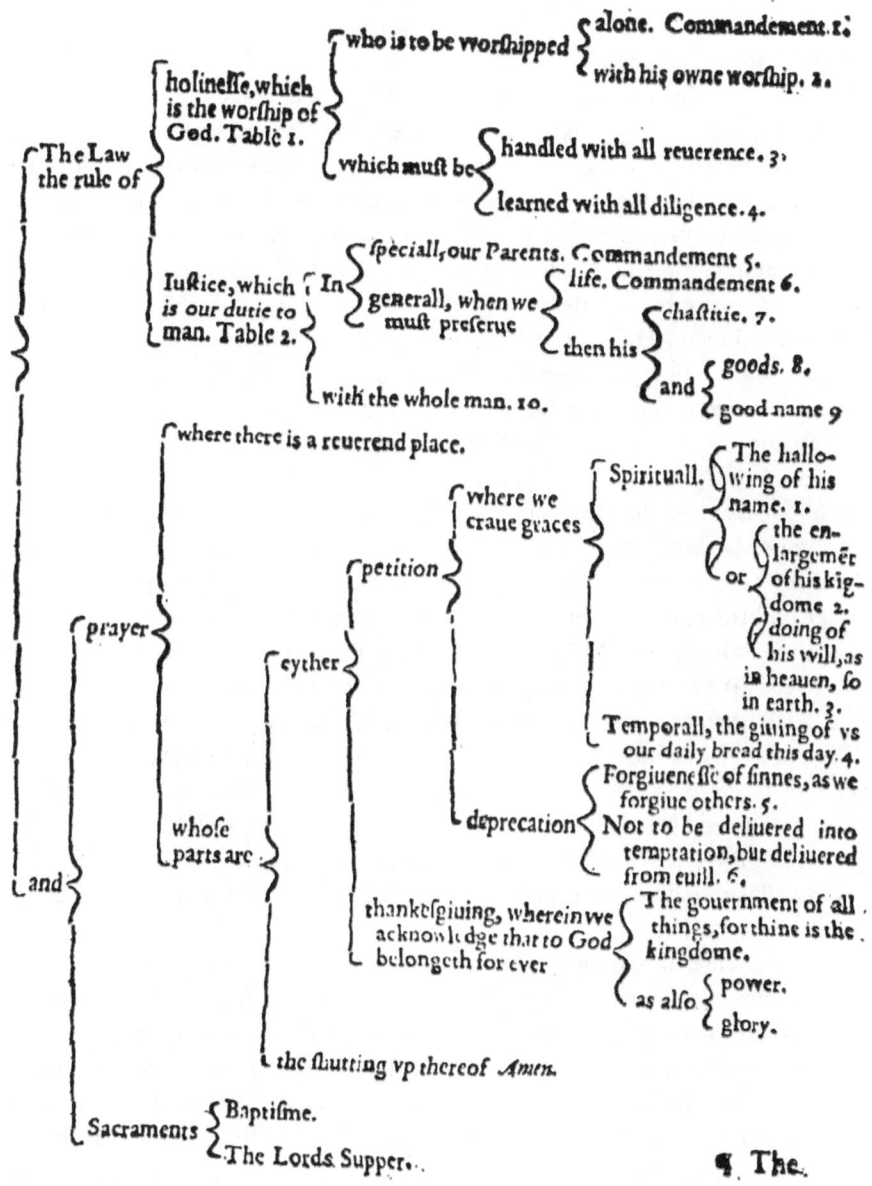

Figure 1 (continued)

Yates was a Puritan minister in Norfolk who, along with Nathaniel Ward, helped stir up a 1624 controversy in Parliament over the writings of the Laudian Richard Montagu.[17]

Ramism undoubtedly influenced Emmanuel College, the founders of New England, and Puritan academia in general. It offered a useful, concise schematization of all knowledge especially suited for pedagogy at the lower levels. However, Calvinist academics never replaced Aristotelian logic with Ramist teaching, because to do so would have put them at a fatal disadvantage in controversy with Catholic thinkers. As Howard Hotson has put it, "Ramus offered a cheap, effective and extremely versatile basic tool for solving practical domestic problems; Aristotle on the other hand offered an expensive, high-technology weapon for international theological warfare."[18] Thus, Calvinist scholars such as Perkins and Johann Heinrich Alsted often adopted an exciting Ramist package for their work, while retaining an essentially Aristotelian content.[19] The Emmanuel Book of Orders, which included Ramism in the curriculum while giving preference to Aristotle, attested to the hybridization of Ramist and Aristotelian approaches in the English universities.

Yet this provision of the Orders only applied to lectures. What can be said of the content of tutorials at Emmanuel? The little we know is contained in the pages of Richard Holdsworth's "Directions for a Student in the Universitie." Holdsworth entered St. John's College, Cambridge, in 1607; he took his BA, MA, and DB degrees there and became a fellow of St. John's from 1613 to 1623. He later served as Master of Emmanuel from 1637 to 1643.[20] We do not know when Holdsworth wrote his "Directions." The surviving copy includes a reference to a book published in 1647, but Holdsworth left Emmanuel in 1643. Thus the "Directions" may relate to Holdsworth's tenure as Master of Emmanuel, or, as seems more likely, they may have been written during his period as a St. John's fellow and redacted later by someone else.[21] In either case, since Holdsworth's pedagogical approach proved agreeable enough to the fellows of Emmanuel that they elected him Master, the "Directions" give us at least some idea of what Emmanuel tutors imparted to their students.

Holdsworth's teaching program had one foot firmly in the medieval scholastic past, while at the same time catering to the desire of an increasingly genteel student body for humanistic studies like rhetoric and history. His approach was fairly simple: mornings were devoted primarily to logic, with a lesser component of ethics, and a smattering of natural philosophy. In logic, Holdsworth was not averse to assigning Ramus or semi-Ramists like Bartholomaus Keckermann (ca. 1571–ca. 1609) and Molineus (Pierre du Moulin, 1568–1658). However, he insisted on supplementing these with the thoroughly Aristotelian survey of Burgersdicius (Franco Burgersdijk, 1590–1635), which Holdsworth said "contains a more perfect, & usefull Log[ic]: than most doe: it aqu[ain]ts yo[u] with Aristotles termes. […] It hath w[ha]t:ever is deficient in Molinus, Kekerman, Rhamus, &c."[22] We find partial confirmation that Holdsworth already employed his method while at St. John's in the autobiography of Sir Simonds d'Ewes, a Suffolk baronet who had Holdsworth as his tutor during his studies at St. John's between 1618 and 1620. D'Ewes remembered reading through Keckermann's and Molineus's logic with Holdsworth, along with the 1545 *Dialectica* of John Seton, a pre-Ramist but humanistically inspired text.[23] D'Ewes also recalled reading the work of the second-century writer Aulus Gellius and of Alessandro Piccolomini (1508–1578), a prolific Catholic commentator on Aristotle, for moral philosophy.[24] This does not match Holdsworth's recommendations for ethics in the "Directions," which included the Aristotelian commentators Bernard Morisan, Eustachius a Sancto Paulo (another Catholic) and Burgersdijk. Nevertheless, it is clear that these morning philosophical studies—in ethics even more than in logic—had an Aristotelian bent. As Holdsworth commented, "The reading of Aristotle, will […] crown all your other learning, for he can hardly deserve the name of a Scholar, that is not in some measure acquainted with his works."[25]

Afternoons, however, Holdsworth devoted to "the Greek & Latine toungs History Oratory, & Poetry." He explained that without these more humanistic pursuits, "all the other Learning though never so eminent, is in a manner voide & useless, without those you will be bafeld in your disputes, disgraced, & vilified in Publicke examinations, laught at in speeches, & Declamations. You will never dare to appear in any act of credit in the University, nor must you look for Preferment by your Learning only."[26] In other words, classical and humanistic studies were necessary for success not only within the scholastic framework of the university, with its numerous oral disputations and public exercises, but also in one's career after taking a degree. The classical authors whom Holdsworth assigned—with Cicero given pride of place, but also including Demosthenes, Livy, Terence, Vergil, Homer and Seneca—were those with which an educated public man needed to be familiar in order to impress his audience.[27]

Nathaniel Ward's later works, written after his return to old England from Ipswich, Massachusetts, in 1646, suggest that some such program of study was already in place at Emmanuel by the later years of Elizabeth I (he took his BA in 1600 and his MA in 1603).[28] In his published 1647 sermon, *A Religious Retreat Sounded to a Religious Army*, Ward managed to cite at least eight different works of Cicero—in the original Latin, though somewhat erroneously, suggesting he was quoting from memory—as well as texts by Tacitus, Terence, and Quintus Curtius Rufus.[29] Most of these dealt with political subjects, indicating the usefulness of the humanistic side of the curriculum in supplementing the political studies that took place under the rubric of moral philosophy. In a 1647 fast-day sermon before the House of Commons, Ward claimed, "If my observation and memory misuse me not, I thinke I might give you Presidents from Classicall Authors of 66. Empires, Kingdoms, Dukedoms, and Provinces" which had suffered from political anarchy or tyranny.[30] Ward's confidence in his classical erudition was most likely founded on his humanistic studies at Emmanuel.

On the other hand, if we define scholasticism as the use of certain logical tools, like the syllogism, combined with medieval academic practices like public disputations, we can say that Cambridge in the early seventeenth century was still recognizably scholastic. Simonds d'Ewes, for example, noted that he attained knowledge "by the ear as well as by the eye, by being present at the public commencements […] at problems, sophisms, declamations, and other scholastical exercises."[31] The enduring elements of medieval scholasticism in the Reformed universities seem to contradict the anti-Catholic disclaimers which Protestant scholastics typically added to their works, but in fact they made such ritualized anti-Catholicism even more necessary as scholars sought to employ originally Catholic methods without damaging their Reformed credentials.

But rather than reopening a fruitless debate about the predominance of scholasticism or humanism in the early modern university, let us consider what this evidence suggests about the Puritan leadership formed at Emmanuel and the attitudes they brought to the project of founding settlements in the New World. Protestant scholastics were neither pragmatists nor utilitarians, yet—like Puritan ministers who typically included a section on the "use" or application of their doctrine in every sermon—they prized ideas partly for their usefulness and practical benefits. For example, Johann Heinrich Alsted, who taught at the Reformed High School of Herborn in the County of Nassau–Dillenberg, said that schools should perform "a function which is not only theoretical, but practical also." Alsted emphasized the relationship of pedagogy, as "a separate practical discipline," to the state; it was the duty of the magistrate "to found and guard the school." Alsted would later be praised by Cotton Mather and widely read at Harvard College during the seventeenth century.[32]

Puritan intellectuals were practical because they were primarily interested in hastening the onset of the Kingdom of God. Every human construct and adherence was secondary to this goal, so English Reformed leaders happily borrowed ideas and inspirations from whatever traditions lay to hand—including scholasticism, Ramism, Ciceronian humanism, common law, civil law, the *prisca theologia* (the notion that traces of God's law were handed down by the descendants of Noah and could thus be found in all cultures), even alchemy and Baconian experimentalism—anything that could be made consistent with their theological beliefs and that would help promote their spiritual and social goals. Then, too, we should remember that these "isms" are scholarly constructs which in reality were never hermetically sealed from each other. Ernst Kantorowicz's seminal work on corporatism shows how the concept developed while being batted back and forth like a shuttlecock among theologians, logicians, encyclopedists, legal scholars, popes, rulers and other politicians.[33]

During the early modern period the demographics of the English universities changed, as numerous gentlemen's sons with no intention of taking holy orders began flocking into Oxford and Cambridge, giving rise to the tutorial system and an increasingly complicated pecking order among students. Puritan academics like John Preston, who made a career out of teaching the wealthiest and best-born of this newly gentrified student body, welcomed this development—which was especially pronounced at Emmanuel College—because it gave them an opportunity to influence the next generation of magistrates to support godly goals.[34] Thus, while retaining the Aristotelian approach to logic so necessary for theological education and controversy, Emmanuel and other Cambridge colleges like St. John's introduced studies meant to appeal to men destined for legal and political pursuits. These were predominantly humanistic, but not exclusively so: moral philosophy as a scholastic discipline became more prominent because of the increased gentry presence in the universities.[35] Emmanuel College intended to promote a "close alliance of 'magistracy and ministry,'" according to its most recent historians, and its integration of scholastic and humanistic pedagogies was designed to do just that.[36]

Besides the objection based on the supposed prevalence of humanism, there are other reasons why scholars object at times to an emphasis on Protestant scholasticism. Some historians, who have fought long and hard to establish the "new religious history" and make this field of inquiry respectable again in American history departments, see any interest in scholasticism as a way to denature Puritan studies and deny their distinctively

Reformed theological content. I have no interest in pursuing such a project. I want to do justice to the Puritan ideology, meaning the way that both Reformed theology and Protestant scholarship informed political thought and action in old and New England, and how the ideology was in turn modified by developments "on the ground" during the New England experiment. I am employing Karl Mannheim's "non-evaluative general total conception of ideology":

> This approach confines itself to discovering the relations between certain mental structures and the life-situations in which they exist. We must constantly ask ourselves how it comes about that a given type of social situation gives rise to a given interpretation. Thus the ideological element in human thought, viewed at this level, is always bound up with the existing life-situation of the thinker. According to this view human thought arises, and operates, not in a social vacuum but in a definite social milieu.

Puritan ideology was informed both by the general social context, which affected all English people in the Elizabethan and early Stuart eras, and by the influence of educated Puritan ministers seeking to form a "godly" people, who played the role of what Mannheim calls an "intelligentsia," presenting theological doctrines but also providing criteria for the use of practical reason. Puritan ideology combined the dogmatic certitude of an older worldview with the interest in experiment and experience that would become characteristic of later scientific thought (it was not for nothing that John Winthrop called his early spiritual journal the "Experiencia").[37] In other words, it was incarnational, especially in its thoroughgoing corporatism.

Looking deeply into the records of the communities founded in New England during the seventeenth century, one finds much that is surprisingly "relevant" to present-day concerns. In this connection I have been preceded and inspired by scholars such as Barry Levy and Brian Donahue, who have shown that the Puritans created sustainable communities that were designed to look after the needs of all their members.[38] In his analysis of John Winthrop's sermon aboard the *Arbella*, "A Modell of Christian Charity," Abram van Engen found that Winthrop was trying to convey "a principle of sympathy that forms good communities through the reciprocity of fellow feeling."[39] This very famous text also, I believe, shows how seamlessly the Puritans combined their theological convictions with their academic formation in elaborating their vision of Christian community.

Like most members of the Puritan elite in England, John Winthrop was linked to Cambridge, albeit not so intimately as some of the figures featured in this book. His father, Adam Winthrop, had been appointed the auditor of Trinity College in 1592, which required him to visit Cambridge every year to audit Trinity's books. On one of these trips in late 1602, John Winthrop accompanied his father and enrolled in Trinity. He officially matriculated in the Easter term of 1603, but dropped out within two years in order to marry Mary Forth. Winthrop never took a degree, but afterward inherited his father's position as college auditor.[40] Winthrop's writings, including the "Modell of Christian Charity," show that he was quite familiar with the terminology and concepts of Protestant scholasticism.

The "Modell" is best known for its thesis statement—"God Almightie in his most holy and wise providence hath soe disposed of the Condicion of mankinde, as in all times some must be rich some poore, some highe and eminent in power and dignitie;

others meane and in subieccion"—and for its ringing peroration in which Winthrop predicted that New England "shall be as a Citty vpon a Hill, the eies of all people are vppon vs," so that if their project should fail they would become "a story and a by-word through the world." Those who read what comes between are almost sure to be surprised. The newly elected governor of the Massachusetts Bay Colony explained, first, that God had instituted social hierarchy in order "to shewe forthe the glory of his wisdome in the variety and differance of the Creatures and the glory of his power, in ordering all these differences for the preservacion and good of the whole." This reflected the traditional worldview based on the notion of a "great chain of being"; modern people might call it an argument from diversity. Winthrop also referred to the "distribution" of people into "riche and poore," alluding to the Aristotelian notion of distributive justice to which we will return frequently in subsequent chapters.[41]

Winthrop's second reason was that God showed the power of his Spirit by "moderating and restraining" both social groups, "soe that the riche and mighty should not eate vpp the poore, nor the poore, and dispised rise vpp against theire superiours." But Winthrop entered the heart of his message with his third point: God created both haves and have-nots

> that every man might haue need of other, and from hence they might be all knitt more nearly together in the bond of brotherly affeccion: from hence it appeares plainely that noe man is made more honourable then another or more wealthy etc., out of any perticuler and singuler respect to himselfe but for the glory of his Creator and the Common good of the Creature, Man.

Here the governor insisted on the primacy of the common good in political and social life over individual prerogatives, in keeping with the scholastic tradition, while introducing the theme of affection and Christian love among the colonists. He went on to distinguish between the two laws that applied to social relations, "the lawe of nature and the lawe of grace, or the morrall lawe or the lawe of the gospell." Reformed Christians located the scholastic concept of natural law, or the law of God for human nature, in the various covenants made by the Hebrew people with God and especially in the Ten Commandments. Winthrop pointed out, correctly, that the command "to loue his neighbour as himselfe" belonged to the natural or moral law of the Old Testament; this law required not only that "every man afford his help to another in every want or distresse," but that this must be done "out of the same affeccion, which makes him carefull of his owne good." The gospel law, the covenant of grace, demanded more: "there is a time when a christian must sell all and giue to the poore as they did in the Apostles times. There is a tyme allsoe when a christian (though they giue not all yet) must giue beyond theire abillity." The gospel law also "teacheth vs to put a difference between Christians and others" in the order of charity, something which of course played out in the history of New England, where life could be quite pleasant for those who embraced the dominant ideologies, religious teachings, and cultural assumptions, but miserable for people who did not fit the prevailing *habitus*.[42]

Winthrop went on to make it clear that a Christian must lend to a "brother" whether or not he had means to repay. If the borrower had the ability to pay back the debt, then the transaction could be carried out according to the just rules of commerce, but if not, "then is hee an obiect of thy mercy thou must lend him, though there be danger of looseing it." In either case, if the debt came due and "if he haue noething to pay thee [thou] must forgiue him (except in cause where thou hast a surety or a lawfull pleadge)." In times of common peril, believers had to show even "more enlargement towardes others and lesse respect towards our selues, and our own right." The governor buttressed these fairly stern guidelines with scripture from the Old Testament, the Gospels, and the New Testament epistles: "cast thy bread vpon the waters" (Ecclesiastes 11:1); "Lay not vpp for yourselues Treasures vpon earth" (Matthew 6:19); "he whoe hath this worlds goodes and seeth his brother to neede, and shutts vpp his Compassion from him, how dwelleth the loue of god in him" (1 John 3:17).[43]

Winthrop's Scriptural and scholastic reasoning reached its climax when he introduced St. Paul's image of the church as Christ's body from 1 Corinthians chapter 12, the basis also of corporatism, in which other social bodies—nations and lesser corporations—are seen as "bodies politic," analogous to the church as the mystical Body of Christ.

> There is noe body but consistes of partes and that which knitts these partes together giues the body its perfeccion, because it makes eache parte soe contiguous to other as thereby they doe mutually participate with eache other, both in strengthe and infirmity in pleasure and paine, to instance in the most perfect of all bodies, Christ and his church make one body: the severall partes of this body considered aparte before they were vnited were as disproportionate and as much disordering as soe many contrary quallities or elements but when christ comes and by his spirit and loue knitts all these partes to himselfe and each to other, it is become the most perfect and best proportioned body in the world.

Each community in New England, I hope to show through a careful consideration of town records, took up Winthrop's challenge to create a well-proportioned body politic in keeping with Scripture and Protestant scholastic teaching. But "the ligamentes of this body which knitt together," Winthrop concluded simply, "are loue." The rest of the sermon was an ecstatic meditation on love, which in the colony would be expressed "by a mutuall consent through a speciall overruleing providence [...] to seeke out a place of Cohabitation and Consorteshipp vnder a due forme of Goverment both ciuill and ecclesiasticall." In this body politic united to Christ, "the care of the publique must oversway all private respects [...] for it is a true rule that perticuler estates cannott subsist in the ruine of the publique"—words which, as I write this during the COVID-19 pandemic of 2020, I wish could be emblazoned on every mind.[44]

Speaking of the history of the church, Winthrop praised "the sweete Sympathie of affeccions which was in the members of this body one towardes another [...] how liberall they were without repineing." To Winthrop, this called to mind the "State of Wedlock," in which "there be many comfortes [...] but let such as haue tryed the most, say if there be any sweetnes in that Condicion comparable to the exercise of mutuall loue." In his magisterial work *State Formation in Early Modern England*, Michael Braddick suggested that English Puritans sought to inscribe patriarchy in their communities, and Winthrop's words seem to bear that out. However, the rest of the sermon complicates what our concept of patriarchy might have meant to the Puritan migrants of 1630. First, Winthrop made it clear that among the "patterns" for the formation of Christian social bodies, Christ's action in "becomeing a parte of this body [of the church], and being knitt with it in the bond of loue" took precedence over any other instance one might care to name, including the creation of Christian households through marriage. Winthrop cited Adam and Eve as one example of how "the soule which is of a sociable nature," according to the scholastic idea of natural sociability, desired union with others; but he also mentioned David and Jonathan, as well as Ruth and Naomi.[45]

Before Winthrop embarked on his voyage, he wrote to his friend Sir William Spring in the same vein.

> The apprehension of your love and worth togither hath ouercome my heart, and remoued the veil of modestye, that I must needes tell you, my soule is knitt to you, as the soule of Jonathan to Dauid: were I now with you, I should bedewe that sweet bosome with the tears of affection: O what a pinche it will be to me, to parte with such a freinde![46]

In his "Experiencia" journal for 1611/12, Winthrop had recorded that in a dream about Christ, "I was so ravished with his love towards me, farre exceeding the affection of the kindest husbande [...] as I was forced to unmeasurable weepings for a great while."[47] The annotations in the margins of the Geneva Bible for Ephesians 5:30 made it clear that "this our coniunction with Christ must be considered as Christ is the housband, and we the wife."[48] For the godly migrants, the marriage of Christ to his body, the church, was conceptually prior to the patriarchal marriage of husband and wife: this was "the more neare bond of mariage, betweene him and vs, wherein he hath taken vs to be his after a most strickt and peculiar manner."[49] Their culturally conditioned notions of the family no doubt informed the Puritans' sense of the mutual obligations of the members of the social body, but did not exhaust it. As a result, would-be patriarchs found their behavior constrained by the demands of their divine "housband."

John Winthrop will make only brief appearances in the remainder of this book; rather, I will focus on a group of town-founders who opposed many of the first governor's policies. However, all these leaders shared Winthrop's fundamentally corporatist view of society, rooted in scripture and Protestant scholasticism; such adherence was in some sense necessary in a colony founded by a business corporation, the Massachusetts Bay Company.[50] As Francis J. Bremer put it, Winthrop's sermon presented "the social gospel that had long been proclaimed in the Stour Valley and elsewhere in England"; that the text went generally unnoticed for many years only underscored that "the ideas which have struck so many later commentators as original and influential were commonplaces of the time."[51] Corporatism provided the metaphysical basis for the ideology that justified their migration and animated their founding of towns in New England, many of which are still in being, and have served in turn as the inspiration for other migrations and other foundations.

ACKNOWLEDGMENTS

First, I would like to thank Mrs. Evelyn Coney at the Albany State University Library for her efficient, professional, and friendly handling of my numerous interlibrary loan requests. This book would not have been possible without her help. Thanks also to my department chair, Dr. Babafemi Elufiede, for his assistance in funding conference travel.

Thanks to the staffs of the British Library Manuscripts and Archives department, the National Archives at Kew, the Cambridge University Library Manuscripts and University Archives department, the Bodleian Library, the Lincolnshire Archives, the Suffolk Record Office (Bury St. Edmunds branch), the Essex Record Office, and the East Riding (Yorkshire) Archives, as well as the librarians of Emmanuel College and St. John's College, Cambridge.

I am very grateful to Linda L. Koutoulas, City Clerk of Haverhill; Austin Simko, Town Clerk of Andover; Leslie Haley, Newbury Town Clerk; Janice Forrest, Newbury Assistant Town Clerk; and Susan G. Hazen, Rowley Town Clerk. I also wish to acknowledge the assistance of the Ipswich Town Clerk's Office and the staff of the Massachusetts Historical Society and the Massachusetts Archives. And I would like to express gratitude to the Church of Jesus Christ of Latter-Day Saints for being so far-sighted as to microfilm and then digitize the town records of New England, and to the staff of the Genealogy Room at the Washington Memorial Library in Macon, Georgia, where I consulted the LDS FamilySearch database.

Thanks to those who generously offered me hospitality during my New England research trips, especially the Congregation of the Holy Cross at Stonehill College, Easton, Massachusetts; Saint Benedict Abbey at Still River, Massachusetts; and the Campion Center at Weston, Massachusetts. My gratitude also to Dr. Kevin Fleming for vital aid that made my travels possible.

For assistance with and permissions for images, thanks once again to Haverhill City Clerk Linda L. Koutoulas, as well as Gordon Harris at Historic Ipswich; Jennifer Hornsby of the Phillips Library at the Peabody Essex Museum; Clive Coward, Images Manager at the Tate Gallery; and the staff of the National Portrait Gallery Portrait Picture Library.

Profound thanks to my mentors at Saint Louis University who have continued to provide extraordinary support for me even after my graduation: Dr. Silvana Siddali, Dr. Lorri Glover, Dr. Damian Smith, Dr. Hal Parker, Dr. Nathaniel Millett, and Dr. James Hitchcock. Thanks also to my friends from my graduate program for their support, including Stephen Kissel, Richard Allington, Joe Reidy, Matt Morgan, Luke Ritter, Andrew Jones, and Adam Hoose. Many thanks to David Powers and Matt Stanley for reading sections of this work and for their encouragement, and to David Gilbert as well.

I'm very grateful to everyone at Anthem Press, especially Acquisitions Editor Megan Greiving and Prof. Thomas Adam, editor of the Intercultural Transfer Studies series.

Thanks to my mom, Patricia McDermott, for putting up with me all this time, and to my friend Diane Thompson, an irreplaceable part of my life for the past 36 years.

This book would not have been written without the affirmation, goading and encouragement of my colleague Prof. Patrick Whitehead and my writing accountability partner, Fr. Michael Wurtz, CSC, to whom I owe a deep debt of gratitude.

Ad Majorem Dei Gloriam (For the Greater Glory of God)
On the feast of the Holy Innocents, December 28, 2020

A NOTE ON DATES

In the Old Style calendar that was used before 1752 in the English Empire, the year began on the Feast of the Annunciation, March 25. For example, the date which we would call February 12, 1631, would for the people of that time have been February 12, 1630. In this book I have adopted a composite form, so that that date would be rendered as February 12, 1630/31. March was considered the first month and February was the twelfth month under the Old Style calendar; the date on which I am writing this, January 3, 2021, would have been called "the third day of the eleventh month" in a letter written by one of my Puritan protagonists.

Chapter One

PURITANS AND SOCIETY IN THE STOUR VALLEY

This chapter will take readers on a journey through the Valley of the River Stour in the English region of East Anglia to meet clerical members of the Ward/Rogers family: Nathaniel Ward, his brothers Samuel and John, his stepfather Richard Rogers and his stepbrothers Daniel and Ezekiel Rogers, and their kinsman John Rogers of Dedham and his son Nathaniel. Along the way the reader will encounter issues of great concern to ordinary people and their ministers in the early seventeenth century: land use patterns and the spread of enclosure, moral economy and the right of resistance, the problem of vagrancy, economic depression, and attempts by Puritans and other local leaders to address these issues through a combination of moral regulation and poor relief. Any disorientation the reader may feel is intentional, mirroring the sense of rapid demographic, economic, and agricultural change observed by people of the time, and replicating the lived experience of Puritan mobility in early Stuart England. This included "gadding about" to sermons by the godly faithful, and the even more striking peregrinations of their clerical leaders, leaving home to attend university or to pursue legal studies at the Inns of Court, perhaps relocating for a time to learn from a Puritan spiritual teacher like John Cotton, to whom the Protestant scholastic John Preston sent his pupils (as Cotton Mather put it) for "seasoning," then moving from one ministerial post to another, possibly even leaving the country to escape persecution or pursue Calvinist connections on the continent.[1] Such strategic religious removals set the stage, not only for the Great Migration, but also for the emergence of a full-blown politics of place within New England, as leaders like Thomas Dudley and Thomas Hooker relocated in order to make political statements.

For the past century and a half, discussion of Puritans' motives for migration to New England has centered on whether they emigrated primarily for religious or economic reasons, and historians' responses have predictably followed their own ideological proclivities. In recent decades scholars have valiantly attempted to construct datasets of migrants that would provide a more objective foundation for addressing this question. Results have been inconclusive, to say the least. In his study of migrants from East Anglia, N. C. P. Tyack declined to generalize about the economic origins of migrants, given the lack of hard evidence, but linked waves of migration to periods of economic distress among clothworkers in the region, as well as "pressure on the land," the threat posed by enclosing landlords to those common rights that had survived earlier enclosures.[2] Anthony Salerno went further in his study of Wiltshire emigrants. Finding that young, unmarried servants and urban artisans predominated in his sample, Salerno suggested that his migrants fit the profile of seasonal economic migrants within England, commonly stigmatized as vagrants. On the other hand, Virginia DeJohn Anderson's cohort inclined her to agree with Puritan apologists who trumpeted their religious motives for emigration; her typical migrants were "mature couples, generally in their thirties," economically secure and often of urban origins. Alison Games split the difference between Salerno and Anderson; her 1635 migrants to New England included a surprisingly large number of Londoners and servants, but the majority of emigrants traveled with family members.[3]

T. H. Breen and Stephen Foster had offered an emigrant profile similar to Anderson's, featuring mature "nuclear families" whose presence helped account for "social stability" in early New England. Their data from 1637 depicted migrants who were also predominantly urban and far from destitute, but instead of discounting the economic motive as a result, Breen and Foster argued that since urban tradesmen were also likely to be Puritans, it made no sense to dichotomize religious and economic motives. Emigrants likely experienced both types of pull, and the determining factor might often have been something quite individual like local disagreements, family connections, or personality quirks.[4] Roger Thompson took this analysis a step further; in his sample from "Greater East Anglia"—Essex, Suffolk, Norfolk, Lincolnshire, and Cambridgeshire—Thompson found that, rather than having a tendency toward vagrancy, his migrants were "typically *deeply* rooted" in their English communities, so that their experience in moving to the New World "must have been profoundly traumatic."[5]

If these findings were not entirely contradictory, neither were they particularly coherent. However, there was one subset of migrants who had undoubtedly shown a propensity for mobility even in England. Thompson pointed out that "there is one group among the emigrants from Greater East Anglia who are exceptions to this settled pattern, the clergy." Puritan ministers left their homes to attend university, usually Cambridge, and then followed their vocation to various postings; hostile interventions by Archbishop William Laud and other anti-Puritan bishops often required them to relocate suddenly, sometimes even to go into hiding or to accept exile in the Netherlands. University-educated ministers often provided the final impetus which sealed a decision to emigrate, and many migrants went to England in one of the "ministerial companies" led by famous Puritan preachers such as Thomas Hooker, Thomas Shepard, or Nathaniel Rogers.[6]

This would seem to tip the balance in terms of motivation toward the religious thesis, which the early tracts justifying emigration to New England tend to support as well. For example, in his letter to Bridget, Countess of Lincoln, Thomas Dudley discouraged the "poorer sort" from coming to Massachusetts while urging "godly men" to emigrate for "religious ends."[7] However, Puritan ministers were themselves often quite sensitive to the economic challenges of migrants under their care. From his rectory at Stondon Massey, Essex, Nathaniel Ward wrote to John Winthrop in January 1629/30, entreating the Great Migration's leader

> to reserue roome and passage in your shipps for 2 families, A carpenter and Bricklayer the most faithfull and dilligent workmen in all our partes, one of them hath putt of a good farme this weeke and sold all, and should be much dammaged and discouraged if he finds no place amongst yow. he transports himselfe att his owne charge. there is a paire of sawyers also specially Laborious.[8]

From this letter it is impossible to pinpoint the economic condition of these migrants, except that either the carpenter or the bricklayer was prosperous enough to pay his own way across the Atlantic—begging the question of who bought the other three men's passage. One thing is certain, though: all of these men turned for help to their minister, whose teachings may also have helped to inspire their decision to move to New England.

Both Thomas Dudley and Nathaniel Ward made their homes in Ipswich, Massachusetts, for a period of time, becoming key members of the local elite, Dudley as a magistrate and Ward as the town's pastor. Considering the ideas and actions of Ward, Dudley and their close associates in New England town-founding will show that Breen and Foster were right to question "the traditional either/or dichotomy—*either* religion *or* economics." However, as Alison Games pointed out, the end of the religion versus politics debate has fed "a recent trend, to attribute motivations for emigration to such a melange of variables that it is impossible and, apparently, undesirable to make any conclusion about why some people left England while others of comparable belief and social background remained."[9] I hope to redirect the focus of the migration debate to a Puritan ideology that encompassed religious, economic, intellectual, and social factors in its justification for mobility. Scholars of New England have avoided engaging with Puritan ideology in recent years for a number of reasons. Justifiably, historians feared falling into the "Whig interpretation of history," the idea that all of history merely constituted a preparation for the emergence of Anglo-American democratic institutions.[10] More recently, the attempt by David Barton and other evangelical historians to portray the United States as an originally "Christian nation" has provided a strong disincentive among mainstream American academics to any consideration of Puritan political thinking.[11]

Such a reevaluation is desperately needed; in its absence, we are left either with determinism (geographic or demographic) or mere confusion in accounting for the Great Migration. Since 1990 British historians have responded brilliantly to the late Dr. Collinson's call for a "social history with the politics put back in."[12] A similar move in colonial New England studies is long overdue. This book will present the ideology of mobility developed by Ward, Dudley, and other Puritan intellectuals, an ideology that provided a justification and an incentive for other members of the godly community to emigrate. (Indeed, the rank-and-file Puritans were used to traveling to hear their favorite ministers preach; this was called by their detractors "gadding about to sermons," and it helped to create extensive networks of community that contributed to the formation of ministerial companies during the Great Migration.[13]) I will focus on the communities they helped establish, beginning with Ipswich and its satellite towns in Essex County, including Rowley, Haverhill, Andover, and Newbury. While I will not address the question of economic motives for migration from England, in considering those New England communities I will present considerable evidence bearing on the economic effects of the migration, and how the need for land and resources required by the settlers' mixed-farming regime drove further migrations within New England and the founding of numerous towns. All this became part of the Puritan ideology of mobility as developed by its elite theorists, modified by the actual experience of settlement and the political give-and-take within New England towns, and (unsuccessfully) reexported back to the mother country during the English Civil War.

Nathaniel Ward was the quintessentially mobile Puritan minister, as peripatetic as any Aristotelian philosopher, though his academic influences ranged beyond the Aristotelian strain in Protestant scholasticism. Following his travels will shed light on the various preoccupations that migrants brought into the enterprise of founding their New World communities. It will also introduce the members of his extended family, which Kenneth Shipps has called "the most important family of Puritan clerics in England," four of whom also came to Essex County as ministers and town-founders.[14]

Ward was born ca. 1578 in Haverhill, Suffolk, to John and Susan Ward. John Ward was a noted Puritan preacher, and in addition to Nathaniel, the couple had two sons who became ministers, Samuel and John. The Stour River, which for much of its course provides the boundary between Suffolk and Essex, bends northward just east of Haverhill, which lies at about the halfway point on the road from the market town of Colchester to Cambridge. Sometime during the 1590s, Ward moved his family north to the Suffolk town of Bury St. Edmunds.[15] After John Ward's 1598 death, Susan married Richard Rogers, the staunchly Puritan lecturer of Wethersfield in Essex (and father of Daniel and Ezekiel Rogers).[16] However, by this time Nathaniel had already left home, having entered Emmanuel College in 1596. Nathaniel Ward then studied law at Lincoln's Inn, one of the London Inns of Court—in fact, he would become one of only three men in early Massachusetts who had been called to the English bar—but lived at least part of the time in Ipswich in southeastern Suffolk.[17]

Ward's next remove took him to the continent of Europe, probably in 1616, to serve as a minister for the Eastland Company, based in London. This corporation traded with the Baltic region through its staple in Elbing, a city that fell under the overlapping jurisdictions of the Duke of Prussia and the King of Poland.[18] However, Ward must have left Elbing before June 1622, since he attested in his most famous book, *The Simple Cobler of Aggawam* (1647), that he had met the Protestant scholastic David Pareus, who died in that month. (In the Algonquian tongue, Aggawam or Agawam was the name of the area that later included Ipswich, Massachusetts.) On this grand tour of international Calvinism, not only did he meet Pareus, presumably at Pareus's home in Heidelberg, but he also hobnobbed with Elizabeth, daughter of King James I of England, and her husband Frederick, the Elector Palatine and ill-fated Winter King of Bohemia, whose usurpation of the Bohemian throne in 1618 provided the spark for the Thirty Years' War. Ward recalled holding the Elector's son Rupert in his arms and receiving Rupert's promise to be a "good Prince." That Rupert, born in late 1619, could already talk, suggests that Ward followed Frederick and Elizabeth to the Netherlands where they took refuge at the Hague in 1621.[19]

Ward's whereabouts then become unclear until February 1625/26, when Sir Nathaniel Rich presented him to the living of Stondon Massey, southwest of Chelmsford in Essex.[20] Ward became embroiled in a major 1624 political controversy at Westminster, signing a petition urging Parliament to condemn the Laudian author Richard Montagu. In 1646, Samuel Gorton recalled that Ward had once served as lecturer at St. Michael's, Cornhill, in London; possibly Ward held this position at the time of the 1624 Parliament.[21] Ward served at Stondon Massey until he emigrated to New England in 1634, settling in Ipswich before returning to England in 1646 and becoming rector of Shenfield, near Stondon Massey, where he lived until his death in 1652.[22] Ward's son John (Emmanuel College—BA 1626/27; MA 1630) also emigrated and became a founder of the Essex County village of Haverhill.[23]

Ward's brothers and stepbrothers were well-connected Puritan ministers in their own right in southern Suffolk and northern Essex, very much involved with what Tom Webster has called the "network of noble professors" in the region, Puritan gentry like the powerful Barrington and Rich families.[24] They were also Protestant scholastics. Samuel Ward went up to St. John's College, Cambridge, where he received his BA in 1597. He then transferred to the new foundation of Sidney Sussex College, where he became one of the first fellows in 1599, earning his MA in 1600 and his DB in 1607.[25] The *Annalls of Ipswche* [sic] for 1605 record that the Assembly of the Town of Ipswich appointed Samuel Ward lecturer at the church of St. Mary-le-Tower.[26] In addition to his preaching skills, Thomas Fuller declared that Samuel Ward of Ipswich "had a sanctified fancy, dexterous in designing expressive pictures, representing much matter in a little model."[27] Ward's printed works frequently contained a frontispiece which he drew himself.[28] One of Samuel Ward's political/religious cartoons led to a serious brush with the law. Ward's drawing featured the pope, the cardinals and the king of Spain conferring with Satan, flanked on one side by a depiction of the destruction of the Spanish Armada in 1588 and on the other by the foiling of the 1605 Gunpowder Plot.[29] The image was provocative enough to land Ward in jail in early 1620/21 when the Spanish Ambassador, Count Gondomar, complained.[30] After his release, as Joseph Mead wrote to Sir Martin Stuteville, Ward was "silenced for preaching any more at Ipswich," but must have been reinstated, as he continued to serve as lecturer in Ipswich until 1635.[31]

Nathaniel Ward's younger brother John became rector of Dennington, Suffolk, in 1624. It later transpired that Ward had obtained the living with the help of a cash payment to the incumbent, most of which was provided by Nicholas Bacon, the brother of Nathaniel Bacon (recorder of Ipswich and scribe of its *Annalls*) and nephew of Sir Francis Bacon. Thus, the Court of High Commission deprived John Ward of the Dennington post on grounds of simony. But Ward, believing that he had been persecuted because of his Puritanism, was restored to the ministry upon the downfall of Archbishop Laud. He then became rector of St. Clement's church in Ipswich.[32] Due to confusion with other John Wards, it is not clear where this John received his academic formation, but a published sermon reveals his commitment to Protestant scholasticism, particularly with respect to the natural law. Addressing the Long Parliament in 1645, John Ward announced that in speaking of political matters he did not need to rely on scriptural revelation, because

> there is a light of it shining in mens minds by nature. Whence els was it, that the very heathens *without God in the world* did sacrifice to God, make triall by Auguries, and consult with the Oracles, in all great undertakings [...] doubtlesse there was some religion in their superstition, and some truth in their very fables.[33]

This was nothing new in the Puritan tradition; William Perkins, the great Elizabethan scholar of Christ's College, Cambridge, linked natural law to the Ten Commandments but insisted that it was inwardly accessible to all men. "Morall law concernes duties of love, partly to God and partly towards our neighbor: it is contained in the Decalogue [...] and it is the very law of nature written in all mens hearts."[34]

Nathaniel Ward's stepbrothers both attended Christ's College, Cambridge. Daniel Rogers matriculated in 1591/92, during Perkins's tenure, taking his BA in 1595/96, his MA in 1599 and his DB in 1606; Ezekiel Rogers received his BA in 1604/5 and his MA in 1608.[35] Daniel Rogers led a relatively quiet life for a staunchly Puritan minister. His father, Richard Rogers, had died in 1618 and was followed by Stephen Marshall as lecturer of Wethersfield. When Marshall was offered a position as vicar of nearby Finchingfield, a clerical conference helped him resolve his scruples about accepting the offer, and for good measure recommended that Daniel receive the lectureship. Thus in 1625 Daniel Rogers returned to Wethersfield and took up his father's position as lecturer. Daniel Rogers survived being suspended by Laud and remained in Wethersfield until his own death in 1652. He also helped persuade his son Samuel not to emigrate to New England.[36]

Ezekiel Rogers, destined to become the founder of Rowley, Massachusetts, was more typical of the family in terms of mobility. In his first important post, Ezekiel served as chaplain to the Barrington family of Hatfield Broad Oak, Essex, from 1610 to 1621, when Sir Francis Barrington appointed him to the living of Rowley in the East Riding of Yorkshire. The Barringtons were an ancient family who, after a period of conflict with the *nouveaux riche* Rich clan (who received the earldom of Warwick in 1618), decided to ally with the Riches; working together, the two families became the leaders of the Puritan gentry in Essex. Ezekiel Rogers served in Rowley, Yorkshire, until his emigration to New England with a company of followers in 1638.[37] Another emigrant to Essex County, Nathaniel Rogers, was the son of John Rogers, perhaps the most famous of the entire clerical dynasty. This John Rogers was supported at Emmanuel College by his uncle Richard Rogers of Wethersfield, until he sold his books and spent the money he received for them. Richard Rogers was prepared to "cast him off utterly," according to another kinsman, Giles Firmin, when Susan Ward Rogers intervened and persuaded her husband to forgive his nephew. After a brief stint ministering at Haverhill, "Roaring" John Rogers went on to become the most renowned Puritan preacher in England from his headquarters in Dedham, Essex.[38] His son Nathaniel Rogers also attended Emmanuel College, taking his BA in 1617 and his MA in 1621. He married Margaret Crane of the clothing town of Coggeshall, Essex, and came to Massachusetts in 1636, replacing his step-cousin Nathaniel Ward as pastor of Ipswich in 1637/38. There he remained until his death in 1655, which Cotton Mather blamed on a "flood of *rheum*" caused by quitting smoking.[39]

What conditions formed the consciousness of these men as they grew up and ministered in the Stour Valley and its environs during the late sixteenth and early seventeenth centuries? First, the consequences of enclosure of land loomed large. To grasp the significance of enclosure, it is essential to understand land use patterns in England—a topic that has generated an extraordinary amount of first-rate scholarship, especially when compared with the almost total lack of attention that field systems have garnered in American historiography. We must rid ourselves of the modern American concept of what constitutes a family farm, namely a contiguous plot of land, rectangular or square, bounded by a fence. In England during the early 1600s, an enclosed field would have been called a "close" or a "croft" and surrounded by a thick hedge. In certain regions of England—including East Anglia, home of the Ward/Rogers family—such "enclosures" had been part of the landscape for centuries, but in the "open-field" areas of the Midlands and elsewhere, enclosure was not the norm and seemed to many like a dangerous innovation that threatened to push poor farmers off the land. Rather than farming a continuous piece of land, tenants on a typical manor would be allotted separate strips of land in common fields. They also received rights to use common pasture and woodland, and sometimes they would receive strips of meadow land which they could mow for hay. Lords of the manor and freeholders had more freedom to enclose land if they wished, though this could lead to protest if an enclosure threatened common rights, but many continued to follow the strip-farming method into the late eighteenth century. The strips were often widely dispersed, but the system provided farmers with the various types of resources they needed: arable land on which to grow crops (as well as dung to fertilize it), meadow and pasture to feed livestock, and woodland, where pigs could forage and fuel could be gathered.[40]

In the most classic model of common-field farming, a community divided its arable land into three different open fields to permit crop rotation. In a particular year one of the three fields would be sown with winter wheat; a second would be planted in spring with other crops like peas, beans, vetches and tares (a type of pea), or oats and barley. The third field lay fallow and was subject to common grazing which, of course, also brought the revitalizing application of manure.[41] Strips would be allotted so that each farmer had a roughly equal proportion of land in each of the three fields, to make sure that at least some of his land would bear crops in a given year. This was the typical "three-field" system as it evolved in the Midlands; in more backward areas, a two-field system persisted in which half the land lay fallow at any given time. Certain regions produced far more complex arrangements with numerous smaller fields or an "infield-outfield" layout, in which less fertile soils would be farmed as arable for a few growing seasons and then put down to grass for several years. A visible "ridge and furrow" pattern still exists on the land in parts of England as a reminder of the plowing of open-field strips.[42]

The planting cycle on a manor was worked out in the manorial courts. The "court baron" was primarily responsible for defending customs and developing agricultural by-laws, but the "court leet" also involved itself in prosecuting offenders against the plan agreed upon by the tenants and the lord of the manor. Brodie Waddell has shown the ongoing vitality of the manor courts well into the early modern era, especially in common-field areas.[43] Individual farmers had to follow the plan exactly, because after the harvest, fields could be thrown open to grazing as "lammas lands." A tenant who tried to grow winter wheat in the spring planting field would find their crop consumed and trampled by livestock. For the same reason tenants could not enclose their strips, because the other tenants, as well as the manorial lord and the freeholders, had the right to "shack"—grazing after harvest—on their lands.[44] Nor would they necessarily want to enclose, because the genius of the open-field system was that it kept the land fertile by providing manure without requiring labor-intensive carting of dung onto the strips.

Why, then, would anyone wish to enclose at all? Enclosure became desirable when a shortage of meadow or pasture occurred. This could happen when farmers increased their flocks and herds to produce wool or meat for the market, or because increased human population made it necessary to turn waste or pastureland into arable for growing crops—and the population of England increased by 75 percent between 1561 and 1651. A farmer who enclosed land was no longer forced to plant wheat or "spring corn" when what he really wanted was grass to feed his livestock. Thus enclosure was more desirable in predominantly "pastoral" rather than "arable" regions. Enclosures also permitted farmers to experiment with more complex rotations which included new crops such as turnips, leading to an "Agricultural Revolution" that dramatically improved the productivity of the soil over time.[45] Sometimes enclosures took place by mutual agreement, but often they provoked anger, protest, and even violence as poorer farmers defended their right to common pasture, shack, and woodland. Thus commoners would "break hedges" planted to enclose lands. Enclosing landlords were widely blamed in the sixteenth and seventeenth centuries for the depopulation of a number of villages where the smaller husbandmen and farm laborers could no longer survive on diminished common resources.[46] Displaced villagers would often move to forest or fen areas, where common rights survived intact and it was possible to eke out a living on a small parcel of land, or they would migrate to towns or cities in hopes of finding work, contributing to the widespread perception of an increase in vagrancy under the Tudors and early Stuarts.[47]

Enclosure had made early inroads in East Anglia, but the perception of the region as entirely "old-enclosed" is not accurate.[48] Enclosure would have been very much a live issue for the members of the Ward/Rogers family and their contacts among the gentry; in fact, it had helped cause the early conflict between the Barringtons and the Riches. The Barringtons were the hereditary woodwards of Hatfield Forest. In 1566, Sir Thomas Barrington obtained the manor of Hatfield Broad Oak priory, gave up his office of forester, and was permitted starting in 1576 to make enclosures from Hatfield Forest. This caused tension with the forest's owner, Lord Robert Rich, and with the possessors of common rights to the woodland. Resentment against the Barrington enclosures simmered for decades; in 1611, when Sir Francis Barrington made a new enclosure, 130 local residents destroyed its hedges. However, despite the forest enclosures, common rights in the forest still existed as of 1757, its court leet functioned until 1845, and more than a thousand acres of forest were still unenclosed as of 1854. Furthermore, some open fields persisted at Hatfield into the early modern period, and at least nineteen commons survived in the parish as late as 1841.[49]

Nor was the Ward family's home town of Haverhill largely enclosed during our period. In his 1618 *Breviary of Suffolk*, Robert Reyce stated unequivocally that "The westerne parts [of Suffolk are] either wholly champion [i.e., open-field] or neer, the feilding abounding by tillage or flockes of sheep, doe from thence emprove their greatest commodities."[50] According to Joan Thirsk, southwestern Suffolk was part of a sheep-corn area that extended northward beyond Bury St. Edmunds, across the northern edge of Norfolk and back south to the eastern coast of Suffolk. There was an active cloth industry in southwestern Suffolk, especially in Haverhill, but "the sheep-corn region was first and foremost an arable area and corn was the main interest of both large and small farmers." Furthermore, "the class structure of the sheep-corn region was typical of a manorialized society living in nucleated villages, and practising co-operative husbandry."[51]

The Suffolk Historic Landscape Characterisation map clearly reveals a sizeable area of historic open fields stretching northeast of Haverhill to the River Stour, as well as the remnant of a large green to the north of the town, which would have had common pasture rights during the early modern period. As late as March 3, 1648/49, at a court baron held by the lord of the manor of Haverhill and Horsham with Helions, Thomas Cole, there is a reference to arable land "in a common field called Halesfield." Stewards' records from 1659 describe William Sharpe receiving a "Crofte of pasture" of about five acres, but also a tiny plot of half an acre of arable in a common field called Marshfield. Another common field, West Field, was mapped in 1733, showing that some holdings had been consolidated and enclosed by "Quick Fences," that is., hedges, but unenclosed narrow strips remained. A map of 1825 depicted eight named commons still in process of enclosure. Despite this reorganization of fields, as late as 1854, land including open-field arable remained to be enclosed by Parliamentary act in Haverhill, and a map generated during this process still showed five commons.[52] The area around Haverhill represents a northward extension of the agricultural regime in northwestern Essex, the "Essex Till," which remained a "champion" district into the era of Parliamentary enclosure—in 1795, agricultural improver Charles Vancouver could still refer to the region as "this open part of the county." Wethersfield, where Richard Rogers raised his children, lay on the southeastern border of this region.[53]

So the members of the Ward/Rogers clerical dynasty spent their earliest years in a region where open-field communal agriculture was very much alive. At some point during Nathaniel Ward's youth his family moved to Bury St. Edmunds, a textile-producing town and the main urban area of northwestern Suffolk, a sheep-corn area.[54] Richard Blome in 1673 could still say that "the parts about *Bury*, and from thence Northwesternly, are *champaign* or *fielding*, abounding with excellent corn of all sorts." Field systems were irregular in this region, but manorial landlords had the right of "foldcourse" or pasturage for their flocks over arable fields after harvest or under grass ("ley" land), even when the field was enclosed. The foldcourse system retarded enclosure and required extensive communal cooperation so that strips subject to the foldcourse at a given time would not be sown with crops.[55]

When Ward matriculated at Emmanuel College, Cambridge, in 1596, he exchanged one open-field milieu for another. Cambridgeshire lay at the very heart of the Midlands three-field system; the town of Cambridge and its environs, only 20 miles from Haverhill, remained fielden during Ward's university days. As of 1794, 132,000 of 147,000 arable acres in the county still lay in open fields. Agricultural reformer William Gooch in 1811 took Cambridgeshire to task for "being the worst cultivated in England" because "the open-field state and system" had hitherto hindered all progress. Modern historians concur; B. A. Holderness affirms that the three-field system was "scarcely disturbed before 1750" because "even piecemeal enclosure was inhibited by the strength of manorial custom and collective action in Cambridgeshire."[56] Early modern writers often spoke of people being "born" in a certain place but "bred" at the college they attended; Nathaniel Ward spent this crucial formative period in an open-field environment.[57]

My point is not that the Ward/Rogers family brought an "open-field" mentality to their New World settlements. A later chapter will seek to debunk the type of deterministic thinking by which settlers' geographic origins in England supposedly determined their preferences in New England. What this evidence shows is that land use patterns in England were considerably more complex and harder to characterize than a facile geographic determinism would suggest. Even in Dedham, an indisputably enclosed area by the time of John Rogers's arrival, older customs endured. Dedham's custumal protected grazing rights in "lammas" lands:

> by the Custome noe p[er]son or tenn[an]ᵗ shall or may plow upp any Lay land [ley, i.e. under grass] in any Com[m]on ffeild w[i]ᵗʰin the p[ar]ish of Dedham aforesaid until Candlemas day [Feb. 2] and that noe p[er]son shall take theirupon or upon the Com[m]on Meadowes more then one Cropp in one yeare soe that all the mowings [...] or stubbles of suche Lands & Meadowes aforesaid are ffree for the Inhabitants of Dedham aforesaid to ffeed or Com[m]on upon until Candlemas-day then following.

This applied to arable land after harvest and meadow after hay-making. The date is uncertain, but as late as 1650, a Parliamentary survey noted that "the tenants of the sayd Mannoʳ do also clayme to have Priviledge of Com[m]onage with all Cattle Com[m]onable, in the Hall field, and Broad meddow from the tyme that the last sheafe of Corne is carryed out of the ffeild until the second day of February."[58] Enclosure and the accompanying extinction of common rights were hardly a *fait accompli*, even in East Anglia, during the late sixteenth and early seventeenth centuries. New England town founders of the Ward and Rogers family, as well as their followers and dependents, would have been aware of the benefits of enclosure as well as the suffering that accompanied it; in New England they would show that they were neither dogmatically averse to enclosure nor insensitive to common rights. Like the Barringtons, they favored enclosure in certain settings and maintained open-field customs in other circumstances.

For Puritans, following their great teacher William Perkins, decisions about practical matters such as land use were simply "cases of conscience," which fell under the rubric of *"practicall understanding."* Perkins saw conscience as "a natural power, [or] facultie" of the mind whose function was "to iudge of the goodnes or badnesse of things or actions done." Here Perkins collapsed the distinction made by his intellectual mentor Thomas Aquinas, who saw conscience as an act of the mind informed by *synderesis*, the habit or disposition that made it possible to grasp the principles of natural law. Perkins elevated conscience to the level of a mental habit, while at the same time referring to it as an act, as in his famous syllogism, so typical of Protestant scholasticism:

> *Everie murtherer is cursed*, saith the mind:
> *Thou art a murtherer*, saith conscience assisted by memorie:
> ergo, *Thou art cursed*, saith conscience, & so giueth her sentence.

Here we see that human conscience operates on multiple levels for Perkins; in the major premise as a mental habit ("the mind"); in the minor premise, cooperating with the faculty of memory, while in the conclusion, conscience as act "giueth her sentence." Placing conscience at both levels, of *synderesis* and of act, endowed Puritan decision-making with human agency and flexibility as well as divine power.[59]

Thus, Perkins could refer to conscience in homely fashion as "a Notarie, or a Register that hath always the penne in his hand," or as "a Iudge that holdeth an assise," or "(as it were) a little God sitting in the middle of mens harts." Perkins's successor as the most respected Puritan casuist, William Ames, tried to roll back the implications of Perkins's theoretical move, insisting that "the rule of this triall or judgement, must not be our *naturall reason*, the *custome of others* or the like; but the *Law*, or *revealed* will of God." Ames's *De Conscientia* appeared in Latin in 1630, when the Great Migration was already well under way; the first English version was published in 1639, but it is likely that New England's intellectual elite were familiar with Ames's views even before 1630, and Ames's high scripture-based moralism undoubtedly had great appeal in Massachusetts Bay. As we will see, in resolving the "cases of conscience" they faced with respect to land distribution, Essex County settlers would combine Perkinsian flexibility with Amesian moral rigor.[60]

For the Puritans of our period, in keeping with Protestant scholastic views, human laws, rules, and procedures bound the conscience, but not absolutely. They bound, Perkins said, insofar as they "tend to maintain the peaceable estate and common good of men [...] so far forth as they are agreeable to Gods word, serue for the common good, stand with good orders, and hinder not the libertie of conscience." This was in keeping with the scholastic idea of the common good as the object of politics, as well as the teaching of Thomas Aquinas on the right of resistance; Thomas wrote that "a law has as much force as it has justice. If, however, in some point it conflicts with the law of nature it will no longer be law but rather a perversion of law." In other words, as Perkins put it, all binding ordinances had to be consistent with "common equitie [...] made according to the lawe or instinct of nature common to all men."[61] (We shall see how equity became one of the controlling concepts of land policy in colonial Ipswich, Massachusetts.) For this reason David Pareus, whom Nathaniel Ward had encountered on his European tour, famously taught the right of resistance in his commentary on Romans 13:1:

> Those whose task it is to constitute magistrates, also have the task of restraining monstrous criminal acts, or to remove the magistrates, if they do not cease to transgress against God, and against the republic. Magistrates are constituted either by the senate, or by other magistrates. Therefore they do rightly, when they restrain or remove transgressors.[62]

This gave Puritans considerable latitude to follow or depart from laws or policies as their practical reason instructed them. For example, when King Charles I levied the "Forced Loan" of 1626–27, widely seen as a form of illegal taxation in violation of English constitutional tradition, resistance centered on the heavily Puritan villages of the Stour Valley. In excess of three hundred Essex residents were reported to the Privy Council for evading the loan, and more than thirty of them lived in Dedham, where John Rogers whipped up the opposition.[63] Puritan practicality was reflected in their response to other contemporary issues besides enclosure, including vagrancy, poor relief, unemployment in the cloth trades, and food shortages. But we should be cautious about applying to the Puritans John Bohstedt's suggestion that a "politics of provisions" superseded traditional ideas of moral economy during the early modern period.[64] For Puritans also respected the "languages of legitimation" which were used to justify social policies of the time, and they were reluctant to transgress the limits that these languages set to what was politically possible. Such legitimizing discourses included notions of moral economy as well as Protestant scholastic and humanist precepts, ancient customs, legal principles, Reformation ideals of Christian liberty and morality, everyday social values like neighborliness—all part of the prevailing "world-picture" of the period.[65]

The problem of vagrancy in the sixteenth and earlier seventeenth centuries tested the limits of commonly held beliefs about Christian charity. Enclosures were not the only factor leading to increased migration. The practice of primogeniture which prevailed in most of the kingdom forced younger siblings to go out into the world to seek their fortune; as Sir Thomas Wilson put it in 1600, "younger brethren" had to "apply ourselves to letters or to arms," while the oldest brother stayed "at home like a mome." The same problem affected many landholders of lower status.[66] However, in regions where partible inheritance was common, landholdings frequently became fragmented into tiny parcels that could not support a family. Those unable to survive on available resources might be pushed into the stream of migrants trekking long distances in search of employment; at best, such persons would have to travel locally to seek work as farm laborers.[67] In the Stour Valley and in other cloth-producing districts, another option was available: land-poor husbandmen or cottagers could spin thread or weave cloth at home as part of the "putting-out" system. However, this left them vulnerable to downturns in the clothing industry which periodically resulted in massive unemployment or underemployment. A 1629 report of the Essex JPs, describing a depression that had struck the cloth industry in the Stour Valley, claimed that there were more than three thousand people in Dedham alone, and "above 100,000 persons" in the region, who "are like to be utterly undone and ruinated if some speedy course be not taken."[68]

Such people could easily find themselves in the ranks of what Peter Clark called "subsistence migrants," forced to travel long distances looking for work, as opposed to "betterment migrants" who moved shorter distances in search of opportunity. Apprentices were the classic betterment migrants; John Patten's study of apprentices in Norfolk and in Ipswich, Suffolk, showed that the majority had traveled between 8 and 20 miles to take up their apprenticeship.[69] However, Clark himself has cautioned against an overly rigid distinction between betterment and subsistence migrants; apprentices often found themselves in informal arrangements with little job security. In any case, they rarely stayed in the town where they were apprenticed and could easily find themselves in the ranks of long-distance migrants.[70]

Historians seem to agree that mobility was generally high in Elizabethan and Jacobean England; as Peter Clark and David Souden put it, "Mobility was so pervasive that it was seen as much a natural part of the life cycle as being born or dying." However, much of this movement seems to have taken place locally or over relatively short distances.[71] The label of "vagrant" was chiefly applied to long-distance subsistence migrants, who were seen as a threat to social order and distinguished from "strangers" who may have traveled to a neighboring village to perform seasonal labor, or taken up an apprenticeship in a nearby town. Another marker of the "vagrant" was "illegal or immoral activity" such as theft or premarital sex. It is difficult to tell whether the rising number of vagrancy prosecutions reflects an actual increase in long-distance migration or simply a greater determination to identify and eliminate vagrants, but in any case they loomed large in the nightmares of Puritans and their associates like Sir Francis Bacon.[72] Bacon, though no Puritan, was willing to accept support from Puritans when he needed it, and key features of his "Great Instauration" of the image of God in man through learning would be adopted by Puritan scholastics.[73] In a 1611 memorandum to King James, Bacon attacked "vagabonds" and "sturdy beggar[s]," since "it is that kind of people that is a burthen, an eye sore, a scandal, and a seed of peril and tumult in a state." Bacon proposed to expand "houses of correction," also known as bridewells, a new and rapidly spreading accompaniment to poor relief. Ipswich and Norwich had bridewells by the 1560s, and in 1598 a scheme for creating 23 new bridewells in Essex was proposed.[74]

The Puritans' visceral and deep loathing for long-distance subsistence migration must have had origins deeper than any actual threat posed by "vagrants." For one thing, Puritans themselves were often tarred with the brush of excessive mobility, criticized for their habit of "gadding about to sermons." A 1629 letter from Samuel Collins, vicar of Braintree, offers a Laudian perspective on "gadding about": discussing Bishop of London William Laud's attack on Thomas Hooker's Chelmsford lectureship, Collins hoped "my L[ord]. of London will be carefull who suceed in the lecture there. None will please them but a man of Mr Hookers choise. they must have one who may drawe tumults & troupes of the Countrey to their faires & shopps w[hi]ch a regular man cannot doe." Even some modern historians have accepted Collins's implication that Puritans promoted long-distance travel to hear sermons for economic rather than spiritual reasons.[75] In addition, the popular literature about vagabonds spun fanciful tales about "uncomely companies" of vagrants, describing migrant criminals as a "crafty company of Cozeners and Shifters." Such tales presented a whole taxonomy of "Knaves" including "rufflers," "upright-men," and "rogues," accompanied by "doxies" and other female accomplices.[76] In the same way that, as Michael Braddick has argued, witches provided an "antitype" to contemporary ideas of a properly ordered society, vagrants seemed to mock the Puritan tendency to form themselves into companies and corporations to promote their idea of the common good, such as ministerial conferences, the Dorchester Company (created by Rev. John White to promote poor relief and moral reformation in Dorchester, but later an engine for colonization), and indeed the Massachusetts Bay Company.[77] Given that such companies promoted Puritan migration, it became necessary to construct a new ideology of mobility, perhaps partly to purify the concept of its unsavory associations in the literature of vagabonds. The construction of this ideology will be the subject of the next chapter.

Puritan paranoia about vagrants was undoubtedly exaggerated. That only about 10 percent of those apprehended as vagrants were actually punished suggests that the vast majority of migrants posed no threat to anyone. Many were actually given money and told to move on.⁷⁸ However, the apparent surge of subsistence migration during the period inspired fear, reflected in comments like that of John Rogers of Dedham, who in his *Treatise of Love* thanked God for "having freed vs from that intolerable burthen of the Rogues, that swarmed like Locusts all over the Land; whose burthen lay on vs very heavie; as they that be of yeares can remember, which yet yeelded small comfort, the greatest part of them being a cursed generation of idle and sinfull Varlets."⁷⁹

Rogers's uncle Richard of Wethersfield (Figure 3) saw the pernicious mobility of vagrants as a threat to the liberty of law-abiding people to travel. In his 1615 *Commentary vpon the Whole Booke of Iudges*, Rogers gave thanks that "wee may safely trauell and passe throughout all places and countries of this dominion, by the protection of good lawes," observing that Christians must "praise God highly for such liberties" since only recently "the high waies lay vnoccupied."⁸⁰ Nathaniel Ward inherited his stepfather's concern for protecting the right to be mobile; Ward's 1641 Massachusetts law code, the Body of Liberties, explicitly guaranteed every man's liberty "to remove both himselfe, and his familie" out of Massachusetts.⁸¹

It is also noteworthy that East Anglia seems to have attracted more than its share of long-distance subsistence migrants; while the typical pattern of migration was from the north of England toward London, East Anglia drew migrants from the southern as well as northern part of the kingdom. Perhaps it is no coincidence, then, that in 1566 Thomas Harman listed Essex, Suffolk, and Norfolk among the counties most attractive to migrants as "the chief and best shires of relief."⁸² During the reign of Elizabeth, poor relief was the subject of a series of laws, culminating in the great act of 1601. Whereas previously poor relief had been carried out largely by manorial courts, aided by monasteries and religious guilds which no longer existed, the Elizabethan poor laws awarded responsibility for poor relief to the parishes. However, it would take decades before the structure of poor relief in the parish, including vestries, churchwardens, and overseers of the poor, took shape. In the meantime, there was room for a great deal of flexibility at the local level in collecting poor rates and/or managing relief; indeed, the poor laws themselves grew out of such local initiatives in places like Bury St. Edmunds and Ipswich.⁸³ In many places the leet courts continued to play a vital role, but so did corporate entities like boroughs and guilds. In some places, like Dorchester, companies were organized to help deal with the problem, and elsewhere quasi-corporations like clerical conferences also got involved.

Everywhere the strategy was similar: to distinguish the "impotent" poor, local residents who were unable to make a living through no fault of their own, from vagrants and the "thriftless" poor whose vices were to blame (it took time for officials to recognize the problem of the laboring poor, those who lived hand to mouth from farm labor, neither paying poor rates nor receiving them). In 1616, for example, John Winthrop donated part of his manorial waste so that a cottage could be built "for some impotent poore p[er]son beinge [an] ynh[abi]tant of the s[ai]d parrishe."⁸⁴ While those deemed "inhabitants" might have their needs addressed, communities intensified their efforts to "warn out" migrants who, they feared, would become a charge on the parish poor rates. Such undesirables were sent back to their parishes of origin. In practice, however, discerning the "impotent" from the "thriftless" poor, and local residents from interlopers, was beset

Figure 2 John Rogers of Dedham, after unknown artist, mid-seventeenth century. © National Portrait Gallery, London

Figure 3 Richard Rogers, after unknown artist, 1650. © National Portrait Gallery, London

with difficulty. Thus in 1598, the Essex Justices of the Peace issued a set of orders "for the Reliefe of the poore and punishment of Roages and Vagabonds," partly in order to make sure that "no persons (other than Roages or Vagabondes) shalbe removed from their presente habitacions, either to their birthe places or last aboade." Mentioned in the document are Puritan justices Roger Harlakenden of Earls Colne and Sir Harbottle Grimston from the Colchester area.[85]

In this connection, it is worth remembering that John Rogers of Dedham uttered his criticism of traveling "Rogues" in the context of an exhortation "to relieue our owne true poore."[86] Early efforts at poor relief in Dedham had been made by the Dedham Classis, a conference of area ministers linked to the "Presbyterian" movement during the 1580s. The relationship of Elizabethan Presbyterianism to its Scottish inspiration, the reformed kirk, raises issues that are central to Puritan ideology and must be considered at some length.

When the newly widowed Queen of Scots, the Catholic Mary Stuart, returned to rule her homeland in 1561, she chose to treat the Reformation then occurring in Scotland as a *fait accompli*. Aside from securing for herself the right to assist at Mass, she made no real attempt to impede the goals of John Knox and the other reformers, and focused instead on her main goal: securing the succession to the throne of England. This meant that a presbyterian system was free to evolve without interference from either a Catholic ruler or from a force that might have been even more disruptive, a Protestant monarch suspicious of presbyterianism.[87] It is true that the kirk reflected and enforced an all-inclusive national covenant. But this does not mean that in pursuing its goals, which included the establishment of moral discipline as one of the hallmarks of the church, the kirk acted solely from the top down with no trace of congregationalism or voluntarism. In fact, the seeds of the new structure were "parish kirks," which had functioned more or less clandestinely at the local level prior to the Reformation Parliament of 1560. These were voluntary organizations that sought to redirect popular religious energies away from guilds that purchased masses for the dead and performed other ecclesial functions. The unfolding Reformation was driven largely by the kirk sessions or consistories, committees of ministers, deacons and lay elders who enforced moral discipline in each parish. As Jane Dawson has argued, the kirk sessions could not have functioned without a "passive consensus" of ordinary people who wanted to see moral standards enforced for reasons of "communal welfare"—for instance, to prevent the breeding of bastards who might prove a charge on the parish. Against the theorists of "confessionalization" in early modern Europe, Margo Todd went so far as to assert that the kirk sessions helped to make Scottish Calvinism "genuinely a religion of the people."[88]

Nevertheless, the kirk was relatively free, even after Mary's deposition in favor of her Protestant son James VI, to develop organically into a national church. The presbyteries, intermediate councils of ministers and elders that occupied a level between the kirk sessions and the General Assembly, emerged by 1581. The peculiar circumstances of the kirk's founding fostered what has been called the "two kingdoms" theory, the idea that the church should be entirely free from state interference in religious matters and should even have the power to rebuke royal misdeeds (thus King James's squawk of protest against "Puritan–Papists"). However, even Pope Gelasius I, whose letter in 494 to the Emperor Anastasius provided the ultimate source for this viewpoint, would of course not have condoned the church/state separation that the doctrine seems to imply. Kirk leaders certainly did not. While the Crown and great magnates gradually surrendered patronage powers over church benefices and tithes, local dignitaries were normally chosen to serve as elders and thus played an ongoing role in decision-making within the kirk.[89] The genius of the presbyterian system was to domesticate the growing cadre of educated and reformed gentlemen, giving them status within the kirk, putting them to work promoting its goals rather than interfering with them and exploiting church resources from on high. For it would have been impossible to implement the kirk's program, especially the tightening of moral discipline, without the support of the governing class.

The "classical" movement in England during the 1580s, which featured godly ministers meeting in "classes" in an attempt to promote some form of the presbyterian discipline, was obviously subject to an entirely different set of pressures. The ministers were already leaders of an at least partly reformed Church of England and, as such, subject to episcopal discipline. They were also citizens of a state whose Protestant queen had very decided views on ecclesiology and little inclination to tolerate open dissent. Unable to take over the existing church apparatus, and in spite of their efforts to create regional and national structures, the classical movement inevitably became, as Patrick Collinson put it, "a purely voluntary discipline" that in fact helped give rise to congregationalism.[90] Thus, while some members of the Dedham classis disliked the idea of a congregation's "reiecting and receyving their pastors wthout counsell of others," most agreed "that a Paster shuld haue his owne people" (though they were reluctant to say so publicly). Dedham's lecturer Edmund Chapman hoped that the classis' rulings might be shared with other churches "that there might be as much conformity as might be," but when a member brought up the issue of what to do when another classis ruled differently on an issue than their own had, the question was "deferred" and apparently never taken up again.[91]

But the most anomalous thing about the Dedham classis was that it was, in fact, strictly "presbyterian," being made up entirely of ministers. Local political leaders obviously could not participate in an organization that was probably illegal, and without the participation of local magistrates, the ministers could not implement their program of moral reform. It would have been impossible, for instance, to set up a functioning consistory in a parish, when anyone disciplined or excommunicated by such an unsanctioned group would only have to appeal to the ecclesiastical courts for redress. There was another alternative—the godly ministers could have given up on their social goals and concentrated solely on spiritual matters, cultivating interior piety and holiness in their flocks and seeking to reform the church from within. That this approach was never even considered shows how central social activism was to the "presbyterians" and to Puritans in general.

On religious issues such as what to do about parishioners with separatist leanings, the Dedham conference acted decisively, but in dealing with social problems the classis had no choice but to appeal to lawyers and magistrates, and its minutes reveal that it did so on numerous occasions. Taking up a motion concerning "the multitude of roges wherwth the cuntrey was charged," they refused to intervene as a group, "except the creditt of any were such as to deale wth some Magistrate for it, and then to deale as a private man in it." Even a witch should be referred "to some Justice to examyne it."[92] Future Archbishop Richard Bancroft accused the classical movement, under Scots influence and according to the "two kingdoms" model, of taking action "'without the assistance or tarrying for the Magistrate.'" In reality this was not an option for the English presbyterians, precisely because they were unwilling to jettison their goal of reforming the broader society as well as the church.[93]

The strategy of cooperation between religious leaders and prominent townspeople was enshrined in the famous "Orders" adopted by Lecturer Chapman, Vicar Richard Parker, and "the Aunceints of the Congregation of Dedham to be diligently obserued and kepte of all persons whatsoeuer dwellinge w^{th}in the said Towne." The document established a regular meeting on Tuesdays after every communion Sunday between the two clergymen and the "aunceints" to discuss "matters concerninge the good gouernment of the towne." With respect to poor relief, the Orders reflect Puritan preoccupations: four times a year clergy, ancients, and at least one constable were to "visitt the poore and chiefly the suspected places, that understandinge the miserable estate of those yt wante and the naughtie disposition of disordered persons, they may provide for them accordinglie." Alongside this rather fear-driven form of charity were provisions for warning out those "not havinge any callinge" and for the public humiliation of married couples known to have engaged in premarital sex. But poor individuals accepted as part of the town enjoyed an unusual privilege:

> Item yt so many as be of habilitie invite to their howses one couple of such of their poore neighbors as haue submitted themselues to the good orders of the Churche, and walke christianly and honestlie in their callinges, and others of lesse hability any one such person providinge no more for them then ordenary and so longe as they shall thankfully accepte of the same.[94]

Richard Rogers of Wethersfield was involved in the Presbyterian movement as an active member of the Braintree classis.[95] His Judges commentary offered a homely twist on the "two kingdoms" theory: Rogers asserted that "the Church and Common-wealth are friendly neighbours, each bordering vpon other, both compast with one wall, and both yeelding mutual aids & defences each to other." "Therefore let the Magistrate backe the Minister with authoritie, and by the sword of iustice, sharpen the edge of the sword of the word." (An anecdote about Queen Elizabeth, though no doubt apocryphal, may have been on Rogers's mind: on progress in Suffolk and seeing its Justices of the Peace, "every one of them having his Minister next to his body," the monarch supposedly observed that "her County of *Suffolk* was better governed than any other County. [...] It must needs be so [...] where the Word and the Sword go together."[96]) Rogers repeatedly invoked the corporatist metaphor of society as a body, within which order would be guaranteed if every member of the body, from magistrates and ministers down to lowly husbandmen, would be faithful to their callings. "God hath dealt with the societies of men as with the members of the bodie; giuing to euery member a distinct facultie, that they might all agree to the good of the whole, seeing that none could well be spared without blemish."[97]

The belief in natural sociability was based on Aristotle's dictum that "man is by nature a social and political being." Rogers appealed to natural sociability even in relations with outsiders: "one man should be sociable with another, yea with stangers (seeing euery one is our neighbour,)" but should be suspicious of strangers who might infect the body with ungodliness. "[A] sore or wound in the bodie, though neuer so good salues be laid thereto, is not healed thereby, vnlesse the corruption and hurtfull humours be first drawne out." It is chiefly the magistrate who "stands in the gap to stay Gods hand from being reuenged vpon the whole body for the disorder of a few bad members." The godly should beware of following the example of the Israelites,

> for euen as they failed in suffering the Canaanites to remaine amongst them, and did not expell them; so doe we suffer them who are little better then Canaanites in their behauiour and manners to abide therein, till they corrupt and taint them that dwell among them; as if an infection were dispersed round about to poyson mens bodies.[98]

Rogers understood, however, that migrants could be produced by "oppression, extortion, violence, or fraud." He condemned "rackings of mens rents, that they neuer regard how the tenant with all his toile may, in any poore sort, be maintained; by they are forced by necessitie to leaue their farmes, and some to run cleane away." He also acknowledged that some "strangers and aliants [sic]" could "be made members of this bodie, and citizens of this Citie."[99]

Here he spoke of the church as the Body of Christ, but it is remarkable how easily Rogers throughout this text glided from individual bodies to social bodies to mystical bodies. In any case, the duty of a Christian toward someone who achieved membership in any of these analogous bodies was clear. The godly must take care of those "that be of the same household and body, whom it most concernes vs to looke to, hauing charge of such poore given vs by Christ." Rogers deplored "that Christians, through selfeloue, or worldlinesse should be too fast handed, scantie and nigardly towards other their poore brethren."

> Though in the corrupt practise of this wicked world, we see euery one is for himselfe, as the prouerbe speaketh; posting off the regard of the needy to others: yet if we enter into the Lords sanctuary [...] wee shall finde it odious, vnnaturall, and highly displeasing in the sight of God, that there is not compassion in one to another, and care in one ouer another, as equity and band of duty requireth.

Even the desire to provide for one's own children should not take precedence over obligations to the needy, lest the conscience should suffer "torment [...] to remember that they haue increased their childrens portions with the complaints of the poore." Rogers's concern about vagrancy and immorality did not overwhelm his fealty to the precepts of moral economy and Christian equity.[100]

Richard Rogers's nephew John, ministering in Dedham to a later generation, operated within the same mental framework but took the obligations of charity to new levels in his *Treatise of Love*. Dedicating the book "to my loving neighbours of Dedham," John Rogers celebrated the town's Puritan tradition in a corporatist vein, rejoicing "wherin both the head and body of the Congregation looking one way, much ill hath been hindred, and much good done and maintained." He also appealed for an ordered charity in his definition of love as "a sanctified affection of the heart, whereby whosoever is indued withall, endevoureth to doe all the good he can to all; but especially, to them that be nearest vnto him." Thus charity should "beginne with our own family," then extend "to our kindred [...] then to our owne Towne, then to strangers, as farre as we can" (though Rogers also teaches that we should love "the Saints before our naturall kindred, that be but carnall").

Such an ordered love is the "bond of perfection" of Scripture, which "binds vp all the duties that wee owe to our neighbour, which are many. [...] It tyes societies together and families. Its the strength of Kindgomes, Cities, Corporations, and Villages." Rogers urges the rich to recall the parable of Lazarus and Dives and give to the poor, not only because of the "commandement of God" but also in keeping with the "Law of nature."[101]

However, Rogers introduces a new motive of love beyond scripture and natural law, suggesting that we love another person because our recognition of God's image in him or her "ought to draw our hearts vnto it."[102] Thus although "our loue must begin at those that be neerest us," nevertheless "[w]ee must loue all other men. Not onely our kindred, friends, acquaintance, or neighbours [...] but even all that dwell vpon the face of the earth, high, low, rich, poore, men, women, young, old, bond, free, without or within the Church, that eyther are or ever may be the people of God." Such an enthusiastic love leads the godly to "loue the meanest that feare God, and not neglect them. The meanest member of the body is regarded by the greatest [...] nothing is more comely, than to see wealthy ones to be affable, and to speak kindly, and to the hearts of the poore that be godly." Thus the rich must abandon all "covetous pinching, neglect of giving where cause is, of free lending, by reason of vsurious lending." They should not only bestow alms, giving of their excess in situations of ordinary want but "of our maine substance" in emergencies; prosperous Christians must also "lend freely to them that be a degree aboue the poorest." Rogers laments, "How backward are most in giving to the poore any more than needs must? what contentions at making of rates." To those who say, "My goods are mine owne, Ile doe with them what I list," he retorts, "God hath but committed them to thee of trust, and reserved a right in them, commanding thee to dispose of part of them to the poor." Love, for Rogers, moves through distributive justice into an all-embracing communion: "Loue is *bountifull, beneficiall* and *helpfull*, not keeping what it hath to it selfe, but ready to *distribute* and *communicate* to the good of others, whether spirituall or temporall gifts."[103]

This expansive, inclusive love brings us back to the national covenant. Just as it is untrue that the Scottish kirk, based on the national covenant, entirely lacked congregationalist elements, it is also incorrect to suggest that the English Puritans, forced into congregationalism because of their ecclesial situation, abandoned the idea of the national covenant entirely. The question of the national covenant raises the issue of "preparation for salvation"—whether members of a national church, who might or might not be among the Calvinist elect, can do good works, and in what sense they are in covenant with God. This in turn leads us to Perry Miller's much-discussed essay "'Preparation for Salvation' in Seventeenth-Century New England." Numerous authors have rebutted one caricature or another of what Miller actually said in his seminal article. Most recently, Baird Tipson took Miller to task for his treatment of Thomas Hooker's theology of preparation. Tipson portrayed Hooker's views on how God prepares believers to receive justification as

> more extreme, more "Calvinistic" [...] than Calvin's. "Preparation" is misunderstood as humans doing something to provoke a response from God (Miller's imagining the prepared as "those who most strove to prepare themselves"). Rather, it was the preacher, as God's

agent, who "prepared" initially unresponsive hearers by overcoming their resistance with his rhetoric.

Tipson acknowledges Hooker's argument that believers could bring forth "good fruit" during the stage of preparation prior to justification by faith, and even that this shows an "affinity with the medieval Catholic tradition he [Hooker] abhorred." But he emphasizes that for Hooker, these good works were produced by God, not the believer, because "during this period the hearer was only the passive recipient of the Spirit's work."[104]

For our purposes it is especially important to understand Hooker's doctrine of preparation because he was so closely associated with the Ward/Rogers clan. In fact, John Rogers of Dedham was one of Hooker's closest friends and, arguably, his ego ideal. Two of Hooker's most important publications on preparationism and the national covenant, *The Faithful Covenanter* (ca. 1629) and *The Danger of Desertion* (1631), were originally sermons he delivered at Rogers's Dedham lecture; it is unclear whether Hooker learned his preparationism from Rogers or vice versa. Hooker contributed an introductory epistle for Rogers's *Doctrine of Faith* in which he credited Rogers with having "determine[d] the controversie" over preparation by his argument that "in the hungrings & thristings of the soul there is as it were the spawne of Faith, not yet brought to full perfection."[105] There is also a very significant connection between Hooker and John Rogers's son Nathaniel, who served as curate of Bocking (a village bordering on Braintree in Essex) until Hooker convinced Rogers in 1631 to stop wearing the surplice and the Dean of Bocking sent Rogers packing. Interestingly, several of what John Winthrop called "mr Hookers company" of emigrants came from Bocking and Braintree, though Hooker was in Holland at the time of their 1632 departure and joined them in Newtown (Cambridge), Massachusetts, only later.[106] Hooker was also close to Nathaniel Ward, who signed a November 1629 petition to Bishop of London William Laud urging that Hooker not be suspended from ministry as both Daniel Rogers and John Rogers of Dedham had recently been. In a July 1628 letter to William Sancroft, encouraging him not to be backward in signaling his willingness to accept the mastership of Emmanuel College after the death of John Preston, Ward wrote, "Had yow bene att home Mr Hooker & my selfe had bene wth yow this day." Once both men arrived in New England they would become political allies in opposition to John Winthrop's emphasis on magisterial discretion.[107]

Tipson is correct to emphasize the agency of the preacher as part of Hooker's doctrine of preparation; for Puritans, effective preaching was one of the chief means of grace which God had made available, at least in some places, within the Church of England. It is also true that Hooker insists on the soul's passivity during the process of preparation, so that any "good fruits" are attributable to the Holy Spirit. Hooker never departed from the Reformed doctrine that salvation is entirely a free gift of God's grace that cannot be earned or merited (in fact, Perry Miller himself agrees that Hooker and the other early preparationists were at pains to avoid the imputation of Arminianism or salvation by works; he attributes the development of a more reciprocal sense of covenant, in which God is bound to save people as a result of their actions, to later generations of New England theologians, beginning with John Norton, who served as teacher of Ipswich, Massachusetts).[108]

However, Tipson overlooks a crucial distinction that Hooker makes between the "inward" and the "outward" covenants. Hooker makes it clear that the outward covenant is not the legal covenant with Adam, which is impossible of fulfillment; it pertains to the Covenant of Grace. Nevertheless, those in the outward covenant are not necessarily justified.

> *Externally those are within the covenant*, who expressing their repentance, with their profession of the truth, ingage themselves to walk in the waies of God, and in the truth of his worship, though they have not for the present that sound work of Faith in their hearts, and may be shall never have it wrought by Gods spirit in them.[109]

These are the ordinary baptized Christians of the Church of England who have been exposed to Christ's saving ordinances through the ministry of that Church but who may or may not be saved. (If the distinction between inward and outward covenant seems like scholastic logic-chopping, well, it is. It is no accident that Hooker called the work just cited *A Survey of the Summe of Church-Discipline*, *Summe* meaning *Summa*. He even offered an apology for the book's dense scholastic logic.[110]) In a similar way John Preston could speak of "a conditionall Couenant of Grace, which is common to all."[111]

In *The Faithful Covenanter*, Hooker takes a dimmer view of those in the outward covenant. "The wicked are in Covenant with the Lord outwardly, but not inwardly; the heart closes not with God, they are not humble: The *Iewes* were Gods people in outward Covenant, but were disobedient and stubborne against the Lord." While Hooker does not explicitly say that such people are to blame for their unsaved status, he does suggest that their punishment will be severe, especially those who (like the Dedhamites) had the benefit of what he called elsewhere a "powerfull Ministry."

> A Dedham drunkard, or hypocrite, carelesse carnall Gospeller, or covetous one; the devils will rejoyce for him; when he comes to hell; they will make Bonefires, and make it holiday for him, stand upon their tiptoes to look on him, and say, What, are you come hither after all Prayers, and Sermons, and Sacraments, and Admonitions?

Hooker also calls the inward covenant a "Covenant of being in God, which is called the Covenant of faith." The covenant that embraces the "generall frame of the nation," however, is "a Covenant of walking before or with God [...] this is the covenant of new obedience or of thankfulnesse, which the Lord reveals, requires, and exacts of all that have given their names unto him"—that is, all who belong to the national church. It was this outward, national covenant and its social consequences that Perry Miller was concerned about, how it provided an "incentive for righteous conduct" for the non-elect or not-yet-assured-of-election, rather than salvation per se.[112]

Hooker's clearest statement on the national covenant came in his sermon *The Danger of Desertion*. Although his "Far[e]well Sermon" was not in fact preached just prior to Hooker's 1633 departure from Europe, but on Maundy Thursday 1631, it does offer an important ideological justification for Puritan mobility.[113] In this powerful work, Hooker raises the specter of God's departure from England. Hooker's doctrine is *"That God may justly leave off a people, and unchurch a Nation.* Israel suspected it, and feared it." Hooker explains that God cannot "cast off his elect eternally; but those that are onely in outward covenant, with him he may." Thus God had left the Jewish nation with its merely "outward vocation, and for such God may cast them off"—as he could now cast off England for its unfaithfulness to the national covenant. While Hooker has to be discreet about calling for the faithful to depart from England before God does, he makes it clear that believers should seek out the place where "Gods ordinances" are enjoyed, "for he is principally there where his ordinances are in the purity of them." Meanwhile, Hooker depicts forlorn Englanders pleading with God to remain. "Thou hope of Israel, doe not leave us: they beset God with their prayers, and watch him at the Townes end that he might not goe away."[114]

English Puritans did believe in a national covenant centered on the Church of England, in spite of its imperfections. In his Judges commentary, Richard Rogers, speaking of "this couenant which the heads of Israel must keepe toward the Lord," concluded "that Christian Magistrates are by their authority to pull downe all Idols, and abolish superstition both of the infidels and heretickes." But in practical terms, given their embattled position within the Church, Puritans had to further their spiritual and social goals by instituting private, voluntary covenants, what Rogers called "couenant[s] of loue." Speaking of David and Jonathan, Rogers emphasized the need for Christians to "renue their covenant of love oftentimes, as they two did."[115] In his most popular work, *Seauen Treatises*, Rogers recounted how about twenty of his parishioners met in a private home during the Armada year, 1588, "for the continuance of love, and for the edifying one of another." The group drafted and agreed to a "covenant to turne to God by repentance."[116]

Reading this document, one might almost be tempted to think that Puritans were interested only in "practical divinity" or inward piety, since it contains little mention of social matters, and that their social activism was something they undertook merely as citizens, separate from their spiritual lives. It is also true that the "reformation of manners" which took place in early modern England was not a Puritan monopoly. For example, the "Company of the Four and Twenty" which ruled Braintree in the early seventeenth century was led by Samuel Collins, the vicar who advised Laud about how to get rid of Thomas Hooker, and this group vehemently pursued the campaign against vagrancy, premarital pregnancy, and other Puritan concerns. Nevertheless, the Puritans, with their belief in the national covenant and hatred of hypocrisy, did have special motives to engage wholeheartedly in the moral crusade.[117] And they tended to analogize rather than compartmentalize. If a group of Puritans like Rogers's parishioners formed a corporate body so as to develop their spirituality, they did so not in order to drop out of society; rather, their attempt to reform their small corporation from within was analogous to the broader effort to restore the whole body politic in keeping with the national covenant, in keeping with the scholastic "analogy of being."

Modern people have lost the habit of analogical thinking, so we may be tempted to see the concept of the body politic in purely metaphorical terms: "society is a body," "society is a mystical body [like the body of Christ, the Church]," "a minister is an eye for the social body." But early modern people conceived these relationships as analogies, not metaphors: "a minister is to society as an eye is to the body," "as the head is to the human body, so is the King to the social body, and so is Christ to the Church."[118] The various corporate entities were nestled inside each other like Russian dolls; each had its own autonomous being springing from the terms of its covenant, but what applied to one held true, *mutatis mutandis*, for all the others, according to the principle of proportion.[119] There was no separation between the religious, the intellectual, the political, and the social among Puritans.

The assertion that Puritans adhered to the scholastic analogy of being is problematic because Puritan academics avoided using this phrase, reserving the word analogy for the "analogy of faith," a principle of biblical exegesis.[120] But the word analogy comes from the Greek word for proportion, and it was in the context of proportionality and distributive justice that the analogy of being entered into Puritan thought.[121] In his *De Regno Christi*—a work cited approvingly by both Samuel Ward and Nathaniel Rogers—Martin Bucer offered a classically Aristotelian discussion of distributive justice, "according to which there is attributed to everyone the task, honor, and emolument which is due to him for the utility of the entire commonwealth in proportion to his nature, ability, virtue, and industry."[122] In other words, the body politic must be well-proportioned according to the status of its various members and the dignity of the estates, guilds, universities, and other lesser corporate bodies to which they belong, all of which stand in an analogical relationship to each other and the entire body politic. Similarly, In his *Whole Treatise of the Cases of Conscience*, William Perkins spoke of distributive justice as "that, which keepes a proportion in giuing to euery man that honour, dignitie, reuerence, reward or punishment, that is due vnto him." In keeping with this line of reasoning, he offered an extensive defense of distinctions in clothing as proper and necessary for maintaining social hierarchy.[123] The Puritans' concern for social proportion would become an obsession once they removed to colonial New England, as town records presented in future chapters will show.

A Puritan's attempt to reform their inner self, and a Puritan prayer group's agreement to help purify each other, were analogous to the efforts of organized Puritans to regulate society. However, when it came to charity for the poor, there was a more direct link, namely commutative justice, the counterpart of distributive justice. When commutative justice applied, all people were supposed to be treated equally without respect of persons. Perkins's thought also embraced commutative justice in the form of "Christian Equitie […] a rare and excellent vertue, whereby men use a true meane, and an equall moderation, in all their affaires and dealings with men, for the maintaining of iustice and preservation of peace." The magistrate had power to judge according to equity rather than the letter of the law, especially "when the mittigation stands with the lawe of nature." More than once Perkins mentioned "leases"—land tenure—as a type of transaction which should be informed by equitable considerations, "rents" being another. "The laws of men, are policie," Perkins stated pithily, "but Equitie is Christianitie."[124]

The concept of equity informed Puritans' frequent interventions to promote "moral economy" in situations of unemployment, dearth of food, shortage of land, or elimination of common rights.[125] In a similar vein, Ethan Shagan has pointed out the influence of the "Aristotelian ideal of virtuous mediocrity" in fostering "social moderation" in early modern England. This was a theme dear to both Protestant scholastics and Christian humanists. Sometime between 1553 and 1565, Elizabeth's Lord Keeper Sir Nicholas Bacon wrote a poem entitled "In Commendacion of the Meane Estate," which concludes thus:

> Of thre estates twooe [wealth and poverty] are escheude,
> As twooe extremes by reasons lore,
> And the meane state is sett before,
> Who bringes and bredes theis Juells three,
> Saftye, Quiette and Libertye.[126]

Nicholas Bacon fathered not only Francis Bacon (whose mother Anne Cooke patronized Puritan ministers) but also Sir Nathaniel Bacon, the staunchly Puritan magnate of Stiffkey, Norfolk. (Sir Nicholas Bacon's son, also named Nicholas, became the father of another Sir Nathaniel Bacon, a painter whose *"Cookmaid with Still Life of Vegetables and Fruit,"* ca. 1620–25, from the collection of the Tate Gallery, is the cover illustration for this book.) Indeed, we are not surprised to find this ideal of mediocrity expressed by Puritan writers such as Richard Rogers, who asked, "Why do few godly Christians enioy any great portion of outward blessings in comparison, (for it is so) euen because the Lord prouideth a better thing for them, when he giueth them a mediocritie in them all, as of maintenance, of credit, account and fauour with their betters." Rogers went on to employ an agricultural metaphor for the desired golden mean: "The earth which is too strong and lusty, runneth vp into weede and stalke, but the well tilled and compassed, bringeth forth a plentifull crop. And rare is the man, whose fruites are not more gratious and constant in a moderate estate, then in a mighty."[127] The ideals of moderation and equity converge in Puritan thought, providing an example of godly resourcefulness in drawing on and synthesizing whatever sources lay to hand, whether biblical, scholastic, or humanistic.

Such invocations of mediocrity, however, have suggested to "post-revisionist" historians that Puritanism represents the rise of, if not a "middle class," at least a "middle sort" bent on imposing what Shaw's character Alfred Doolittle called "middle class morality" on previously fun-loving peasants, merrily skipping around maypoles and enjoying other harmless recreations passed down from ideally cohesive medieval communities.[128] David Underdown commented, "Rural society was dividing, with a minority of middling property-owners acquiring a sense of identity which detached them from the previously relatively homogeneous village community, and led them to devise new mechanisms for imposing their own conception of order on those below them." Similarly, Keith Wrightson diagnosed "social polarization," "a differentiation of attitudes and values [...] within local communities."[129] In his dissertation, H. R. French bravely questioned the emphasis on this "middle sort" by Wrightson, his thesis advisor, pointing out that those promoting the early modern reformation of manners liked to call themselves the "chief inhabitants" or the "better sort" rather than the "middle sort." This is readily apparent in many documents written by Puritans and their magisterial allies; for instance, in the 1629 description of the cloth depression cited above, the Essex Justices referred to the "many poor" in Braintree, "and those of the better sort are not able long to maintain them." With respect to Bocking, the JPs commented "that town abound[s] with poor whereof many are very unruly and having no employment will make the place very hazardous for men of better rank to live amongst them." French's data suggested that local leaders were not entrusted with public office because they were wealthy or of the "middle sort," but rather that the prestige associated with office-holding helped local leaders on their path toward gentry status.[130]

The association of the Puritan contribution to the reformation of manners with class warfare on the part of an incipient bourgeoisie ultimately does not account for all aspects of this movement. As Margo Todd remarked, Puritanism may have appealed to a "hypothetical middle class," but it also displayed considerable "social activism and progressivism."[131] Whether Puritans' advocacy for the poor sprang from a patronizing condescension, from the notion of equity, or from genuine Christian love is less important than the fact of their consistent solidarity with the poor according to the precepts of moral economy. That it did not come entirely from a (somewhat wishful) sense of *noblesse oblige* is suggested by the apparent adherence of sizable numbers of poor people to Puritanism. The remainder of this chapter will present the evidence for Puritan activism on behalf of the poor during times of dearth and economic hardship.

In late 1622, a depression struck the East Anglian cloth industry, due partly to Spanish restrictions on English imports during a period of tension between the two nations.[132] Food rioting took place that December in the Stour Valley; the Essex justices of the peace wrote to their counterparts in Suffolk charging that "the principal outrages" had been committed by inhabitants of Sudbury in Suffolk. The JPs, led by Puritan magnates the Earl of Warwick and Sir Francis Barrington, requested help from the Suffolk commission of the peace in "repressinge" these "disordered people," and promised "to sceecure yor Countie from anie like vnlawfull attempts by anie the Inhabitants of ours."[133] While this clearly brings out the "law and order" aspect of Puritan social thought, the largely Puritan bench in Essex must have also assisted in efforts to alleviate the distress of unemployed clothworkers. On December 22, 1622, King James ordered the enforcement of the Book of Orders first issued in 1586, according to which "the Justices of Peace in all Parts of the Realm are directed to stay all Ingrossers Forestallors and Regrators of Corne, and to direct all Owners and Farmors, having Corne to spare, to furnish the Markets." Under the Book of Orders, JPs were empowered to search stocks of grain for evidence of hoarding, prohibit grain exports, regulate public markets to make sure that corn was available to the poor and exhort merchants to sell grain below market prices.[134]

As the dearth spread into Lincolnshire during the spring of 1623, Sir William Pelham sympathetically recorded its effects, claiming that "our country was never in that want that now it is, and more of money than corn, for there are many thousands in these parts who have sold all they have [...] and cannot get work to earn any money. Dog's flesh is a dainty dish," Pelham continued, "also such horse flesh as hath lain long in a deke for hounds. And the other day one stole a sheep who for mere hunger tore a leg out, and did eat it raw."[135] This compassionate observer had, at least, Puritan leanings. His wife Frances's sister was Lady Brilliana Harley, married to the staunch Puritan Sir Robert Harley. When Lady Harley heard that the minister of Pelham's family home,

Brocklesby, had died, she wrote to recommend a Puritan candidate for the living; Pelham told her that "if he sawe he weare painefull, it was likely he would consider him."[136] However, Pelham's Christian conscience eventually compelled him to take the King's side in the Civil War, since he had sworn an oath to support the monarch upon receiving a post at court. Although Pelham never abandoned the Royalist cause, he nevertheless sheltered the Puritan minister Symon Patrick at Brocklesby during the Civil War.[137] His distant cousin Herbert Pelham III became an important resident of the Massachusetts Bay Colony; Herbert Pelham's sister Penelope married Massachusetts governor Richard Bellingham, a sometime Essex County resident and key supporter of Nathaniel Ward and his Body of Liberties.[138]

Better documentation has survived for the official response to the more serious crisis of 1629–31, caused by another downturn in the cloth industry that affected East Anglia and other textile-producing areas, and exacerbated by a bad harvest in 1630. In his study of crowd actions in early modern England, Buchanan Sharp estimated that more than half of the food riots between 1586 and 1631 took place during this two-year period of dearth. The situation was so dire that the Privy Council issued three different Books of Orders during the crisis which, to a certain extent, represent a reevaluation of the traditional policy. Innovations included the creation of a special commission made up of Privy Councillors to supervise the nationwide relief effort, as well as a new emphasis on implementing the Elizabethan poor laws and vagrancy statutes and on the creation of bridewells and other institutions to house the poor and set them on work. However, as Paul Slack has put it, "that did not mean that there was any general desire to abolish the government's corn policy, lock, stock and barrel"—rather, "there was a deliberate search for improvements and embellishments," including even an increased advocacy of "price-fixing."[139]

The burden of enforcing this flurry of edicts fell, of course, primarily on the justices of the peace. Both Michael Braddick and Steve Hindle have suggested that the Orders of 1630–31 were unpopular and that pushback from local officials signaled the beginning of the end of traditional ideas of moral economy. Norfolk magistrates complained to the Privy Council that forcing farmers to bring their corn to local markets instead of selling it to corn merchants for shipping to London and other places, as they were accustomed to do, was "toylesome to the Corne master & fruitleese to the poore."[140] Even the Essex justices balked when the Council requested that towns "unable to maintain their own poor" should receive contributions from neighboring communities, but they resisted simply because the entire Stour Valley was suffering the same severe hardship.[141] However, the Essex commission of the peace showed their real commitment to the Orders when they received a petition from the weavers of Bocking (where Nathaniel Rogers was serving as curate) and Braintree in October 1629, charging that local clothiers were putting the poor out of work by employing too many apprentices. The justices immediately began issuing warrants to jail textile manufacturers throughout the region who refused to dismiss their apprentices; when clothiers of Coggeshall complained, two royal assize judges issued an order "to stay all further proceedings." On December 2 the justices protested this injunction, ending their letter with the warning that "if somewhat be not presently done, we shall not be able to keep these poor people in quiet, which we assure ourselves will be very displeasing to his Majesty and the lords." The letter was signed by Sir William Maynard, Sir Thomas Wyseman, Sir William Maxey, Drue Deane, and James Heron.[142]

Interestingly, the first signatory, Maynard, was an Arminian and friend of Archbishop Laud, while Thomas Wyseman [Wiseman] was in fact a church papist who was presented as a recusant in 1626. William Maxey's religious affiliations are not known, but he joined with Wiseman in an ill-fated plot to rig a 1628 Parliamentary election to exclude the Earl of Warwick's candidates, the Puritans Sir Francis Barrington and Sir Harbottle Grimstone.[143] However, Drue Deane came from a prominent Puritan family. His father, Sir John Deane, was an ally of the Earl of Warwick who had written to the Privy Council to express concern for the plight of the poor during the 1622–23 cloth trade depression. After the death of Sir John's father, his mother Anne Deane remarried Sir John Tyndal; their daughter Margaret would become the third wife of John Winthrop. That the Deanes and the Winthrops became closely allied is suggested by the fact that Sir John Deane's sister Anne chose John Winthrop as the executor of her estate. As for James Heron, his affliations are obscure.[144]

Thus far anti-Puritan JPs seem to have taken the lead in poor relief efforts during the crisis; indeed, Wiseman and Maxey continued their aggressive enforcement of the orders in late 1630. They reported on December 21 that in Lexden Hundred and its environs, they had conducted a thorough search of grain stockpiles, told all those possessing corn how much grain they should take to market and attended the markets themselves, "so as whereas before there was a great scarcitie and want of graine in every Markett and the price every Daie risinge, nowe by these orders the Marketts are fully served w[i]thout any want and the princes of Corne decreasinge." This letter was also signed by John Wakeringe. That Wakeringe may have had Puritan leanings is suggested by the career of his son Dionysius, who served in the First and Second Protectorate Parliaments and on the Essex commission of the peace under Cromwell.[145] And on the same day, the prominent Puritan Sir Thomas Barrington notified the Council that elsewhere in Essex, magistrates had aggressively enforced the Orders against "Badgers, Millers, &c [...] som of them being bound to ye sessions, others ouerlooked wth a strict eye [...] we haue furthermore taken care [...] that the poorer sort be prouided for" at reduced grain prices.[146]

Another report of the Essex Justices, dated April 19, 1631, brought out even more strongly the depth of Puritan commitment to the norms of moral economy. It invoked the Puritan obsession with proportion: "wee have assessed euery man that had Corne, to carry the same p[ro]portionably to the Marketts. [...] And have not only delt with the able men of p[ar]ishes to p[ro]vide and laie in Corne for p[ro]vision of the poore at vnder:Rates, but did cause them to raise stockes & meanes to sett their poore on work." The justices cautioned against "a second search" which they feared would create an impression of scarcity and thus raise grain prices; rather, they recommended measures be taken to improve the cloth trade so that poor weavers could return to work. This missive was signed by the Earl of Warwick, Sir Thomas Barrington and their staunchly Puritan ally Sir Harbottle Grimston, as well as by John Wakeringe. Wiseman and Maxey signed, but so did Puritan magnates Sir Henry Mildmay and Sir William Masham, as well as Warwick's brother-in-law Sir Thomas Cheke. Mildmay's grandfather Walter Mildmay founded the Puritan stronghold of Emmanuel College, Cambridge (the family was also connected to the Winthrops by marriage); Masham married Elizabeth Barrington, daughter of Sir Francis and Lady Joan Barrington.[147]

I have not had time to make an exhaustive survey of all documents that have survived the crisis and are relevant to the theme of moral economy, or to research all signatories in depth; even if I had, there is obviously no way to quantify this data, to prove that either "Arminians" or "Puritans" took the lead in enforcing customary economic norms, or to show that the different groups emphasized different aspects of traditional precepts. We can say, following Buchanan Sharp, that in Essex between 1630 and 1631 "the justices of the peace consistently and conscientiously enforced those aspects of the Book of Orders intended to insure that stocks of grain in private hands were surveyed and brought to market, the market supervised, and the needs of the poor attended to first."[148] This seems to have been true regardless of a justice's religious bent; Puritan and anti-Puritan leaders who had shown themselves to be political enemies cooperated fully in enforcing these norms with no sign of dissension. Certainly the Puritan magistrates did nothing to suggest that they represented the needs of an incipient middle class or that they were on the cutting edge of capitalism in the Stour Valley. Although some East Anglians began to offer criticism of traditional procedures for enforcing moral economy, as Paul Slack has said, "that did not imply any widespread acceptance of *laissez-faire*. Criticism of, and action against, regrators and forestallers continued amidst almost unanimous approval."[149] If such critiques gained ground later in the 1630s, perhaps that process was aided by the departure of many Puritan magistrates and ministers for New England.

Puritans did not bring capitalism to the Stour Valley. Is it possible that, in fact, the converse might be true—that the reason the Stour Valley was so heavily Puritan has something to do with Puritans' defense of moral economy—that Puritanism was a genuinely popular religion in the region? This contradicts the post-revisionists, who anticipated the "confessionalization theory" that emerged from studies of Calvinist regimes on the continent of Europe, arguing that Puritan magistrates and ministers sought to impose their vision of social order on the ordinary people (as in Keith Wrightson's and David Levine's discovery of horizontal "polarization" in the village of Terling, Essex).[150] However, there is room for doubt as to whether confessionalization theory, developed from studies of thoroughly Calvinist governments, can apply to the situation in England, where Puritan magistrates, however dominant their position in localities, occupied a rather marginal place in the nation as a whole. While Wrightson's model might have some relevance for the most completely Puritanized places like Terling, none of the English village studies surveyed by Martin Ingram replicated Wrightson and Levine's findings. Ingram suggested that where polarization existed, as in the village of Keevil in Wiltshire, "the splits were as much vertical as horizontal."[151] Margaret Spufford also questioned the model of horizontal polarization, since poor people too were known to manifest Puritan religiosity. Believe it or not, Spufford suggested, "the 'poorer sort' may have had their own religious convictions.'"[152]

Unless Puritanism had a large popular following in the Stour Valley, many contemporary accounts become hard to comprehend. We have seen that the vicar of Braintree, Samuel Collins, charged that merchants desired Puritan lecturers in order to "drawe tumults & troupes of the Countrey to their faires & shopps." John Rogers of Dedham alluded to this accusation when he wrote "of an abuse amongst us, that they which bring in here (because of the concourse of people) their commodities to sell, raise the prizes, and sell dearer than in any of the Market Towns round about us, whereby they wrong the poor here [i.e., in Dedham] [...] yea, and also raise an evil name on the Gospel."[153] If such large crowds of people flocked to Puritan lectures, as is attested by both Puritans and their opponents, could this really have been the cult of a relatively small "middle sort"? Why did a gallery (balcony) have to be built in the church at Dedham to accommodate the enormous attendance at Rogers's lectures?[154] Dr. Henry Sampson (d. 1700) recorded that during one of Rogers's sermons, the gallery "gave a grievous crash, which affrighted the whole company, the floor and gallery being exceeding full, as it used to be in his time"; yet miraculously the balcony did not completely collapse. A more contemporary and presumably more exact account was given by Emmanuel Downing in a letter to John Winthrop. Downing places this event at Rogers's 1636 funeral:

> I was at mr. Rogers of Dedham his funerall, where there were more people than 3 such Churches could hold; the gallery was so over loaden with people that yt sunck and crackt and in the middle where yt was Joynted the tymbers gaped and parted on from another soe that there was a great Cry in the Church [...] but yt pleased God to honour that good man departed with a miracle at his death, for the gallerie stood.[155]

These accounts suggest that the lower ranks of the English population did not spend all their spare time drinking ale and performing morris dances. Puritan lectures seem to have been as "popular" as any other popular activity, at least in the Stour Valley during the early seventeenth century.

An event of 1636 demonstrates that just as Puritan leaders sought to defend the people's well-being, ordinary citizens could at times take action to protect their Puritan ministers. In 1635, the Laudian Matthew Wren was named Bishop of the see of Norwich, which had jurisdiction over Ipswich, Suffolk. In November 1634, Samuel Ward of Ipswich was summoned before the ecclesiastical Court of High Commission, on charges which included (in William Prynne's words) "*saying, that the Church of England was ready to ring the Changes,*" and "*saying, that Religion and the Gospel stood on tiptoes ready to be gone.*"[156] On trial between January and June of 1635, Ward did not endear himself to High Commission when he defended the right of the people to choose their own ministers, based on precedents from the church fathers Leo, Cyprian, and Augustine.[157] Found guilty, suspended from ministry, and imprisoned in November 1635, Ward prepared a form of submission which Bishop Wren deemed inadequate.

Wren sent ecclesiastical visitors to Ipswich in April 1636, who found the town in an ugly mood. Greeted by a mob which refused to let the ecclesiastical commission into the Church of St. Mary-le-Tower, the visitors responded by suspending four ministers for various liturgical irregularities. When Wren himself appeared in Ipswich on Trinity Sunday, June 12, 1636, passersby cursed and threw stones while boys approached the Bishop and rudely tried to stare him down. Wren had placed himself in a bind. At his own trial Wren would later say that he would have appointed another lecturer for Ipswich to replace Ward, "if they had desired any but him." Not only did the residents of Ipswich refuse to accept any lecturer besides Samuel Ward, but one of the town's elected officials, Portman William Cage, also petitioned the King for the restoration of their ministers and the right of borough officials to continue selecting the town's clergy. The stage was set for Wren's next visit to Ipswich, on August 11, 1636, when a mob of about one hundred citizens, including "apprentices, ship carpenters and sailors," broke into Wren's residence and forced Wren and his wife to flee Ipswich. This affront inspired proceedings in Star Chamber against Cage and the entire magistracy of Ipswich for inciting the mob to riot, which dragged on until the Long Parliament put an end to them. Upon his release from prison, Ward fled to the Netherlands; he returned in 1638, still deprived of his post, and died in Ipswich in 1640. That same year, the burgesses of Ipswich elected William Cage to Parliament.[158]

The career of the Ward/Rogers nexus along the border of Suffolk and Essex demonstrates that Puritans were committed to cultivating their inner life, but they were also determined to transform their society. Writing of the Earl of Warwick and his associates during the 1630s, Karen Kupperman has astutely observed that "Puritanism, rather than causing them to restrict their outlook, seems to have given them a zest for life and endeavor. For leading puritans, religious commitment meant empowerment."[159] But as Charles I instituted his "personal rule," governing without Parliament after 1629, the Puritan agenda met with seemingly insurmountable obstacles. Many English Puritans began to consider whether their religious and social ideals could be more effectively deployed in a colonial setting. Yet departing from England, and detaching themselves from the various institutions in which they were imbricated, required some theoretical justification in order to satisfy their orderly minds.

Chapter Two

THE PURITAN IDEOLOGY OF MOBILITY

Puritans produced their ideology of mobility by applying certain key principles available to the English godly in the early seventeenth century, especially corporatism and covenant, so that they could live out their beliefs in the political, religious, and social context of the time. It was a very unlikely development, not only because long-distance migrants in England were feared and stigmatized as vagrants, but also because a covenanted, corporate body, once created, was seen as a living organism that people should not depart from with impunity. Prior to the Great Migration, the most common rationales offered for mobility by the godly were to obtain religious teaching, to partake in fellowship with other believers, and to enjoy a ministry that was sound by Puritan standards. After removal to New England, justification for mobility centered on the health of the social bodies created by the settlers. A corporate body could become diseased or distempered if the elements that composed it fell out of balance. This might happen if a town's location did not afford enough of the resources required, including arable land, forest, meadow, and pasture, to sustain the "mixed farming" regime for all inhabitants. Political and religious disagreements also threatened the health of a social body. In all these cases it might become necessary for some of the members of the body to withdraw to another place, creating a new social body in order to save the collective life of the original body.

In order to create this ideology, Puritans first had to redefine mobility, chipping away at its negative connotations in seventeenth-century England. But they also had to develop an institutional framework to make mobility possible, based on the already existing ideological concept of corporatism. Before turning to the ideology of mobility proper, I would like to discuss its organizational underpinnings.

Patrick Collinson made his appeal, referenced in the last chapter, for a "social history with the politics put back in" as part of his discussion of the 1596 Swallowfield Articles. Leaders of the parish of Swallowfield, straddling the border of Wiltshire and Berkshire, drew up this document to address social problems and regulate communal life. In reprinting this document, Steve Hindle called it "a milestone on the road from manor to vestry."[1] Here he referenced one of the major themes of early modern English historiography, the transfer of local governance from manorial courts to parish vestries as a result of the Elizabethan poor laws, which gave control of poor relief to parishes. There were two types of vestries: "open" vestries, which allowed for greater participation by ordinary parishioners, and "close" or "select" vestries, self-perpetuating groups of the more prominent members of the parish. Sidney and Beatrice Webb provided the classic narrative of this transition in volume 1 of their landmark series *English Local Government*.[2]

Indeed, the Swallowfield leaders stated their intention to deal with matters "consernynge the Churche, the poore or the parrishe," suggesting their kinship to a vestry. The problem is that they never referred to themselves as a vestry, although the term was certainly in use by that time, calling themselves instead "the chieffe inhabitants" and, repeatedly, a "companye."[3] Hindle is aware that the transition from manor to vestry was a long and drawn-out process, lasting into the eighteenth century. The Webbs' own research had suggested this; for instance, they note that the "Four-and-Twenty" of the parish of St. Michael's, Alnwick, did not start calling itself a select vestry until 1800. Nevertheless, Hindle seems determined to join the Webbs in retroactively labeling any organized body of inhabitants that legislated for their community a vestry; he suggests that the Swallowfield "chief inhabitants" were in fact "a primitive form of parish vestry or 'town meeting.'"[4]

Hindle seems to be suggesting that Swallowfield's was an open vestry, but applying the term "vestry" (and especially "select vestry") to a group of "chief inhabitants" conjures up the image of a self-perpetuating oligarchy which was a law unto itself, with little sense of responsibility to the whole community. As Gervase Rosser argues in his account of similar groups during the Middle Ages, this is a mistake:

> The chief pledges of Westminster [...] were, by the later Middle Ages, the self-identified "better sort" of the various trades and professions of the town, admitted to office by co-option. In Aristotle's sense of the word, they constituted an aristocracy. Yet it is an assumption of historians far more than of contemporaries that the few "more discreet" individuals necessarily sacrificed communal interests in the selfish pursuit of their own. The Aristotelian ideal, after all, was that these should be the few men best suited to act on behalf of all.[5]

Rather than adopting the idea of the close vestry as a *telos* toward which all English communities were tending, I would like to explore the rich variety of corporate forms available in early modern England for regulating village and parish life, rooted in the robust corporate ethos of the medieval period. Groups of this sort did often adopt the name "vestry" over time, primarily in order to gain legal sanction for their actions according to the poor laws. But such groups had institutional descendants besides the vestry; namely, the corporations and companies of settlers who formed communities in New England, informed by their experiments with local organization in England.

In an age when the word *corporation* conjures up images of global conglomerates like Nissan, Apple, or Amazon, it is difficult to grasp what it meant for Europeans in the Middle Ages, when corporations took many forms and often served to anchor local communities. Colleges and universities were corporations; Henry S. Turner reminds us that the most common word for a corporation in early modern law was *universitas*.[6] Any collection of individuals that was united, or united itself, into one body for a particular purpose could become a corporation: cathedral chapters, monasteries, craft guilds and confraternities or religious guilds were common varieties. In addition, the monarch was a *corporation sole*, a corporation with only one member, whose natural body was conceptually distinguished from his body politic, the nation as a whole.[7]

The rediscovery of Justinian's *Digest* in the late eleventh century and the recovery of the Roman law of corporations led to stunning developments. In Italian cities, religious confraternities transformed themselves into urban communes; since corporations had the right to make regulations binding their members, the communes could use the Roman private law of corporations to claim public political power. After losing a war against the Lombard League of cities operating under communal government, Emperor Frederick I had to acknowledge their de facto independence in the 1183 Peace of Constance.[8] As the Middle Ages went on, people organized into guilds continued to claim a role in urban politics based on corporatist thinking; for example, in fourteenth-century Florence a federation of guilds obtained sovereignty over the commune.[9] Corporatism allowed for a measure of self-government because the Roman law maxim "quod omnes tangit ab omnibus approbetur" applied to corporations—what touches all should be approved by all. As Hwa-Yong Lee has pointed out, the "q.o.t" rule did not mean that every individual in an organization would have to consent to every measure, but rather that decision makers would consider the rights and interests of those affected. In practice a *maior et sanior pars* of a corporation or community—its "greater and better part," like the "chief inhabitants" at Swallowfield—could represent the interests of the whole.[10]

The vexed question of "the reception of Roman law" in England has led some very great British historians, like F. W. Maitland, to say some rather foolish things, but the prevalence of corporate forms in medieval towns is one concrete indication that the Roman law of corporations, at least, had an impact in Britain.[11] An interesting example comes from thirteenth-century Berwick-upon-Tweed, then part of Scotland, where all the guilds already existing in the town combined themselves into one guild which became the town government. The purpose of this merger, according to the guild's statutes, was "so that through many bodies joined in one place, [each] one of them in the relation of one to another may strive for one will and a firm and sincere love." Day-to-day government would be in the hands of 24 "proborum hominum," honest men.[12] It is not surprising that Scotland, which of course did not follow English common law, would be influenced by Roman law, yet when Edward I conquered Berwick temporarily in 1296, he allowed this system of government to stand. And after the English definitively took control of Berwick in 1482, the privileges of the guild continued.[13]

The typical pattern in England was somewhat different. As Stella Kramer documented in her brilliant and neglected 1905 dissertation, the Crown after the Norman conquest created guilds-merchant to regulate trade in towns. Soon, however, competing craft guilds began to emerge, so that the guild-merchant often morphed into the town government and then disappeared, superseded by borough governments which typically left craft guilds in charge of business regulations under the supervision of the town. Thus there was always a close connection between the craft guilds and the local government, but as Gervase Rosser argues, it is incorrect to see guild membership as a burden imposed from above. Guilds were essentially voluntary organizations that helped workers survive by providing them with a social network through which they could obtain credit and social respectability; towns generally allowed guilds to regulate themselves.[14]

This leads to another feature of corporatism in medieval and early modern England, its multiplicity. Individuals were often members of numerous corporate bodies; as Samuel L. Thomas put it, they "saw themselves as members of a range of communities simultaneously. These ranged from the international Protestant (or Catholic) communion, the English nation, or a particular county, region, parish, neighborhood, or prayer meeting."

They could also be members of guilds, confraternities, or local elite groups entrusted with decision-making powers. Henry Turner argues that the "many overlapping and often competing corporate bodies" created "a pluralistic public space—a space composed of multiple publics and associations." Corporations nestled inside corporations, as when members of the corporate body known as Parliament represented corporate boroughs.[15] This would provide an important precedent for the settlement of Massachusetts, where corporate towns existed within a colony that was itself a corporation, the Massachusetts Bay Company.

Historians have been reluctant to admit this; David Thomas Konig insisted that New England towns could not have seen themselves as corporations because according to the common law, one corporation could not create another.[16] From a purely legal perspective Konig is quite correct; William Sheppard, one of Lord Protector Cromwell's legal officials, said as much in his 1659 book *Of Corporations, Fraternities, and Guilds*. Yet Sheppard also indicated that "A Corporation may be made up of natural persons, or it may be made up of persons or bodies incorporate and political."[17] Only the Crown and Parliament, strictly speaking, had the power to incorporate, yet towns did sometimes use this language in recognizing guilds, as when Hull in 1680 decreed that the city's Company of Tailors would "stand and be incorporated into a Brotherhood by such name as heretofore in ancient time they have been."[18] We see here the power of prescription, whereby an "ancient" organization could claim a quasi-corporate status. As Sheppard—a Puritan who, during the Interregnum, affiliated himself with the conservative faction of Independents, led by John Owen and greatly influenced by the New England congregationalist experiment—put it: "That which hath been, and continued time out of mind, a good Corporation; and hath had all the Incidents and Badges of a good Corporation, shall continue so, albeit they cannot shew any Charter for it: For this doubtlesse was by Charter at first, the which hath been since lost." Most groups in England were self-created; upon finding their legal status in doubt, they might appeal to a legitimate corporation, like a borough, to acknowledge their claim to corporate existence "time out of mind," and thus acquire at least a limited autonomy.[19]

The New England settlers—who, in their primitive state of organization, were hardly particular about legal niceties—followed this rather nebulous precedent.[20] New England towns, as covenanted communities, were acknowledged by their colonies' governments, which tacitly delegated corporate powers to them. In 1647 Nathaniel Ward, speaking to the House of Commons, would appeal to the concept of "consociate bodies" as the underpinning of the Puritan vision of an orderly and harmonious state: "There is no establishing of Kingdomes, but by Order. [...] Order is unity branched out into all the parts of consociate bodies to keep them in unity and perfection; where Order failes they are disjoynted and convulsed; *Symmetry* and *Harmony* are the two supporters of the world."[21]

In recent years, scholars such as Eamon Duffy have emphasized social bodies like guilds and religious confraternities as sites of agency for lay people within Catholic parishes.[22] The development of the doctrine of transubstantiation, and the creation of the feast of Corpus Christi in 1264, provided a vital link between confraternities, guilds, and local governments which cooperated to sponsor processions and pageants to honor the Body of Christ on the feast day (one of the earliest records of a Corpus Christi pageant in England occurs in Ipswich, home of Samuel Ward and, for a time, of his brother Nathaniel—in 1325 the city's guild merchant transformed itself into a Corpus Christi guild of which all the burgesses were members).[23] In a seminal 1983 article, Mervyn James showed that local English leaders seized on the feast as a way of conferring symbolic legitimacy on the social body of the town (Natalie Zemon Davis had already made a similar argument in her study of Lyon in the sixteenth century). As Henry S. Turner has suggested, there was a "mystical idea of the corporate body, sourced in a metaphysics that can be broadly but coherently described as 'Aristotelian'"; this "*mystical* ontology" of the social body had its root in the Body of Christ, which was celebrated in Corpus Christi festivals. Accordingly, as David Crouch has argued for York, the Corpus Christi procession was "in essence, a civic occasion." Crouch documented that the religious and craft guilds of Beverley, York, and Wakefield cooperated to produce Corpus Christi plays (Gail McMurray Gibson has shown that the same was true in Bury St. Edmunds in Suffolk). In York, the town government firmly controlled the entire performance, and membership in the Corpus Christi guild became a key step on the path to public office—something that was also the case in Coventry.[24]

Gervase Rosser has shown that Corpus Christi conferred a sacred aura even on secular guilds during the Catholic era in another way. As the doctrine of transubstantiation spread, communions became less frequent; with the consecrated host now understood as the literal body of Christ, lay people seemed less worthy to receive it. Accordingly, parishes began distributing blessed but non-consecrated bread at the end of Mass which the laity felt freer to consume. Guild feasts benefited from a perceived analogy to this blessed bread and thus took on a "paraliturgical" dimension.[25] With Rosser's argument in mind, it is intriguing that when religious guilds and confraternities were abolished by the Chantries Act of 1547, they often continued in a secularized form, either through a reconstituted secular guild or through the town government. This was especially true when confraternities had played a role in poor relief. York again provides an example: its Corpus Christi guild dissolved in 1547, but one of its projects, the hospital of St. Thomas, maintained control of guild estates for almost thirty years in spite of royal efforts to confiscate them. Eventually, the city secured control of these properties and continued to use them for poor relief. Similar subterfuges proved successful in Coventry and in Richmond, Yorkshire. In Bury St. Edmunds, the Candlemas Guild morphed into an interim town government between the destruction of the Benedictine abbey, which had formerly controlled the town, and Bury's incorporation as a borough in 1606.[26]

Historians have given the most attention to Norwich, where craft and religious guilds had been closely linked for centuries. Norwich seemed determined to hang on to its traditional ways for as long as possible, not out of loyalty to the old faith but from reluctance to lose the civic benefits which Corpus Christi and the religious guilds had conferred. In a short-lived attempt to save the city's Corpus Christi procession, its terminus was changed from St. Mary in the Fields church to the town's Common Hall (a former Dominican house where craft guilds met). The religious guild of St. George had already effectively merged with the town government in 1452; the city's outgoing mayor was automatically appointed guild alderman, while all the aldermen were inducted into the guild. After the

Chantries Act, the guild was secularized, losing its Catholic devotions but playing much the same role in urban politics as before.[27]

One prominent historical narrative about early modern guilds admits that guilds were extremely important promoters of social harmony, poor relief, and moral economy during the late Middle Ages, but it suggests that they became obsolete under the Tudors and Early Stuarts, due to religious and economic changes. Their role was taken over by the developing bourgeoisie of the towns, who created a new "public sphere" to serve their own interests.[28] Current scholarship has questioned this account.[29] Avril Leach concedes that the guilds' economic importance declined but argues that they continued to play a key role in transmitting civic values. She documents the ongoing and very close links between the Drapers' and Tailors' Company in Canterbury and the urban government. Jeffrey Hankins shows how "guild and town fathers" in Colchester "merged [...] into a legitimate and potent authority" during the late sixteenth and early seventeenth centuries.[30]

Phil Withington has enriched the discussion immeasurably with his introduction of the concept of "company" in early modern England, broadening the focus from guilds to other types of associations.[31] In the context of Protestant scholasticism, "company" was an expression of Aristotelian natural sociability, which took numerous forms. D. M. Palliser's study of York uncovered guilds that transformed themselves into companies, perhaps to avoid the negative associations acquired by religious guilds. There were the failed attempts to set up corporations in several counties in order to regulate the textile industry and put the poor to work, and a successful bid by the newly formed Dorchester Corporation to obtain the property formerly belonging to a religious confraternity of the Virgin Mary so that they could use it to promote Puritan goals.[32]

Indeed, the residents of early modern English towns did not have the option of waiting for the bourgeoisie to emerge so that they could deal with pressing social problems. Someone had to fill the gap in poor relief, the policing of morals and dispute resolution left by the disappearance of the monasteries and the religious guilds. Efforts to address these social issues show both continuity and change during the transition from late medieval to early modern England. There was continuity since the concerns were essentially the same. Ben McRee showed that medieval religious guilds undertook to regulate behavior in ways that were quite similar to the later efforts of groups like the Dedham classis and the Chief Inhabitants of Swallowfield. Marjorie Keniston McIntosh's brilliantly executed studies revealed that moral enforcement, hostility to vagrancy, and warning out cottagers who might need poor relief—in short, all the concerns associated with the supposedly Puritan "reformation of manners" during the early modern period—were addressed by manorial courts, craft guilds and religious confraternities during the late Middle Ages.[33] Change also took place, however, since early modern England proved fertile ground for the creation of new forms of association, such as the dubiously legal groups of "Chief Inhabitants" and Presbyterian classes, and the adjustment of other types of corporations to address social goals. Puritans were especially creative in this regard—for instance, organizing the "Feoffees for the Purchase of Impropriations" in 1625 to buy up advowsons so that they could bestow church livings on Puritan ministers; organizations like the trustees of the grammar school in Puritan Dedham could also play a major role in public life.[34]

However, McIntosh has shown that non-Puritan elites could exercise this type of creativity in her remarkable study of Hadleigh, Suffolk—remarkable because she resists the temptation to call Hadleigh's company of Chief Inhabitants a "select vestry." Hadleigh, a cloth-making town nine miles west of Ipswich and eight miles south-southeast of Bury St. Edmunds, followed the pattern of other communities discussed above: local leaders managed to secure control of the property of religious guilds, continued to use it to support poor relief and other civic efforts, and thus became the real political authority in the community. Hadleigh provides the clearest example of how religious guilds were not so much annihilated as transformed into new corporate forms:

> The body of Chief Inhabitants appears to have grown out of three previous groups, which in practice probably had heavily overlapping memberships: the "most honest persons" of Hadleigh, whom Rector and Archdeacon William Pykenham had named in 1497 as the present and future feoffees of the land that supported the almshouses he established; the feoffees who held the market property; and the men who headed Hadleigh's pre-Reformation religious guilds or fraternities.

The Chief Inhabitants held power from 1547 into the early years of the seventeenth century; by the end of that period, their poor relief activities should have been carried out by the local parish, yet the group did not style itself a vestry because it was not, in fact, a vestry, but another animal entirely.[35] William Sheppard, writing in 1659 well after the rise of vestries, does not see groups of "inhabitants" as vestries or as belonging to a parish at all, but as the corporate representatives of a town: "That Cities, Town-ships, and Villages may be, and are incorporated, some by one, and some by another name. [...] Some by the name of the inhabitants, or good men, or the men of date."[36]

Braintree's "Company of Four and Twenty," which had been ruling the town since at least 1565, did officially become a select vestry, but not until 1612 when Dr. John King, the Bishop of London, awarded it that status. King's decree cited a petition from the parish which alleged that "the inferiour and meanest sort of the parishioners and inhabitants" of Braintree were trying to crowd into vestry meetings to interfere with the group's "good proceedings." It is not clear whether this refers to the meetings of the Four and Twenty, or perhaps to open vestry meetings which were taking place alongside the Company meetings. If the latter, then Vicar Samuel Collins may have agreed with the 24 headboroughs to allow the Company to become the vestry. Based on the timing it also seems likely that the Four and Twenty thought it would be advantageous to align itself with the parish in order to conform with the Elizabethan poor laws in continuing its mission of poor relief and moral regulation. In other words, the group was not conceived as a vestry; that title came later, as an afterthought, and the Braintree's Company should properly be seen as part of the broader universe of corporate forms which appeared in English towns during the early modern period. Braintree's Company records also reveal the presence of a very elaborate social hierarchy within the town. The group's members were precisely ranked according to the stools they occupied in the Company's pew in the parish church. There were eight rows of three stools; a new member would be assigned to the lowest stool and had to work his way up in the pecking order. Later chapters will show how attempts like this one to create a fully articulated social body, a system which specified the exact status of each member of the body relative to the others, would be recreated in colonial New England.[37]

In Clare, a village 17 miles from Braintree and 6 miles from Nathaniel Ward's birthplace of Haverhill in Suffolk, a parish vestry existed in tandem with a group of headboroughs deriving its authority from the court leet; there was also a third group that administered a common pasture bestowed on the town by Queen Katherine of Aragon, the proceeds of which financed poor relief. A cloth-producing town of long-standing, Clare in the early seventeenth century had a strong Puritan connection through Sir Nathaniel Barnardiston. A cadet branch of the Barnardiston family held Clare's Priory manor, but Sir Nathaniel exercised preeminence over the entire area from his seat at Kedington between Haverhill and Clare. Barnardiston's personal chaplain, Samuel Fairclough, was born at Haverhill in 1594; his father was vicar there after John Ward. Samuel Ward, later of Ipswich, was then serving as lecturer in Haverhill, acted as Fairclough's godfather, and subsequently exercised a great influence on Fairclough. In a 1636 letter to John Winthrop Jr., Sir Nathaniel sent his love to Nathaniel Ward, among others, and he showed his great interest in New England by leaving a bequest to Harvard College. The Wards, from Haverhill, would have been well aware of the corporatist form of government being administered in nearby Clare. Under the Barnardistons' sway, Clare developed a method of governance that was more flexible and creative than the "select vestry" stereotype would indicate. The Clare vestry made regulations for the town, the headboroughs enforced them through the leet, and the feoffees of the pasture helped provide financing; but in fact the membership of all three groups was practically identical. The "cheife Inhabitants," as they sometimes styled themselves, simply wore different hats as needed to accomplish their various social goals.[38]

I have tried to show that the "road from manor to vestry" was by no means straight and that it had multiple forks and branches. Corporatist creativity was especially pronounced in market towns like Dedham and Braintree, which were not incorporated boroughs. Larger cities like Samuel Ward's Ipswich, which had been incorporated since the time of King John, had complicated and intrusive governmental systems that enabled them to step in and deal with social problems like vagrancy and poor relief, which the Ipswich government effectively monopolized from the mid-1500s; but the smaller towns were freer to devise original structures to address public concerns.[39] Nor was the "select vestry" the only endpoint on this road; the manifold experiments in corporate governance undertaken in early modern English towns would also bear fruit in New England land corporations and towns. The organizations founded by Puritans often sought to address local problems, but they also expressed a "godly" identity that transcended locality. As such they were in keeping with their predecessors, the religious guilds of the Middle Ages. As Gervase Rosser has put it, "the diversity and mobility of medieval society created both extended and highly localized affiliations [...] to which the guilds alone were able to give a definite form."[40]

New England towns would thus be invested with the corporatist mystique, according to which—in Paul Halliday's words—"images of the human body invoked one flesh and one mind, creating a moral and legal imperative for unanimity." Another attraction of corporatism was that it gave life to social bodies that were immortal in law.[41] Puritans did not, of course, believe that the Eucharist was the literal Body of Christ, but they did adhere to the Pauline trope of the Church as Christ's body, and (according to the analogy of being) the political bodies they created retained the mystical ambiance of the "Corpus Christi" long after the official commemoration of the Eucharist under that title was banned. In this way the principle of corporatism provided a metaphysical basis for the establishment of communities in colonial New England.

Samuel Ward's published 1618 assize sermon, *Iethro's Iustice of Peace*, brings out the intellectual ramifications of Puritan corporatism. This volume included Nathaniel Ward's first published works, written during his stay in Elbing, Prussia: a postscript to his brother's sermon and an "Epistle Dedicatory" in which Ward referred to the "body politique" and the "Nationall body." The work was dedicated to Sir Francis Bacon, who represented Ipswich in the House of Commons in the last two Elizabethan parliaments of 1597–98 and 1601 and in the lengthy first parliament of James I, which met several times between 1604 and 1610. Ward indicated that Bacon still had some religious credibility among Puritans—"you haue not let fal your name of religion in getting vp"—and thanked him for "a fauour [...] greater then your Honour knowes of, or I can expresse."[42]

Bacon's reputed hostility to scholasticism, both Catholic and Protestant, seems to make him an unlikely patron for a work in which Samuel Ward refers to Aristotle as "the great Dictator of reason." The notion of Bacon's contempt for Aristotle springs partly from his early biographer William Rawley's reference to Bacon's "dislike of the philosophy of Aristotle."[43] In Bacon's own writings one finds a more nuanced approach to the scholastics. In *The Advancement of Learning*, first published in 1605, Bacon did offer a critique of the schoolmen and "Aristotle their dictator" (Ward seems to have borrowed this epithet while softening it), but he also criticized humanism, which "grew speedily to an excess, for men began to hunt more after words than matter." Bacon declared that "knowledge derived from Aristotle, and exempted from liberty of examination, will not rise again higher than the knowledge of Aristotle." However, he added a significant qualification:

> Notwithstanding, certain it is that if those schoolmen to their great thirst of truth and unwearied travail of wit had joined variety and universality of reading and contemplation, they had proved excellent lights, to the great advancement of all learning and knowledge; but as they are, they are great undertakers indeed, and fierce with dark keeping.

Bacon did not want to destroy scholasticism, but to bring its latent power—"fierce with dark keeping"—into the light and to put it to work for the good of humanity. Like his Puritan allies, he sought to apply learning "to use, and not to ostentation." Bacon indeed promoted the humanistic curriculum in the universities—"histories, modern languages, books of policy and civil discourse"—because he wanted to train leaders in practical understanding for usefulness to the state; but he also complained that European colleges were "all dedicated to professions, and none left free to arts and sciences at large":

> For if men judge that learning should be referred to action, they judge well; but in this they fall into the error described in the ancient fable, in which the other parts of the body did

suppose the stomach had been idle, because it neither performed the office of motion, as the limbs do, nor of sense, as the head doth; but yet notwithstanding it is the stomach that digesteth and distributeth to all the rest. [44]

With this oblique reference to distributive justice, Bacon endorsed a humanistic education that was useful but not utilitarian, within which purely scholastic pursuits would continue to be held valuable in themselves: in other words, an approach very similar to that enjoyed by Nathaniel Ward and promoted by Richard Holdsworth at Cambridge, as described in the preface.

For his part, Samuel Ward showed his sympathy with the Baconian program by declaring that his goal was "to repair these ruines of this dying world" by "renew[ing] gouernment to the primitiue beauty of it." This was in keeping with Bacon's "Great Instauration," his desire to restore the image of God in man, damaged in the fall, through the discoveries of experimental science.[45] Crucially, as Peter Harrison has noted, Bacon believed it essential "that natural philosophy be a corporate activity." (Bacon would have been aware of the more humble form of corporatist creativity carried out by his father, Sir Nicholas Bacon, as the leader of the feoffees for the town lands in Bury St. Edmunds, which evolved from the suppressed Candlemas guild to become the town's governing body prior to Bury's 1606 incorporation as a borough.[46]) In his *New Atlantis*, posthumously published in 1627, Bacon imagined a utopian "Society of Salomon's House" or "College of the Six Day's Works," devoted to recovering "the true nature of all things" that was known to Adam but subsequently lost to humanity.[47] Here we see that Bacon's thought should not be stereotyped as purely "progressive" or "modern" science, since he was part of a broader movement aimed at rediscovering and reconstructing the ancient knowledge called the *prisca theologia*, supposedly passed down from Adam to Noah and then spread throughout the world through Noah's sons. *Prisca theologia* was a way to reconcile natural law thinking with the Old Testament by suggesting that people had access to the "light of nature" not only intuitively but also through transmission from the Hebrew patriarchs. Samuel Ward gave a nod to this tradition when he referred to "*Moses* himselfe [...] father of all Law-giuers, of the thrice great *Hermes*, *Lycurgus*, *Solon*, *Plato*, *Iustinian*, & the rest." Adherents of the *prisca theologia* believed that Moses had taught the ancient wisdom to Egyptian initiates including Hermes Trismegistus ("thrice great"), who then passed it on to Plato and the Greeks.[48]

Protestant scholastics who pursued the quest for the ancient knowledge included Jan Amos Comenius, John Dury, and Samuel Hartlib (who, interestingly, was from Elbing, although there is no evidence that he and Nathaniel Ward encountered each other there).[49] In his *Via Lucis*, Comenius called for "A Catholic College among the learned men of the whole world," echoing Bacon's call for a corporatist approach to the search for wisdom; in a similar vein, Nathaniel Ward would later speak of human society as "Christs Academy."[50] These corporate academic enterprises also provided a crucial justification for mobility to the New World. The frontispiece of Bacon's *Great Instauration* (1620 edition) included a quote from Daniel 12:4, "Multi pertransibunt et augebitur scientia"—"Many shall go to and fro, and knowledge shall be increased" (Figure 4).

Figure 4 Frontispiece to Francis Bacon, *Instauratio Magna*, 1620 edition, with epigram from Daniel 12:4, "Multi pertransibunt et augebitur scientia"—"Many shall go to and fro, and knowledge shall be increased."

Hartlib, Dury, and Comenius all supported a failed effort to create a learned "college of Antilia" with Virginia as a possible location.⁵¹

Comenius and his associates were also profoundly interested in John Eliot's mission to the Indians in Massachusetts; in his 1668 dedication to *Via Lucis*, Comenius recalled that the occasion of his visit to England in 1641 had been "the propagation of the Gospel unto the nations of the world, and in particular the sowing thereof so happily made then in New England." Proponents of the Instauration supported the missions in hopes of gleaning traces of primordial knowledge of plants, herbs, minerals, and roots that could be used in medical and alchemical preparations.⁵² This was also the primary motive for John Winthrop Jr.'s town-founding efforts and frequent removes throughout New England, starting in Ipswich. The younger Winthrop, who became an early fellow of the Royal Society, maintained a correspondence with Samuel Hartlib, who in 1660 urged Winthrop to disclose "what kinde of talents the Lord has entrusted you" in the alchemical field, for "you cannot believe what secret reports I have heard of you of which I would be so willingly informed onely of the general truth and reality both of the medicin and the tincture." Referring to "reall vestigia magni elixiris either quoad sanitatem [...] or transmutationem" ["real traces of the great elixir either for the purpose of health [...] or transmutation"], Hartlib declared his desire "to know whether there be such a reall work itself or only an approximation elsewhere that I may be instrumentall by the will of God to bring old and new england closer together for the perfecting and improving of so great a talent."⁵³

As Zachary McLeod Hutchins has argued, the promotional literature for New England shows how a commitment to the Baconian Instauration helped justify mobility to the New World. Robert Cushman, who was involved in the founding of Plymouth colony, invoked the Baconian goal of useful knowledge. Those "wanting opportunitie" to do good in England

> should lift vp their eies and see whether there be not some other place and countrie to which they may go to doe good and have vse towards others of that knowledge, wisdome, humanities, reason, strength, skill, facultie, &c. which God hath giuen them for the servuce of others and his owne glory.

Boston minister John Cotton argued that "wee may remove for the gaining of knowledge. Our Saviour commends it in the Queene of the south, that she came from the utmost parts of the earth to heare the wisdome of *Salomon*." According to Hutchins, Cotton is claiming "that the knowledge New England will reveal about the natural world [...] will draw the Puritans closer to their goal of Solomonic wisdom," according to the example of the biblical Queen of Sheba.⁵⁴ Hutchins has also pointed out that Anne Bradstreet, in her poem "The Vanity of All Worldly Things," took on the persona of Solomon himself.⁵⁵ Bradstreet moved to Ipswich along with her father Thomas Dudley in 1635, and with her husband Simon later became one of the founders of Andover, Massachusetts. Her early poems were strongly influenced by the work of Guillaume du Bartas, whose link to *prisca theologia* has been documented by Peter Harrison. In Bradstreet's "The Four

Elements," Earth takes credit for promoting mobility across the seas as well as the pursuit of natural wisdom:

> But hark you wealthy merchants, who for prize
> Send forth your well-manned ships where sun doth rise,
> After three years when men and meat is spent,
> My rich commodities pay double rent.
> Ye Galenists, my drugs that come from thence,
> Do cure your patients, fill your purse with pence;
> Besides the use of roots, of herbs and plants,
> That with less cost near home supply your wants.
> But mariners where got you ships and sails,
> And oars to row, when both my sisters fails?
> Your tackling, anchor, compass too is mine,
> Which guides when sun nor moon nor stars do shine.[56]

Returning to Samuel Ward's sermon, in order to "renew government" to its "primitiue beauty," Ward suggested adopting the advice of Moses's father-in-law Jethro, who in Exodus 18 suggested a scheme of government based on the appointment of "rulers of thousands, and rulers of hundreds, rulers of fifties, and rulers of tens."[57] Interestingly, New Englanders would only put this plan into full operation in the "praying towns" of Indians converted through John Eliot's ministry.[58] But it bore a strong resemblance to long-standing English custom, as updated by Puritans and others bent on promoting good order in towns. Under the ancient English system of frankpledge, initially administered by the hundred courts, the realm was divided into "tithings," groups of ten men who were collectively responsible for each other's good behavior.[59] Ruling groups of headboroughs and "chief inhabitants" partially resurrected this system by assigning each of their members a neighborhood to supervise; for example, in Braintree the chief inhabitants split up the town into "walkes," each assigned to one of the 24 to keep an eye on.[60] Later, some colonial New England towns would appoint tithingmen who were responsible for policing a certain "beat." In 1677 the Massachusetts General Court, using the language of proportionality, ordered "that the selectmen, constables, and tithingmen, in euery toune, doe, once euery quarter of a yeare, so proportion and diuide the precincts of each toune, and goe from house to house," to determine who had not taken the oath of fidelity to the colony. "Tything men" were also empowered to inspect alehouses.[61]

Samuel Ward explicitly linked the Jethro scheme to the "view of frankpledge" when he compared "Tything-men or Deciners, to their rulers of tens." Invoking Aristotelian distributive justice, Ward emphasized that he was addressing all public officials from the highest to the lowest:

> Let mee, as the third part of my text, and the distribution of Magistracy requires, tell you to whom all this hath beene spoken: not to Iudges and Iustices of peace onely, as I feare most haue imagined in hearing it: but to all from the highest and greatest, to the lowest and least

Instrument of Iustice, from the Gouernour of the thousand, to the Centurion, from him to the Tithingman or Decinour.

In fact, the lower officials were even more necessary for the promotion of Puritan social goals than the higher ones, because it is "the lowest and neerest orbs that gouerne the *world*."[62] Ward's proposed system of surveillance might have intruded on the privacy of the lower ranks of town residents; on the other hand, it would have required even greater popular participation in governance, in a nation where ordinary people's involvement was already essential for legal proceedings.[63] He supported popular participation when he urged his hearers to "stand fast in your lawfull liberties of election" and affirmed "that cottages and ploughes have brought forth as able men for the gowne and sword, as Pallaces and Scepters."[64]

Samuel Ward continued the corporatist tone established by his brother, referring to the "common body." But his text offered a more obscure allusion to the history of corporatism by twice commending the *De Regno Christi* of Martin Bucer, written and dedicated to England's King Edward VI while Bucer held the Regius Professorship of Divinity at Cambridge University in 1550.[65] *De Regno Christi* also influenced other members of the Ward/Rogers family. For instance, in 1644, Nathaniel Rogers, the son of John Rogers of Dedham and a resident of Ipswich, Massachusetts, cited the reformer of Strasbourg in a letter to a member of Parliament. Rogers praised Bucer, "whose piety in his works *de Regno Christi*, is worth the reading and observing at this time"; he beseeched his correspondent to follow Bucer's example and "not suffer any Parliament privileges, or rights and liberties of subjects to be taken away."[66]

The adamantly scholastic and humanist Bucer repeatedly cited Aristotle, Cicero, and especially Plato in support of the reforms he proposed to Edward VI (in Chapter One I quoted his summary of Aristotelian distributive justice).[67] Bucer's connection to corporatism lay in his position as a major urban reformer. As discussed earlier in this chapter, the corporate origins of many European cities sprang from the rediscovery of Justinian's *Digest* in the late eleventh century, which made the Roman law of corporations available to support the claims of urban communes to public privileges. Bucer drew heavily on the Roman civil law, frequently citing Justinian's *Corpus Iuris Civilis* (which Samuel Ward cited when referring to "*Hermes, Lycurgus, Solon, Plato, Iustinian* ...").[68] As Bernd Moeller has pointed out, Bucer brought the civic humanist consciousness of the urban communes into the Reformation; furthermore, corporations and guilds frequently drove the urban reformation. Thomas A. Brady Jr. refers to the "sacral corporatism of the Reformation era" in the cities.[69] Long before Samuel Ward, Bucer suggested the adoption of the Jethro model of government, with rulers of tens, fifties, and so on.[70] With his Platonic republicanism, Bucer was even more insistent than Ward that the purpose of this ruling hierarchy was "that there may be nothing unsupervised." On the other hand, he attacked enclosure and other forms of social greed, including usury.[71] Poor relief was a duty for Christians, provided that it was extended judiciously, and only to the deserving poor.[72] Bucer's call for increased social surveillance went hand in hand with the necessity of greater participation in the church and public life.[73]

Up to now this chapter has presented the institutional grounding of mobility in the theory of corporatism. Corporate groups like the Massachusetts Bay Company (as well as land corporations that were formed within New England) helped make mobility possible by organizing migrations; they could also be transformed into governing bodies for newly founded colonies and towns. However, in another way the notion of corporatism would seem to work against mobility. The individual "members" of a corporate body like a town, parish, or nation were seen as part of a living, organic unity. People who abandoned a social or religious body to which they belonged could, and did, receive criticism. For example, when in 1634 Thomas Hooker applied to the Massachusetts General Court for permission to move his large clerical company from Newtown (Cambridge) to Connecticut, John Winthrop commented "they ought not to departe from vs. beinge knitt to vs in one bodye."[74] The remainder of this chapter will focus on how Puritans were able to justify mobility, bestowing a positive value on it and even arguing that it might be necessary to leave a social body in order to save it.

In England, Puritans were often ridiculed for their mobility in "gadding about" to lectures outside their own parishes. This practice was all the more unacceptable because "gadding" of any sort was coded as a bad feminine habit akin to "gossiping."[75] Puritans fought this stereotype by redefining this type of mobility in terms of natural sociability and Christian fellowship. In letters from his parish in Yorkshire, Ezekiel Rogers constantly nagged his patron Lady Joan Barrington for not approaching "your neighbours for converse, many being such as could helpe you by telling what God had done for their soules."[76] John Rogers of Dedham lamented that the "dutie of neighbourly dealing, inviting, visiting, these are decayed" partly because of covetousness. He suggested that Christians' duty to their own families should not make them forgetful of their duty to others: they should "striue who shall doe most dutie each to other; husband to wife, neighbour to neighbour." Neighborly conversation should consist of

> taking to heart their spirituall wants, instructing the ignorant, counselling the doubtfull, comforting the afflicted, admonishing them that be out of the way, exhorting them that begin to faint or stagger in the way, and praying for all.[77]

His uncle Richard Rogers of Wethersfield (whose promotion of natural sociability was mentioned in Chapter One) offered similar arguments in praise of good neighborhood, but went beyond them by emphasizing the necessity "to seeke and ioyne our selues in acquantaince with the religious and godly"; here Rogers made no suggestion that such fellowship should be limited to those of one's own neighborhood.[78] Rogers also made an effort to revalue this kind of public engagement as something masculine, saying that

> it is a goodly sight to behold Captaines in warre, and Gouernours and Magistrates in peace; and more particularly [...] Headboroughs in townes, and the fathers of families, to be lights in religion and holy practise, to the rest, and examples in the seruice of God: and the inferiours to follow, euen as the flocke followeth the bell-weather.[79]

(Yet interestingly, a wether was, properly speaking, a castrated sheep.) And he went farther than John Rogers in making godly fellowship a justification for "remoouing our dwellings," something that might be necessary in order to seek "the true knowledge of God, which now is to be attained of vs by a sound ministery"—a logical extension of "gadding about to sermons." We have already seen that Thomas Hooker told the hearers of his "Danger of Desertion" sermon that they should seek out "Gods ordinances" in the New World. John Dane of colonial Ipswich decided to emigrate when he opened the Bible to the passage "Cum out from among them, touch no unclene thing, and I will be your god and you shall be my pepell." Rogers added that in these circumstances, the new dwelling place was "seldome without some whose companie is to bee desired, and whose acquaintance may make our liues sweet and ioyfull." Profit was rarely a sufficient justification for changing one's dwelling, but the desire to "set vp an alter, that is, retaine Gods true worship" was. Rogers invoked Baconian usefulness as well as Christian charity as a rationale for relocation:

> What know we what God hath appointed to be done by vs in another place? It may bee wee may bring some to God by our remoueing, and bee seated among such as shall bee like our selues, or may be our good conuersation which they shall see, be turned vnto vs. Which two things we should principally aime at, and endeauour vnto when we must change and remoue our dwelling.[80]

In his posthumously published *Survey of the Summe of Church-Discipline*, Thomas Hooker offered a pithy justification as to why covenanted social bodies could be sundered in certain circumstances. Although "*cohabitation*" was the norm within the social body, "the Church may send out *some*, either to begin plantations, in case the body require it, or to help on some others who want able guides to succour them in their beginnings, before they can attain a Church-state."[81] The latter clause could be taken to apply to the colonists' oft-stated goal of missionizing the Indians, but Hooker did not list the conditions under which "the body" might "require" out-migration from a community. However, the history of Hooker's departure from Newtown offers an example of the two most typical reasons. The first was scarce resources: in 1635, John Winthrop told Simonds d'Ewes that Hooker wanted to leave Newtown because it was not large enough to support all of Hooker's followers and their cattle.[82] The second was religious or political disagreement: in Hooker's case, his alignment with the faction in Massachusetts, led by sometime governor Thomas Dudley and Nathaniel Ward and centered in Ipswich, which disagreed with John Winthrop's preference for magisterial "discretion" as the basis of law in the colony, and successfully promoted the Body of Liberties, Massachusetts' first law code, to protect public rights and restrain magisterial power.[83]

For example, in November, 1633, Thomas Dudley sent Hooker and John Haynes as his emissaries to Governor Winthrop during one of their numerous disputes.[84] In January 1635/36, Haynes (who would join Hooker in Connecticut), defending Dudley's approach to jurisprudence, attacked Winthrop for dealing "too remissly in point of Iustice."[85] Hooker's son-in-law, Thomas Shepard, who remained in Newtown as its minister, pointedly rejected Winthrop's theory of discretion in his 1638 election sermon, observing that "w[he]n lawes rule men do not."[86] Fittingly, Shepard joined Nathaniel Ward and Thomas Dudley on the committee that produced the Body of Liberties.[87]

Hooker himself has provided the best evidence for a political motive for his exodus from Massachusetts. In 1635/36, the General Court finally acknowledged "some reason & grounds" for Hooker and his entourage to "remove from this oʳ com[m]onwealth & body of the Mattachusetts."[88] In a fiery 1638 letter he sent to Winthrop from Connecticut, Hooker offered a blistering attack on the idea of magisterial discretion.[89] Conceding that judges must have authority over all judicial matters, Hooker nevertheless asked "what rule the Judge must have to iudge by." Winthrop's view that "the sentence should lye in his [the judge's] breast, or be left to his discretion," in Hooker's opinion, would lead "directly to tyranny, and so to confusion." A judge must "not ask what his discretion allowes, but what the Law requires." "Had not the law overruled the lusts of men, and the crooked ends of iudges many tymes, both places and people had been in reason past all releif in many cases of difficulty." Winthrop had complained to Hooker that the Connecticut settlers were "referring matter of counsel or judicature to the body of the people," instead of following the *maior et sanior pars* principle—"the best part is always the least, and of that best part the wiser part is always the lesser." Hooker retorted with a version of the "quod omnes tangit" maxim, "ad omnes spectat, ab omnibus debet approbari"—what pertains to all should be approved by all.[90] Clearly Hooker was practicing a politics of place, signaling his opposition to Winthrop's leadership in Massachusetts by taking refuge in Connecticut.[91]

Hooker's doctrine, justifying removal from a community "in case the body require[d] it," provided a powerful justification for mobility. It was fitting that in his *Wonder-Working Providence* another ally of the Ipswich leaders, Edward Johnson of Woburn, praised Hooker for his various migrations:

Come, Hooker, *come forth of thy native soile:*
    Christ, I will run, says Hooker, *thou hast set*
My feet at large.[92]

Mobility is a trope of the *Wonder-Working Providence*; Johnson repeatedly referred to the Puritan settlers of New England as "wandering Jacobites"—a term that should not be taken to mean they were partisans of the Stuart kings. Rather, New Englanders followed in the footsteps of the peripatetic patriarch Jacob, who in the book of Genesis migrated from Canaan to Haran and back again, then to Egypt.[93] In a somewhat opaque passage, Johnson suggested that migration to New England would ultimately redound to the benefit of the social and religious body of old England:

> Of purpose he causeth such instruments to retreate as hee hath made strong for himself: that so his adversaries glorying in the pride of their power, insulting over the little remnant remaining, Christ causeth them to be cast downe suddenly forever, and wee find in stories reported, Earths Princes have passed their Armies at need over Seas and deepe Torrents. Could *Caesar* so suddenly fetch over fresh forces from *Europe* to *Asia, Pompy* to foyle? How much more shall Christ who createth all power, call over this 900 league Ocean at his pleasure, such

instruments as he thinks meete to make use of in this place, from whence you are now to depart.

In other words, the colonists were engaging in a strategic "retreate" to New England so that they could strengthen their "Armies" for a return to "this place," Old England, to deliver it in due time from God's "adversaries."[94]

The Puritans took the model of the social body very literally, and believed that corporate bodies, like human bodies, were subject to disease, "distemper," infection and contagion.[95] On a more mundane level, the "wellfare of a bodye"—as John Winthrop put it in 1629—"consistes not so muche in the quantitye, as in the proportion and distribution of the partes."[96] If a town had too little meadow, pasture, or arable land to support its people, it had fallen out of proportion; or if it had six millers, no blacksmith and only one man fit for a leadership role, then distributive justice could not operate properly, and a removal of some members of the body might be necessary. More dramatically, if the social body were infected with religious or political dissent, and the voluntary departure of the offending members could not be obtained, an involuntary exile might be called for. This became manifest most clearly during the Antinomian crisis of 1636–38, when Anne Hutchinson and some of her circle were banished from Massachusetts. In his preface to John Winthrop's *Short Story of the Rise, reign, and ruine of the Antinomians, Familists & Libertines*, Thomas Weld spoke of antinomianism as a disease of the body politic: "Multitudes of men and women [...] were streight infected before they were aware, and some being tainted conveyed the infection to others: and thus that Plague first began amongst us."[97] Thomas Shepard said that Newtown had been chosen as the site of Harvard (and endowed with its new name, Cambridge) because it had been "kept spotless from the contagion of the [antinomian] opinions."[98] In justifying the General Court's decision to exile the antinomians, Winthrop, of course, appealed to the corporatist image of the body politic, in scholastic terms. He asked "what is the essentiall forme of a common weale or body politic such as this is." Winthrop's answer was "the consent of a certain companie of people, to cohabite together, under one government for their mutual safety and welfare"—so that anyone who threatened that safety and welfare could be expelled from the social body.[99]

The idiom of corporatism came so naturally to everyone involved in the New England colonial enterprise that it seems to have been used reflexively, almost unconsciously. In his "Discourse on Arbitrary Government," John Winthrop made a distinction within the "bodye politike" between the General Court and the larger body of freemen, noting that authority had been given to the Court while the freemen enjoyed "the power of Liberty." The Deputies objected to "the distinction therein made of the bodye Polit[ic], and the members thereof," for in the corporatist model, the body and its members were part of an organic unity. Winthrop denied that he had intended to "distinguish betweene the wholl and the parts," but only among the various members of the social body—a move which was in keeping with the principle of distributive justice.[100] Even ordinary settlers like Edward Elmer, a Hartford farmer, were imbued with the ethos of corporatism. In a 1649 letter to John Winthrop Jr., asking his support as a magistrate for a town-founding enterprise, Elmer mused, "what is a body with out a head what is a poeple without a guide[?]"¹⁰¹

The language of corporatism was flexible enough that the leaders of the Massachusetts Bay Company could make it clear that they were starting a new and distinct body politic, while still claiming to belong to England and its national church. In his letter to Lady Lincoln, Thomas Dudley apologized for recounting so many "matters of small moment" on the grounds that "small things in the beginning of natural or politic bodies are as remarkable as greater in bodies full grown."¹⁰² But in the "Humble Request" composed on board the Great Migration's flagship *Arbella* in 1630, the leaders claimed to be still "members of the same body," namely the Church of England. The notion of analogy or proportion among different corporate bodies made this verbal sleight of hand possible. The "Humble Request" also employed the metaphor of parentage, which would have a long life in relations between the "mother country" and its colonies: "we desire you would be pleased to take notice of the principals and body of our Company, as those who esteem it our honor to call the Church of England, from which we rise, our dear mother."¹⁰³

John White, the minister of Dorchester and guiding spirit of the Dorchester Company, perfectly balanced the parentage metaphor with the corporatist model in his promotional book *The Planters Plea* (1630). White was heavily involved in the Massachusetts Bay Company's deliberations before the Company transferred itself to the New World in 1630, and seems to have had a connection to Nathaniel Ward: in a meeting on November 25, 1629, White recommended that the Company seek the counsel and support of certain ministers, including "Mʳ Nathaniell Ward, of Standon."¹⁰⁴ In his justification for mobility to the New World, White showed his sympathy for the Baconian criterion of usefulness when he quoted David Pareus: "He [God] commands [humanity] therefore to fill the earth, not only with respect to generation and dwelling, but preeminently with respect to the power of cultivation and use"—a precept that was still binding on "the body of mankind."¹⁰⁵ White also appealed to the desire to convert the Indians, who he hinted had had some contact with the Jews in times past, since "they separate their women in the times appointed by the Law of *Moses*." He argued that emigration was necessary when "a few men flourish that are best grounded in their estates," while "the rest waxe weake and languish, as wanting roome and meanes to nourish them," a situation that would lead to "couetousnesse [...] idlenesse, wantonnesse, fraud, and violence, the fruits of well-peopled Countreys." Anticipating an objection from proponents of the reformation of manners, White denied that simply establishing order through better supervision of "inferiour Magistrates" would solve the problem of unemployment and idleness; the resources of the New World were needed to set England's superfluous population to work. However, since "ill humours soone overthrow a weake body," it was necessary that the mother country allow not only vagrants and the underemployed to emigrate, but also the well-born:

> A State that intends to draw out a Colony for the inhabiting of another Country, must looke at the mother and the daughter with an equall and indifferent eye; remembering that a Colony is a part and member of her own body [...] which therfore she should labour to

further and cherish by all fit and convenient meanes; and consequently must allow to her such a proportion of able men as may be sufficient to make the frame of that new formed body: As good Governours, able Ministers, Physitians, Souldiers, Schoolemasters, Mariners, and Mechanicks of all sorts.

This was even more necessary because "the first fashioning of a politicke body is a harder taske then the ordering of that which is already framed."[106]

Thus for White the New England body politic was "unsetled," a "rude and incohaerent body," a fetus that had to be nourished by its mother.[107] Proper proportion was necessary if the new body were to grow into a daughter with its own autonomous being. The early records of the Massachusetts Bay Company show this same concern for "preporc[i]on" whenever they discuss land distribution, and it was the keynote of Nathaniel Ward's political thinking. In his 1650 work *Discolliminium*—or "de-necking," a protest against the execution of King Charles I—Ward wrote that *"a mixt frame of Government well-temper'd, and proportion'd, must support this State* [England]."[108] The next chapter will show how land distribution helped to nurture the social body of colonial Ipswich according to the principle of proportionality as an expression of distributive justice.

Chapter Three
LAND DISTRIBUTION IN COLONIAL IPSWICH

Why did the founders of many New England towns apparently lean toward the open-field model of mixed farming, avoiding enclosed individual farms while allotting multiple strips in common fields? The "town studies" of the 1960s and 1970s addressed the issue. Sumner Powell argued that Sudbury implemented common fields because "almost half" of its residents came from open-field areas of England, begging the question of why the majority of settlers would reject their ancestral models. Kenneth Lockridge astutely suggested that Puritan ideology had something to do with the settlers' preference, but reduced this ideology to nostalgia for an "imaginary golden past"; T. H. Breen and Stephen Foster drew a similar conclusion.[1]

This viewpoint provided a welcome antidote to the Turnerian and Whig interpretations of New England towns as progressive proto-democracies, but it failed to do justice to the Puritan ideology. Implying that open-field farming resulted from a knee-jerk reaction against incipient modernity, the authors of the town studies relegated Puritans to the realms of mystical obscurantism caricatured by Vernon Parrington and H. L. Mencken. Furthermore, the nostalgia thesis could not withstand the evidence provided by Stephen Innes and John Frederick Martin that land entrepreneurs, sometimes acting as absentee landlords, played a major role in New England town founding.[2]

While this issue was in dispute, geographical determinism continued to provide a popular explanation for land use patterns in New England, even for those towns which were less committed to the open-field model. Chapter 5 of David Grayson Allen's *In English Ways* represents a brave attempt to trace the English origins of settlers in Ipswich and Watertown as a way of explaining the patterns of land use that developed in those towns. Focusing on Allen's analysis of Ipswich will give us a sense of the difficulties besetting this approach. Allen argues that most of the settlers in Ipswich came from the East Anglian counties of Suffolk and Essex, where enclosure of land was reputedly far advanced, and as a result they avoided the open-field arrangement and set up "an active and thriving market in land," as proprietors sought to consolidate their holdings even more, just like enclosing English landlords.[3]

Other historians have taken up this line of argument, frequently citing Allen's analysis of Ipswich land patterns. William Cronon, while admitting that "early land divisions had been done communally" in New England, claimed that "later divisions were generally made through the abstract mechanism of land speculation." He specifically cited Allen's work in developing his theory of the commodification of land in the New England colonies. John Frederick Martin called Allen's book "among the most informative works" on local history in seventeenth-century New England; Edward T. Price accepted Allen's geographic determinism in his influential book *Dividing the Land*. *In English Ways* was also cited in *Peoples of a Spacious Land* by Gloria L. Main, who not surprisingly argued for early enclosure in New England and a "lively land market" in such towns as Deerfield, Connecticut. Robert Friedeburg's article on "social and geographical mobility" in New England towns drew on Allen's work to show the "social stratification" of Ipswich.[4] In working toward a synthesis of scholarship on New England's land use patterns, therefore, a reconsideration of Allen's data seems necessary.

Allen's list of Ipswich residents is based on a 1642 record of "commoners"—inhabitants who enjoyed common rights to meadows, pastures, and woodlands.[5] This fact in itself should suggest that the reality of land use in Ipswich was more complex than Allen's picture of a proto-capitalist land market allows. If land entrepreneurs really intended to make maximum profits from town land, they would have monopolized as much of the vital meadow and pasture resources as possible, rather than allowing them to lie in common.[6] Also, Ipswich was first settled in 1633, so that Allen's list of early settlers includes numerous people who came to the town well after the system of land distribution was established. Even if we were to grant, for the sake of argument, that most early Ipswich settlers came from enclosed areas primarily in Suffolk and Essex—a very dubious assertion, as we shall see, based on the evidence Allen provides—we need to ask which settlers were on the ground early enough and in a position to influence the first distributions of land. Who was present in Ipswich during what Douglas R. McManis called "a critical stage in landscape evolution," the period of "group decisions about settlement sites, land use, and physical structures … before any changes are made in the landscape"?[7]

Fortunately, the evidence on this point is quite a bit clearer for Ipswich than for most other New England towns. On April 1, 1633, the Massachusetts General Court helpfully listed all the men who were already in residence at "Aggawam"—the Indian name for Ipswich—and forbade anyone else to move there.[8] The names were John Winthrop Jr., Thomas Clarke, Robert Coles, Thomas Howlett, John Gage, Thomas Hardy, William Sargent, William Perkins, "Mr Thornedicke," and John Biggs. However, the last three names do not appear in the first recorded land distributions of 1634, nor in any subsequent town records, so presumably they died or moved away.[9] The early town meeting records also document that John Gage was appointed to a committee to help allot lands, along with Henry Short, John Perkins (probably the elder of the two men by that name who were allotted land), and Robert Mussey; Robert Coles was also specifically asked to help Perkins and Short "view a piece of land."[10] Also influential, no doubt, were the ministers present in Ipswich, Thomas Parker and Nathaniel Ward. Parker was about to move on to found Newbury, but as a church elder his opinion would have been taken seriously. In addition, the General Court on March 4, 1634/35, appointed John Winthrop Jr., John Humfry, and John Endecott "to devide ye lands at Ipswitch, within 4 myles of the towne […] as in equity they shall thinke meete."[11]

Based on the evidence, then, it would seem that of all the early Ipswich residents, those most involved with deciding how land would be allotted were the town's main founder Winthrop Jr., John Gage, Henry Short, John Perkins, Robert Mussey, Robert Coles, and William Sargent. Also well placed to influence decisions on land distribution were the three other 1633 settlers who received land in Ipswich: Thomas Clarke, Thomas Howlett, and Thomas Hardy. In addition, two commissioners, besides Winthrop Jr., were empowered to distribute land in Ipswich, namely John Humfrey and John Endecott. Finally, there were the ministers Thomas Parker and Nathaniel Ward. Examining the English origins of these men complicates Allen's picture considerably.

Of all these men, John Winthrop Jr. fits Allen's argument most comfortably. He grew up in Groton, Suffolk, which was firmly in an early-enclosed, wood-pasture region of dairy farming, where his father was, of course, the lord of the manor.[12] Many farmers in this part of Suffolk moonlighted in the textile industry as part of the "putting-out" system, and Groton was producing cloth as early as the 1460s.[13] Characteristic of the enclosed wood-pasture region was a loss of manorial control, leading to less communal regulation and a more open market in land, as described by Allen; however, given the senior Winthrop's high-handed sense of the power of magistrates, one wonders how far advanced this process could have been in Groton itself.[14] And although ancient field systems had disappeared with the onset of enclosure in this region, considerable common grassland, meadow, and pasture continued to feed the area's cattle as late as 1650.[15] Still, the younger Winthrop's origins might have influenced him toward a system of enclosed family farms, promoting land entrepreneurship in Ipswich, if he were really that concerned at all about land policy there—something that is rather questionable, given his lack of long-term commitment to the community. Biographer Robert C. Black calls it "a matter for wonder" that Winthrop made five trips to Boston for meetings of the Court of Assistants "in the course of the first crucial months" of Ipswich settlement. By 1634 Winthrop was in England, accepting a commission to organize the Saybrook Colony in Connecticut on behalf of Lord Brooke and Lord Saye and Sele. From this point forward, Winthrop Jr. focused mainly on town-founding in Connecticut, to which he moved permanently in 1646.[16]

As mentioned in Chapter Two, the junior Winthrop's various removes within New England had to do with his quest for minerals, herbs, and Indian lore that would assist his alchemical and medical pursuits.[17] Winthrop Jr.'s brief residence in Ipswich seems to fit the model of the entrepreneur as absentee landlord, as portrayed by John Frederick Martin in *Profits in the Wilderness*, but actually demonstrates the widespread resistance that absenteeism met in many places in New England. First the Ipswich inhabitants complained to the General Court about Winthrop's nonresidence (Figure 5), then the town meeting tried to lure Winthrop back to Ipswich by offering him "Castle Hill and all the meadow and marsh lying within the creeke provided y^t he lives in the Towne." This was in keeping with the town's standing order that everyone admitted as an inhabitant had to stay at least three years in Ipswich. By February 1637/38, Winthrop Jr., under pressure, sold his initial land grant, Argilla Farm on Labour in Vain Creek, to Samuel Symonds (Figure 6—the two men had married sisters); Winthrop would soon move on to Connecticut, and in 1644–45 sold Castle Hill to Symonds as well.[18] There is no surviving evidence that Winthrop sold, leased out, or otherwise profited from any other Ipswich land grants.[19] The younger Winthrop was an important town founder, but if he ever intended to become a land entrepreneur in Ipswich, his ambitions were thwarted.

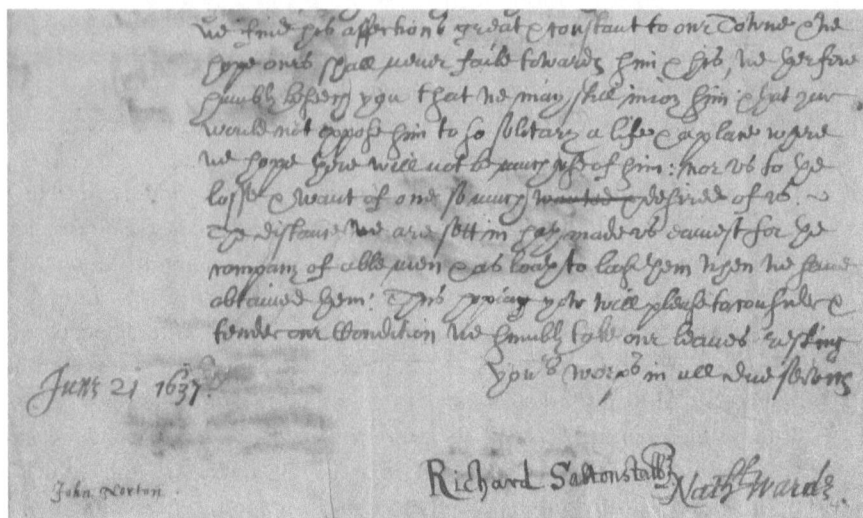

Figure 5 Detail of 1637 Petition to the Governor and Council of Massachusetts remonstrating against the removal of John Winthrop Jr. from the town of Ipswich, Massachusetts, MSS 413, Phillips Library, Peabody Essex Museum. Note signatures of ministers Nathaniel Ward and John Norton.

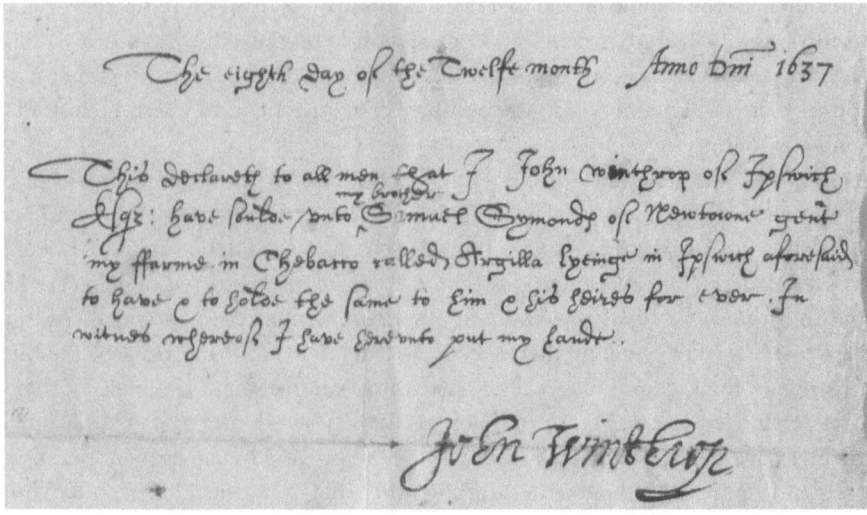

Figure 6 Deed of farm called Argilla in Ipswich from John Winthrop Jr., to Samuel Symonds, February 8, 1637/38, MSS 413, Phillips Library, Peabody Essex Museum. (Since the year began on March 25 in the English Empire prior to 1752, March was considered the first month of the year, making February the twelfth month.)

Although Winthrop, given his frequent absences, was in no position to exert an overriding influence on land distribution in Ipswich, he would undoubtedly have had some influence. Given that the younger Winthrop was, above all else, an intellectual, it seems fitting to examine scholarly influences that might have affected his preferences with respect to land policy, rather than just his geographical origins. Although no editions of Aristotle survived in Winthrop's library as it was handed down to his descendants, we know that John Winthrop Sr. apologized to his son in 1622 for being unable to fulfill his promise to procure one of the Greek philosopher's works, "because your vncle Fones is not at London to buye it, and I know not whither you would have latine or Greeke."[20] Works published before 1633 that Winthrop is known to have had in his library include *Christian Oeconomie* by William Perkins, the *Corona virtutum moralium* by the German Lutheran scholar Johannes Magirus, an English translation of *De optimo Senatore* by the Polish Catholic political thinker Laurentius Grimaldus Goslicius, and a 1622 edition of the classic Calvinist resistance treatise *Vindiciae contra tyrannos*, probably written by Philippe du Plessis-Mornay (bound with Machiavelli's *Prince*). In addition, Winthrop owned Daniel Rogers's 1640 *Two Treatises*, which I mention despite its late date because Rogers was the stepbrother of Nathaniel Ward, so that ideas from the portion of the book called the "Practical Catechisme," first published in 1632, could well have been circulating in early Ipswich.[21] These works suggest that Winthrop, far from being influenced by proto-capitalist individualism, operated within the traditional mental universe of corporatism, where social hierarchy was necessary so that the social body would remain in proportion, but Aristotelian distributive justice was balanced by Christian equity.

Of greatest relevance in the 1609 edition of *Christian Oeconomie* owned by Winthrop is the "Epistle Dedicatorie" by Thomas Pickering, who argues that the family is "the Seminarie of all other Societies," so that its laws should "prepare and dispose men to the keeping of order in other gouernments" including those of "Church and Commonwealth." Pickering emphasizes the hierarchical nature of the family, in keeping with the concept of distributive justice: "the Superiour that faileth in his priuate charge, will prove vncapable of publike employment," while "the Inferiour" must accustom himself or herself to "Oeconomicall subiection" as well as "the yoke of ciuill obedience." Pickering invokes corporatism when he claims that "an error in the foundation [i.e., the family], puts the bodie and parts of the whole building in apparent hazard." Therefore it is essential that "al estates" must govern their families so as to provide "fit grounds for the commo[n] good in more publike and open courses."[22]

The 1601 edition of Johannes Magirus's *Corona Virtutum moralium* provides an Aristotelian amplification of this picture of communal life. Commenting on the *Nicomachean Ethics*, Magirus glosses Aristotle's maxim "homo natura est animal politicum"—man is by nature a political animal—by saying that happiness

> should not only be assessed based on our [individual] person, as when we judge as a matter of course that we are happy when we have enough for ourselves alone [...] in fact neglecting others, but indeed those who pertain to us should be included beneath our own person, to whom either by the law of nature, or by reason of our office, we ought to do good to: as parents, children, neighbors, friends, domestics, and our fellow-citizens.[23]

In his analysis of Book Five of the *Ethics*, Magirus offers a deeper scholastic insight into the relation of family to the political community. For Magirus, distributive justice, "properly speaking, is the action of rightly distributing good and evil things on the basis of outward condition, merit, and the dignity of persons. [...] However, commutative justice is properly the action of justly and rightly exchanging something, so that after the transaction each party has an equal portion." Thus distributive justice pertains to people in their "publicam personam," political standing, while commutative justice has to do with "domestic administration," and "is called economic."[24] Aristotle had said that "the just is something proportionate"; Magirus comments that distributive justice operates according to geometric proportion, an unequal distribution based on differing social status, while commutative justice is in arithmetic proportion, governing fair dealing among individuals. All "proportion is equality of ratios," as Aristotle put it, but arithmetic proportion is what most modern people would consider equal or equitable.[25]

However, early moderns under the influence of scholasticism—Protestant or Catholic—would have seen both types of proportion as "equal." Another work in Winthrop's library, the book by Laurentius Grimaldus Goslicius which was Englished as *A Common-wealth of Good Counsaile*, effectively collapses the distinction between distributive and commutative justice without using those terms. Goslicius's "Counseller" should

> in bestowing offices, honours and gifts obserue equalitie [...] this iustice is defined by the Philosophers, to be an habit of the minde destined to common vtilitie, giuing to euerie man the honour he deserueth. [...] Let the Counsellor therefore haue the skill of that equalitie which proceedeth from reason and iudgement, whereby he may conceiue what is due to each man, what honours should be giuen, what giftes bestowed, what offices d[i]stributed. [...] This equalitie is assuredly a notable thing, and for the seruice of euerie state, exceeding necessarie.

Here distributive justice appears to have become equity. Speaking of Poland, however, Goslicius makes it clear that the distinction of the different "estates" of the realm is essential for the survival of "the bodie of our commonweale," so that "if that same bodie be deuided or dismembred, that state becommeth of all others the most lame, imperfect, and infortunate."[26]

Similarly, in the *Vindiciae contra tyrannos*, Mornay makes it clear that the "Estates" [*Comitia*] of a kingdom can act on behalf of the whole social body, according to the *maior et sanior pars* principle:

> as it is lawful for the whole people to oppose [tyranny], thus also the leaders [*Principibus*] of the kingdom, who represent the whole, and are none other than councillors for the benefit of the body [*decurionibus pro corporis vtilitate*], may join forces. As that is truly referred to the whole which is done publicly by the major part [*maiorem parte(m)*], all that which the major part of the leaders or optimates should do, is said to be done by the whole people.[27]

This was true not only of kingdoms but also of lesser political units like towns and cities: "What we say of the whole people [...] we would say of those who legitimately represent the whole people in each kingdom and city."[28] Here we find a clear emphasis on distributive justice; in fact that principle lies at the heart of Mornay's notion of the dual "covenant" [*foedus*] which constitutes society, the first between God, the King, and the people, and the second between the King and the people. If the ruler does not live up to the conditions of these covenants, the people are absolved from allegiance; the condition of the covenant with God is "if you observe my law," and the condition of the covenant between King and people is "if you distribute to each person their right."[29]

Thus Mornay's thought combines corporatism and covenant to empower social bodies at all levels, which (in contrast to individual rulers) enjoy the privilege of perpetuity. "Even if Kings die, the people however never dies, nor does any other *Vniuersitas*."[30] The Puritan emphasis on covenant, as an agreement of individuals to create a social or religious body, has often been seen as an individualistic and ultimately secularizing development, but David P. Henreckson has recently demolished this way of thinking in his book *The Immortal Commonwealth*. For Henreckson, covenant in the early modern period meant neither secularization nor theocracy; it was a rational technique which had not lost its religious moorings. According to Calvinist political thought as informed by federal theology,

> we can recognize a good political order by whether it accords with the the terms of an antecedent covenantal relationship. For Mornay and other covenant theologians, this antecedent relationship is constituted by the express desire of the divine sovereign to make his creatures his beloved people, and to provide them with rational principles and laws that direct them toward a good and blessed end.[31]

A careful reading of the *Vindiciae* bears out Henreckson's argument, as in the passage where Mornay acknowledges the national covenant: "The whole people is bound to keep the law of God and maintain the law of the Church, so as to eliminate on the contrary the idols of the Gentiles from the land of Canaan, which requirement cannot pertain to individuals, but only to the whole."[32] The whole is constituted by individual people, but once the covenant is sealed, it can never again dissolve into a mere conglomeration of individuals.

Nathaniel Ward would become the chief apostle of this corporatist and distributist way of thinking in colonial Ipswich. In his *Simple Cobler*, Ward observed, "When rotten states are soundly mended from head to foot, proportions duly admeasured, Justice justly dispenced; then shall Rulers and Subjects have peace with God and themselves."[33] However, he would remain committed to the scholastic notion of the common good as the object of politics. This view was strongly reflected in his stepbrother Daniel Rogers's "Practical Catechism," which Winthrop Jr. acquired sometime after 1640. "Let men also seeke the good of a Common-wealth, not a private," wrote Rogers. "The proverb is, *Every one for himselfe*: and in this age, selfe-love hath corrupted mutuall commerce exceedingly." The true Christian, however, must "practise innocency and harmelessnesse" to neighbors, specifically avoiding "wrongs to each other in common cases of each others grounds, fences, cattell, and commodities." Furthermore, "in Townes-matters, not ayming at over-ruling others, treading our inferiours under-feete [...] but carrying equal mindes, and doing as we would be done to." Here the emphasis is on equity in its social rather than individual aspect. This then was the vocabulary that the founders of Ipswich worked with as they sought to balance hierarchy and equity, distributive and commutative justice, the common good and the rights of the individual.

The case of John Winthrop Jr. has become too complex to fit easily into the picture painted by Allen. How well do the others in a position to influence Ipswich land distribution accord with Allen's model? Allen places John Gage's origin in Polstead, Suffolk—albeit with a question mark—a few miles southeast of Groton. This attribution is based on the far-from-reliable antiquarian works of Charles Edward Banks and James Savage, as well as a genealogical article by a descendant, Arthur Gage. Savage, however, only said that Gage was from Suffolk, not Polstead, and Arthur Gage simply disproved that his ancestor was from Stonham in central Suffolk.[34] Even if we were to allow that John Gage came from Suffolk, this would not necessarily mean that he came from a predominantly enclosed region; according to the preeminent scholar of English field systems, the late Joan Thirsk, "in Suffolk, only the wood-pasture region in the central sector of the county was enclosed early, and the corn-growing brecklands to east and west contained many common fields, some of which lingered into the eighteenth century."[35] But we cannot even be sure Gage came from Suffolk: the definitive authority on New England genealogy, Robert Charles Anderson, lists Gage's origins as "Unknown."[36]

Henry Short's specific birthplace is also unknown, but he was almost certainly a member of Thomas Parker's ministerial company from southwestern England (not East Anglia) and had moved to Parker's settlement of Newbury by 1638. Parker's English origins will be treated below.[37] John Perkins senior and junior both came from Hillmorton, Warwickshire, a village right on the border between the dairying district in the Forest of Arden and a classic "fielden" area of arable strip farming; they would have been familiar with "assarts," enclosures from forest land, as well as the open-field model prevalent in south Warwickshire.[38] Allen does not claim Robert Mussey as a native of Suffolk or Essex, placing him in South Stoneham, Hampshire, near the city of Southampton. While open fields of a somewhat irregular type (not the classic Midlands two- or three-field systems) were present through much of Hampshire, the area around Southampton was certainly pastoral and enclosed early, although as usual, common rights to pasture endured. However, Anderson considers Mussey's origins to be unknown, as are those of Robert Coles and William Sargent.[39]

So far, among the early settlers known to have been involved in land distribution, only Winthrop Jr. was undoubtedly from an enclosed region. Considering the three remaining men from the cohort of the first Ipswich settlers who received land grants does not alter this picture. Allen claims that Thomas Clark, a tanner, came from Westhorpe in largely enclosed central Suffolk. He cites Savage and an article by G. Andrews Moriarty. However, the pages cited from Savage include no information about a Thomas Clark of Ipswich. Savage does laconically reference a Thomas Clark in Ipswich—"freeman 1674"—but this Thomas Clark was almost certainly a different person, and in any case Savage offers no information about county of origin. Moriarty's article refers to Thomas Clarke of Westhorpe, Suffolk, father of the John Clarke who left Boston for Rhode Island as a result of the Antinomian Controversy; this was a completely different family from that of the tanner of Ipswich. Anderson and his coauthors list Thomas Clark's origins as unknown.⁴⁰ Allen places Thomas Howlett in South Elmham, Suffolk, with a question mark, based on Banks; Anderson classifies his origins as unknown. If Howlett was from South Elmham, however, historic landscape characterization reveals that he came from a region on the northeastern border of Suffolk where most arable was early enclosed, but which retained some open fields in the seventeenth century, as well as extensive commons and greens.⁴¹ These common pastures were not enclosed until the eighteenth century or later by Parliamentary act; in fact, as late as 1855, Parliament ordered the enclosure of a green in South Elmham. As for Thomas Hardy, his origins are a mystery.⁴²

Nor did the General Court's commissioners for land distribution in Ipswich, aside from the younger Winthrop, come from enclosed regions of East Anglia. John Endecott's origins, surprisingly for such an important settler, remain unknown. Francis Bremer suggests that "it is likely that he was from the southwest, probably Devon."⁴³ John Humfry was a native of Chaldon, near Dorchester in Dorset, and a member of the Dorchester Company organized by the Rev. John White to promote New England settlement from the West Country. The striking fact about Dorchester and its environs at the time of Humfry's departure was the multiplication of sheep, so that by the 1720s, Daniel Defoe could claim "there were 600,000 Sheep fed within Six Miles of the Town every way." The increase in commercial sheep farming obviously produced pressure to enclose throughout Dorset, which had traditionally been an area of common strip farming on the three-field model. While much enclosure did take place, common grazing land remained plentiful in the seventeenth century. Humfry also had a strong connection to Lincolnshire through his wife, Lady Susan, sister of Theophilus Fiennes Clinton, the Earl of Lincoln.⁴⁴ Not only did Lady Susan accompany Humfry to New England, but the Earl's onetime steward Thomas Dudley, along with his daughter—the poet Anne Bradstreet—and her husband, Simon Bradstreet, also moved to Ipswich in 1635. This happened largely because of Dudley's political opposition to John Winthrop—another instance of a politics of place in colonial New England.⁴⁵ Since the Earl of Lincoln's circle had multiple opportunities to influence land use patterns in Ipswich, it is necessary to consider the model of farming prevalent in the area of Sempringham, the Earl's estate.

Sempringham and nearby Horbling (the birthplace of Simon Bradstreet) lie on the eastern verge of the Kesteven Plateau, just west of the edge of the South Lincolnshire fens. This was an open-field area where some early enclosure took place, but in general, the movement made little headway until the eighteenth century. Horbling seems to have had a simple two-field system (with one field always fallow) as well as extensive common grazing in the fen areas.⁴⁶ A deed of February 6, 1574/75, recorded in the Horbling Town Book, refers to a "house [...] w[i]ᵗʰ sarteyn Land arrable [...] com[m]on balks com[m]on lands town meddowe." Surviving documents show that the enclosure of Horbling took place primarily between 1765 and 1771.⁴⁷ In his study of late eighteenth-century enclosures in the area, which did not take place without controversy, W. H. Hosford reported that a common pasture "certainly existed" at Horbling "down to about 1910."⁴⁸ In the mid-sixteenth century, John Leland described "Champaine Ground, fertile of Corne and Grasse"—"Champaine" meaning champion or open-field arable land—in the vicinity of Sempringham.⁴⁹ As steward, Thomas Dudley would no doubt have found this land-use pattern congenial; he hailed from the city of Northampton, in the heart of David Hall's "Central Region" of open-field Midlands farming.⁵⁰ Leland recorded that "From *Welingburne* to *Northampton* 8. Miles al be Champaine Corne and pasture ground."⁵¹ Even in the borough itself common rights were extensive and jealously guarded; the last common pasture rights were finally extinguished in 1882.⁵²

Turning to the ministers of Ipswich, its first teacher, Thomas Parker, did not remain long, but brought an enormous entourage of mostly West Country migrants. In May 1634, John Winthrop Sr. minuted that "mr Parker a minister & a Company with him beinge about 100: went to sitt downe at Agawam."⁵³ Winthrop's language makes it clear that this was a clerical company very much under Parker's sway, so his English antecedents become even more relevant to the disposal of land in early Ipswich. Parker had served as master of the grammar school at Newbury, Berkshire, prior to emigrating. This was a clothing town, home to the legendary clothier of the early sixteenth century, "Jack of Newbury" (John Winchcombe), whose establishment spawned many tall tales as to its scale.⁵⁴ Newbury lies in the Vale of the River Kennet, a narrow pastoral area surrounded by the North Wessex chalk downs, which in the seventeenth century was an open-field arable region. The Vale of Kennet itself was a pastoral area devoted to livestock-rearing and industry. Whether or not open fields endured in Newbury itself during our period, the manorial courts remained vital throughout the period of the Civil War; among other activities, they continued to appoint the officers traditionally charged with enforcing regulation of common fields and grazing areas. As Anne Wallis Chapman put it, "The election of a hayward on the marsh, Northcroft, and market-place may be simply the survivals of obsolete customs [...] but the existence of a strong agricultural element in the community is implied in such rules as those for the driving of the common fields and the infliction of fines on persons grazing more than the lawful number of sheep there." The former common pasture now known as Victoria Park was not enclosed until 1846.⁵⁵ However, Thomas Parker spent his early years at Stanton St. Bernard, Wiltshire, where his father, the famous Puritan Robert Parker, served as rector before fleeing to the Netherlands. This parish lay on the western edge of the chalk downs enveloping the Vale of Kennet, part of a sheep-corn area of open-field arable. Stanton St. Bernard seems to have used the classic Midlands three-field system in its open fields, at least on its demesne arable. Much of Stanton St. Bernard's pastureland was enclosed ca. 1610, but enclosure of its arable fields did not begin until October 1792.⁵⁶

So far, aside from John Winthrop Jr.—who set the intellectual tone for the founding of Ipswich before quickly absenting himself from the town—we have found no discernible influence on Ipswich land distribution by people from old-enclosed areas of Suffolk and Essex, the supposed key factor in determining its land-use system. Residents came from Lincolnshire and the Midlands, with its largely traditional agricultural regime, as well as the southwestern counties of Wiltshire and Dorset, where enclosure had made some progress by the early Stuart period but was nowhere near completion; enclosed fields and sheep downs shared the landscape with open arable fields and extensive common pastures. The very persuasive presence in Ipswich of Nathaniel Ward, whose roots lay entirely in Suffolk and Essex, might seem to alter this picture; but as I have shown in Chapter One, Ward's life prior to his appointment at Stondon Massey was spent entirely in open-field environments. As for Stondon Massey, this was located in a dairying region of wooded hills which was certainly old-enclosed, where settlement followed the pattern described by W. G. Hoskins of dispersed farmsteads circling a green or common, rather than nucleated villages. We seem here to be in Thirsk's stereotypical pastoral area, where dispersed settlement and weakened manorial control led to greater individualism or, at least, to the organization of society around kin groups. But the lords of the manor at Stondon Massey, including Nathaniel Rich, were generally in residence and quite active during the sixteenth and seventeenth centuries, and the necessity of sharing grazing land among the different hamlets would have required at least some cooperation.[57]

It is possible, however, that Nathaniel Ward was converted to the merits of enclosure during his time at Stondon Massey and brought that predilection to Ipswich, exerting a defining influence on the process of land distribution there. If this were the case, one would be hard-pressed to describe such an influence as determined by geography, since Ward spent his formative years surrounded by open fields; Ward's liking for enclosure, on such a theory, must have sprung from his seeing it as more consistent with the Puritan social ethic in some way, perhaps because it discouraged the poor from depending on their common rights and thus promoted industriousness. We would then have to believe that Ward's opinions overrode the predilections of all the other early Ipswich settlers with their varied origins, including the numerous followers of the other minister in the town, Rev. Thomas Parker. Before we embark on such speculation, however, it would be well to consider whether Allen's argument—that Ipswich decisively rejected the open-field model—is in fact consistent with the evidence.

The records of Ipswich, and of many other New England communities, show that settlers were inclined toward an open-field model of land use early on, regardless of whether the majority of settlers came from open-field or enclosed areas of England. However, the prospect of eventual enclosure was always envisioned. Enclosure on a large scale was generally postponed until settlers could be certain that they had enough resources in arable land, woodland, meadow, and pasture to provide for all of a community's inhabitants for the foreseeable future. There were many unknown factors at the time of a town's creation that had to be taken into account. The town founders did not know how fertile the arable land would prove to be or how nutritious the grasses used to feed their livestock. They had no way to estimate life expectancy or typical family size. Accordingly, town founders were usually reluctant to distribute common lands in large enough tracts to create self-sufficient farms, and they maintained the open-field model for a period of time, even after its lack of utility in the New World became evident. This was not based on nostalgia; towns waited to distribute land until they could be sure that they had enough resources to guarantee sustainability for the long term. Here mobility came into the equation. If a town could convince the General Court to allow it to create a satellite community to absorb its excess population, large land distributions and subsequent enclosure became a live option. However, towns tended to err on the side of caution when they considered liberalizing land policies and distributing common resources, and this was especially true of Ipswich.

Ipswich was a hybrid of land use patterns from the start. Houselots were laid out in the town proper, situated on the banks of the Ipswich River. There were two common planting fields, one north and one south of the river, where individual plots were generally somewhat larger and more contiguous than strips in a typical English open field, although some were small and narrow enough to be described as strips.[58] Settlers also received allotments of meadow and woodland. And beyond the common fields, larger tracts of land were distributed to the more prosperous inhabitants. These were "farms" in the modern sense. However, of the 11 men we have identified as most influential on Ipswich land distribution, only John Winthrop Jr. and Robert Coles received farms. Winthrop held 300 acres on Labour in Vain Creek—but as we have seen, if Winthrop intended to become a "land entrepreneur" in Ipswich, "Labour in Vain" was an appropriate description of his efforts. Robert Coles had a smallish farm, 200 contiguous acres. Nathaniel Ward was granted 600 acres, which later formed the nucleus of the town of Haverhill, but this farm came from the General Court, not the town of Ipswich.[59] Most of the lot-layers were middling men, and Thomas Howlett's grant was typical: 30 acres of "upland" (planting ground), 10 of meadow plus 10 additional acres "towards the Reedy marsh," 6 acres on the river, 6 acres "part meaddow, part upland," and a houselot; in a separate grant he received 2 acres of meadow and 2½ acres of marshland, as well as 6 acres in a plot which he shared with Thomas Clarke and John Manning. The more prosperous Robert Mussey came close to receiving a self-sufficient farm, 100 acres plus 16 acres of upland and 10 acres of meadow adjoining it, but he also was allotted a narrow strip in the common fields only 40 rods (660 feet) broad, as was Henry Short.[60]

"Enclosure" in the classic English sense did not exist during the first 25 years of Ipswich settlement. However, neither did the settlers rigidly rule out the possibility of enclosure. In 1637/38, the town voted to build a common fence around the common field north of the Ipswich River, to be maintained by those holding land within that field in proportion to the size of their plots.[61] Two years later, on January 13, 1639/40, the town "agreed that where many planting Lottes are layde out together yf the maior p[ar]t agree to fence them in it shall binde all the rest to doe the lyke." In other words, if the majority of proprietors of land within each common field voted to fence their particular plots, the rest would have to follow suit. Interestingly, the Massachusetts General Court copied this provision in a 1643 ordinance. But the fencing of all the particular plots in the common fields never happened in Ipswich.[62] Indeed, the historian of Ipswich, Thomas Franklin Waters, recorded in 1914 that "in the North Common the lots still remain unfenced for the most part"; Waters also believed that even the larger farms were unfenced in early Ipswich.[63]

There were two reasons why towns were reluctant to allow proprietors to enclose their individual plots of land within the common fields. The first was the clear expectation that English land use patterns would persist in the New World. As we have seen, in a typical open-field system, individual parcels of land could not be enclosed because the whole community had rights of "shack" or grazing on the stubble of a field before planting and after harvest. Various orders make it clear that this right existed in Ipswich. For example, in its 1643 agreement with the keepers of the common cattle herd, the town stipulated that "the her[d]smen are to bring the herd into the Towne every night when the Corne feilds are open."[64] However, as Brian Donahue has shown, this arrangement ultimately proved impractical in New England conditions. With snow on the ground throughout much of the winter, there was little forage to be had.[65]

Another factor that should have worked against grazing on the common fields was the desire to grow winter wheat, which germinated beneath the soil during the cold months, in the same field as spring corn without letting the land lie fallow. (In early New England, the spring and summer crop was Indian corn, maize, not wheat.) In an English three-field system, the cattle would only have been turned into a fallow field on winter nights, not one sown with winter wheat. But the colonists seem to have believed that a field planted in Indian corn, when fertilized with fish, did not need to lie fallow in winter.[66] As Robert Walcott has pointed out, New Englanders never adopted the full system of English crop rotation. Consequently, in Ipswich, some attempt was made to plant wheat, which they called "English corn," in autumn in fields that had just been harvested. But when this was done, cattle were still allowed on the common fields to eat the remnants of the maize crop; this was only done when snow was on the ground and, presumably, their hooves would not uproot the wheat. An order ca. 1640/41 provided that "it shall not be Lawfull for any man to putt in any Cattle in the said Com[m]on fields vnder the penalty of 5ˢ a peece unles the Towne make an order [...] soe to doe when snowe is vpon the ground that the Cattell may eate the Indian Corne stalks without spoyling the englishe corne."[67] The founder of Ipswich, John Winthrop Jr., confirmed this practice in a paper submitted to the Royal Society of London in 1677: "The Stalks of this [Indian] Corn, cut up before too much dryed, and so laid up, are good Winter-fodder for Cattle. But they usually leave them on the Ground for the Cattle to feed on."[68] The settlers seem to have been reluctant to abandon the practice of "shack" despite its limited utility in New England, and this promoted the survival of the common fields.[69]

The second reason against enclosure was simply the need to conserve wood resources. This may seem strange, given that North America in the seventeenth century must have appeared to an Englishman to have almost unlimited forest. But the English consciousness of wood as a scarce resource died hard, partly because settlers tended to locate towns and plant crops on land that had already been partly deforested thanks to the Indian use of burning for forestry management.[70] The coastal areas of Essex County were one such place. Rev. Francis Higginson, who arrived as Salem's minister in 1629, wrote that

> though all the Countrey bee as it were a thicke Wood for the generall, yet in divers places there is much ground cleared by the *Indians*, and especially about the [Salem] Plantation: and I am told that about three miles from us a Man may stand on a little hilly place and see diuers thousands of acres of ground as good as need to be, and not a Tree in the same.[71]

Even in heavily forested areas there was still good reason for prudence, given the typical family's vast wood consumption: William Cronon estimated that each household required 30–40 cords of firewood annually, "which can best be visualized as a stack of wood four feet wide, four feet high, and three hundred feet long," consuming an acre of forest.[72] The main reason for fencing was to keep cattle and other livestock out of growing crops, and in Ipswich the outlying farms had little need for this, since Ipswich was blessed with several "necks" of land, peninsulas that could easily be fenced where common herds and flocks were kept.[73]

In addition, throughout its first 50 years Ipswich jealously guarded its wood resources; the town records are filled with regulation after regulation restricting the cutting of timber on common lands. One such order, issued by the town meeting on February 20, 1665/66, declares that "the commons wood & timber is much wasted and destroyed, for want wherof this Town in a very little time will inevitably be destressed."[74] Two ordinances of 1649 specifically prohibited fencing plots within the common fields. On November 10, the town ordered that "the select men shall not give licence to any Ynhabytant to take off the com[m]ons any timber for posts & rayles to erecting or mainteineing of any ynward fences that lyeth not open to the common." Wood could be cut for common fences but was restricted to two rails, except for houselots, orchards, gardens, and yards. Perhaps because the selectmen balked at the time-consuming procedure of issuing licenses for felling timber, which they found "burdensom," the town felt the need to repeat its order on December 11, insisting that "all insyd fences are wholy restraynd."[75] Thus, we see that while the town meeting often ordered proprietors to keep their portion of the common fences mended, the enclosure of individual plots was frowned upon.[76] Ipswich timber restrictions help explain John Dane's account of how, after his house burned in 1661, he had to wade through the swamps in winter to get lumber for his new house, even though he "had bene ill." Dane considered it one of God's "prouedensis" that his health actually improved in spite of the wetting.[77]

Another very intriguing provision was adopted when, in 1644, the selectmen were tasked with assessing land for tax purposes. They expressed their desire "to do that which may be equall [...] & that every one man beare his due p[ro]p[or]c[io]n in the said rate." They distinguished between land within three miles of the town and that on the outskirts, rating the former at four shillings per acre and the latter at only three, and they also ordered "all ground fenced w[i]'hin the bounds of Ipswich to be valewed 3^s more by the acre."[78] (Thus, fencing one's particular planting lot within the common fields would have resulted in higher taxes, a clear discouragement of the practice.) In a similar vein, the town meeting in February 1671/72 forbade the felling of any timber more than 3½ miles from the meeting house. Wood within that radius could be taken, as long as it were done without "spoyle or wast."[79]

These provisions are strongly reminiscent of the undated, unsigned "Essay on the Ordering of Towns," which offered recommendations for town-founding in Massachusetts. The essay begins by arguing that any structure, however "magnificent" or "bewtefyed," "yet the same wanting its due proportion, declyneth the principall of its worthy Comendacions. So in all pragmaticall imployments [i.e., matters of practical understanding], the Fownedacions to be disposite, that the peraedifications [...] may orderly be proceeded in: is a thing necessarely Required." This pretentious language of Protestant scholasticism suffuses the document as it offers a blueprint for land use in the colony based on the master concept of "due proportion." The author suggests that towns should be six miles square, centered on the meetinghouse, and divided into two concentric areas. The area within 1½ miles of the meetinghouse would be "distributed and employed vnto the houses within the Cumpas of the same, orderly placed to enioye compfortable Communion. Then for that ground lyeing without the neerest circumferance may be thought fittest to be imployed in farmes." The farms in the outer ring would be divided "vnto such proportions, as ech of them may well, and in convenient tyme Improve." The essayist envisions "none expectacion of sudden incloseing," but foresees that the farmers will eventually take advantage of the "benefit of incloseing"; he accepts the existence of common fields "in the Interim." However, the author hopes to minimize the existence of unused common lands by distributing the "wholl towne [...] into portions" as soon as it decides how many inhabitants to admit. As a corollary he calls "vnwarantable" the "greate extent of Townes."[80]

John Stilgoe pointed out that the laying out of towns according to "due proportion" is meant to image and uphold "the divinely sanctioned social hierarchy," but he believed the essay had little actual impact on land distribution in New England. It is clear, however, that the essay had a discernible influence on New England town-founding, at least in Ipswich.[81] The match is not exact; in Ipswich, houselots were indeed located at the town center, but the common fields also lay within the essayist's inner radius, while larger individual farms were farther from the meetinghouse. However, the vision is similar: a central area better suited to "Communion" among the townsfolk and an outer ring which would, eventually, feature enclosed farms. The essayist's language and preoccupations are remarkably close to surviving statements by elite residents of early Ipswich. Speaking of the division of land in the outer ring, the essay states that "euery man may haue his due proportion, more or lesse according vnto his present or apparent future occasion of Imployment; and so the meane ones not to be neglected." Here "due proportion" takes on a chronological dimension, so that potential status is taken into consideration in land distribution. Similarly, in a 1646/47 letter to John Winthrop, Ipswich magistrate Samuel Symonds commented on God's purpose in founding New England: "To exercise the graces of the ritcher sort in a more mixt condiccion, they shall have the liberty of good government in their hands yet with the abatment of their outward estates. And that the poorer sort (held vnder in Engl:) should have inlargement."[82] Equity supplemented and corrected "due proportion" in Ipswich land distribution.

The essay comes even closer to the thought of Nathaniel Ward, whom we have already identified as one of the prime movers in Ipswich land distribution. Ward echoed the essayist's concern that towns be kept small in a letter to John Winthrop, ca. April 1640:

Our neighbour Townes are much greiued to see the lauish liberality of the Court in giving away the Countrye. some honest men of our towne affirme that in their knowledge there are 68 townes in England within as litle compasse as the bounds of Ipswich: I know neere 40 where I dwelt. [...] We should incourage many to come ouer if many plantations were not spoiled by the extreame largnes of those that are already giuen.[83]

It is worthy of note that although Ipswich originally lay in a vast and unbounded tract, the General Court authorized Winthrop, Humfry, and Endecott to distribute land only "within 4 myles of the town [...] as in equity they shall thinke meete." And after its various satellite towns were subtracted from its land area, Ipswich ultimately covered 41 square miles—remarkably close to the 36 square mile norm of the essayist.[84] However, not all Ipswich residents agreed with Ward's preference for limits on town land. While Topsfield was in the process of separating from Ipswich in 1645, Ipswich appealed to the General Court to save its lands; "but it was Answeared," wrote John Winthrop,

> a principall motiue which ledd the Court, to grant them & other Townes such vaste boundes was, that (when the Townes should be increaced by their children & servantes growing vp &c) they might have place to erecte villages, where they might be planted, & so the lande improved to the more Comon benefite.[85]

This is a very important statement to which we will return later.

In addition, the author of the essay was of one mind with Ward on the subject of social "proportion"; in fact, it is no exaggeration to say that Ward was obsessed with this concept and the Aristotelian notion of "distributive justice." When justice is administered "to every man to his true *suum*," as Ward once put it—that is, according to his social status—there is distributive justice or geometric proportion.[86] Elsewhere Ward wrote that "there is no duty more natural, morall, and politicall, then for Subjects to see their Government and Governors exquisitely constituted, and exactly carried on in a just line of Succession or Election; I mean in their due stations and proportions."[87] And the preamble of the Body of Liberties, Massachusetts' 1641 law code written primarily by Ward, insists that "liberties Immunities and priveledges" are "due to every man in his place and proportion."[88]

The complementary concepts of proportion and equity played a prominent role in Ipswich throughout the seventeenth century. Granted that proportion is a common word, the noun and its variants appear in the Ipswich town records with the frequency of an *idée fixe*, and in contexts where its use seems almost gratuitous. For example, the town meeting in February 1671/72 "voted to choose a committy to considder of some convenient way for shareing out a p[ro]portion of timbar & wood to the ynhabitants."[89] Equity was a concept dear to the town's founders; in *Iethro's Iustice of* Peace, the 1618 collaboration between Nathaniel Ward and his brother Samuel, Samuel Ward twice approvingly mentioned this social virtue.[90] Equity lingered in the town's consciousness, as evidenced in the controversy over John Winthrop Jr.'s sale of Castle Hill to Samuel Symonds. As Symonds reported to Winthrop in a 1647 letter (Figure 7), the town challenged his title to the estate in court (the Essex County Quarterly Court held in Ipswich on July 28, 1647). When their attempt to cast doubt on the written land title failed, the town pled "poynt of Chancery or equity […] that you left the Towne when Mr. Ward was leaving his place, the Church settling our present officers, & the Church ready to crack."

However, the magistrates (of whom Symonds was one) declined to use their equitable jurisdiction to remedy this perceived wrong, and the sale stood. Related to this case was the only recorded instance in colonial Ipswich of fence-breaking, a common form of direct popular action against enclosure in England. In the same court session Symonds sued William Story and John Dane for trespass for "breaking down fence." Given that the dispute over Castle Hill was happening simultaneously, this seems to be more than a dispute between neighbors; most likely Story and Dane acted in the interests of the town.

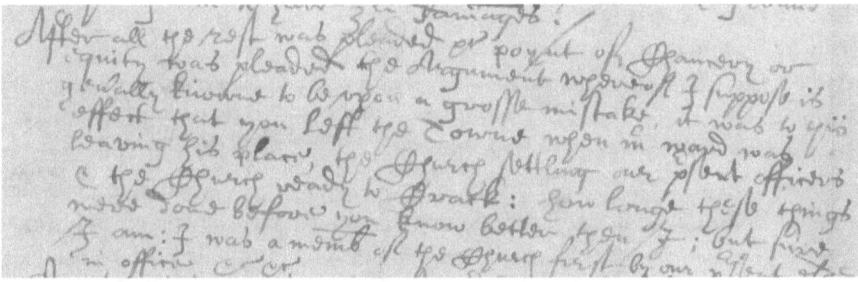

Figure 7 Section of letter from Samuel Symonds to John Winthrop Jr., 1647, MSS 413, Phillips Library, Peabocdy Essex Museum. The handwriting is difficult for a modern reader because the letter is written in a seventeenth-century script, "secretary hand."

The town records of the dispute survive only in a late nineteenth-century copy of what must already have been badly damaged pages, but they reveal that in June 1647 a committee was "chosen to try the Title" of "the Neck whereon Castle Hill stands; that April, the selectmen had already reimbursed John Dane "for going to Castle Neck." Symonds proved his title in court, receiving £3 damages and the repair of his fence. However, the town seems to have shown its approval for Dane's action by entrusting some surveying business to him in December 1648.[91]

But Symonds himself would find occasion to plead equity against what he saw as an abuse of the idea of proportion when, as a magistrate, he issued a ruling in the 1657 case of *Giddings v. Brown*. In 1655, the town voted to levy a tax of £100 to build a home for its new minister, Rev. Thomas Cobbet; each taxpayer had to pay his or her "p[ro]portion." Some residents refused to pay the tax, arguing that a public work like a minister's house should belong to the town and not to Cobbet. When the town marshal, Edward Browne, confiscated the pewter of George Giddings, one of the dissidents, Giddings sued.[92] In his decision, grounded primarily on the natural law of property, Symonds appealed directly to the principle of equity: "The law construeth things with equity and moderation; and therefore restrayneth a generall act, if there be any mischief or inconveniency in it."[93]

The ethic of social proportion was so deeply ingrained in colonial Ipswich that it made itself felt in almost every decision. In 1641/42, for example, as flocks and herds increased and wolves became a problem, the town required the wealthier inhabitants to acquire a dog; but those rated at more than 500 pounds net worth had to obtain "a sufficient mastive Dogg or such one as shalbe alowable," while those worth between 100 and 500 pounds only had to get "a sufficient hownde, or beagle."[94] But a concern for equity balanced the need to maintain social hierarchy. This made itself felt in homely ways, as when the town made it clear that Samuel Appleton's malt house had to charge "such rates as shalbe thought equall from tyme to tyme," as well as in greater matters such as the setting of tax rates. When two men were entrusted with the task of making a rate in 1644, they solemnly declared that "we desire to make as equall a rule as we can attain."[95] In fact, the two concepts were inseparably linked; when the town ca. 1646/47 levied an annual tax of £140 to support the ministry, "it was alsoe voted that it shall be p[ro]portined eqally in a rate or p[ro]portion."[96] Nathaniel Ward forged a similar link between equity and proportion in the *Simple Cobler*, written around the same time, when he argued that "Equity is as due to People, as Eminency to Princes; Liberty to Subjects, as Royalty to Kings."[97]

Considering the Ipswich land records in light of the principles of Protestant scholasticism and Puritan communal practice, a new synthesis of scholarship on land use patterns in colonial New England becomes possible, one that may apply not only to Ipswich but also to other communities. David Grayson Allen was quite right to challenge the impression left by the "town studies" of the 1970s that colonial New England towns were normally committed to common fields, even if this only had to do with nostalgia or wishful thinking. Ipswich had common fields from the beginning, an arrangement that promoted a rich corporate life by requiring the commoners to work together for the common good, but it also provided large, contiguous farms to wealthier residents as a way of respecting "due proportion." Further, Ipswich never definitively ruled out the possibility of enclosing even the small plots within the common fields. The common fields remained open during the town's first 30 years not so much for dogmatic as for practical reasons: a perceived timber shortage made "particular" fences seem wasteful, and farmers were reluctant to preclude completely the possibility of common grazing and dunging of fields, even though this proved less workable in New England conditions. All of this was in keeping with the Protestant scholastic categorization of all such concerns as matters of the practical understanding.[98] Thus, decisions about land distribution and maintenance of common resources were guided by precepts from the Gospel as well as the natural law—including the maintenance of social hierarchy as well as the obligation of charity to neighbors—but they were also considered to be human, prudential judgments, which could be suspended or altered for equitable reasons, such as concerns about sustainability.

Ipswich was never locked in to a rigid system of communal land management; nevertheless, in its first 30 years, it erred on the side of caution in departing from the common-field model. Here Allen gives a false impression, lumping Ipswich together with Watertown, where he claims "no hint of common arable field regulations exists, except for the very earliest years." Later he has to backtrack with respect to Ipswich, admitting that the town's selectmen "issued countless bylaws" including "agricultural regulations."[99] Indeed there were far fewer regulations than one would find on an English manor that practised a typical system of crop rotation, but we have already seen that the town did provide for common grazing on arable fields. The voluminous legislation relating to the use of timber has already been discussed as well. The town also jealously guarded its common meadows and pasture lands. This is surprising because Ipswich was known for its abundant salt marshes, crucial for haying, before the first European settlers even arrived in the town. In his 1631 book, *Advertisements for the Unexperienced Planters of New England*, Captain John Smith admonished, "Be carefull in the Spring to mow the swamps, and the low Ilands of Auguan [Agawam, the Algonquian name for Ipswich] where you may have harsh sheare-grasse enough to make hay of, till you can cleare ground to make pasture."[100] And in 1634, as the town was being settled, William Wood praised its "great

Meads and Marshes."[101] Nevertheless, the town generally behaved as if meadow were as scarce a resource on the Essex County coast as it had been in England.

One of the town's first acts, in January 1634/35, was to set aside "the Necke of Land next adioininge vnto Mr Rob[er]t Coles his land extending vnto the Sea [...] for Com[m]on use vnto the Towne." At the end of this record, which refers to Jeffrey's Neck (present-day Great Neck), comes a symbol that looks like E^r; both transcriber George Schofield and historian T. F. Waters render this as "forever" ["eternaliter"]. This symbol does not appear in standard dictionaries of medieval and early modern abbreviations, but the reading seems plausible.[102] Philip Fowler and six other men did receive four acres each of "meadowe and marsh ground" north of town, but the recorder hastened to add that "the marsh is not limitted unto them." (In addition, Fowler got to share a hill containing 30 acres of land with four other men—providing a typical example of numerous, small and scattered holdings.[103] Occasionally in the early records there is evidence of settlers trying to create larger, contiguous farms, as when Joseph Medcalfe in 1640 asked for some land "lyinge betweene his meadowe & his vpland"; but the recorder in Medcalfe's case made sure to add that it would only be granted "if it be not iudged inconvenyent for the Towne." Medcalfe got his land, but Fowler's landholdings—seven non-contiguous plots—conformed more closely to the Ipswich norm.)[104]

Common grazing lands were numerous, diverse, minutely regulated and zealously defended. The great "Cow pasture" or "Cowe Commons"—west of town, divided by the Ipswich River so that about two-thirds of the land lay north of it—was set aside by the town meeting on February 20, 1636/37. It fed "working cattle," that is, dairy cows and mature bulls (and, at times, some horses) that had to stay closer to the homelots; they were led to the common at night by the two herdsmen for the north and south herds. There were also two "Impounders" for the north and south grazing areas whose job was to round up beasts that were not supposed to be on the commons.[105] Nonworking cattle, such as steers (castrated bulls) more than 2 years old—that is, oxen—and dry cows, were taken farther afield, to places like Jeffrey's Neck, as were young bulls and (as of 1655/56) sheep. Swine were relegated to even remoter areas such as "hogg yland," and, not surprisingly, the number of pigs one could graze was proportional to one's net worth: under £100, two hogs; £100–£500, 3 hogs; above £500, four hogs.[106]

Presentments for violations of grazing rules were not numerous in early Ipswich; this could indicate that the rules were not strictly enforced, or simply mean that the townspeople accepted them so thoroughly that they were rarely violated. Some prosecutions were recorded, however, as when eight residents were presented in 1664 for sneaking some cattle onto a common arable field on Sunday; since it was a first offense, they got off with an admonition. In December 1641, two of the most prominent local leaders, William Hubbard and Simon Bradstreet, were presented along with three other men for "keeping cattell w[i]^thin the Com[m]on field contrary to an order"—presumably the order of 1640/41 designed to protect the winter wheat experiment. A verdict was not entered into the record.[107]

Complaints about local residents encroaching on the commons were more frequent. When in November 1665 it was reported that "some persons towards Newberry have incroached upon the Com[m]on by taking in much land w[i]^thout any title," the town took action to recover the land. Similarly, in March 1667/68, the town noted that a Mr. "Boynton yncrocht on the common."[108] Grazing was guarded so strictly that even the grassy areas around common roads were policed. A 1641/42 complaint that people when repairing their fences "Doe Incroach vpon the high-wayes, and [...] rimove the bounds" makes more sense in the context of an order a year earlier that the road to Chebacco would be maintained from the proceeds of the grass growing next to it.[109] The town's determination to protect its commons remained constant, from 1641, when it took steps to "p[re]serve the Com[m]on from incroachm[en]'" from those who had taken over more land than their grants entitled them to, to 1669/70, when the town ordered its selectmen to "prosecute against all incrochments vpon the commons Lands woods et."[110] For example, in 1667, the town's selectmen addressed a strongly worded petition to the General Court against the "incrochment of some of their neighbours"—that is, neighboring towns—on their meadows and thatch banks, against "the constant practice of such as were chosen to lay out any grants of Land" who "left such places as Com[m]on."[111] Rather than doling out all available land to private citizens, the town continued to create new commons; for example, a "new common for dry cattle" was set aside on May 4, 1656, and as late as 1668 a committee pointed out several areas of thatch banks "that we finde noe grant of the Towne for and soe common."[112]

At one point, in 1640/41, the town appointed the seven selectmen on condition "that they give noe Lands, nor meddle with Dividinge, nor stinting of the Com[m]ons."[113] However, a glaring exception seems to appear in the records on February 25, 1644/45, when 3,244 acres of the north cow common "was presented vnto the freemen of the Towne." The freemen then immediately granted the land to the town "inhabytants [...] to be imp[ro]ued." This odd legal fiction springs from an ambiguity in the early period of town settlement in New England, before the commoners or "inhabitants"—those possessing common rights—began meeting separately from the town meeting. Prior to the last two decades of the seventeenth century, when this trend became evident, the town meeting made decisions about the common lands, even though technically only the commoners had rights in them. Here the commoners wished to divide up and improve some excess lands on the common, so they gave the land to the town who then authorized that it be distributed to individual "inhabitants" for improvement, presumably meaning enclosure.[114] Given that in 1831, Ipswich contained only 7,423 acres of "pasturage," not counting hay meadows and marshes, this would have represented a considerable land grab by the commoners if a wholesale distribution had actually taken place.[115] However, there is no mention of this issue again until 1651, when the town meeting ordered the selectmen to "take care that there be no yncrochment made vpon the Cowe Commons either by bui[l]ding felling timber or feeding or any other ymprouement." Another record of around the same time reads as follows:

> Granted that all small p[ar]sells of Land soe inclosed by p[ro]priatyes as they are therby made useles to the Cowe Commons be refered to a commity to sell or lett as they shall see meet [...] for the use of the Towne p[ro]vided the said p[ar]sells of land exced not one p[ar]sell.[116]

This most likely means that although the town had been empowered in theory to distribute part of the cow commons for enclosure, it hadn't, but some of the commoners had taken matters into their own hands and created enclosures on the basis of the former decision. By 1651, the town felt the need to conserve the rest of the commons, so it signaled that no more distribution would take place; any enclosures that had already been made would be sold or leased for the benefit of the town—presumably to those who had enclosed it—provided that not too much land was lost to the commons. This represents another victory for the town meeting and common rights over the so-called lively land market in colonial New England.

The town also took a decisive step toward protecting its commons in 1659, when for the first time it took up the issue of who actually was entitled to the right of commonage.[117] A list of commoners had been produced in 1641/42, based on the distribution of houselots, but since then some families had built additional homes on their outlying lands.[118] That it was not the original intention of the town for those living in such "farm" houses to have the right of commonage may be inferred from the case of Daniel Denison, who came to Ipswich in 1635 and received a houselot and a medium-sized farm of 150 acres at Chebacco. In 1639 the town refused to make Humphrey Griffin an "inhabitant [...] the Town beinge full." Thus the town signaled its intention of defending common rights, but Griffin stayed on in Ipswich, perhaps as a tenant, until 1641 when Denison sold Griffin his houselot and, presumably, went to live at his farm. As a result, Denison was not included in the list of commoners compiled in 1641/42. The town decided in 1643 to grant him a commonage, presumably to keep him in Ipswich fulfilling his role as the captain of the militia.[119] The assumption seems to have been that a farm of 300 acres or more could be laid out in such a way as to contain sufficient grazing and mowing ground for the farmer's livestock, even if someone who did not have a houselot—and, thus, a commonage—had inherited or was running the farm. However, it appears that over time some residents of newly constructed farm houses claimed an extra commonage in addition to the one that belonged to their family's houselot. On March 15, 1659/60, Ipswich put a stop to that.

> Forasmuch as it is found by dayly experience y^t the common Lands of this Towne are ouerburdened by the multiplyeing of dwelling houses contrary to the intent [...] of the first ynhabitants in granting of houselotts. [...] Yt is ordered that no house henceforth erected shall haue any right to the common Lands of this Towne.

The town then declared its intention to petition the General Court for confirmation of the order. Once again, Ipswich showed itself in the vanguard of towns trying to maintain common rights when the Court on May 30, 1660, decreed that "no cottage or dwelling place shallbe admitted to the priviledge of com[m]onage [...] but such as already are in being or hereafter shallbe erected by the consent of the toune."[120]

As time went on, the town's determination to prevent new dwellings from claiming commonage merged with its long-standing animus against undesirable inhabitants. This dated back at least to December 1635, when Nathaniel Ward wrote to John Winthrop Jr.: "Our Towne of late but somewhat too late haue bene carefull on whome they bestowe lotts, being awakned thereto by the confluence of many ill and doubtfull persons, and by their behauiour since they came in drinking and pilferinge."[121] In February 1668/69, the town recast its former order with a new emphasis on restricting population.

> Wheras order hath beene taken that the number of inhabitants of this Towne might not be increased to the preiudice & damage of the commoners, notwithstanding which divers dwelling houses have beene built, and more intended yt is heerby ordered, that noe p[er]son not admitted & entred as a com[m]oner in this Towne shall directly or indirectly make use of [...] the Towne commons.[122]

By 1673, paranoia on this point had increased to the point that the town began "warning out" undesirable residents or collecting bonds from their employers or landlords lest they become a "charge" upon the town. This was a common practice in colonial New England; it was part of what Barry Levy has called the "political economy of the town" which helped protect rights and resources of town inhabitants, thus preventing an exploitative system of labor such as that found in the southern colonies.[123] Obviously it worked against the desire of wealthier citizens to bring in tenants or hired labor. In his first published study of labor in colonial Essex County, Daniel Vickers claimed that tenant families accounted for up to 25 percent of total families, but in this calculation Vickers extrapolated from the existing evidence on the assumption that "all landowners in the top decile of the population [in terms of wealth] hired at least one tenant." In his book *Farmers and Fishermen*, however, Vickers took a more conservative approach and came up with an estimate that tenants made up 5–15 percent of the county's inhabitants. The truth is that given what William Cronon has justly described as the "astonishingly sloppy" state of land recording in the early colonial period, we will never know how many tenants there were in colonial Ipswich.[124] What we can say is that, like practically everything else, tenancy was regulated by the town so that landlords and employers did not have carte blanche to rent land to whomever they wanted. If they tried, they came up against stern warnings like that issued by the Ipswich town meeting on November 17, 1673, against those who, for their own "p[ar]ticular advantage," should "lett out land or tenements to such p[er]sons as are no way desireable or may prove burdensom."[125]

In spite of its determination to protect the commons, there were two occasions in the first half century of Ipswich when the town seemingly preferred individual interests to common rights. The first experiment began, surprisingly, at the same town meeting of March 15, 1659/60, which decreed that newly built farm dwellings would not earn their builders a commonage. Perhaps to soften this blow, the town also allowed five men to lease and enclose three acres of common meadow land apiece, provided that in the last year of the lease they sowed "4 bushells of good hay seeds." Soon others were granted the same arrangement.[126] This was indeed a policy in keeping with the proto-Agricultural Revolution in England, but the town stood to benefit as well, in two ways. First, as Thomas F. Waters sensibly pointed out, cultivating the land for a period of time was a way to eliminate weeds that may have affected the quality of the hay. The more important reason had to do with a broader problem in New England as a whole, since (as was also the case in England) livestock required large quantities of hay to get through the winter. However, the native grasses were not so nutritious as English hay. The town fathers were ahead of their time in their efforts to promote the cultivation of what the selectmen called "good Ynglish hay," which was not widespread in New England until the eighteenth century.[127]

However, the town was also careful to correct any impression that widespread enclosure of common lands would become the "new normal" in Ipswich. When some of the beneficiaries of the new policy enclosed more land on Jeffrey's Neck than they were actually granted, the selectmen fined them 20 shillings apiece unless they agreed to sow English hay, "remove there fence & leave it out into the common of the sayd neck as before"; that is, accept eviction. Several months later, in February 1662/63, the town "voted that the selectmen shall not have any further liberty to lett out any more of common for yeares to plant."[128] In 1666, the selectmen took steps to repossess the leased portions of the commons by ordering the lessees to sow their English hay seeds and prepare to vacate or else face a lawsuit. Due to a summer drought, the order was amended that August to allow the fences to remain for another year for the sake of the hay; in the absence of any further evidence, presumably these enclosures were dismantled and returned to the commons in 1677.[129]

However, a more radical proposal was floated when in 1663/64 a committee was created "to consider of devoiding the common." A year later the town meeting voted to divide Plum Island, Hog Island, and Castle Neck among the commoners "according to the p[ro]portion of foure six eight." This meant that those who paid less than 6s. 8d. in taxes "in a single countery rate" would receive one share, those who paid between that amount and 16s. would get a share and a half, and those who paid more than 16s., as well as all magistrates and elders, would receive two shares.[130] As it turned out, however, a survey revealed that the entire distribution would amount to only "about eight hundred acres of marsh or upland beside heathes and sand hills," so that a single share would be three acres, a share and a half four acres and a double share only six acres. Considering that in 1831 Joseph Felt estimated Ipswich's total acreage at 21,267, while John Henry Sears in 1905 placed the total at 26,240 acres, what might seem like an organized gobbling of the commons by greedy inhabitants really amounted to an insignificant nibble.[131] However, it did give the town an opportunity to rearticulate its social body by putting Aristotelian geometric proportion into action.[132]

Nearly a half century into the corporate life of Ipswich, the town's statements on the subject of common rights seemed to become more, rather than less strident. The word *enclosure* made its first appearance in the town records, in far from triumphant fashion, in the selectmen's decision of May 1676: "that all horses that shall trespase upon inclosiers or com[m]on field or any neate cattell swine and sheepe being taken in any com[m]on field or inclosier shall be liable." Fittingly, even as it confirmed the existence of enclosures and the rights of their owners—a possibility that had always been envisioned in Ipswich—it also protected common rights. A year later, however, the selectmen took steps to prevent unlawful enclosures that damaged the commons. "Wheras there are severall persons that yntrude upon the common by making severall yards or pens, which afterwards are made use of, for Gardens & planting, and are preiuditiall to the Towne and an occation of calling that into question, wh is to lye free for com[m]on use," the selectmen decreed a significant fine of 5s. per week for every rod of ground "so taken in or ingrossed." Finally, in April 1682, the selectmen posed a question to the town meeting which, in its unusually general scope, sounds like a calculated warning shot across the bows of those expecting further distributions of the commons. They asked "whether any commoner or ynhabitant may take vp and inclose land upon the common or highwayes as he or they shall see good for tobaco yards or other vses." Not surprisingly, the town "Voted in the Negative."[133]

One important data set remains to be addressed, Allen's study of the surviving land deeds of early Ipswich, which he uses to support his point that "the traffic in land sales in East Anglian [...] Ipswich was extraordinary." Allen found 104 deeds from the period before 1660 "involving Ipswich men and Ipswich land, twice as many as in Newbury and over ten times the number entered by Rowley men."[134] I count 108 such deeds using the same records, with seventy different individual sellers. This would indeed have been a brisk rate of land transfer in the old country; whether it was "extraordinary" in a newly-founded and sizeable town is open to interpretation. The 1641 Ipswich commoners' list contains 111 names. In addition, there were undoubtedly landowners who were not commoners because of the New England practice of partible inheritance. For example, when Robert Mussey died in 1642 he left land to his sons Joseph and Benjamin and, surprisingly, bequeathed his houselot to his daughter Mary after his wife's death. Mussey also stipulated that "the commonage ptayning to my howse & land I leave to be divided betwixt my wife & children according to the discretion of my overseers." This means that two out of his three children would have become landowners without the right of commonage. Besides the large number of landowners there would have been other people in Ipswich—sons excluded from inheritance, tenants, laborers—looking to buy land. Population estimates for colonial Ipswich are elusive, but Arlin I. Ginsburg has described mid-seventeenth-century Ipswich as "a large town and still growing," while Susan L. Norton found that a "tremendously high" growth rate during the early years of settlement. That, in this town of several hundred people, only 70 Ipswich landholders sold any part of their land in the first 25 years of the town's existence actually seems rather surprising.[135]

Reading these deeds fails to produce the impression that early Ipswich was a seething hotbed of proto-capitalist land speculation. Five of the sellers, accounting for eight of the deeds, transferred land to close family members; for example, John Coggeswell between 1651 and 1652 sold land to his two sons and his son-in-law, after which John Jr. deeded his land purchase to his brother William.[136] Two transactions resulted from the deaths of landowners, and one wonders whether Thomas Firman's three separate transactions of 1647 were made in preparation for his death in early 1648. Thomas Scot of Stamford, Connecticut, made three separate sales of land that he had inherited from his father. Technically, that would make Scot an "absentee landowner," but one could hardly label him a land speculator; nor was Thomas Brigden of Charlestown, who sold land in 1659 that his wife, Mildred Carthrick of Ipswich, had inherited from her brother.[137] The only land seller who may fit the picture of the wealthy absentee landowner was William Payne, who lent money to several people in Essex County, but it is not clear whether Payne actually moved to Boston or stayed in Ipswich.[138]

In fact, one might expect the Ipswich land market to have been considerably more bustling than it was, given that a number of towns—Newbury, Haverhill, Rowley, Andover, Topsfield, and North Brookfield, among others—were settled largely or partly from Ipswich. But my own data support Edward Perzel's conclusion that most out-migrants must have owned little or no land. Only 18 of the 70 land sellers definitely left Ipswich, while four more probably did so.[139] It stands to reason that those settlers unable to obtain land in Ipswich, or to obtain a sufficient portion of the various types of land necessary for survival, would have moved on to other towns.[140] Thus out-migrants generally had little land to put on the market, while those who remained in Ipswich, especially householders with families to provide for, had little reason to sell. And given the state of the Essex County land records, the existence of fewer deeds from towns like Rowley and Newbury than from Ipswich, which Allen uses to bolster his argument about the Ipswich land market, means little. As early as 1652, Richard Browne, testifying in a Newbury land dispute, complained that "much of the town book was lost long ago."[141] As for Rowley, the compilers of the town records, Benjamin Mighill and George Blodgette, stated that "the book used for recording the general affairs of the town of Rowley from 1638 to 1672 is much worn, mutilated, and nearly illegible, many leaves are missing, so that nothing remains of record before August, 1647." A seemingly complete land survey survives, dated 1643/44, but that does not mean that the town's deeds are complete.[142] In 1640, the General Court required the recording of land conveyances, but as David Thomas Konig has shown, the 1648 Laws and Liberties of Massachusetts (a revision of Ward's Body of Liberties) specified that deeds only had to be recorded when the seller, mortgager, or granter, for some reason, continued to live on the land. In any case, as Edward Perzel points out, deeds from before the establishment of the Essex County Probate Court in 1640 "were recorded only if the persons holding them made an effort to have them recorded."[143] Under these circumstances, no quantitative comparison of deeds from the various Essex towns could possibly be meaningful.

Decisions about land distribution and land policy in colonial Ipswich were made on the basis of practical reason, but they had deeper ramifications. As Sarah Irving has argued, in a Baconian sense Puritans felt an obligation to use the land to benefit humanity and help hasten the onset of the Kingdom of God. To leave the land in its wilderness state would mean "that humanity had shirked its responsibilities toward the rest of the creation."[144] This raises the issue of Puritan misunderstandings of Indian land use practices, which the settlers used to justify the appropriation of Indian land, but that is properly a subject for another book. In addition, to distribute land was to perform a social ritual that fully articulated the social body of a town. It was also, in a sense, to spiritualize the land by incorporating it into the town's body, which was analogous to the Body of Christ, in a way akin to the Puritan devotional practice of "spiritualizing the creatures."[145] Here Puritan practice was in keeping with John Norden's remarkable statement in the 1618 edition of his *Surveyor's Dialogue*: "Is not every Manor a little commonwealth, whereof the Tenants are the members, the Land the body, and the Lord the head?"[146] The next chapter will investigate how this metaphysics of land use gave rise to further mobility in colonial New England, as settlers from Ipswich broke away from that town's body to form new organic and living communities elsewhere.

Chapter Four

TOWN-FOUNDING IN ESSEX COUNTY
The Communities around Ipswich

The first social body to be birthed from Ipswich, Massachusetts, was Newbury to its north. Newbury was something of an outlier among New England towns, first of all because its ministers, Thomas Parker and his cousin James Noyes, had decidedly Presbyterian leanings and rejected the emerging Congregationalist model, perfected by Thomas Shepard, in which believers had to offer evidence that they were among the predestined "elect" in order to be admitted to full church membership and become communicants. In his 1646 *Hypocrisie Unmasked,* Plymouth's sometime governor Edward Winslow cited the toleration of Parker and Noyes as evidence that the New Englanders did not ruthlessly crush religious dissent.[1] Newbury's land-use patterns also evolved atypically, because in 1642 the Newburyites, "well weighing the streights they were in for want of plough ground, remoteness of the Common, scarcity of fenceing stuffe & the like" decided to relocate their houselots to a "new Towne" about three miles north. This seems to have artificially accelerated the transition from open-field farming to enclosure in an anomalous way.[2]

Accordingly, David Grayson Allen focused on Newbury's pronounced social hierarchy rather than its system of land use, pointing to inequalities in the allocation of common rights in Newbury. Allen argued that this stratification replicated conditions of inequality in the counties of Wiltshire and Hampshire, which provided most of the members of Parker's company.[3] I would suggest that the thoroughgoing Protestant scholasticism and corporatism of Parker and Noyes had at least as much to do with it. In his biography of Parker, Cotton Mather labeled him "Scholasticus" (although he claimed that after devoting himself to "school divinity" early in his Newbury pastorate, Parker "afterwards laid it all aside, for the 'knowledge of Jesus Christ crucified.'").[4] Whether or not this is true, Parker received a thorough formation in Protestant scholasticism, first from his father, the famous Puritan Robert Parker, alumnus of Magdalen College, Oxford (author of the 1607 *Scholasticall Discourse against symbolizing with Antichrist in Ceremonies*), and later at Trinity College, Dublin—also John Winthrop Jr.'s *alma mater*—where Parker matriculated in 1610.[5]

James Noyes attended Brasenose College, Oxford; his published works relentlessly deploy the corporatist image in defense of Presbyterian polity. The first words of Noyes's 1646 *Temple Measured* are as follows: "The Militant Church of Christ upon earth, is one integral Body visible, and hath power to act in Synods and Councels to the end of the world." Arguing for the unity of the Church against Congregationalist particularism,

Noyes insists that "many and all Churches [...] are but one Church" just as "many Corporations under one King, are but one Body Politick." *Moses and Aaron* was published posthumously in 1661, with a dedication to King Charles II and an epistle "To the Reader" by Thomas Parker. In this work Noyes nuances his view of the networks of social bodies to which people might belong:

> One visible covenant implied in the profession of faith doth make one visible Church, one mutuall covenant in a republick makes one politick body, one mutual covenant of many Cities, make one repu[b]lick, many perfect republicks, may become one by mutuall covenant, The church is so one body, that every member hath freedom in every congregation.

Nevertheless, the various bodies are concentric, ending in the ultimate unities of the Church (under its visible head, Christ) and of the State (ruled by its monarch). Invoking the scholastic language of proportion, Noyes argues, "If Christ be not a visible head, the visible church is a body without a head proportionate." In other words, hierarchy—here in the form of headship—is necessary so that the body retains its proper proportion. But Congregationalism destroys the unity of the body under its head: "Independency doth teare the coat, the body of Christ into pieces. It cuts, hacks and hews the fat olive into chips or blocks."[6]

Newbury's shortage of resources and collective move northward had much to do with the founding and rapid expansion of nearby Rowley. Antiquarians and historians have consistently offered the same picture of colonial Rowley: under the thumb of its dictatorial first minister Ezekiel Rogers, Nathaniel Ward's stepbrother, the community adhered to the open-field model with unusual strictness. The conventional wisdom is that the origins of many settlers in the open-field region around Rowley, Rogers's Yorkshire parish, led the New World Rowley to adopt common-field strip farming. But following Rogers's death in 1660/61, we are told, the town lost cohesion and after a bitter church fight, proved helpless to resist the secession of Bradford and Boxford and the fragmentation of its communal ethos.[7] I hope to show, first, that some of the most influential members of Rogers's company came from the Leeds area, which was not an open-field district; second, I will suggest that the departure of Bradford and Boxford was not only accepted, it was actually foreseen from the beginning as part of Rogers's eminently practical plan to guarantee subsistence to his cohort for generations to come; and finally, that from the beginning colonial Rowley showed even less hostility to enclosure than Ipswich.

Rowley in Yorkshire was not a town but a very large parish that included several villages. It lay on the border between the Wolds district and the region of Holderness, surrounding the city of Hull, in Yorkshire's East Riding. Both the Wolds and Holderness featured nucleated villages and extensive open fields well into the seventeenth century; unlike other areas of Yorkshire, corn, and not cattle, provided most farm revenue in the Wolds. Large areas of common grazing land and open fields were enclosed in the parish in 1803–4, including 1,677 acres at Little Weighton and 1,413 acres in Riplingham. M. W. Beresford's analysis of glebe terriers (a glebe consisted of lands which belonged to a parish) revealed that Rowley's glebe was still in open fields as of 1685, while the deanery to which it belonged, Harthill, remained 65 percent unenclosed at the end of the seventeenth century.[8] Furthermore, the core of the Rogers company did indeed come from the Rowley region. Several emigrants were connected to the village of Holme-on-Spalding-Moor, which according to Brodie Waddell "continued to grow most of its crops on three large town fields until the 1770s."[9]

Among those early settlers in Rowley, Massachusetts, who did not come from the East Riding, the most significant hailed from the area around Leeds in the West Riding of Yorkshire: Matthew Boyes from Leeds and the Jewett brothers, Maximilian and Joseph, from nearby Bradford. Maximilian Jewett served repeatedly as a Deputy to the Massachusetts General Court as well as a deacon in the church, while Ezekiel Rogers praised Boyes as a pillar of the community, saying he "hath bene faithfull among vs and approoued [...] so y^t haue made good vse of him in o^r Church & Towne, where he hath long bene one of o^r Seauen-Men for ordering o^r affaires: & one of o^r Deputyes in ye Generall Court [...] it being o^r Parliament."[10] Boyes was also appointed by the General Court in 1641 to help lay out the boundaries of Haverhill, and by the town of Rowley to settle a dispute with Robert Haseltine, William Wild, and John Haseltine over "what vplands meadowes & other accom[m]odations they were to haue of the Towne." Since Boyes seems to have been a significant player in land policies, some consideration of land use in his area of origin seems necessary.[11]

The Leeds region was a pastoral area with very little arable, which lacked the nucleated villages characteristic of the East Riding. Historic landscape characterization reveals the presence of open fields in Bradford as late as 1854, but the process of enclosing the arable was well under way by the early seventeenth century. However, there were immense tracts of common pasture where common rights were jealously maintained. An Inquisition of 1612 refers to "a certain moor, waste or common" in Bradford on which freeholders and copyholders had had "common of pasture and *turbary* [the right to cut turf or peat], time out of mind." And at nearby Manningham, also during the reign of James I, copyholders sued in the Duchy Court over infringement of their common rights.[12] In addition, most residents were involved in the burgeoning textile industry in the area, so that by the 1720s Daniel Defoe could claim that its clothiers "not only supply all the Shop-keepers and Wholesale Men in *London*, but sell also very great Quantities to the Merchants, as well for Exportation to the *English* Colonies in *America*." As David Hey put it, in this relatively barren district, "to obtain a living it was necessary to have a dual occupation and generous common rights." Martha Ellis has shown in her study of Halifax Parish that while some enclosures were "probably greeted with enthusiasm," at other times "some of the inhabitants were antagonistic to the enclosure movement."[13]

Enclosure was also a live issue in the Wolds district from which most of the Rogers party emigrated. Rowley itself may have been enclosed shortly after Rogers's departure. An entry in the parish register states that Jeremiah Northend "went with Mr Rogers in to America, when about 12 Years old. & staid there about 9 years" before returning to old Rowley. "The Enclosure at Rowley was made in his absence." This would suggest that a major enclosure took place at Rowley between 1638 and 1647, one that seems likely to have been discussed prior to the Rogers company's departure.[14] And while the accusation that Rowley was depopulated because of the Rogers exodus is unfounded, the phenomenon of "deserted villages," which in the early modern period was commonly blamed on enclosure, had caused concern in the East Riding for centuries.[15] To sum up, a simple geographical determinism does not appear to account for the origin of Rowley's open fields or the way they were managed. As discussed in Chapter One, in his upbringing and early ministry Rogers was exposed to both open-field and enclosed areas, then removed to Rowley, where open fields were the norm but apparently came under threat during his tenure. Other key founders of Rowley, Massachusetts, came from the district of small and increasingly enclosed farms around Leeds, surrounded by huge areas of a crucial common resource, pasture land. Furthermore, the Leeds area increasingly formed part of far-flung marketing networks in the textile industry, and even Rogers himself, supposedly a rock-ribbed traditionalist defender of Puritan communal ideals, was far from hostile to entrepreneurialism. In his 1646 letter from Massachusetts to the prominent Hull merchant, William Sykes (who had invested £100 in the Rowley enterprise at its outset), Rogers boasted of Rowley's and the colony's business promise. "O^r trade of Fishing is come to be a rich benefitt already: Greate hope of a very rich trade of Bever: we make many & greate Shipps." Rogers went on to explain that the town was sending Matthew Boyes as an emissary to England to promote "some way of Trading out of Englande."[16] Rowley would later acquire a reputation as a leader in the colony's nascent textile industry. Circa 1660 Samuel Maverick referred to "a large and populous Towne called Rowley" where "the Inhabitants are most Yorkshiremen very laborious people and drive a pretty trade, makeing Cloath and Ruggs of Cotton Wool, and also Sheeps wooll."[17]

Rogers was thoroughly imbued with his stepbrother Ward's corporatism and proved one of the most feisty proponents of a law code to restrain magisterial powers and promote moral reformation. Using corporatist terminology, Rogers informed John Winthrop in 1639: "A body of Lawes is now of all much desired; and all maturenes of proceeding therin wished."[18] Rogers again displayed his corporatism a month later as he continued to nag the Governor: "Truly Sir we are not yet (the body of the land, I meane) as we must be. And if magistracy and ministry preuaile not to clense our mixtures and filth, a sore scourge we shall most certainly haue."[19] In 1643 he offended Winthrop with his election sermon in which he warned voters against choosing the same man as governor twice consecutively (Winthrop noted gleefully that in spite of Rogers's sermon, he was reelected).[20]

In addition to his interest in promoting entrepreneurship, Rogers showed himself a master negotiator as he strove to accumulate as much land as possible to meet the needs of his company. It helped his bargaining position that other New England communities, including New Haven and Salem, were eager to attract Rogers and his cohort to join them.[21] John Winthrop's comment is revealing: because "many of quality in England did depend upon his choice of a fit place for them," Rogers insisted on so many "propositions and cautions" that the New Haven deal fell through. It was clear that only a new plantation would offer resources ample enough to satisfy Rogers's determination to provide for his companions.[22] Accordingly, the General Court in March 1638/39 offered Rogers the site of Rowley, near the Atlantic Ocean between Ipswich and Newbury, and "8 miles every way into the countrey, where it may not trench upon other plantations already setled." Because some of the land near the town site had already been laid out to landowners from Ipswich and Newbury, the Rogers company had to purchase it at the cost of £800.[23] Rogers later claimed that the cost was "at least 900li" and hinted that the entire town should be immune from taxation because of the expense; it is further proof of Rogers's prestige and persuasiveness that the Court soon guaranteed that Rowley would be completely tax-free for two years.[24]

However, Rogers was not yet satisfied. In March 1639/40 he complained of those who would "depriue vs of our measure of lande": "the Court doe giue vs but three miles of the eight, that we go into the Country, yet we heare that some woulde take somwhat of[f] from that."[25] Rogers was determined that Rowley's bounds would extend northward all the way to the Merrimack River, and insisted that Winthrop and the Court had promised him that they would. On the strength of this promise, he said, "the sound of Merimack we made not a little vse of" in advertising the town-founding enterprise back in England. However, the fledgling town of Andover had already been granted land along the south shore of the Merrimack, and in any case the eight-mile radius from Rowley did not reach any available land along the river. (Rogers's attempted land grab inspired the already cited complaint from his stepbrother Nathaniel Ward, who was heavily involved in the settlement of both Andover and Haverhill, about "the lauish liberality of the Court in giving away the Countrye.")[26]

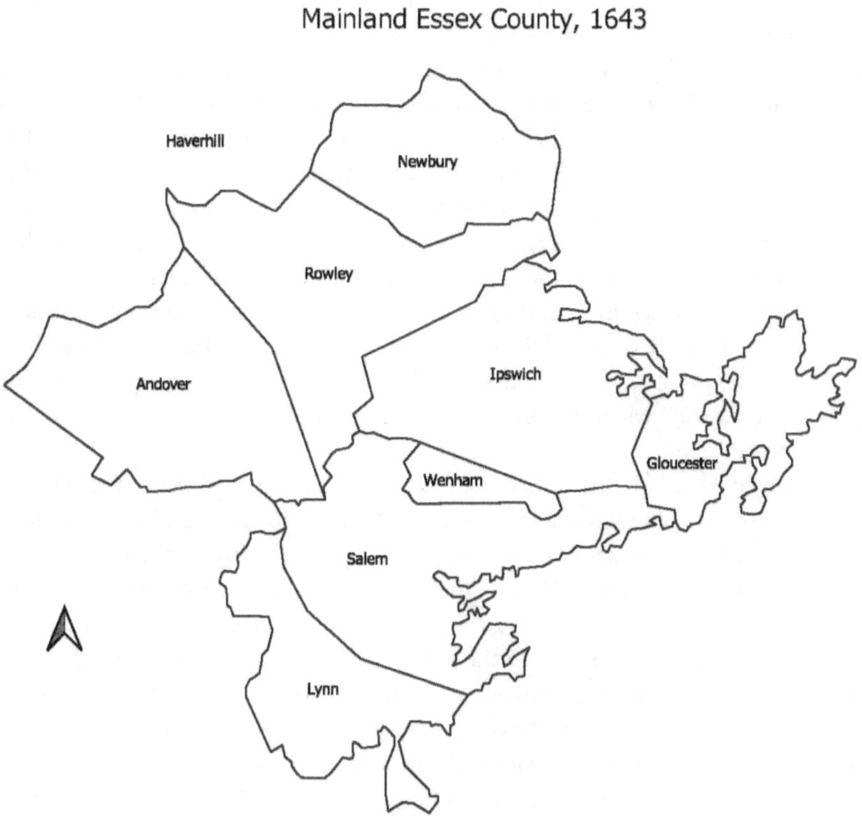

Figure 8 Boundaries of Essex County towns in 1643, when Haverhill became part of Norfolk County.

Obligingly, the General Court agreed to measure the eight miles not from Rowley itself but from a spot farther west on the Ipswich River. However, when it turned out that this point was farther than eight miles from the Merrimack, Rogers went ballistic. Flying into a "passionate distemper," he threatened to inform his fellow church elders of the Court's perfidy and stormed out. This appeal to the Church over the State was seen as "menacing," so Rogers was compelled to return. When he "did freely and humbly blame himself" for his fault, the Court, astonishingly, "freely granted what he formerly desired," giving Rowley the Merrimack lands (see Figure 8).[27] As the icing on the cake, Rogers demanded 100 acres of precious meadowland which had been claimed by Andover, in exchange for some land within Rowley's grant that had already been assigned to former governor Henry Vane, much to the disgust of Andover's future minister, John Woodbridge.[28]

It isn't clear whether Rogers won that battle, but he undoubtedly won the war, namely his struggle to provide enough arable, meadow, pasture, and woodland for the members of his ministerial company for the foreseeable future.[29] But why would Winthrop and the General Court cave in to Rogers's demands, given the intense interest of other powerful colonists like future governor Simon Bradstreet (another founder of Andover) and Nathaniel Ward in preventing Rogers from engrossing all the available land in Essex County? A possible answer is that Ezekiel Rogers shared Winthrop's vision of how settlement should proceed, quoted in Chapter Three: ideally towns should have "vaste bounds" so that when the original settlements became overpopulated, they could "erecte villages" on their remaining land, "& so the land improved to the more Comon benefite." Rogers unwittingly echoed this in an offhand remark he made to Winthrop: "Neither doe we purpose to keepe this lande vnimployed so long by halfe, as others haue done."[30] Looking at the vast extent and boomerang shape of Rowley's original bounds, it is obvious that the far-flung lands between the Ipswich and Merrimack Rivers were of no use whatsoever to inhabitants of Rowley for planting or pasturage—the daily "commute" would have been an impossibility. Rogers and the other Rowley leaders must have already envisioned the creation of separate towns in that part of their grant, new settlements to absorb the overflow from Rowley when the original community ran out of resources near enough to be consumed.

The clearest proof of this is that in the southwestern part of the grant, which later became the town of Boxford, land was set aside for a "Ministers farm," which "shall belong to the Minister at that place when thei haue an orthodox minister setled there."[31] In a 1673 petition to the General Court, the Boxford inhabitants declared that their "land was sold to us as village land, free from any engagement to the town of Rowley, ellse we had not purchased it."[32] Similarly, in the northwestern portion of Rowley's grant which became the town of Bradford, 40 acres were laid out "for the use of the ministrie."[33] On January 2, 1653/54, the Rowley town meeting created a committee to "proportion all the lands apoynted for a uillage within the bounds of Rowley unto the inhabitants of the same towne acording to purchase."[34] These lands on the Merrimack were clearly intended from the beginning to form a separate "uillage," and when Bradford petitioned in 1668 to be recognized as a town, the General Court's response was in keeping with that expectation:

there is liberty granted the petitioners by the toune of Rouley to provide themselues of a minister, & also an intent to release them from their toune ship when they are accordingly prouided, and therefore [...] this Court may grant their petition to be a touneship, provided they doe gett & setle an able & orthodox minister.[35]

As for Rowley itself, the town records reveal that far from being a bastion of rock-ribbed conservatism in its land use patterns, it followed the same trajectory as Ipswich, only faster and more deliberately. One interesting detail lacking in Ipswich, but in keeping with the English practices discussed in Chapter Two, is that the town was broken into eight "Devisions," also called "Companyes," each of which had to provide a bull.[36] Rowley did start with the open-field model of agriculture and extensive commons. The town itself—the cluster of houses near the bottom of the map in Figure 9—was well-sited, with plenty of arable upland nearby. The common arable field mentioned most frequently in the records was the Northeast field, adjacent to the town; to the east of this field lay "Mst Dumers farme," land that had been originally assigned to Richard Dummer by the town of Newbury but later purchased by Rowley. This area, labeled on the map as "Salt Meadow," was indeed mostly marshland good for haying, but also contained some arable.[37] Like the Ipswich residents, the Rowleyites thought of their grant in terms of concentric circles. In a ca. 1660 copy of the earliest town records that are now lost, the town "Commons" was defined as "fiue mills from the Towne Euery way wher we haue propriatie."[38] The land beyond this outer circumference was set aside for the two proto-villages of Bradford and Boxford, but it also included most of the large farms granted to Rowleyites, such as the 300-acre tracts bestowed on Samuel Phillips and Ezekiel Rogers

Figure 9 Detail of Plan of Rowley surveyed by Joseph Chapin, December 1794, from Massachusetts Archives, in Digital Commonwealth.

in the Merrimack lands in 1658.[39] The heart of Rowley lay within a 1½-mile radius—as envisioned in the "Essay on the Ordering of Towns"—which was often referenced in town records. Thus "Catle horses and sheep" that got into "the north East feild and farme and other common corne feilds withing a mile and one half of the towne" were to be impounded; any timber felled within the 1½-mile limit had to be removed within six days, and no lumber could be obtained there "except for building or Railes."[40]

The term "proportion" occurs in the Rowley records in every imaginable context, from the dividing up of fencing responsibilities around the common fields in proportion to landholdings, to determining the differing sizes of the yokes that had to be inflicted on swine to keep them from rooting up plants, according to their age and bulk.[41] Preeminently, however, the number of animals each inhabitant was allowed to pasture on the commons, as well as each householder's share of future land divisions, were determined by the number of "gates" they held, and gates were distributed in proportion to the amount of money contributed by that inhabitant to pay off the original £800 debt. All New England historians owe a great debt of gratitude to John Frederick Martin for being the first to explain, in *Profits in the Wilderness*, how this type of system worked.[42] In Rowley, to use Magirus's terms, gates were earned not in arithmetic proportion but in geometric proportion. Thus a payment sufficient for an acre and a half houselot also earned 1½ gates, a two-acre houselot came with 4½ gates, a three-acre lot brought 13½ gates, a four-acre lot included 22 gates, and the largest houselots of six acres came bundled with a whopping 45 gates. Ezekiel Rogers and his cohort shared Nathaniel Ward's commitment to social hierarchy and Aristotelian distributive justice—but it is interesting that they also used the language of equity to describe the allocation of gates: the system was designed "to the end euery man may haue an equall share in the Commons," equal, that is, "according to purchase." The Rowleyites, like the founders of Ipswich, saw no contradiction between social equity and social proportion.[43]

As in Ipswich, the open fields of Rowley reflected the settlers' expectation that their animals would need the right to "shack," grazing in arable fields in the winter and after harvests. In Rowley we can spot the moment when this practice outlived its usefulness—apparently the Rowleyites conducted their own experiment with winter wheat, planting rye in the Northeast field. But the town meeting on February 16, 1651/52, noting that since "their is hurt Done yearly by Cattell eating and treading on mens Rye in the northeast field in wintertime upon sudden thaughes and at breaking vp of frosts at spring," any animal found on the field in winter would be impounded.[44] Even before this shift in policy, the Rowleyites clearly envisioned the possibility of enclosure. We have seen that in the Ipswich records, the word *enclosure* did not appear until 1676, but the term appears on page one of the ca. 1660 copy of the earliest records: "It is ordered that all house Lotts That are or shall bee Laid out shall fence against all Common Pastiers and Inclosures which are not laid out for house lotts."[45]

Other references to enclosures are numerous, and the reason is suggested by an entry that probably dates to the early 1670s:

> Whereas it is aparent by experience that diuers persons haue fenced of[f] there gates from the Common with a fiue Raile fence intending to preserue them from swine and other small cattell

and yet they haue a considerable Numbers of swine and sheepe and such small creatures goeing vpon the Commons where other mens wholle share lieth in common vnfenced it is therfor ordered that the owners of all such pastures shall only be secured by ther fence and shall Recover noe dammage nor poundage by Swine nor other small Cattell except the owner of such swine or other small cattell be knowne to put them in or any by there order.[46]

(Notice that the term "cattell" included not only cows, bulls and oxen but several other kinds of domesticated animals, such as sheep and swine.) The tone of this record is not very friendly to the enclosers, who are held liable for damage inflicted within their enclosures by stray animals from the commons, but it accepts enclosure as part of the town's "experience" (in keeping with Puritan practical reason). What is unusual is that in Rowley, enclosers apparently felt free to erect a "fiue Raile fence," something which, as we have seen, was forbidden in Ipswich. Here as in other matters, we see Ezekiel Rogers's foresight in providing the town with an abundance of the resources it needed. The taking of timber was regulated in Rowley, as in the two ordinances previously mentioned, and common rights were also preserved.[47] But such regulations were far more lenient, and their tone less strident, than those of the more straitened Ipswich community. The simple fact that timber was far more plentiful in Rowley made enclosure much more practical. So did the abundance of common meadow and pasture.

Only two provisions in the Rowley records indicate qualms about the advancement of enclosure. The first has to do with an ordinance permitting anyone "to fence in or inclose any of ther meadows or vpland [...] eyther within or without the common fence." But this record is crossed out, which normally indicates that it was repealed at some point.[48] Apparently the Rowleyites explictly endorsed enclosure in their town meeting early on, and the later repeal of this provision did little to halt enclosure in the community. The second dates to the 1660s and asserts that "ther shalbe noe more deuissions of land on the townes Commons nor noe more Adission of Gates nether by Giueing leting or selling except it be for the nessesery of the towne to accomodate teaching elders."[49] This vote was probably a reaction to the selling of common lands after Ezekiel Rogers's death, in order to buy back Rogers's lands from his heir, also named Ezekiel Rogers, son of Nathaniel Rogers of Ipswich; this occurred around the same time as a distribution of common lands to the inhabitants at the ratio of one acre per gate.[50] But the ban on further reduction of the commons was a dead letter from the beginning. On January 15, 1666/67, "it was agreed by voat that the common marsh at hog iland should be Devided according to Gates." (Hog Island was not an island but a swampy area at the east of Rowley's grant, just across from Plum Island, which blocked the town's access to the Atlantic; Rowley's portion of Plum Island had already been distributed to the inhabitants by vote of the town meeting on December 28, 1657.)[51] By the end of the 1670s, the Rowley commons would be effectively extinguished. At a landmark town meeting on February 24, 1673, the Rowleyites voted to distribute their commons—"two thirds of it [...] more or less"—not just to inhabitants who owned gates, but to all town ratepayers. Each gate would receive two acres, while a 20-shilling assessment in the previous year's ministry tax rate would garner four acres. Less than a month later the town meeting increased the quantity of land to be distributed.[52] Finally, on February 27, 1659,

Rowley voted to distribute all of "the right that every man hath in the Deuision of the Comons acording to Towne grants that remaineth yet unsatisfyed," reserving only a few small parcels as "free common for ever."[53] When Joseph Chapin made his survey map of Rowley in 1794, he commented in the margin that "there be little or no common lands in Rowley, except the roads."[54]

This is a radically different picture than we have hitherto received of land policy in colonial Rowley, but it is not necessarily a tragic one. The Rowleyites accepted enclosure not because they fell victim to a proto-capitalist land market, but as part of a strategy to guarantee sufficient resources for all their inhabitants down to the second and third generations. What made this strategy practical was that their first minister, Ezekiel Rogers, had a talent for raising hell. By browbeating and manipulating the Massachusetts General Court into submission, Rogers brazenly managed to grab a large portion of the remaining land in Essex County, rich in all the resources needed for the mixed-farming regime, not for personal gain but to make his community sustainable for the long term. Rogers's vision, a triumph of Puritan practical reason without a trace of nostalgia, included the founding of two new towns, Bradford and Boxford, to siphon off the excess population from Rowley so that by the 1670s Rowley was able to complete its process of enclosure without causing hardship to its inhabitants. The imperative of organizing migration to new towns—creating new social bodies in order to ensure the long-term viability of the original, founding body—was a crucial part of the Puritan ideology of mobility. It was fitting that the epitaph for Rogers in Mather's *Magnalia Christi Americana* began "*Abi, Viator*":

Traveller, depart!
Stand by his grave, and learn that thou must die;
Then trace his shining path to yonder sky.[55]

The settlement of Andover, Rowley's Western neighbor, remains somewhat obscure because of the total disappearance of all town records before March 9, 1656, when the inhabitants created a "New Towne booke, the old being rent and in many places defective and som graunts lost."[56] Nevertheless, it provides a useful illustration, not only of the pitfalls of historical generalizations based on incomplete land records, but of the development of the Puritan ideology of mobility as new towns were founded. For the migration was instigated by the highly articulate leaders of the political movement, based in Ipswich, that supported the adoption of Nathaniel Ward's Body of Liberties, including Ward himself and the family of Thomas Dudley. The intellectual leaders of the Andover settlement were Dudley's sons-in-law Simon Bradstreet and John Woodbridge, as well as the poet Anne Dudley Bradstreet (wife of Simon).

By December 22, 1639, Nathaniel Ward had decided to leave Ipswich and start a new plantation on the Merrimack River, either at Cochichawick on its southern shore or at Pentucket on its northern bank. He asked John Winthrop to make sure those lands remained available "till my self and some others either speak or write to yow about it." Giles Firmin, husband of Ward's daughter Susannah, explained in a letter that the plan was partly meant to provide Firmin with means of support. Firmin had been practicing medicine at Ipswich, but complained of "my want of accommodation here (the ground the Towne hauing giuen mee lyinge 5 miles from mee or more) and that the gaines of Physick will not finde mee with bread." Firmin then mysteriously alluded to "some temptations" which dogged Ward in Ipswich—perhaps related to the "naturall infirmity (himselfe being best privy unto)" which Edward Johnson cited as the reason for Ward's leaving the ministry in the late 1630s.[57] In the spring of 1640 Ward reported to Winthrop "concerning the plantation [...] our company increases apace from diuers townes, of very desirable men wherof we desire to be very choise." Anthropologist Elinor Abbot put it well when she wrote that "the main features of the company [...] is that it is hierarchical, headed, and purposeful."[58] Ward's emphasis on the "choise" nature of his potential settlers may indicate that he was unhappy with the social composition of Ipswich and hoped to create a better-proportioned social body in his new town.[59]

However, there was a roadblock in the way of Ward's plan to provide for Firmin and his family: Ipswich had granted Firmin 100 acres "vpon this Condition that I should stay in Towne 3 yeers, or else I could not sell it." One might expect the community-minded Ward to favor such a provision, but applied to a member of his own family, it rankled: "now my father [Ward] supposes [...] that it is more then they cann doe to binde mee so when as others haue not beene so, but range from place to place on purpose to liue vpon the Country." This illustrates the Puritans' dual take on mobility: it was undesirable to have migrants "range from place to place," but there were certain members of the community—we might call them the "estate of town founders"—who were entitled to leave one social body and start another when this was necessary for some compelling reason. Clearly, Ward felt that it violated distributive justice that Firmin, one of the Ipswich social body's more exalted members, should have his movements restrained. In light of Ward's 1635 comment (Figure 10) that "we consider our Towne [Ipswich] [...] had neede to be strong and of a homogeneous spirit and people, as free from dangerous persons as we may"—is it fanciful to see this estate of town founders as the "spirit" animating the social body, guiding its lesser "people," endowing them with its own privilege of transmigration as needed for the health of the community?[60]

The postscript of Ward's spring 1640 letter to Winthrop, in which he complained of his stepbrother Ezekiel Rogers's hunger for land, probably explains why he decided to turn his attention north of the Merrimack to Pentucket, which became the town of Haverhill. In December 1641, the General Court granted Ward 600 acres that later became part of Haverhill. Leadership of the Andover enterprise shifted to Simon Bradstreet and John Woodbridge, who helped bring in a number of settlers from Newbury, Massachusetts, most originally from Wiltshire and Hampshire. Also involved were some settlers with roots in Bishop's Stortford, Hertfordshire, who had followed John Norton to Ipswich when he became the town's teacher in 1638.[61] There were settlers at Andover by May 1643, when the General Court officially designated Cochichawick as part of Essex County. In October 1645, Woodbridge was ordained as pastor of the new Andover congregation.[62]

As the Bradstreets' in-law and Thomas Parker's nephew, Woodbridge provided a link between the Ipswich and Newbury emigrants at Andover. Like Parker, Woodbridge hailed from open-field Wiltshire, and it is tempting to suggest, with Philip Greven, that

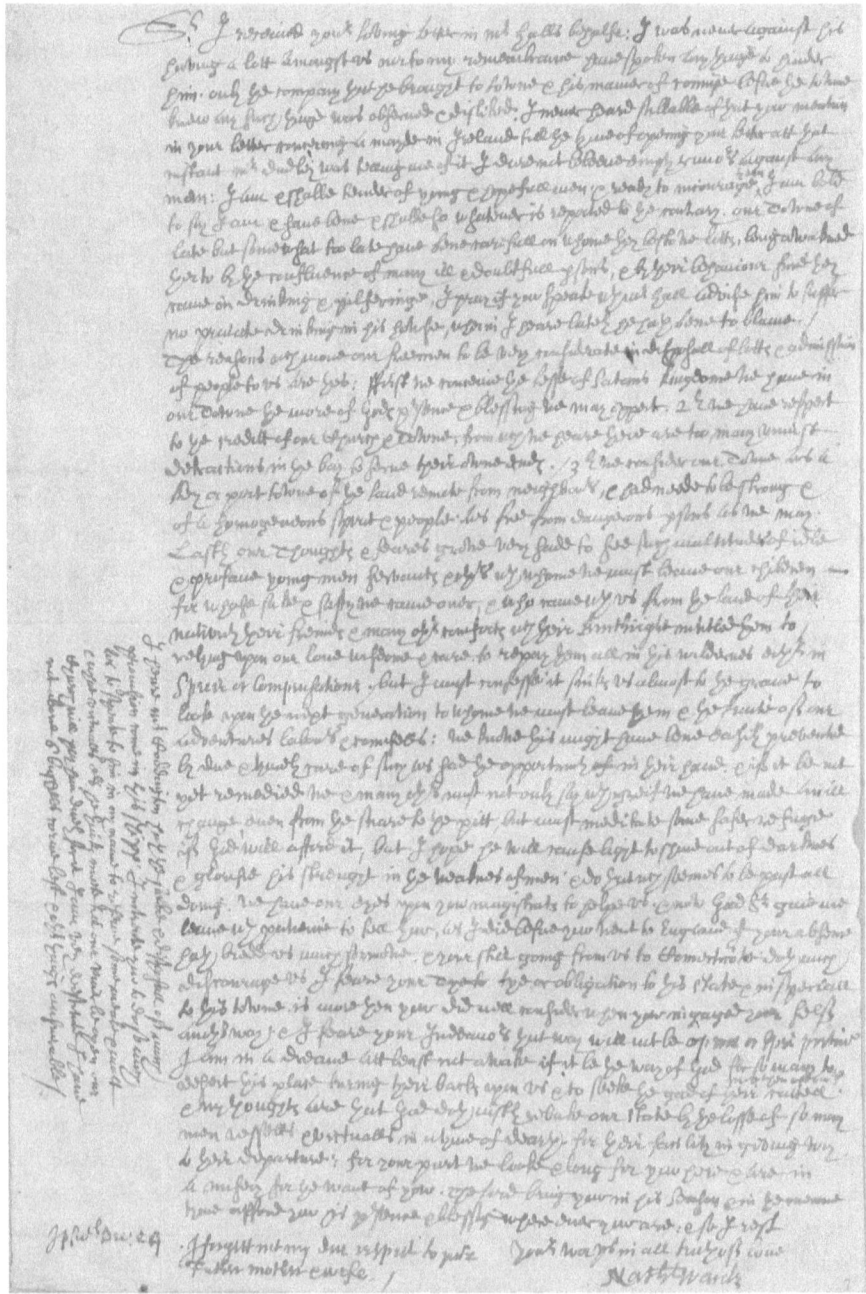

Figure 10 Nathaniel Ward's "spirit and people" letter to John Winthrop Jr., 1635. Phillips Library, Peabody Essex Museum, MSS 413.

the "Hampshire, Lincolnshire, and Wiltshire" origins of Woodbridge, Bradstreet, and other Andover settlers determined the town's initial land use pattern, which undoubtedly included common fields. However, the extremely sketchy state of the land records from colonial Andover does not permit any detailed reconstruction of the trajectory of land use there—nor can it be taken to provide proof that Andover fathers were especially inclined to "patriarchalism" in withholding land from their grown sons.[63] The little evidence we have suggests that the Andover founders shared the emphasis on social proportion tempered by equity in constructing the social body of the town through land distribution. On January 18, 1663/64, the town meeting declared that Andover, at the time of its founding,

> did Covenant and agre[e] [...] to giue euery Inhabitant whome they receiued as a Townsman an house lott proportionable to his estate, or otherwise as he should reasonably desire, with suteable accommodations thereunto of meadow, and all other divisions of upland & ploug[h]ing ground, that should afterwards be divided. [...] Indeauoring and intending to make all mens accomodations as suteable and equall as they Can according to their seuerall proportions.[64]

Indeed, it is of interest that even in describing Andover's physical setting, Edward Johnson falls into the language of corporatism, saying that the town lay "about one or two mile distant from the place where the goodly river of Merrimeck receives her branches into her own body, hard upon the river of Shawshin, which is one of her three chief heads."[65]

The Andover settlers seem to have gone farther than other communities like Rowley in the direction of equity in allocating resources; as Greven points out, Andover's hierarchy was flatter than the norm. Instead of creating a system of gates, Andover distributed unusually large houselots, the size of which determined the householder's commonage and share in subsequent land distributions. The smallest houselots contained an ample 4 acres while the largest were only 20 acres. This relative egalitarianism may have had something to do with the comparatively small number of the original householders, probably less than half of the total in Rowley. It was also in keeping with what Greven calls "the settlers' reluctance to parcel out the land in great tracts," an attitude no doubt influenced by their consciousness of being hemmed in by Rowley.[66]

However, this parsimony did not last long—by 1658 the third division of land in Andover awarded each householder four acres of land for each acre in their houselot, and in the fourth division of 1662, the town meeting bestowed no less than twenty acres of land per houselot acre. This distribution of large, recognizably modern farms clearly indicates a move toward enclosure, so it is not surprising to find records from the early 1670s which speak of fenced plots as the norm. The most revealing provision required "euery man that hath any land lying unfenced, either upon other men or by it self, shall take one of his neighbours with him, and renew ye boundmarks." Land "by it self" seems to refer to larger farms, while "upon other men" seems likely to have meant land in common fields and meadows.[67] Other records from this period show inhabitants clearly striving to consolidate their holdings; for example, three consecutive entries documenting the land swaps and purchases which made Edward Whittington's acreage more contiguous, or the "libertie" granted John Abbott "to lay his land in a long square."[68]

The timing of Andover's apparent acceptance of enclosure as a model of land use roughly coincides with the death of Anne Bradstreet in 1672 and her husband Simon's subsequent remarriage and removal to Salem.[69] Simon Bradstreet, a longtime member of the Court of Assistants, was a consistent ally of Ward and the group of Ipswich leaders who promoted the Body of Liberties. Bradstreet, who had attended Emmanuel College, Cambridge, joined Thomas Dudley's very political move to Ipswich in 1635. In 1643 he cosigned a letter with Ward, Ezekiel Rogers, Nathaniel Rogers, and others denouncing John Winthrop's offer of assistance to the Frenchman Charles de la Tour in his struggle for power in Acadia. In 1646, Bradstreet and another of Ward's allies, future governor Richard Bellingham, dissented from the large fine (£50) imposed on Dr. Robert Child (a close friend of John Winthrop Jr.) for writing a "Remonstrance" attacking the New England Way from the Presbyterian viewpoint. Bellingham was also from Lincolnshire, having served as a member of Parliament for Boston; in November 1639, the General Court awarded Bellingham a farm in the northwestern part of the Salem grant, near the borders of both Ipswich and Rowley, although he later moved back to Boston. Finally, in 1645, Bradstreet joined Ward and Bellingham on a committee based in Ipswich that was tasked with reviewing the Body of Liberties for republication.[70]

Anne Bradstreet's poetry reflects how fully immersed she was in the corporatist ethos surrounding Nathaniel Ward and establishes her role as an intellectual leader in her own right in Ipswich and Andover. In 1647, the minister of Andover, Bradstreet's brother-in-law John Woodbridge, took ship for England bearing the manuscript of her poems.[71] (Woodbridge's son Benjamin later married Mary Ward, Nathaniel Ward's granddaughter, while another son, Joseph Woodbridge, would wed Nathaniel Rogers's granddaughter Martha.[72]) Three years later Woodbridge succeeded in publishing Bradstreet's work under the title *The Tenth Muse Lately sprung up in America*, "without whose [Bradstreet's] knowledge, and contrary to her expectation."[73] The book featured a curmudgeonly prefatory poem by Nathaniel Ward, who proclaimed, "It half revives my chill frost-bitten blood, / To see a woman once do ought that's good."[74]

Ward's doggerel highlighted not only his close friendship with Bradstreet but also the superior quality of Bradstreet's verse. In "Of the Four Humours in Man's Constitution," Bradstreet portrayed the reconciliation of the four bodily humors, melancholic, phlegmatic, sanguine, and choleric, and the elements from which they derived, in terms that the drafter of the Body of Liberties must have appreciated:

> Nor jars nor scoffs, let none hereafter see,
> But all admire our perfect amity;
> Nor be discerned, here's water, earth, air, fire,
> But here's a compact body, whole entire.[75]

Granted, Bradstreet's more scholastic poems fail to reach the beauty of her masterpiece "Contemplations," but her frequent references to traditional academic learning should not be ignored. Everywhere in her work one finds echoes of scholastic teachings: praise for "wise Aristotle," for example, and the invocation of the "common good."[76] In her letter "To My Dear Children," Bradstreet reported that she knew of the existence of God from reason, because of "the wondrous works that I see [...] the order of all things [...] the preserving and directing of all to its proper end." Bradstreet's natural theology here was highly reminiscent of Thomas Aquinas's fifth argument for the existence of God based on "the governance of the world."[77] Bradstreet's "Meditations Divine and Moral" offered a critique of arbitrary power, that is, "Authority without wisdom." Bradstreet observed, in corporatist terms, "A sore finger may disquiet the whole body, but an ulcer within destroys it; so an enemy without may disturb a commonwealth, but dissentions within overthrow it." And Meditation 62 gives important insight into the Puritan ideology of mobility: "As a man is called the little world, so his heart may be called the little commonwealth; his more fixed and resolved thoughts are like to inhabitants, his slight and flitting thoughts are like passengers that travel to and fro continually." Puritans embraced mobility, but not for its own sake. The goal of mobility and the founding of new social bodies was to enable people to move from being aimlessly mobile "passengers" to becoming "inhabitants," the term that was most commonly used for householders with common rights in a New England town, fully provided with ample natural resources for the foreseeable future.[78]

Given the presence of corporatist thinking like Bradstreet's in Andover, it is not surprising that from time to time, the community expressed misgivings about the transformation to an enclosed landscape. The town meeting of March 1, 1660/61, produced a strongly worded condemnation of settlers who moved their homes to farms at a distance from the town center: "taking into consideration the great damage that may come to the To[wn] by p[er]sons liueing remote from the Towne vpon such Lands as were giuen them for ploughing or planting," the meeting fined anyone who moved their residence away from their original houselot the considerable sum of 20 shillings a month.[79] In 1686/87, the town seems to have suffered a fit of remorse about the progress of enclosure, ordering that "for the future the Towne shall change noe Land with any man, but with the Consent of euery inhabitant of ye Towne: they hauing sufficiently experiencd the damage thereby already," and setting aside four separate tracts as common sheep pasture.[80] But in Andover as in Rowley, by the early 1670s, enclosure was clearly the new normal, and it would seem that Andover had allocated its resources with sufficient farsightedness that the transition caused minimal hardship. Records of land transactions ca. 1670, after the town had changed its policy toward newcomers, provide evidence for this. Henceforward new arrivals could buy only 20-acre plots that, unlike the original houselots, did not entitle their owners to a share in future land divisions. But they did come with ample common rights to grazing and timber, a sign that the town was not experiencing a shortage of communal resources—aside from an anxiety to conserve its arable land.[81]

Nathaniel Ward's plantation north of the Merrimack, Haverhill, became part of Norfolk County in 1643, but when the province of New Hampshire was created in 1679, Haverhill remained in Massachusetts and returned to Essex County.[82] In spite of Ward's grumbling about his stepbrother Rogers's engrossment of land for Rowley, Haverhill also received a very ample allotment. Even after losing territory to Methuen and Lawrence as well as four towns in New Hampshire, Haverhill still had a length of nine miles, a breadth of three miles, and contained 17,920 acres as of 1903.[83] Taking their cue from Rowley, the Haverhill settlers were assiduous in their efforts to augment their landholdings whenever possible, earning a gentle reproach from Edward Johnson: "This Town is of a large extent [...] there being an over-weaning desire in most men after Medow land, which hath caused many towns to grasp more into their hands then they could afterward possibly hold." (He hastened to add that although the Haverhill settlers were "laborious in the gaining of the goods of this life, yet are they not unmindful also of the chief end of their coming hither," namely religion.)[84]

It appears that Giles Firmin never moved to Haverhill—the Boston congregation dismissed him to the Ipswich church shortly before his return to England in 1644—but Ward's son John became the longtime minister of Haverhill, until his death in late 1693. John Ward, who took his BA from Emmanuel College in 1626/27 and his MA in 1630, was steeped in Protestant scholasticism.[85] It is not surprising, then, that variants of the word "proportion" appear with stunning regularity, and in every conceivable context, in the surviving records of Haverhill.[86] In his poem praising John Ward, Johnson commented that "whereas thy father left, / Left hath he not, but breaths for further strength" in his son.[87] The privilege enjoyed by members of the estate of town-founders, that of moving from place to place, seemed to confer on them the gift of ubiquity—indeed, a sort of immortality.

The original town ordinance regarding land allocation, probably from 1643, reflects the ethos of distributive justice in typical fashion:

> Voted That there shall be three hundred acres laid out for houselots, and no more, and that he that was worth two hundred pounds should have twenty acres for his houselott and none to exceed that number, and so every one under that sum to have acres proportionable for his houselot together with meadow and common and planting ground proportionably.[88]

From this it may appear that land distribution in Haverhill was a simple arithmetical calculation, with net worth translating into a fixed number of acres. However, the truth is more complex. Haverhill introduced an intriguing refinement, very much in keeping with the idea of distributive justice, with their second division of arable land in 1652. The town voted that each acre of houselot would garner four acres of "ploughland [...] according to our true meaning: each man being to have his proportion either in the quality or quantity of his lot." In other words, inferior soil would require a larger allotment, while someone receiving richer earth would need a smaller plot. In this way, the town hoped, "each man's proportion" would be "laid out according to order and true meaning."[89] In certain cases, the size of a houselot would also be gauged to the owner's "quality" rather than the quantity of his wealth; potential settlers with useful skills were offered larger "accommodations" than their net worth would appear to merit. In addition, the listing of "each man's accommodations" at the time of the second division of arable reveals that a Haverhill settler's accommodation, unlike an accommodation in Andover, did not necessarily match the size of their houselot. For example, Stephen Kent had a 20-acre houselot but his "accommodations" number was 22½ (Figure 11).[90]

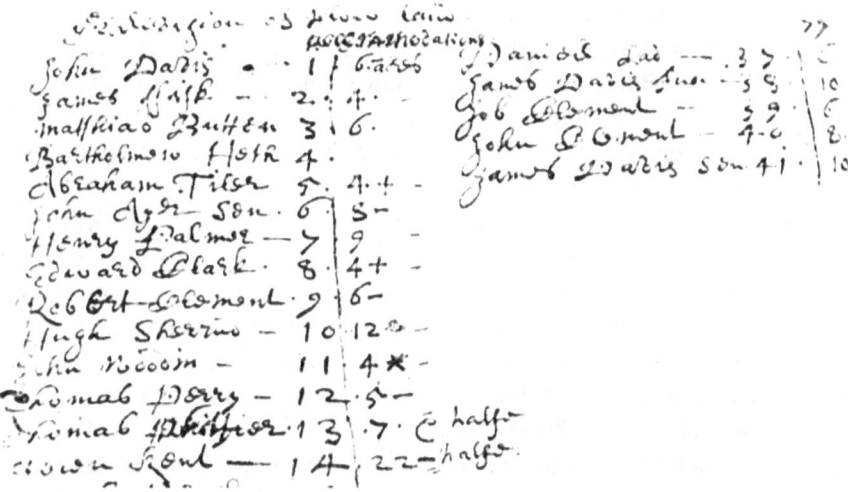

Figure 11 Part of the chart listing each householder's proportional share of Haverhill's second division of "plow land" in 1652. The number in the left column shows the order in which the plots would be surveyed, as determined by lot; but the second column contains the value of each settler's "accommodation," which determined their portion of land in this and subsequent land distributions. Charts like these graphically represented where each "member" of the community stood in relation to all others, and were of crucial importance in articulating the social body of a New England town. Haverhill Town Meetings, 1643–60, page 77; courtesy Haverhill City Clerk's Office, Haverhill, MA.

The calculus involved is obscure, based on the records, but the operative principle seems to have been the inhabitant's overall worth to the community. For example, the town's tanner, Job Clement, originally had a three-acre houselot—presumably all he could afford—but in 1645 was awarded three additional acres "with proportionable accommodations," so that in the 1652 list his accommodation number was six. The median for the 39 inhabitants with an accommodation number was seven; Clement had been elevated into the middle ranks of the community, no doubt because of his useful niche as a tanner. Indeed, Newbury at one point attempted to entice Clement and his tannery to their town, but Clement remained in Haverhill, which had shrewdly made it worth his while to stay.[91] Similarly, in 1653, John Webster, a lowly blacksmith, was offered a six-acre accommodation if he would ply his trade in Haverhill for five years. The proprietors of the town's sawmill were repeatedly granted lands and special privileges— the right to take timber within a mile of the mill, violating a previous ban on harvesting trees within three miles of the town; 10 acres of meadowland which the mill owners had already illegally started mowing; up to 80 acres of land across a stream from the mill, then 8 additional acres nearby. But such perks came with conditions, for example, "that when the sawmill shall cease to go for the benefit of the owners and town then this land is to return to the town again." That is just what happened in 1648 when the town "declared, voted & granted that all the former privileges granted to the Sawmill or Mills are forfeited & accordingly taken into the town's hands."[92]

By the time of Haverhill's settlement, its inhabitants had the example of several nearby communities on which to draw, including Ipswich, Andover, Rowley, Newbury, and Salem. Thus in spite of their corporatist convictions, the founders of Haverhill seem to have realized that the English open-field model would not endure in the New World. The town was sited on the banks of the river, and in its early years, all the arable land was located in one large field called "the Plain."[93] This indicates that no attempt was made to create multiple fields which could have supported the standard open-field system of crop rotation. There is no mention in the Haverhill records of the privilege of "shack" or grazing after harvest—since the settlers had made sure to get ample meadow, presumably there was no need for shack, and thus no reason to discourage fencing or ban enclosure. Indeed, these practices seem to have sparked little discussion in the town meetings; one casual reference gives all the inhabitants "liberty to fence in their meadows" as well as neighboring plots of "upland."[94] Less than a year after the second division of arable land, a third division took place "at the rate of twelve acres to an acre of accommodation." This means that James Davis, Senior, with an accommodation number of 10, should have received 120 acres of arable land; in fact he was granted 220, suggesting the land he received was of inferior quality. In any case, the generous third division in Haverhill produced a large number of good-sized farms eminently suitable for enclosure.[95] At only one point in the early town records did anxiety about enclosure appear. In February 1662/63, the "proprietors of the ox common" voted to divide the common among themselves. Three of them, however, including Rev. John Ward, "did enter their dissent."[96]

Haverhill thus provides the clearest example of the realist streak in Puritan land distribution policy in New England. As we have seen, New England town founders saw such decisions, in keeping with the teachings of Protestant scholasticism, as matters of practical understanding. They were strongly influenced by the corporatist and distributist aspects of their Puritan ideology, but they did not cling to a particular model of land use out of nostalgia for their regions of origin or an attachment to a vanishing open-field England. They wanted to preserve the option of continuing practices, like "shack," which had proven useful in the old country, but whenever and wherever it became clear that such procedures did not work in their new context, they abandoned them and drew on other models. However, John Ward's dissent in the matter of the ox-common should remind us that the estate of town-founders in New England never lost their overriding concern with the health of the entire social body, the well-being of the whole community. In 1650s Haverhill, for example, all inhabitants were "compellable to attend town meetings," and forbidden to harbor new "town: dweller[s] without the consent of the town."[97] The turn toward enclosed farms in colonial New England does not necessarily represent a drift into proto-individualism, but rather a considered policy made possible by solid decisions about shared resources at the beginning of each town's common life.

Epilogue

THE FUTURE OF CORPORATISM
AND THE IDEOLOGY OF MOBILITY
IN AMERICA

After the founding of early Massachusetts towns during the Great Migration of the 1630s, the next major expression of the Puritan ideology of mobility was, oddly enough, a massive repatriation to England triggered by the onset of the Civil War.[1] Some New Englanders wished to fight for the Parliamentary cause, while university-educated men were attracted by ministerial opportunities which suddenly opened for Puritans in the old country. Perhaps one-fourth of colonists with a university degree, and a larger percentage of the early graduates of Harvard College, returned to England, creating a "brain drain" from New England as the Great Migration sputtered to a halt.[2]

Nathaniel Ward's *Simple Cobler of Aggawam*, written in Massachusetts but published as Ward returned to England in 1647, reflected this new development in the ideology of mobility. In his *Magnalia Christi Americana*, Cotton Mather labeled Ward "our St. Hilary," referring to the hilarity of Ward's humorous and highly original writing style, which has earned Ward 606 citations in the online *Oxford English Dictionary*. However, Mather would also have been aware that St. Hilary of Poitiers had been exiled to Phrygia for four years because of his intransigent opposition to Arianism—applying this to Ward's case, Mather implied that his hatred of Arminianism propelled Ward to New England.[3] In the *Simple Cobler*, Ward supported the necessity of the Great Migration, speaking of those who "necessarily abide beyond *Jordan*, and remaine on the American sea-coasts," and encouraging those "whom necessity of Conscience or condition thrusts out [of England] by head and shoulders" to come to New England. On the other hand, he declared that "it ill becomes Christians anything well-shod with the preparation of the Gospel, to meditate flight from their deare Countrey upon these disturbances," that is, the Civil War. Ward went so far as to argue "that no man ought to forsake his own Country, but upon extraordinary cause, and when that cause ceaseth, he is bound in conscience to return if he can."[4]

This may seem to have undermined the original premise of the Puritan ideology of mobility as it unfolded in New England, namely that the health of an existing social body might require the removal of part of that body in order to form a new, and presumably permanent, communal body. However, when we consider Ward's career after his return to England, it becomes clear that Ward's repatriation was driven by his ongoing adherence to the corporatist metaphor from which that ideology sprang. Ward believed passionately that the English body politic could not survive while deprived of its head, the King, and saw it as his duty to return to that body so that he could use his gifts to promote its health and wholeness. Concern for the "cranium" as a justification for moving back to old England is expressed in one of the *Simple Cobler*'s closing poems:

> *So farewell* England *old*
> *If evill times ensue,*
> *Let good men come to us,*
> *Wee'l welcome them to New.*
> *And farewell loving Friends,*
> *If happy dayes ensue,*
> *You'l have some Guests from hence* [New England],
> *Pray welcome us to you.*
> *And farewell simple world,*
> *If thou'lt thy Cranium mend,*
> *There is my Last and All,*
> *And a Shoem-Akers*
>   *End.*[5]

In a controversal address to the House of Commons in June 1647, Ward told the legislators that in a "Politicall body, The Prince puts life into all Authority, and gives the *Fiat* to all Lawes and Ordinances."[6] He then suggested that the Commons should "lament your constitution, that it is so *Heterogeneus, dissimilar*, and contramixt." Ward was no doubt referring to the presence of M.P.'s from the artisan classes; some army leaders "of a mechanick alloy," Ward lamented, had already "plunder[ed] us of our King."[7] Ward worried that in the absence of its head, the King, the body politic had fallen out of balance, and lesser members were forcing their way to the top. As he put it in the *Simple Cobler*, "Intolerable griefes to Subjects, breed the *Iliaca passio* in a body politicke, which inforces that upwards which should not"—*Iliaca passio* referring to an intestinal obstruction.[8] The 1648 work *Mercurius anti-Mechanicus* has often been ascribed to Ward; I am no longer convinced Ward wrote it, but the book was clearly penned by someone who shared Ward's concern about "mechanick" preachers and wanted to imitate the whimsical style of the *Simple Cobler*. Its unknown author wrote, "let every loyall heart pray for the Royal Head [...] and for the body representative and the universall Politie."[9]

However, Ward's corporatist intervention in English politics proved singularly unsuccessful, not only because of his insistence on the need for monarchical headship but also because of his heresy-hunting bent. In a famous passage, the Cobler "proclaime[d] to the world, in the name of our Colony, that all Familists, Antinomians, Anabaptists, and other Enthusiasts, shall have free Liberty to keep away from us, and such as will come to be gone as fast as they can." His reasoning was typically corporatist: religious dissent created a type of spiritual warfare that "must necessarily kindle Combustions. Fiery diseases seated in the spirit, embroile the whole frame of the body; others more externall and coole, are less dangerous."[10] In the early stages of the Civil War, as David D. Hall put it, English Presbyterians and Independents formed an "improbable alliance," and from his American vantage point Ward hoped that "the Presbyterian and Independent way" could "meet in one." But by the time Ward wrote the *Cobler*, the Independents increasingly sought toleration for religious dissenters, while the Presbyterians were alarmed by the emergence of theologies and ecclesiologies which they found unacceptable—an attitude epitomized in Thomas Edwards's 1646 compendium of heresies, *Gangraena*.[11] For this reason, Ward did not feel free to join other New England congregationalist repatriates in supporting the "Dissenting Brethren," a group of moderate Independents in the Westminster Assembly of Divines, led by Philip Nye, John Owen, and Thomas Goodwin.[12]

By 1650, Ward described himself as "3 quarters Presbyterian, I keep one quarter still Independent." Essentially Ward had painted himself into a corner politically and religiously. In seeking to position himself as a Presbyterian Independent, Ward had followed a tendency so marginal that considerable scholarly discussion has taken place as to whether such personages actually existed.[13] Stephen Winthrop, a committed Independent serving in Cromwell's New Model Army, wrote his father, the elder John Winthrop, that "Mr. Ward hath mad himselfe odious and rediculus heere by books and sermons."[14] And indeed Ward's nuanced position was destined to have little impact on the increasingly polarized English scene; after his 1650 protest against the "Discolliminium" or de-necking of King Charles the previous year, Ward retired from the public eye and served the rest of his days as the rector of Shenfield in Essex.[15]

The corporatist ideology of the New England town founders discussed in this book did not survive the attempt to transplant it back across the Atlantic, and it is tempting to think that it disappeared entirely from American life, as well. Undoubtedly, there are remnants of corporatism in American public life; in recent years, the most notorious has been the Electoral College. The essential meaning of the Electoral College is that Americans do not vote for President as individuals, but in their corporate capacities as members of a state body politic. Nevertheless, by the Jacksonian era, a tide of individualism seemed to be sweeping away the communal ethos of the New England towns. To Alexis de Tocqueville, writing in the 1630s, Americans' relentless mobility revealed a "restlessness" which had nothing to do with building up stable communities; "In the United States, a man carefully builds a home to live in when he is old and sells it before the roof is laid." The drive for equality led Americans to wear themselves out in the pursuit of more worldly goods, following opportunity wherever it beckoned.[16]

However, this picture is incomplete, especially in the context of the Second Great Awakening. Descendants of the Puritans—Congregationalists, Presbyterians, and Unitarians—flocked from New England into the "Burned-over District" of New York, then into the Old Northwest where they cooperated with Methodist missionaries from other regions to build recognizably "godly" communities that would prove especially influential in promoting the antislavery cause. In fact, Puritans had never stopped exporting their communal values to other parts of the country, founding new towns like Midway, Georgia, settled from Dorchester, Massachusetts, in 1752. On the most basic level this was a continuation of the process summed up in 1653 by Giles Firmin: "when other Plantations were erected, for conveniencie of dwelling, (the former Plantations being too full) we would remove and dwell there."[17] In a continuation of Puritan mobility, continued westward migration was essential as New England towns filled up; but for these "Yankee" migrants, marked by their New England heritage, sustainability would never be the sole concern, and an anxiety to spread some version of their forebears' values would never entirely disappear as long as they continued to found new towns.

The staying power of the Puritan corporatist ideology, in spite of all tergiversations of belief, is perhaps best seen in the unusual career of Orestes A. Brownson, born in 1803 in Stockbridge, Vermont, and subsequently passing through phases as a Congregationalist, Presbyterian, Unitarian, Universalist, Transcendentalist, and finally a Roman Catholic. But in his mature Catholic works of political philosophy of 1864–65, "The Federal Constitution" and *The American Republic*, Brownson based the legitimacy of the United States government on the same foundations invoked by Puritans to sanction town-founding in colonial New England. For Brownson, the institution of government reflected metaphysical realities: "The political destiny of the United States is to conform the state to the order of reality, or, so to speak, to the divine idea in creation." This "divine idea," of course, had everything to do with corporatism. "The mystery of the state is [...] analogous to the mystery of the church, what is called the mystic body of Christ, and, perhaps, is only a lower phase of that same mystery." In the context of the Civil War, Brownson used the corporatist image of society—which is complex, as we have seen, involving bodies nestled inside of bodies—to argue for the supremacy of the national body politic while preserving the corporate existence of the states within the federal system. "The life is in the body, not in the members, though the body could not exist if it had no members; so the sovereignty is in the union, not in the states severally; but there could be no sovereign union without the states, for there is no union where there is nothing united." Brownson believed the social contract theory of government was overly individualistic, and saw corporate bodies, which had an organic existence, as the building blocks of the state.[18] His thinking shows the persistence into the nineteenth century of the mental habits of the estate of town-founders in Puritan New England, habits enduringly built into the framework of communities that remain vital to this day.

As much as I might like to, I cannot close this book without addressing the issue of how corporate Puritan towns might have influenced modern-day business corporations. Simply broaching the subject threatens to pull us into the scholarly vortex surrounding the thesis put forward by Max Weber in *The Protestant Ethic and the Spirit of Capitalism*. According to Weber, Puritans and other Calvinists who accepted the idea of predestination were thrust into an "unprecedented inner loneliness," a "disillusioned and pessimistically inclined individualism" since no minister, no priest, no institutional church could help them achieve salvation. However, for the Reformed Christian who had obtained assurance of salvation by experimental means, determined effort in one's calling provided a way of demonstrating confidence in one's divine election. Thus the believer moved out of isolation into social action, a life of "worldly asceticism" that promoted "a systematic rational ordering of the moral life as a whole." If wealth came with the fulfillment of one's calling, this was not to be despised unless it produced overwhelming temptations to unrighteousness; in fact, wealth resulting from careful attention to duty was encouraged. In this way Reformed theology helped to produce the modern capitalist world.[19]

While this syndrome may have appeared in the lives of certain capitalists with devout leanings, my own view is that, although Puritan practical understanding can never be sundered from theology, the determination with which New England Puritans pursued their callings was motivated primarily by the more rational pole of Puritan ideology, particularly the concern for the common good of all members of the community, not by theology.[20] Although my dataset does not allow me to come down on one side or another regarding the Weber thesis, I suspect that New England Puritans did make a significant contribution to American capitalism, not through worldly asceticism but through their corporatism.

A glib way to dispose of this issue might be to say that there is clearly no resemblance between Puritan communities, with their obsessive subordination of individual prerogatives to the common good of the whole, and business enterprises based on the profit motive. Actually, there are quite a few striking similarities.

The modern corporation began with the general incorporation laws passed by a number of American states in the 1840s and 1850s. Previously, corporations had to obtain a special legislative charter that imposed numerous restrictions on the business enterprise. The typical corporation in the early American republic was formed to carry out a public works project—a canal, a turnpike. General incorporation depended on the notion that any group of investors should be able to voluntarily form a business that enjoyed limited liability and the other benefits of incorporation. General incorporation laws at first tried to constrain the size, scope, or duration of corporations, but legislative restrictions were widely ignored and soon obsolete. It would be surprising if the practice of Puritan settlers, who insisted on their right to form a town as a de facto corporation through a voluntary covenant, had had no influence on this development.[21]

Puritan ideology and modern corporate practice also converge in their emphasis on order and organization. When the Standard Oil Trust was formed in 1882, its purpose was to replace dog-eat-dog competition in the oil industry with rational control of production and prices. Soon, however, the weakness of the trust as a horizontal combination of companies with an equal say in business decisions became evident, and large corporations (including Standard in 1899) embraced the New Jersey holding company as a model for consolidation. This opened the way for huge vertically integrated firms such as General Motors, General Electric, and DuPont which imposed order in their market sectors by including the entire production process from the supply of raw materials through merchandising and installation under one corporate umbrella. Historians like Alfred Chandler have described how vertical integration produced a managerial revolution in which ownership was separated from control, stockholders lost their ability to influence corporate actions, and the enormous market power of these firms enabled "organization men" to make momentous decisions that affected entire nations and upset international relations with little constraint from market forces, investors, or elected officials. This hierarchical collectivism resembles the structure of a Puritan town much more than it does a business enterprise of the sort typical in the heyday of laissez-faire.[22]

Other similarities are directly related to the Puritan ideology of mobility. Twenty-first century capitalism is based on the flow of goods and profits across national boundaries. The prototypical corporation of today, Wal-Mart, has become a global behemoth by linking its Southeast Asian supply chain with stores throughout the Western world. If Puritan mobility helped give rise to Tocquevillian restlessness, then it cannot be excused from responsibility for offshoring and other manifestations of globalist corporate mobility.

As we have seen, Puritans justified mobility through their concern for the health of social bodies; at times it became necessary to remove one part of a body politic, which would typically form the nucleus of a new corporate town in a different place, for the sake of the whole. We see a reflection of this in the corporate practice euphemistically known as "rightsizing." While huge vertically integrated firms like GM have set the standard for modern management, they are not the norm, flourishing only in industries where mass production can produce economies of scale and economies of scope. In other industries, companies have quickly reached the point of "diminishing return on investment" where growth no longer makes sense, and giant corporations have increasingly found it necessary to spin off subsidiaries and to outsource elements of the production process. That such moves are made for the sake of the health of the corporate body does not make them any less painful for workers whose jobs are outsourced to other firms in developing nations.[23]

Yet another area of likeness can be found in the emphasis by some business theorists, beginning with Peter Drucker, the founder of modern management science, on the corporation as an organic unity, conceptually prior to its component parts because of its perpetuity. Critics have ridiculed this viewpoint, suggesting that it is absurd to turn the corporation into a "group-personality" (according to the thought of German scholar Otto von Gierke) and condemning the undemocratic nature of corporate groupthink in the absence of effective shareholder input. Yet strangely, in their proposals for restoring shareholder democracy, such writers turn to proposals that New England Puritan settlers would have found highly congenial, such as proportional representation of groups of stockholders (e.g., those invested in a particular mutual fund) on corporate boards.[24]

In spite of these resemblances to modern corporations, corporate towns in colonial New England functioned quite differently from contemporary business concerns in other ways. The power of shareholders in joint-stock companies in seventeenth-century England was already eroding, as company officials were often compelled to make business decisions in far-flung places (like Virginia or India) without consulting investors. However, the Massachusetts Bay Company provided a noteworthy exception; the "transfer of the charter" to the colony itself, which became the company's new headquarters, meant that stakeholders on the ground were able to influence corporate decisions at the General Court. While politics in the colony were undoubtedly hierarchical, a broad spectrum of those affected by collective decisions were able to participate in Court meetings as well as local town meetings. This privilege was enshrined in Nathaniel Ward's Body of Liberties; Liberty 12 provided that

> every man whether Inhabitant or fforeiner, free or not free shall have libertie to come to any publique Court, Councel, or Towne meeting, and either by speech or writing to move any lawfull, seasonable, and materiall question, or to present any necessary motion, complaint, petition, Bill or information, whereof that meeting hath proper cognizance, so it be done in convenient time, due order, and respective manner.

At least in theory, any male resident of Massachusetts Bay, including indentured servants and the enslaved, were empowered to take part on some level in all public deliberations—a far cry from the effective disenfranchisement of shareholders and others affected by modern corporate actions. Communities had an organic life, but not to the extent that a "group-personality" overrode the needs and interests of individual members.[25]

Not only did New England communities provide for greater participation than contemporary corporations, they were also rooted in local place. The point of the ideology of mobility was to promote long-term stability so that all members of a community would eventually come to rest, either in their town of origin or, if land and resources were scarce, in another town founded through the foresight of the town meeting and its leaders. People, animals, forests, meadows, and land were all taken up into a sustainable system of mixed farming which endured for a surprisingly long time—in Concord as described by Brian Donahue, for example, it did not unravel until the early nineteenth century. Part of the eventual problem, as John Frederick Martin pointed out, sprang from the separation of land corporations from town oversight, as proprietors or commoners began having their own meetings distinct from the town meeting; but Martin's own analysis shows that this development did not begin in earnest until the Andros regime of the 1680s and the subsequent Glorious Revolution. Furthermore, when New England towns felt it necessary to engage in "rightsizing," hiving off part of the community to form the nucleus of a new town foundation elsewhere, they did so not with callous disregard for their corporation's current stakeholders (as is the case with modern offshoring of jobs) but precisely in order to provide for those individuals who might otherwise suffer scarcity and dearth. Towns concerned themselves not only with the health of the whole social body but with the well-being of its members.[26]

What has changed, then? One possibility is that the corporate structures pioneered by Puritans in America have been drained of their ideological content. For godly New Englanders there was no separation of religion, society, politics, business, and farming—all were bound up in the flexible mesh of Puritan ideology. However, modern business concerns typically disclaim any ideological motive for their actions—in an introduction to a later edition of *Concept of the Corporation*, Drucker reported that one GM executive dismissed his idealistic vision of corporate life, saying, "We, at GM, have to manage for sales and profits; your priorities are different ones." Scholars analyzing recent corporate structures set up, especially in Western European nations, for the purpose of economic planning have emphasized the pragmatic, non-ideological nature of these bodies. Another issue in the modern world is the lack of Ward's "consociate bodies"—vital corporate entities like churches and universities with the prestige and power to shape corporate thinking along ethical lines. In this landscape, as Weber put it, "the idea of duty in one's calling prowls about in our lives like the ghost of dead religious beliefs." Charles Taylor and Brad Gregory have echoed Weber's vision of a thoroughly secularized modernity, a post-Christian world in which institutions created to serve godly goals continue as dry husks, stripped of their former religious content, which retains only a spectral presence.[27]

For my part, while I realize there is a certain perverse comfort in thinking that the rest of society lies much lower on the moral and spiritual scale than I do, my own failings make it impossible for me to indulge in that line of thinking. True, a corporation like DuPont can amass untold billions from building horrific weapons of mass destruction, but an American president (and a former general at that!) can also warn citizens of the dangers of the "military–industrial complex." Many universities are in the process of "corporatization" on the business model, but a considerable number retain their scholarly independence. In keeping with Tocqueville's conviction that the American tendency to form associations would help mitigate the relative powerlessness of each individual in mass society, corporate pressure groups like the AARP, the NAACP, and the NRA exert tremendous power in the United States, for better and for worse. The federal government has in recent years experimented with the European model of political corporatism, for example, by creating the Consumer Financial Protection Bureau and other agencies in the aftermath of the 2008 financial crisis to help reconcile the interests of citizens with those of the financial sector. Calling such organizations pragmatic rather than ideological does not mean that they are devoid of ethical purpose. Even business corporations, in their response to social movements like Black Lives Matter and #MeToo, have shown themselves increasingly willing to consider the effect of their policies and practices on the broader society.[28]

Finally, it is undoubtedly true that few modern corporations of any sort will reflect Puritan religious values. But I hope I have established that, in their approach to society, Puritan concerns—while inextricably linked to Christian doctrine—operated on the basis of practical understanding, connected with the concept of the law of nature, a concept that underlay the founding of the American republic, and one whose death has been greatly exaggerated. Churches, too, retain at least some of their corporate impact and potential to do good within the body politic, provided that their members understand rightly the moral impulse at the origin of local and national political bodies. Among other reasons, it is in hope of helping the various types of corporations in civil society—universities, business firms, organized interest groups, and churches—to do so that I have written this book.

NOTES

Preface: Protestant Scholasticism and Puritan Ideology

1 David D. Hall, *The Puritans: A Transatlantic History* (Princeton, NJ: Princeton University Press, 2019), 7.
2 Charles Edward Banks, *The Winthrop Fleet of 1630* (1930; repr., Westminster, MD: Heritage Books, 2008), 29–30.
3 John Neville Figgis, *The Divine Right of Kings* (1896; repr., Gloucester, MA: Peter Smith, 1970), 108; Charles H. McIlwain, ed., *The Political Works of James I* (Cambridge, MA: Harvard University Press, 1918), 126.
4 Mark Curtis, *Oxford and Cambridge in Transition, 1558–1642: An Essay on Changing Relations between the English Universities and English Society* (Oxford: Clarendon Press, 1959), 124, 185; Lisa Jardine, "The Place of Dialectic Teaching in Sixteenth-Century Cambridge," *Studies in the Renaissance* 21 (1974): 32–33; see also Walter J. Ong, S. J., *Ramus, Method, and the Decay of Dialogue: From the Art of Discourse to the Art of Reason*, Chicago Press ed. (1958; repr., Chicago: University of Chicago Press, 2004), 132.
5 William T. Costello, S. J., *The Scholastic Curriculum at Early Seventeenth-Century Cambridge* (Cambridge, MA: Harvard University Press, 1958), 1.
6 Scott A. McDermott, "The Opening of the American Mind: Protestant Scholasticism at Harvard, 1636–1700," in *Catholicism and Historical Narrative: A Catholic Engagement with Historical Scholarship*, ed. Kevin Schmiesing (Lanham, MD: Rowman & Littlefield, 2014), 19–46; McDermott, "Body of Liberties: Godly Constitutionalism and the Origin of Written Fundamental Law in Massachusetts, 1634–1666" (PhD diss., Saint Louis University, 2014), in ProQuest Dissertations & Theses.
7 Most notably, Margo Todd, *Christian Humanism and the Puritan Social Order* (Cambridge: Cambridge University Press, 1987); Markku Peltonen, *Classical Humanism and Republicanism in English Political Thought, 1570–1640* (Cambridge: Cambridge University Press, 1995); J. G. A. Pocock, *The Machiavellian Moment: Florentine Political Thought and the Atlantic Republican Tradition* (Princeton, NJ: Princeton University Press, 1975).
8 Costello, *Scholastic Curriculum*, 64.
9 Todd, *Christian Humanism*, 63n28.
10 Diarmaid MacCulloch, *The Reformation* (London: Penguin Books, 2004), 76–77; Ted Booth, *A Body Politic to Govern: The Political Humanism of Elizabeth I* (Newcastle-upon-Tyne: Cambridge Scholars, 2013), 3–5; James M. Blythe, "'Civic Humanism' and Medieval Political Thought," in *Renaissance Civic Humanism: Reappraisals and Reflections*, ed. James Hankins (Cambridge: Cambridge University Press, 2000), 30–74. See also Richard A. Muller, *After Calvin: Studies in the Development of a Theological Tradition* (Oxford: Oxford University Press, 2003), 43, 68.
11 Baker Mss. B., Mm.2.23, 92, Cambridge University Library, Department of Manuscripts and University Archives, Cambridge, UK.
12 Sarah Bendall, Christopher Brooke, and Patrick Collinson, *A History of Emmanuel College, Cambridge* (Woodbridge, UK: Boydell Press, 1999), 1; E. S. Shuckburgh, *Emmanuel College* (London: F. E. Robinson, 1904), 3–4, in Google Books.

13 R. T. Kendall, *Calvin and English Calvinism to 1649* (Oxford: Oxford University Press, 1979), 51.
14 Bendall, Brooke, and Collinson, *History of Emmanuel*, 70.
15 *The Statutes of Sir Walter Mildmay Kt Chancellor of the Exchequer...*, ed. and trans. Frank Stubbings (Cambridge: Cambridge University Press, 1983), 99–112.
16 Ong, *Ramus*, 8–9, 42–43, 89, 101, 114–15, 128–29, 184, 308.
17 John Yates, *A Modell of Divinitie, Catechistically Composed* (London: by Iohn Dawson for Fulke Clifton, 1622), "Table of Religion," [1–2], in Early English Books Online; Francis J. Bremer and Tom Webster, eds., *Puritans and Puritanism in Europe and America: A Comprehensive Encyclopedia*, 2 vols. (Santa Barbara, CA: ABC–CLIO, 2006), s.v. "Yates, John" by Tom Webster, 1:291; John Yates, "Recollections of the 1624 Parliament," in Kenneth Shipps, "Lay Patronage of East Anglian Puritan Clerics in Pre–Revolutionary England" (PhD diss., Yale University, 1971), appendix I, 349, in ProQuest Dissertations and Theses Global.
18 Howard Hotson, *Johann Heinrich Alsted, 1588–1638: Between Renaissance, Reformation, and Universal Reform* (Oxford: Clarendon Press, 2000), 27–29.
19 Wilbur Samuel Howell, *Logic and Rhetoric in England, 1500–1700* (New York: Russell & Russell, 1961), 207; Hotson, *Johann Heinrich Alsted*, 16–17, 21–22.
20 J. A. Venn, *Alumni Cantabrigienses...Part I: From the Earliest Times to 1751* (Cambridge: Cambridge University Press, 1922–27), 2:391; Geoffrey Elcoat, "Richard Holdsworth, Fourth Master of Emmanuel, Vice-Chancellor of the University of Cambridge," *Emmanuel College Magazine* 75 (1992–93): 73–74.
21 Curtis, *Oxford and Cambridge*, 289–90. See also Jardine, "Place of Dialectic Teaching," 47.
22 Richard Holdsworth, "Directions for a Student in the Universitie," in Harris Francis Fletcher, *The Intellectual Development of John Milton*, vol. 2 (Urbana: University of Illinois Press, 1961), 627–33, 634 [quote]; Mordecai Feingold, "The Ultimate Pedagogue: Franco Petri Burgersdijk and the English Speaking Academic Learning," in *Franco Burgersdijk (1590–1635): Neo-Aristotelianism in Leiden*, ed. E. P. Bos and H. A. Krop (Amsterdam: Rodopi, 1993), 151–65.
23 Venn, *Alumni Cantabrigienses...Part I*, 2:38; *The Autobiography and Correspondence of Sir Simonds d'Ewes, Bart.*, vol. 1, ed. James Orchard Halliwell (London: Richard Bentley, 1845), 121, in Google Books; Charles B. Schmitt, *John Case and Aristotelianism in Renaissance England* (Kingston, Canada: McGill-Queen's University Press, 1983), 32–33, 39, 140–41.
24 d'Ewes, *Autobiography and Correspondence*, 121. On Piccolomini's thoroughgoing Aristotelianism, see Philip Gavitt, *Gender, Honor, and Charity in Late Renaissance Florence* (Cambridge: Cambridge University Press, 2011), 82–85.
25 Holdsworth, "Directions," 637, 641, 643.
26 Holdsworth, "Directions," 637.
27 Holdsworth, "Directions," 627–33.
28 Venn, *Alumni Cantabrigienses...Part I*, 4:333; Recepta ab Ingredientibus (Register of Admissions, 1584–1713) [hereafter ECA CHA.1.4(c)], Emmanuel College Archives, Cambridge, UK, 121r; Liber Gratiarum Epsilon, 1589–1620, Cambridge University Archives, Cambridge, UK, 20.
29 Nathaniel Ward, *A Religious Retreat Sounded to a Religious Army* (London: for Stephen Bowtell, 1647), in Early English Books Online. The originals of Ward's citations may be found in the following works: *M. Tulli Ciceronis pro T. Annio Milone ad iudices oratio*, ed. James S. Reid (Cambridge: Cambridge University Press, 1895), 26, in Google Books; *M. T. Ciceronis pars secunda sive orationes omnes ad optimos codices*, vol. 6, ed. N. E. Lemaire (Paris: Nicolaus Eligius Lemaire, 1830), 268–69, 302–3, 365, 369, 362, 298, 133, in Google Books; *The Academica of Cicero*, ed. James S. Reid (London: Macmillan, 1874), 29, in Google Books; Cicero, *Orationes quaedam selectae in usum Delphini...*, ed. Alexander J. Taylor (Philadelphia, PA: Towar and Hogan, 1826), 96, 299, in Google Books; Cicero, *Orationes, with a Commentary by George Long*, vol. 2, ed. George Long and A. J. Macleane (London: Whitaker, 1855), 58–59, in Google Books; *Terence's Comedies*, vol. 2, trans. S. Patrick (Dublin: Gilbert and Hodges et al., 1810), 65, in Google Books; *Selected Orations and Letters of Cicero*, ed. Harold W. Johnston (Chicago: Albert, Scott, 1892), 128–30, in

Google Books; *Ciceronis selectae quaedam epistolae*, ed. M. L. Hurlbut (Philadelphia, PA: H. Perkins, 1836), 95–96, in Google Books; *M. Tulli Ciceronis orationes ex editione Jo. Aug. Ernesti...*, vol. 1, ed. A. J. Valpy (London: A. J. Valpy, 1830), 545, in Google Books; *Q. Curti Rufi historiarum Alexandri Magni Macedonis*, ed. Theodor Vogel (Leipzig: B. G. Teubner, 1875), 240, in Google Books; *The Histories of Tacitus, Books I and II*, ed. Frank Gardner Moore (New York: Macmillan, 1910), 69, in Google Books; Cicero, *De Officiis*, trans. Walter Miller (London: William Heinemann, 1921), 190–91, in Google Books.

30 Nathaniel Ward, *A Sermon Preached before the Honourable House of Commons...* (London: Printed by R. I. for Stephen Bowtell, 1647), 8, in Early English Books Online.

31 d'Ewes, *Autobiography and Correspondence*, 121.

32 Bremer and Webster, *Puritans and Puritanism*, s.v. "Ramist Logic" by Stephanie Sleeper, 1:518; Hotson, *Johann Heinrich Alsted*, 6, 80–88; Robert G. Clouse, *The Influence of John Henry Alsted on English Millenarian Thought in the Seventeenth Century* (PhD diss., State University of Iowa, 1963), 119, 121, 109, in *ProQuest Dissertations and Theses Full Text*; J. H. Alsted, *A Neglected Educator: Johann Heinrich Alsted. Translation, &c. from the Latin of His Encyclopaedia*, trans. Percival R. Cole (Sydney: Government Printer, 1910), 6–7, in Internet Archive; Cotton Mather, *Dr. Cotton Mather's Student and Preacher* (London: for Charles Dilly, 1781), 36, in Google Books; Samuel Eliot Morison, *The Founding of Harvard College* (Cambridge, MA: Harvard University Press, 1935), 157, 159; Perry Miller, *The New England Mind: The Seventeenth Century* (1939; repr., Boston, MA: Beacon Press, 1961), 102.

33 Ernst H. Kantorowicz, *The King's Two Bodies: A Study in Mediaeval Political Theology* (Princeton, NJ: Princeton University Press, 1957).

34 Curtis, *Oxford and Cambridge*, 95, 123, 58–61, 100, 107, 109; V. H. H. Green, *Religion at Oxford and Cambridge* (London: SCM Press, 1964), 100–101; J. H. Hexter, "The Education of the Aristocracy in the Renaissance," *Journal of Modern History* 22, no. 1 (March 1950): 1–20; Lawrence Stone, "The Educational Revolution in England, 1560–1640," *Past & Present*, no. 28 (July 1964): 45, 67; Francis J. Bremer, *Congregational Communion: Clerical Friendship in the Anglo-American Puritan Community, 1610–1692* (Boston, MA: Northeastern University Press, 1994), 25; Joan Schenck Ibish, "Emmanuel College: The Founding Generation, with a Biographical Register of Members of the College, 1584–1604" (PhD diss., Harvard University, 1985), 199–205, 259–62, in ProQuest Dissertations & Theses; Richard Tyler, "The Children of Disobedience: The Social Composition of Emmanuel College, Cambridge, 1596–1645" (PhD diss., University of California at Berkeley, 1976), 99–200, in ProQuest Dissertations & Theses; on Preston's career, see the more extended treatment in McDermott, "Body of Liberties," 39–43, 46.

35 Curtis, *Oxford and Cambridge*, 120, 99, 109, 93, 131; Schmitt, *John Case*, 140.

36 Bendall, Brooke, and Collinson, *History of Emmanuel College*, 68.

37 Karl Mannheim, *Ideology and Utopia: An Introduction to the Sociology of Knowledge*, trans. Louis Wirth and Edward Shils (New York: Harcourt, Brace & World, 1936), 80, 10; see also W. G. Runciman, "Ideology and Social Science," in *Knowledge and Belief in Politics: The Problem of Ideology*, ed. Robert Benewick, R. N. Berki, and Bhikhu Parekh (New York: St. Martin's Press, 1973), 62–63; among other excerpts from Winthrop's spiritual journal in the *Winthrop Papers*, see John Winthrop, "John Winthrop's Experiencia," in *Winthrop Papers*, 5 vols. (Boston: Massachusetts Historical Society, 1929–47), 1:412–13.

38 Barry Levy, *Town Born: The Political Economy of New England from Its Founding to the Revolution* (Philadelphia: University of Pennsylvania Press, 2009); Brian Donahue, *The Great Meadow: Farmers and the Land in Colonial Concord* (New Haven, CT: Yale University Press, 2007).

39 Abram C. van Engen, *Sympathetic Puritans: Calvinist Fellow Feeling in Early New England* (Oxford: Oxford University Press, 2015), 56.

40 Venn, *Alumni Cantabrigienses...Part I*, 4:441; Francis J. Bremer, *John Winthrop: America's Forgotten Founding Father* (Oxford: Oxford University Press, 2003), 5, 68, 80; Victor Morgan, *A History*

  of the University of Cambridge, 1546–1750, vol. 2 of *A History of the University of Cambridge*, ed. Christopher Brooke (Cambridge: Cambridge University Press, 2004), 188.
41 John Winthrop, "A Modell of Christian Charity," *Winthrop Papers*, 2:282–83, 295; Arthur O. Lovejoy, *The Great Chain of Being: A Study of the History of an Idea* (1936; repr., Cambridge, MA: Harvard University Press, 1957).
42 Winthrop, "Modell," 2:283–84; on the connection between natural law and the Decalogue in Reformed thought, see David VanDrunen, *Natural Law and the Two Kingdoms: A Study in the Development of Reformed Social Thought* (Grand Rapids, MI: William B. Eerdmans, 2010), 112–13; Stephen J. Grabill, *Rediscovering the Natural Law in Reformed Theological Ethics* (Grand Rapids, MI: William B. Eerdmans, 2006), 132; Christopher J. Burchill, "Girolamo Zanchi: Portrait of a Reformed Theologian and His Work," *Sixteenth Century Journal* 15, no. 2 (Summer 1984): 187; Stephen J. Grabill, introduction to Jerome Zanchi, "On the Law in General," *Journal of Markets and Morality* 6, no. 1 (Spring 2003): 311.
43 Winthrop's habit of paraphrasing Scripture makes it difficult to determine which of the two popular English Bibles of the day he was using, the Geneva Bible of 1560 or the King James Version of 1611. However, his vocabulary suggests that he was quoting the Geneva version from memory. For example, toward the end of the sermon, Winthrop cited Deuteronomy 30:17 as follows: "if our heartes shall turne away soe that wee will not obey, but shall be seduced and worshipp other Gods our pleasures, and profitts, and serue them [...] wee shall surely perishe." The Geneva verse includes the word *seduced* while the King James does not; "our pleasures, and profitts" was an addition entirely of Winthrop's own. Similarly, Winthrop's rendering of Ephesians 4:16 includes the word *furniture*, present in the Geneva translation of that verse but not in the King James. Winthrop, "Modell," 2:285–87, 2:289, 2:295; on the continuing preference of many English Christians for the Geneva Bible for decades after the introduction of the King James Version, see *The Concise Oxford Companion to English Literature*, 4th edition, ed. Dinah Burch and Katy Hooper (Oxford: Oxford University Press, 2012), s.v. "Bible, the English," 65.
44 Winthrop, "Modell," 2:288–93.
45 Winthrop, "Modell," 2:289–92; Michael J. Braddick, *State Formation in Early Modern England, c. 1550–1700* (Cambridge: Cambridge University Press, 2000), 101–75.
46 John Winthrop to Sir William Spring, February 8, 1629/30, in *Winthrop Papers*, 2:205.
47 John Winthrop, "Experiencia" for 1611/12, in *Winthrop Papers*, 1:166; in this connection see Bremer, *John Winthrop*, 83.
48 *Geneva Bible*, 1560, New Testament 91, column 4.
49 Winthrop, "Modell," 2:293. According to Anthony Fletcher, "the one-sex model of the body invented by Galen of Pergamon proved immensely resilient" during the early and mid-seventeenth century. This theory held that women were men with inverted male genitalia inside the body, with the ovaries taking the place of testicles, the penis as the vagina and cervix, and the scrotum becoming the uterus. Elizabeth Maddock Dillon brings out the deeper implications of the one-sex model, which denied that sex has a fundamental basis in biology, for Puritan thought.

> For the Puritans [...] gender was understood as grounded in the divine hierarchy of God rather than in the bodies of men and women. While the foundations of gender were not biological, gender and sex were nonetheless thoroughly fixed in a divinely ordained hierarchial order. [...] Rather than functioning as the sign of biological sex, then, gender (as well as sex) was a sign of the order of the cosmos,

which, I would add, was conceptually prior to both gender and sex. Anthony Fletcher, *Gender, Sex and Subordination in England 1500–1800* (New Haven, CT: Yale University Press, 1995), 34–35; Elizabeth Maddock Dillon, "Nursing Fathers and Brides of Christ," in *A Centre of Wonders: The Body in Early America*, ed. Janet Moore Lindman and Michelle Lise Tarter (Ithaca, NY: Cornell University Press, 2001), 131.

50 For other examples of corporatism in Winthrop's works, see, e.g., "A Reply in Further Defense of an Order of Court Made in May, 1637," *Winthrop Papers* 3:463–76, and the beginning of the "Discourse on Arbitrary Government" in *Winthrop Papers*, 4:468.
51 Bremer, *John Winthrop*, 179, 175.

Chapter One Puritans and Society in the Stour Valley

1 Cotton Mather, *Magnalia Christi Americana*, 2 vols. (Hartford, CT: Silas Andrus & Son, 1853–55), 1:260.
2 N. C. P. Tyack, "Migration from East Anglia to New England before 1660" (PhD diss., Cambridge University, 1951), 2 vols., 1:231–36.
3 Anthony Salerno, "The Social Background of Seventeenth-Century Emigration to America," *Journal of British Studies* 19, no. 1 (Autumn 1979): 33, 35, 38; Virginia DeJohn Anderson, *New England's Generation: The Great Migration and the Formation of Society and Culture in the Seventeenth Century* (Cambridge: Cambridge University Press, 1991), 22 [quote], 28–29, 31–32, 37–42; Alison Games, *Migration and the Origins of the English Atlantic World* (Cambridge, MA: Harvard University Press, 1999), 30, 49, 53.
4 T. H. Breen and Stephen Foster, "Moving to the New World: The Character of Early Massachusetts Immigration," *William and Mary Quarterly* 30, no. 2 (April 1973): 194 [quote], 195, 197–98, 201, 205.
5 Roger Thompson, "*The Uprooted* or 'Worlds in Motion': East Anglian Founders of New England 1629–1640," *Parergon*, n.s., 11, no. 2 (December 1993): 7, 11 [quote]; Thompson, *Mobility and Migration: East Anglian Founders of New England, 1629–1640* (Amherst: University of Massachusetts Press, 1994), 95–96.
6 Thompson, "*The Uprooted*," 7; Thompson, *Mobility and Migration*, 187.
7 Thomas Dudley to Countess of Lincoln, March 12, 1630/31–March 28, 1631, in *Chronicles of the First Planters of the Colony of Massachusetts Bay, from 1623 to 1636*, ed. Alexander Young (1846; repr., Williamstown, MA: Corner House Publishers, 1978), 324.
8 Nathaniel Ward to John Winthrop, January 16, 1629/30, in *Winthrop Papers*, 2:192.
9 Breen and Foster, "Moving to the New World," 201; Alison Games, "Venturers, Vagrants and Vessels of Glory: Migration from England to the Colonies under Charles I" (PhD diss., University of Pennsylvania, 1992), 140, in ProQuest Dissertations and Theses Global.
10 Herbert Butterfield, *The Whig Interpretation of History* (London: G. Bell & Sons, 1959).
11 David Barton, *The Myth of Separation: What Is the Correct Relationship between Church and State? A Revealing Look at What Founders and Early Courts Really Said* (Aledo, TX: WallBuilder Press, 1989).
12 Patrick Collinson, "*De Republica Anglorum*: Or, History with the Politics Put Back," in *Elizabethan Essays* (London: Hambledon Press, 1994), 11.
13 Susan Hardman Moore, *Pilgrims: New World Settlers & the Call of Home* (New Haven, CT: Yale University Press, 2007), 22; Hall, *Puritans*, 125; Alison Games conceptually links gadding about with New England migration in Games, "Venturers, Vagrants and Vessels of Glory," 139. A. R. Pennie's study of wills from Dedham, Essex, provides hard evidence that the godly "habitually attended services in other parishes." A. R. Pennie, "Evolution of Puritan Mentality in an Essex Cloth Town: Dedham and the Stour Valley, 1560–1640" (PhD diss., University of Sheffield, 1989), 169, in ETHOS. Patrick Collinson records the comment of William Glibery, vicar of Halstead; offended by the drawing power of the sermons of Richard Rogers of Wethersfield, Glibery was willing to bet £20 that "'if I were let alone with these same gadding heads that run about thus to sermons, I would, saith he, in a month bring them to what religion I list.'" Quoted in Collinson, *The Elizabethan Puritan Movement* (Berkeley: University of California Press, 1967), 373.

14 Kenneth W. Shipps, "The Puritan Emigration to New England: A New Source on Motivation," *New England Historical and Genealogical Register* 135 (1981): 85.

15 John Ward Dean, *A Memoir of the Rev. Nathaniel Ward, A. M ...* (Albany, NY: J. Munsell, 1868), 12n5, 14, 17, Google Books; Charles Clay, "Haverhill," *Proceedings of the Suffolk Institute of Archaeology and Natural History* 4 (1874): 104; Janet Cooper, ed., *A History of the County of Essex*, vol. 10, The Victoria History of the Counties of England (Oxford: Oxford University Press, 2001), 1; Shirley Wilcox Harvey, "Nathaniel Ward: His Life and Works" (PhD diss., Boston University, 1936), 3; Bremer and Webster, *Puritans and Puritanism*, s.v. "Ward, Samuel (of Ipswich)" by John Craig, 1:265–266; *American National Biography Online*, s.v. "Ward, Nathaniel" by Mary Rhinelander McCarl, accessed February 6, 2013.

16 Tom Webster, introduction to *The Diary of Samuel Rogers, 1634–1638* (Woodbridge, UK: Boydell Press, 2004), xv.

17 Jean Béranger, *Nathaniel Ward (ca. 1578–1652)*, Études et Recherches Anglaises et Anglo-Américaines 1 (Bordeaux, France: SOBODI, 1969); Harvey, *Nathaniel Ward*, 23; Nathaniel Bacon, *Annalls of Ipswche*, ed. William H. Richardson (1654; repr., Ipswich: for the subscribers by S. H. Cowell, 1884), 461, in Internet Archive; Thomas G. Barnes, "Thomas Lechford and the Earliest Lawyering in Massachusetts, 1638–1641," in *Law in Colonial Massachusetts, 1630–1800: A Conference Held 6 and 7 November 1981 by The Colonial Society of Massachusetts* (Boston: Colonial Society of Massachusetts, 1984), 6.

18 Béranger, *Nathaniel Ward*, 50–51; Harvey, "Nathaniel Ward," 34.

19 Nathaniel Ward, *The Simple Cobler of Aggawam in America* (1647; repr., New York: Scholars' Facsimiles and Reprints, 1937), 39, 61 [quote]; Harvey, "Nathaniel Ward," 44–45.

20 Mary Janette Bohi, "Nathaniel Ward, Pastor Ingeniosus: 1580?–1652" (PhD diss., University of Illinois at Urbana-Champaign, 1959), 51–52, in ProQuest Dissertations & Theses; Barbara Donagan, "The Clerical Patronage of Robert Rich, Second Earl of Warwick, 1619–1642," *Proceedings of the American Philosophical Society* 120, no. 5 (October 15, 1976): 392.

21 Nicholas Tyacke, *Anti-Calvinists: The Rise of English Arminianism c. 1590–1640* (Oxford: Oxford University Press, 1990), 148n129; Shipps, "Lay Patronage," 277n34; Samuel Gorton, *Simplicities Defence against Seven-Headed Policy* (London: by John Macock, 1646), 53, in Early English Books Online.

22 Venn, *Alumni Cantabrigienses ... Part 1*, 4:333; McCarl, "Ward, Nathaniel." American National Biography Online.

23 Béranger, *Nathaniel Ward*, 66–68; Venn, *Alumni Cantabrigienses ... Part I*, 4:332–333; *Winthrop Papers* 4:191–92, 4:221–22; ECA CHA.1.4(c), 136r.

24 Webster, "Introduction," xvi–xvii.

25 Venn, *Alumni Cantabrigienses ... Part I*, 4:334.

26 Bacon, *Annalls*, 424; see also John Wodderspoon, *Memorials of the Ancient Town of Ipswich* (Ipswich, UK: Pawsey, 1850), 372–73, in Google Books.

27 Thomas Fuller, *History of the Worthies of England*, 3 vols. (London: for Thomas Tegg, 1840), 3:186, Internet Archive.

28 On Ward's visual artistry, see John Bruce, "The Caricatures of Samuel Ward of Ipswich," *Notes and Queries* 4th ser., 1 (January–June 1868): 1–2, in Internet Archive.

29 The original drawing does not exist, but a copy was published as Samuel Ward, *The Papists Powder Treason* (London: P. Stent, 1680?), in Early English Books Online. See M. Dorothy George, *English Political Caricature to 1792: A Study of Opinion and Propaganda* (Oxford: Clarendon Press, 1959), 15–16 and plate 3.

30 Samuel R. Gardiner, *History of England from the Accession of James I to the Outbreak of the Civil War, 1603–1642* (London: Longmans, Green, 1883), 4:118.

31 Joseph Mead to Sir Martin Stuteville, February 24, 1620/21, Harley Mss. 389 ff. 22–23, British Library, London, UK; Bacon, *Annalls*, 479; Craig, "Ward, Samuel (of Ipswich)," in Bremer and Webster, *Puritans and Puritanism*, 1:265–66. For more on Joseph Mead, including

his correspondence with Stuteville, see David Randall, "Joseph Mead, Novellante: News, Sociability, and Credibility in Early Stuart England," *Journal of British Studies* 45, no. 2 (April 2006): 293–312.

32 Dean, *Memoir*, 126, 162–64; Matthew Reynolds, *Godly Reformers and Their Opponents in Early Modern England: Religion in Norwich, c. 1560–1643* (Woodbridge, UK: Boydell Press, 2005), 119; Bacon, *Annalls*, i–ii, 535; *Calendar of State Papers, Domestic Series, of the Reign of Charles I: 1637–1638* (London: Longmans, Green, 1869), 497, in Google Books; *Fourth Report of the Royal Commission on Historical Manuscripts, Part I: Report and Appendix* (London: George Edward Eyre and William Spottiswoode, 1874), 64, in Google Books; John Peile, *Biographical Register of Christ's College, 1505–1905*, vol. 1 (Cambridge: Cambridge University Press, 1910), 1:256; Joseph Foster, *The Register of Admissions to Gray's Inn, 1521–1889* (London: Hansard Publishing Union, 1889), 116, in Internet Archive; Venn, *Alumni Cantabrigienses ... Part I*, 1:65.

33 John Ward, *God iudging among the gods* (London: by I. L. for Christopher Meredith, 1645), 14, in Early English Books Online.

34 William Perkins, "A Discourse of Conscience," in *The Works of that Famous and Worthie Minister of Christ ... M. W. Perkins ... Gathered into one volume* (Cambridge: by Iohn Legat, 1605), 622, in Early English Books Online.

35 Venn, *Alumni Cantabrigienses ... Part I*, 3:478; Morison, *Founding of Harvard College*, 60; W. B. Patterson, *William Perkins and the Making of a Protestant England* (Oxford: Oxford University Press, 2014), 41.

36 T. W. Davids, *Annals of Evangelical Nonconformity in the County of Essex* (London: Jackson, Walford and Hodder, 1863), 147, 391, in Google Books; Webster, "Introduction," xiii, xviii; Shipps, "Puritan Emigration," 93; Venn, *Alumni Cantabrigienses ... Part I*, 3:148; Tom Webster, *Godly Clergy in Early Stuart England: The Caroline Puritan Movement, c. 1620–1643* (Cambridge: Cambridge University Press, 1997), 38. Barbara Donagan sees Marshall's decision-making process as an example of Puritan casuistry: Barbara Donagan, "Godly Choice: Puritan Decision-Making in Seventeenth-Century England," *Harvard Theological Review* 76, no. 3 (July 1983): 325–26. Daniel Rogers even hoped to persuade John Winthrop not to leave England: see Deane Tyndal to John Winthrop, October 23, 1629, in *Winthrop Papers*, 2:162–63.

37 Shipps, "Lay Patronage," 109; Arthur Searle, ed., *Barrington Family Letters, 1628–1632* (London: Offices of the Royal Historical Society, 1983), 1–13; Mary-Millicent Egan, "Laudians, Puritans and the Laity in Essex c. 1630–1642" (PhD diss., University College, London, 2001), 204–5, in ETHOS; William Hunt, *The Puritan Moment: The Coming of Revolution in an English County* (Cambridge: Harvard University Press, 1983), 15, 28.

38 Mather, *Magnalia*, 1:415; Venn, *Alumni Cantabrigienses ... Part I*, 3:479; Giles Firmin, *The Real Christian* (London: for Dorman Newman, 1670), 75–76, in Early English Books Online.

39 Venn, *Alumni Cantabrigienses ... Part I*, 3:479; *Oxford Dictionary of National Biography Online*, s.v. "Rogers, Nathaniel" by Michael P. Winship, accessed Feb. 16, 2013; Henry F. Waters, *Genealogical Gleanings in England*, 2 vols. (Boston: New England Historic Genealogical Society, 1901), 1:211–213, 2:1140; George Frederick Beaumont, *A History of Coggeshall, in Essex* (London: Marshall Brothers, 1890), 217; Mather, *Magnalia*, 1:420.

40 On the mixed farming regime imported by settlers to New England, see Donahue, *Great Meadow*, xv, 56–59. On English land use patterns in general, see Joan Thirsk, ed., *The Agrarian History of England and Wales, Volume IV, 1500–1640* (Cambridge: Cambridge University Press, 1967); Joan Thirsk, ed., *The Agrarian History of England and Wales* [hereinafter *AHEW*], *Volume V, 1640–1750; Part I, Regional Farming Systems* (Cambridge: Cambridge University Press, 1984); David Hall, *The Open Fields of England* (Oxford: Oxford University Press, 2014); Patricia Baker, *Studies of Field Systems in the British Isles*, ed. Alan R. H. Baker and Robin A. Butlin (Cambridge: Cambridge University Press, 1973); Brian K. Roberts and Stuart Wrathmell, *Region and Place: A Study of English Rural Settlement* (London: English Heritage, 2002); Joan Thirsk, "The Common Fields," *Past & Present* 29 (December 1964): 3–25; Joan Thirsk, "The Common Fields," in *The Rural*

Economy of England: Collected Essays, ed. Joan Thirsk (London: Hambledon Press, 1984), 35–57; Howard L. Gray, *English Field Systems* (Cambridge: Harvard University Press, 1915), in Internet Archive; Bruce M. S. Campbell, *Field Systems and Farming Systems in Late Medieval England* (Farnham, UK: Ashgate, 2008); C. S. and C. S. Orwin, *The Open Fields* (Oxford: Clarendon Press, 1938); Eric Kerridge, *The Common Fields of England* (Manchester: Manchester University Press, 1992).

41 Gilbert Slater, *The English Peasantry and the Enclosure of the Common Fields* (London: Archibald Constable, 1907), 8, in Internet Archive.

42 For an excellent description of the plowing method which produced the ridge and furrow pattern, see David Hall, *The Open Fields of Northamptonshire* (Northampton, UK: Northamptonshire Record Society, 1995), 2.

43 Brodie Waddell, "Governing England through the Manor Courts, 1550–1850," *Historical Journal* 55, no. 2 (June 2012): 279–315; Denis Stuart, *Manorial Records: An Introduction to Their Transcription and Translation* (Chichester, UK: Phillimore, 1992), 1; William Sheppard, *The Court-Keepers Guide* (London: by James Flesher, 1650), 66–70, in Google Books; see also Warren O. Ault, "Village By-Laws by Common Consent," *Speculum* 29, no. 2, part 2 (April 1954): 378–94; Warren O. Ault, "Open-Field Husbandry and the Village Community: A Study of Agrarian By-Laws in Medieval England," *Transactions of the American Philosophical Society* 55, no. 7 (1965): 1–102; Angus J. L. Winchester, *The Harvest of the Hills: Rural Life in Northern England and the Scottish Borders, 1400–1700* (Edinburgh: Edinburgh University Press, 2000), 26–51, 146–51.

44 E. C. K. Gonner, *Common Land and Inclosure* (London: Macmillan, 1912), 12–13, in Internet Archive; H. R. French, "The Common Fields of Urban England: Communal Agriculture and the 'Politics of Entitlement,' 1500–1750," in *Custom, Improvement and the Landscape in Early Modern Britain*, ed. Richard W. Hoyle (London: Routledge, 2016), 153.

45 On enclosure in general, see Tom Williamson, "Understanding Enclosure," *Landscapes* 1, no. 1 (2000): 56–79; J. A. Yelling, *Common Field and Enclosure in England 1450–1850* (London: Macmillan Press, 1977); Joan Thirsk, "Enclosing and Engrossing," in *AHEW* IV, 200–255; Joan Thirsk, "Tudor Enclosures," in Thirsk, *Rural Economy of England*, 65–83; W. E. Tate, *A Domesday of English Enclosure Acts and Awards*, ed. M. E. Turner (Reading: Library, University of Reading, 1978); J. R. Wordie, "The Chronology of English Enclosure, 1500–1914," *Economic History Review* 36, no. 4 (November 1983): 483–505; John Chapman, "The Chronology of English Enclosure," *Economic History Review* 37, no. 4 (November 1984): 557–59; R. H. Tawney, *The Agrarian Problem in the Sixteenth Century* (London: Longmans, Green, 1912), in Internet Archive; Arthur H. Johnson, *The Disappearance of the Small Landowner* (Oxford: Clarendon Press, 1909), in Internet Archive; Slater, *English Peasantry*. On the "Agricultural Revolution," see Eric Kerridge, *The Agricultural Revolution* (London: George Allen & Unwin, 1967), but also Mark Overton's discussion of the various versions of this theory in Overton, "Agricultural Change in Norfolk and Suffolk, 1580–1740" (PhD diss., Cambridge University, 1980), 2–13. Population increase: Braddick, *State Formation*, 48.

46 Edwin F. Gay, "The Midland Revolt and the Inquisitions of Depopulation of 1607," *Transactions of the Royal Historical Society*, n.s., 18 (1904): 195–244; Steve Hindle, "Imagining Insurrection in Seventeenth-Century England: Representations of the Midland Rising of 1607," *History Workshop Journal* 66 (Autumn 2008): 21–61; Maurice Beresford and John G. Hurst, eds., *Deserted Medieval Villages: Studies* (1971; repr., Gloucester: Sutton, 1989); Maurice Beresford, *The Lost Villages of England* (London: Lutterworth Press, 1954).

47 Paul Slack, "Vagrants and Vagrancy in England, 1598–1664," *Economic History Review* 27, no. 3 (August 1974): 375; Braddick, *State Formation*, 53–54; Clive Holmes, *Seventeenth-Century Lincolnshire* (Lincoln, UK: History of Lincolnshire Committee for the Society for Lincolnshire History and Archaeology, 1980), 20–23. Holmes points out that enclosure for agricultural reform did not force people from the land as mercilessly as enclosure for pastoral purposes often did, because the same number of farm laborers were still required to bring in the crops.

With the extinguishment of common rights that followed enclosure, however, smallholders would be forced to migrate at least locally in search of supplemental income as farm laborers.
48 "By 1750 about half of East Anglia could still be classified as fielden. Only east Norfolk and the Sandlings had changed into predominantly enclosed landscapes in the previous 150 years. Elsewhere active enclosure seldom went so far, and there were few fielden parishes in 1700 with more than one-third, and less than one-tenth, of their acreage in whole-year closes." B. A. Holderness, "East Anglia and the Fens," in *AHEW* V.I, 208. Or as Arthur Young lamented as late as 1797, "Suffolk must be reckoned amongst the earliest inclosed of the English counties, but there are very large tracts yet open, that want the benefit of this first and greatest of all improvements." Arthur Young, *General View of the Agriculture of the County of Suffolk* (London: by B. Macmillan, 1797), 30, in Internet Archive.
49 Searle, "Introduction" to Searle, ed., *Barrington Letters*, 2, 4; Hunt, *Puritan Moment*, 35; Tate, *Domesday*, 113; Felix Hull, "Agriculture and Rural Society in Essex, 1560–1640" (PhD diss., University of London, 1950), 26; W. R. Powell, Beryl A. Board and Norma Knight, eds., *A History of the County of Essex*, vol. 8, Victoria History of the Counties of England (Oxford: Oxford University Press, 1983), 159, 165, 172–73, 174, 177–78.
50 Robert Reyce, *Suffolk in the XVIIth Century. The Breviary of Suffolk* (London: John Murray, 1902), 29, in Google Books.
51 Joan Thirsk, "The Farming Regions of England," in *AHEW* IV, 4, 41, 43, 45; on the cloth trade in the area of Haverhill, see Holderness, "East Anglia," 200–201; Mark Bailey, *Medieval Suffolk: An Economic and Social History, 1200–1500* (Woodbridge, UK: Boydell Press, 2007), 269, 272; Richard Blome, *Britannia* (London: by Thomas Roycroft, 1673), 211, Google Books; D. C. Coleman, "An Innovation and Its Diffusion: The 'New Draperies,'" *Economic History Review* 22, no. 3 (December 1969): 427.
52 "Suffolk Historic Landscape Characterisation Map," Suffolk Heritage Explorer, accessed July 20, 2019; "arabilis ... in Com[muni] Campo vocat[ur] Halesfield": Court roll of Haverhill and Horsham with Helions, 1648–57, E7/26/2, Suffolk Record Office, Bury St. Edmunds Branch, UK; W. E. Tate, "A Handlist of Suffolk Enclosure Acts and Awards," *Proceedings of the Suffolk Institute of Archaeology and Natural History* 25, Part 3 (1952): 259; Stewards' papers [original surrenders and presentments] for Haverhill, 1659, D/DWv M142, Essex Record Office, Chelmsford, UK; Map of West Field Common, Haverhill, 1733, FL 595/13/12, Map of Haverhill, 1825, M547/16, and Map of Haverhill, 1855, M547/17, Suffolk Record Office, Bury St. Edmunds branch, UK; Hull, "Agriculture and Rural Society," 535. On the advantages and disadvantages of using data from the monumental Historic Landscape Characterisation project carried out by English Heritage, see Stephen Rippon, *Making Sense of an Historic Landscape* (Oxford: Oxford University Press, 2012), 54–57. Methodological documents from the project make it clear that its purpose was to characterize the present-day landscape, not to produce historical maps of medieval field systems; however, in those areas of England where twentieth-century agriculture or modern urban sprawl have not obliterated the traces of ancient fields, surviving patterns can indicate when fields were enclosed. Oscar Aldred and Graham Fairclough, "Historic Landscape Characterisation: Taking Stock of the Method," 2003, 7, 21, in Archaeology Data Service; Jo Clark, John Darlington, and Graham Fairclough, "Using Historic Landscape Characterisation," 6–9, in Archaeology Data Service.
53 Thirsk, "Farming Regions," 7; Edward Martin, "Regionality in East Anglian Field Systems," in *Wheare Most Inclosures Be: East Anglian Fields: History, Morphology and Management*, ed. Edward Martin and Max Satchell (Ipswich, UK: Archaeological Service, Suffolk County Council, 2008), 206–7; Charles Vancouver, *General View of the Agriculture in the County of Essex* (London: by W. Smith, 1795), 104, in Internet Archive; Lynn Dyson-Bruce and Alison Bennett, "Essex Historic Landscape Characterisation Project," 20, in Archaeology Data Service; Alison Bennett, "Historic Landscape Characterisation Report for Essex, Volume 1," 18, 20, in Archaeology Data Service; Alison Bennett, "Historic Landscape Characterisation Report for

Essex, Volume 2," 12–13, in Archaeology Data Service; Hull, "Agriculture and Rural Society," 7–8, 13, map facing page 534.

54 Bailey, *Medieval Suffolk*, 269; Diarmaid MacCulloch, *Suffolk and the Tudors: Politics and Religion in an English County 1500–1600* (Oxford: Clarendon Press, 1986), 23.

55 Blome, *Britannia*, 207; Holderness, "East Anglia," 205–6, 227–30; Martin, "Regionality," 195; Overton, "Agricultural Change," 210; Tate, "Handlist of Suffolk Enclosure," 246; K. J. Allison, "The Sheep-Corn Husbandry of Norfolk in the Sixteenth and Seventeenth Centuries," *Agricultural History Review* 5, no. 1 (1957): 12–30; Alan Simpson, "The East Anglian Foldcourse: Some Queries," *Agricultural History Review* 6, no. 2 (1958): 87–96; M. R. Postgate, "The Field Systems of Breckland," *Agricultural History Review* 10, no. 2 (1962): 80–101; Hall, *Open Fields of England*, 69–73, 88–89.

56 W. E. Tate, "Cambridgeshire Field Systems, with a Hand-list of Cambridgeshire Enclosure Acts and Awards," *Proceedings of the Cambridge Antiquarian Society* 40 (July 1939–December 1942): 56–61; Margaret Spufford, "General View of the Rural Economy of the County of Cambridge," *Proceedings of the Cambridge Antiquarian Society* 89 (2000): 77–80; L. F. Salzman, ed., *Victoria History of the County of Cambridge and the Isle of Ely*, vol. 2 (London: Oxford University Press, 1948), 114; William Gooch, *General View of the Agriculture in the County of Cambridge* (London: for Richard Phillips, 1811), 56, in Internet Archive; Holderness, "East Anglia," 210, 206; Frederic W. Maitland, *Township and Borough* (Cambridge: Cambridge University Press, 1898), 1–3, 106–11, in Internet Archive; Sarah Harrison, "Open Fields and Earlier Landscapes: Six Parishes in South-east Cambridgeshire," *Landscapes* 3, no. 1 (2002): 35–54.

57 For a useful example of this distinction, see Mather, *Magnalia*, 2:119.

58 Court book of manor of Dedham Hall, f. 312, D/DU 457/1/2, Essex Record Office, Chelmsford, UK; Pennie, "Evolution of Puritan Mentality," 8–9; Manor of Dedham Hall, Parliamentary Survey, 1650, E 317 Essex/12, National Archives, Kew.

59 Perkins, "Discourse of Conscience," 619, 642; Abraham Stoll, *Conscience in Early Modern English Literature* (Cambridge: Cambridge University Press, 2017), 39–41, 115–16. On Aquinas's influence: as historian H. C. Porter pointed out, Perkins's "Treatise of God's Free Grace and Man's Free Will" cited Thomas Aquinas 5 times and Augustine 12 times, but Calvin and Luther only once each. H. C. Porter, *Reformation and Reaction in Tudor Cambridge* (Cambridge: Cambridge University Press, 1958), 311; on Perkins's scholasticism, see also Patterson, *William Perkins*, 81–82. On Perkins's view of the scope and limitations of humanity's natural freedom of choosing after the Fall, see Richard A. Muller, *Grace and Freedom: William Perkins and the Early Modern Reformed Understanding of Free Choice and Divine Grace* (Oxford: Oxford University Press, 2020), 113–19.

60 Perkins, "Discourse of Conscience," 620–21; William Ames, *Conscience with the Power and Cases Thereof* (London: n.p., 1639), I:27; Hall, *Puritans*, 114; Perry Miller, *The Responsibility of Mind in a Civilization of Machines*, ed. John Crowell and Sanford J. Searl Jr. (Amherst: University of Massachusetts Press, 1979), 178. On Puritan casuistry in general, see Donagan, "Godly Choice," 322–26.

61 Perkins, "Discourse of Conscience," 635–36, 623; Thomas Aquinas, ST q.95, art. 2, in *Saint Thomas Aquinas, the Treatise on Law*, ed. R. J. Henle (Notre Dame, IN: University of Notre Dame Press, 1993), 287; see also Patterson, *William Perkins*, 94.

62 "Quorum est constituere magistratus, eorum etiam est enormiter grassatores cohercere, aut tollare, si non desistant grassari contra Deum, & contra rempublicam. Constituuntur autem vel per senatum, vel per alios magistratus. Ergo hi recte faciunt, cum cohercerent aut tollunt grassatores" (my trans.) Quoted in John Milton, *Political Writings*, ed. Martin Dzelzainis, trans. Claire Gruzelier (Cambridge: Cambridge University Press, 1991), 40n169. On Pareus, see also George W. Whiting, "Pareus, the Stuarts, Laud, and Milton," *Studies in Philology* 50, no. 2 (April 1953): 215–29.

63 Hunt, *Puritan Moment*, 195, 203; Richard Cust, *The Forced Loan and English Politics, 1626–1628* (Oxford: Clarendon Press, 1987), 301; Pennie, "Evolution of Puritan Mentality," 176.

64 John Bohstedt, *The Politics of Provisions: Food Riots, Moral Economy, and Market Transition in England, c. 1550–1850* (2010; repr., London: Routledge, 2016).

65 Braddick, *State Formation*, 89 [quote], 21, 35, 47, 70, 91–93; Steve Hindle, *The State and Social Change in Early Modern England, 1550–1640* (Basingstoke, UK: Palgrave, 2002), 172. On the "world-picture," see E. M. W. Tillyard, *The Elizabethan World Picture* (1944; repr., New York: Mcmillan, 1944); C. S. Lewis, *The Discarded Image: An Introduction to Medieval and Renaissance Literature* (Cambridge: Cambridge University Press, 1964); Basil Willey, *The Seventeenth Century Background* (New York: Columbia University Press, 1958).

66 "Population and Incomes, 1600," in *Seventeenth-Century Economic Documents*, ed. Joan Thirsk and J. P. Cooper (Oxford: Clarendon Press, 1972), 756; Peter Clark and David Souden, "Introduction" to *Migration and Society in Early Modern England*, ed. Peter Clark and David Souden (Totowa, NJ: Barnes & Noble, 1988), 13.

67 A. L. Beier, *Masterless Men: The Vagrancy Problem in England, 1560–1640* (London: Methuen, 1985), 21; Hindle, *State and Social Change*, 41, 47–48; Holmes, *Seventeenth-Century Lincolnshire*, 22; Patricia Fumerton, *Unsettled: The Culture of Mobility and the Working Poor in Early Modern England* (Chicago: University of Chicago Press, 2006), xii.

68 "A Brief Declaration concerning the State of the Manufacture of Wools in the County of Essex, 1629," in *Seventeenth Century Economic Documents*, ed. Thirsk and Cooper (Oxford: Clarendon Press, 1972), 226.

69 Peter Clark, "The Migrant in Kentish Towns 1580–1640," in *Crisis and Order in English Towns 1500–1700: Essays in Urban History*, ed. Peter Clark and Paul Slack (London: Routledge, 2007), 137–38; John Patten, "Patterns of Migration and Movement of Labour to Three Pre-industrial East Anglian Towns," in *Migration and Society*, ed. Clark and Souden, 86–87.

70 Clark and Souden, "Introduction," 31; Patten, "Patterns of Migration," 94; Peter Clark, "Migrants in the City: The Process of Social Adaptation in English Towns, 1500–1800," in *Migration and Society*, ed. Clark and Souden, 269–70.

71 Clark and Souden, "Introduction," 22 [quote], 29, 31; Roger Thompson, "Early Modern Migration," *Journal of American Studies* 25, no. 1 (April 1991): 64; Slack, "Vagrants and Vagrancy," 368–69; Peter Clark, "Migration in England," *Past & Present* 83 (May 1979): 58–59; Beier, *Masterless Men*, 11. On the prevalence of such migration in Europe generally during the early modern period, see Leslie Page Moch, *Moving Europeans: Migration in Western Europe Since 1650* (Bloomington: Indiana University Press, 1992), 1–2.

72 Braddick, *State Formation*, 102, 107; Beier, *Masterless Men*, 3–4; Slack, "Vagrants and Vagrancy," 362, 367–69; Joan R. Kent, "Population Mobility and Alms: Poor Migrants in the Midlands during the Early Seventeenth Century," *Local Population Studies* 27 (Autumn 1981): 36–37 [quote].

73 Julian Martin, *Francis Bacon, the State, and the Reform of Natural Philosophy* (Cambridge: Cambridge University Press, 1992), 33; Charles Webster, *The Great Instauration: Science, Medicine and Reform, 1626–1660* (New York: Holmes & Meier, 1976).

74 Francis Bacon, "Advice to the King, Touching Sutton's Estate," in *The Letters and the Life of Francis Bacon*, vol. 4, ed. James Spedding (London: Longmans, Green, Reader, and Dyer, 1868), 252, in Internet Archive; Beier, *Masterless Men*, 164; Braddick, *State Formation*, 111; Hindle, *State and Social Change*, 164.

75 Samuel Collins to Arthur Duck, May 20, 1629, in Gale Cengage State Papers Online, https://www.gale.com/primary-sources/state-papers-online; Christopher Hill, *Society and Puritanism in Pre-Revolutionary England*, 2nd ed. (New York: Schocken Books, 1967), 98–99. See also Davids, *Annals of Evangelical Nonconformity*, 150; *Oxford Dictionary of National Biography Online*, s.v. "Hooker, Thomas" by Sargent Bush, accessed May 21, 2018; Deryck Collingwood, *Thomas Hooker, 1586–1647: Father of American Democracy* (Interlaken, NY: Heart of the Lakes, 1995), 216.

76 Thomas Harman, "A Caveat or Warning for Common Cursitors, Vulgarly Called Vagabonds" (1566), in A. V. Judges, ed., *the Elizabethan Underworld* (1930; repr., London: Routledge & Kegan Paul, 1965), 63, 67, 69, 74, 105–7; [John Awdeley,] "The Fraternity of Vagabonds" (1561), in Judges, *Elizabethan Underworld*, title page, 53–56.

77 Braddick, *State Formation*, 147, 150–52; David Underdown, *Fire from Heaven: Life in an English Town in the Seventeenth Century* (New Haven, CT: Yale University Press, 1992).

78 Hindle, *State and Social Change*, 169; Clark, "Migrants in the City," 279.

79 John Rogers [of Dedham], *A Treatise of Love*, 2nd ed. (London: by Iohn Dawson for Nathanael Newbery, 1632), 71–72, in Google Books.

80 Richard Rogers, *Commentary vpon the Whole Booke of Iudges* (London: by Felix Kyngston for Thomas Man, 1615), 238, 247, in Early English Books Online, https://about.proquest.com/products-services/databases/eebo.html.

81 William H. Whitmore, ed., *A Bibliographical Sketch of the Laws of the Massachusetts Colony from 1630 to 1686* (Boston: Rockwell and Churchill, 1890), 37, accessed December 14, 2013, in Internet Archive, archive.org.

82 Clark and Souden, "Introduction," 25; Beier, *Masterless Men*, 36; Harman, "Caveat or Warning," 69.

83 Richard M. Smith, "Some Issues Concerning Families and Their Property in Rural England 1250–1800," in *Land, Kinship and Life-Cycle*, ed. Richard M. Smith (Cambridge: Cambridge University Press, 1984), 82; B. W. Quintrell, "The Government of the County of Essex, 1603–1642" (PhD diss., University of London, 1965), 213–14; Hindle, *State and Social Change*, 207–8, 216; Keith Wrightson, *English Society 1580–1680* (1982; repr., London: Routledge, 2003), 219; Clark, "Migrants in the City," 277; Braddick, *State Formation*, 24, 112–13.

84 Hindle, *State and Social Change*, 146, 207; Fumerton, *Unsettled*, 29; Braddick, *State Formation*, 137; Buchanan Sharp, *In Contempt of All Authority: Rural Artisans and Riot in the West of England, 1586–1660* (Berkeley: University of California Press, 1980), 68; License by John Winthrop, September 1, 1616, FL 506/11/8, Suffolk Record Office, Bury St. Edmunds, UK.

85 Beier, *Masterless Men*, 11; Wrightson, *English Society*, 174; "Orders by the Justices of the Peace for the Relief of the Poor in Essex, 3 April, 1598," in *Tudor Economic Documents* vol. 2, ed. R. H. Tawney and Eileen Power (London: Longmans, 1963), 362–63. "Warning out" was not entirely a new development in the early modern period; as William Alfred Morris pointed out long ago, it had its roots in the medieval system of frankpledge, which created "tithings" or groups of ten in each locality who were mutually responsible for each other's good conduct. Supervision of the frankpledge properly belonged to the hundred courts, but in many places the leet courts had acquired the privilege of conducting "view of frankpledge." William Alfred Morris, *The Frankpledge System* (London: Longmans, Green, 1910), 26, 131, 164–65, in Internet Archive. Warning out as a means of protecting members of the local community from liabilities caused by outsiders would later be extensively employed in early New England; the classic work is still Josiah Henry Benton, *Warning Out in New England, 1656–1817* (Boston: W. B. Clarke, 1911), in Internet Archive, archive.org.

86 Rogers, *Treatise of Love*, 71–72.

87 Michael F. Graham, "Scotland," in *The Reformation World*, ed. Andrew Pettegree (London: Taylor & Francis, 2000), 421; Jenny Wormald, *Court, Kirk, and Community: Scotland, 1470–1625* (Edinburgh: Edinburgh University Press, 2018), 146.

88 Hall, *Puritans*, 87, 90; Graham, "Scotland," 420, 425; James Kirk, "'The Polities of the Best Reformed Kirks': Scottish Achievements and English Aspirations in Church Government after the Reformation," *Scottish Historical Review* 159 no. 167, pt. 1 (April 1980): 35; Wormald, *Court, Kirk, and Community*, 155–56; Jane Dawson, *Scotland Re-formed, 1488–1587* (Edinburgh: Edinburgh University Press, 2007), 217–18, 219 [quote]; Margo Todd, *The Culture of Protestantism in Early Modern Scotland* (New Haven, CT: Yale University Press, 2002), 263, 83 [quote].

89 Kirk, "Polities of the Best Reformed," 25, 29, 31, 33, 48–50; Wormald, *Court, Kirk, and Community*, 151–54, 156, 164–65; Dawson, *Scotland Re-formed*, 216–17, 233–34, 223; Graham,

NOTES

"Scotland," 422–23; Rosalind Mitchison, *A History of Scotland*, 3rd ed. (London: Taylor & Francis Group, 2002), 86; McIlwain, "Introduction" to *Political Works of James I*, xxi–xxii.

90 Collinson, *Elizabethan Puritan Movement*, 226, 229, 231 [quote], 319–20; Stephen Foster, *The Long Argument: English Puritanism and the Shaping of New England Culture, 1570–1700* (Chapel Hill: University of North Carolina Press, 1996), 43–44, 46–47.

91 Roland G. Usher, ed., *The Presbyterian Movement in the Reign of Queen Elizabeth As Illustrated by the Minute Book of the Dedham Classis, 1582–1589* (London: Royal Historical Society, 1905), 69, 62, 48, 61, in Internet Archive.

92 Collinson, *Elizabethan Puritan Movement*, 300; Usher, *Presbyterian Movement*, 54–55, 30–31, 38–39, 50, 53, 57, 65, 32, 70; Foster, *Long Argument*, 36–37.

93 Richard Bancroft, "Dangerous Positions," in Usher, *Presbyterian Movement*, 8.

94 Usher, *Presbyterian Movement*, 99–100.

95 Usher, *Presbyterian Movement*, xxix, 67, 98; M. M. Knappen, "Introduction" to M. M. Knappen, ed., *Two Elizabethan Puritan Diaries by Richard Rogers and Samuel Ward* (Chicago: American Society of Church History, 1933), 28; Robert Charles Anderson, *Puritan Pedigrees: The Deep Roots of the Great Migration to New England* (Boston, MA: New England Historic Genealogical Society, 2018), 180–81.

96 Edward Leigh, *A Systeme or Body of Divinity* (London: by A. M. for William Lee, 1654), Epistle Dedicatorie, [3], in Google Books.

97 Rogers, *Commentarie vpon…Iudges*, [Epistle Dedicatory, 6], 807, 9, 60, 12.

98 Aristotle, *Nicomachean Ethics*, trans. Martin Ostwald (Englewood Cliffs, NJ: Prentice Hall, 1962), 15; Rogers, *Commentarie vpon…Iudges*, 323, 707, 72. On the metaphor of infection in the body politic, see Hindle, *State and Social Change*, 37, 147–48.

99 Rogers, *Commentary vpon…Iudges*, 45, 583.

100 Rogers, *Commentary vpon…Iudges*, 312, 315, 259, 275.

101 Rogers, *Treatise of Love*, [Epistle, 1, 3], 24–25, 42–45, 198.

102 Rogers, *Treatise of Love*, 8, 15 [quote], 19.

103 Rogers, *Treatise of Love*, 138, 91–92, 9–10, 172, 62, 71, 227, 61.

104 Baird Tipson, *Hartford Puritanism: Thomas Hooker, Samuel Stone, and Their Terrifying God* (Oxford: Oxford University Press, 2015), 21, 291–92.

105 Tipson, *Hartford Puritanism*, 38–39, 162, 287–90; *Thomas Hooker: Writings in England and Holland, 1626–1633*, ed. George H. Williams, Norman Pettit, Winfried Herget, and Sargent Bush Jr. (Cambridge, MA: Harvard University Press, 1975), 187–89, 221–27; Thomas Hooker, "To the Reader," in John Rogers, *The Doctrine of Faith* (London: by I. D. for Nathanael Newbery and Henry Overton, 1633), [7].

106 Mather, *Magnalia*, 2:416; Winship, "Rogers, Nathaniel"; John Winthrop, *The Journal of John Winthrop, 1630–1649*, ed. Richard S. Dunn, James Savage and Laetitia Yeandle (Cambridge, MA: Harvard University Press, 1996), 79; Collingwood, *Thomas Hooker*, 263, 267; Anderson, *Puritan Pedigrees*, 191.

107 Bohi, "Nathaniel Ward," 61–62; Davids, *Annals of Evangelical Nonconformity*, 464; Bremer and Webster, *Puritans and Puritanism*, s.v. "Hooker, Thomas" by Stephen Foster, 1:131; Shuckburgh, *Emmanuel College*, 73; Nathaniel Ward to William Sancroft, July, 1628, Harley Mss. 3783 f. 11, British Library, London; McDermott, "Body of Liberties," 147–50.

108 Perry Miller, "'Preparation for Salvation' in Seventeenth-Century New England," in *Nature's Nation* (Cambridge, MA: Harvard University Press, 1967), 53–54, 71.

109 Thomas Hooker, *A Survey of the Summe of Church-Discipline* (London: by A. M. for John Bellamy, 1648), I:36–37, in Internet Archive.

110 Hooker, "Preface" to *Survey of the Summe*, [15].

111 John Preston, *The Breast-Plate of Faith and Love* (London: by W. I. for Nicolas Bourne, 1630), 38, in Internet Archive. On this text and other evidences of Preston's "hypothetical universalism," see Jonathan D. Moore, *English Hypothetical Universalism: John Preston and the Softening of*

Reformed Theology (Grand Rapids, MI: William B. Eerdmans Publishing, 2007), 101–3, 110, 113, 117, 124–25.

112 Thomas Hooker, *The Faithful Covenanter* (London: for Christopher Meredith, 1644), 16, 13, 38 10–11, in Early English Books Online; Thomas Hooker, *The Vnbeleevers Preparing for Christ* (London: by Thomas Cotes for Andrew Crooke, 1638), 2, in Early English Books Online; Miller, "'Preparation for Salvation,'" 57; Miller, *New England Mind: The Seventeenth Century*, 410–19, 426–27. See also Andrew Denholm, "Thomas Hooker: Puritan Preacher, 1586–1647" (PhD diss., Hartford Seminary Foundation, 1961), 248–49, in ProQuest Dissertations and Theses. Baird Tipson also notes "Hooker's unceasing attacks on 'covetousness'"; Tipson, *Hartford Puritanism*, 56.

113 *The Puritans in America: A Narrative Anthology*, ed. Alan Heimert and Andrew Delbanco (Cambridge, MA: Harvard University Press, 1985), 63.

114 Thomas Hooker, *The Danger of Desertion: Or a Farwell Sermon....* (London: by G. M. for George Edwards, 1641), 3–4, 8, 7, in Early English Books Online.

115 Rogers, *Commentary vpon...Iudges*, 95, 389.

116 Richard Rogers, *Seauen Treatises* (London: by Felix Kingston, for Thomas Man, 1610), 641–65, in Internet Archive; Anderson, *Puritan Pedigrees*, 184; Collinson, *Elizabethan Puritan Movement*, 381–82.

117 Hall, *Puritans*, 109–67, esp. 146, 129; F. G. Emmison, ed., *Early Essex Town Meetings: Braintree, 1619–1636: Finchingfield, 1626–1634* (London: Phillimore, 1970), v–vii, 1–106.

118 See Kevin Sharpe, *Remapping Early Modern England: The Culture of Seventeenth-Century Politics* (Cambridge: Cambridge University Press, 2000), 44; James Daly, "Cosmic Harmony and Political Thinking in Early Stuart England," *Transactions of the American Philosophical Society* 69, no. 7 (1979): 7; Robert Eccleshall, *Order and Reason in Politics: Theories of Absolute and Limited Monarchy in Early Modern England* (Oxford: Oxford University Press, 1978), 13.

119 Robert Blair St. George refers obliquely the analogy between the various corporate bodies to which Puritans belonged, calling it "metaphoric compression" which led witches to attack houses "because these structures [...] were material metaphors of the human body; because of the extended meanings of the body, the house references malefic assaults against the family unit (the 'little commonwealth,' or dynastic body), the church (Christ's body), government (the political body), and community order (the social body)." St. George, "Witchcraft, Bodily Affliction, and Domestic Space in Seventeenth-Century New England," in *Centre of Wonders*, ed. Lindman and Tarter, 14–15.

120 As in William Perkins, *The Arte of Prophecying* (London: by Felix Kyngston for E. E., 1607), 32, in Early English Books Online. Joyce E. Chaplin comments that in general, in the early modern period, "Nature was a concatenation of animating forces, a web of analogies. [...] A *microcosm* (such as the human body) reflected the structure and meaning of the *macrocosm* or cosmos." Chaplin, *Subject Matter: Technology, the Body, and Science on the Anglo-American Frontier, 1500–1676* (Cambridge, MA: Harvard University Press, 2001), 12.

121 In this discussion of analogy I rely heavily on two neo-Thomist works: James F. Anderson, *The Bond of Being: An Essay on Analogy and Existence* (St. Louis, MO: B. Herder, 1949); Steven A. Long, *Analogia Entis: On the Analogy of Being, Metaphysics, and the Act of Faith* (Notre Dame, IN: University of Notre Dame Press, 2011); see also William F. Lynch, *Christ and Apollo: The Dimensions of the Literary Imagination* (1960; repr., Wilmington, DE: ISI Books, 2004), 179–215. On the Protestant reception of, and resistance to analogical thinking, see Michael McClymond, "Analogy: A Neglected Theme in Jonathan Edwards and Its Pertinence to Contemporary Theological Debates," *Jonathan Edwards Studies* 6, no. 2 (2016): 153–75; Olli-Pekka Vainio, "The Curious Case of *Analogia entis*: How Metaphysics Affects Ecumenics?" *Studia Theologica* 69, no. 2 (2015): 171–89.

122 Martin Bucer, *De Regno Christi* in *Melanchthon and Bucer*, ed. Wilhelm Pauck (Philadelphia, PA: Westminster Press, 1969), 360; Samuel Ward, *Iethro's Iustice of Peace ....* (London: Edw.

Griffin for Iohn Marriot, 1618), 3, 13, Early English Books Online; Nathaniel Rogers, *A Letter, Discovering The Cause of Gods continuing wrath against the Nation* .... (London: by G. M. for Christopher Meredith, 1644), 9, in Early English Books Online. On the Aristotelian origins of distributive justice: Aristotle, *Nicomachean Ethics*, 117–23; see also Samuel Fleischacker, *A Short History of Distributive Justice* (Cambridge, MA: Harvard University Press, 2004), 19–22.

123 William Perkins, *The Whole Treatise of the Cases of Conscience* (Cambridge: by Iohn Legat, 1608), III:149–50, III:95–115, in Early English Books Online; see also Patterson, *William Perkins*, 143.

124 William Perkins, *Epieikeia: Or, a Treatise of Christian Equitie and Moderation* (Cambridge: by Iohn Legat, 1604), 3–4, 10–11, 21, 50, 31.

125 See Patrick Collinson, "Puritanism and the Poor," in *Pragmatic Utopias: Ideals and Communities, 1200–1630*, ed. Rosemary Horrox and Sarah Rees Jones (Cambridge: Cambridge University Press, 2001), 242–58.

126 Ethan Shagan, *The Rule of Moderation: Violence, Religion, and the Politics of Restraint in Early Modern England* (Cambridge: Cambridge University Press, 2011), 222, 224, 228; Todd, *Christian Humanism*, 147, 155; Nicholas Bacon, *The Recreations of His Age* (Oxford: Clarendon Press, 1919), 5–8, in Internet Archive.

127 Lisa Jardine and Alan Stewart, *Hostage to Fortune: The Troubled Life of Francis Bacon* (New York: Hill and Wang, 1999), 30, 32, 34, 204, 515; Peter Harrison, *The Fall of Man and the Foundations of Science* (Cambridge: Cambridge University Press, 2007), 172; H. W. Saunders, ed., *The Official Papers of Sir Nathaniel Bacon of Stiffkey, Norfolk, as Justice of the Peace, 1580–1620* (London: Royal Historical Society, 1915), xl, 195, in Internet Archive; Paul S. Seaver, *The Puritan Lectureships: The Politics of Religious Dissent, 1560–1662* (Stanford, CA: Stanford University Press, 1970), 47, 322–23; Rogers, *Commentary vpon...Iudges*, 190.

128 Shagan, *Rule of Moderation*, 220–21; H. R. French, *The Middle Sort of People in Provincial England, 1600–1750* (Oxford: Oxford University Press, 2007), 1–6. In a brilliant essay, Richard M. Smith undermined such "Marxisant" views by attacking the myth of the "closed corporate community" during the English Middle Ages: Smith, "'Modernization' and the Corporate Medieval Village Community in England: Some Sceptical Reflections," in *Explorations in Historical Geography*, ed. Alan R. H. Baker (Cambridge: Cambridge University Press, 1984), 160, 149.

129 David Underdown, *Revel, Riot, and Rebellion: Popular Politics and Culture in England, 1603–1660* (Oxford: Oxford University Press, 1987), 28; Wrightson, *English Society*, 24, 148.

130 H. R. French, "Chief Inhabitants and Their Areas of Influence: Local Ruling Groups in Essex and Suffolk Parishes 1630–1720" (PhD diss., Cambridge University, 1993), 18, 37, 40, 131–32, 136–38; "Brief Declaration" in *Seventeenth Century Economic Documents*, ed. Thirsk and Cooper, 226.

131 Todd, *Christian Humanism*, 8.

132 "Touching the New Draperies in Essex and Suffolk and Norfolk, 19 December 1622," in *Seventeenth-Century Economic Documents*, ed. Thirsk and Cooper, 23–24.

133 Sharp, *In Contempt of All Authority*, 25; Justices of the Peace of Essex to the Justices of the Peace of Suffolk, January 9, 1622/23, Add. Mss. 39245, f. 70, British Library, London.

134 "A Proclamation for Relief of the Poor, and Remedying the High Prices of Corne," December 22, 1622, in *Foedera, Conventiones, Literae*, 2nd ed., v. 17 (London: J. Tonson, 1727–28), 428–29; Paul Slack, "Books of Orders: The Making of English Social Policy, 1577–1631," *Transactions of the Royal Historical Society* 30 (1980): 3; Braddick, *State Formation*, 119; Bohstedt, *Politics of Provisions*, 69–70.

135 Sir William Pelham to Sir Edward Conway, April 21, 1623, in *Seventeenth-Century Economic Documents*, ed. Thirsk and Cooper, 24–25.

136 Thomas Taylor Lewis, ed., *Letters of the Lady Brilliana Harley* (London: Camden Society, 1854), vii, xii, xv, 107 [quote].

137 Lewis, *Letters of...Brilliana Harley*, 161, 261; Holmes, *Seventeenth-Century Lincolnshire*, 76, 147, 151, 179; *History of Parliament Online*, s.v. "Pelham, George (1635–86), of Gray's Inn" by Paula Watson, accessed July 20, 2020. This very helpful resource reprints articles from the *History of Parliament* series commissioned by the History of Parliament Trust and published by various publishers beginning in 1964.

138 Winthrop, *Journal*, 367; *Winthrop Papers*, 2:315n4; Robert Charles Anderson, *The Great Migration Begins: Immigrants to New England, 1620–1633*, 3 vols. (Boston, MA: New England Historic Genealogical Society, 1995), 3:1417–19; Robert Charles Anderson, *The Great Migration: Immigrants to New England, 1634–1635*, 7 vols. (Boston, MA: New England Historic Genealogical Society, 1999–2011), 5:421; Frances Rose-Troup, *The Massachusetts Bay Company and Its Predecessors* (New York: Grafton Press, 1930); 150–51; *Oxford Dictionary of National Biography Online*, s.v. "Pelham, Herbert" by Robert Charles Anderson, accessed January 8, 2014; Frederick Lewis Weis, *Ancestral Roots of Certain American Colonists Who Came to America before 1700*, 8th ed., ed. William R. Beall and Kaleen E. Beall (Baltimore, MD: Genealogical Publishing Company, 2004), 4; Sidney Lee, ed., *Dictionary of National Biography* 44 (New York: Macmillan, 1895), s.v. "Pelham, Herbert," 248, in Google Books; Joseph Lemuel Chester, "Herbert Pelham, His Ancestors and Descendants," *New England Historical and Genealogical Register* 33 (July 1879): 285–95; McDermott, "Body of Liberties," 183–84, 198–200.

139 Slack, "Books of Orders," 1–3, 5, 13 [quote]; Sharp, *In Contempt of All Authority*, 26.

140 Jeffery R. Hankins, "Crown, County, and Corporation in Early Seventeenth-Century Essex," *Sixteenth Century Journal* 38, no. 1 (Spring 2007): 45; Hindle, *State and Social Change*, 150–51; Braddick, *State Formation*, 121; T. S. Cogswell, ed., "Reasons agst a General Sending of Corne to ye Marketts in ye Champion parte of Norfolke," *Norfolk Archaeology* 20, no. 1 (1917), 18, in Archaeology Data Service.

141 "Letters of the Council to the Deputy Lieutenant and Justices of the Peace in the County of Essex," May 5, 1629, and "Justices of the Peace from Braintree to the Lords of the Council," in *Seventeenth-Century Economic Documents*, ed. Thirsk and Cooper, 227–28.

142 "The Petition of the Weavers to the Justices of Peace at their Quarter Sessions," "Order of Sessions touching Weavers, 1 October 1629," "Justices of Assizes to Sir Thomas Wyseman, etc., 20 November 1629," "A Copy of a Letter from the Justices concerning the Weavers, 2nd December 1629," in *Seventeenth-Century Economic Documents*, ed. Thirsk and Cooper, 228–32.

143 *History of Parliament Online*, s.v. "Maynard, Sir William (1586–1640), of Easton Lodge, Little Easton, Essex" by Paul Hunneyball, accessed July 17, 2020; John Fielding, "Arminianism in the Localities: Peterborough Diocese 1603–1642," in *The Early Stuart Church, 1603–1642*, ed. Kenneth Fincham (Basingstoke, UK: Macmillan Press, 1993), 106; Jeffery R. Hankins, "Papists, Power, and Puritans: Catholic Officeholding and the Rise of the 'Puritan Faction' in Early Seventeenth-Century Essex," *Catholic Historical Review* 95, no. 4 (October 2009): 704, 706, 712; Hunt, *Puritan Moment*, 210–212; Thomas Birch, ed., *The Court and Times of Charles I*, vol. 1 (London: Henry Colburn, 1849), 323, 329, 333, in Internet Archive; Quintrell, "Government of the County of Essex," 33–34; *History of Parliament Online*, s.v. "Grimston, Sir Harbottle, 1st Bt. (c. 1578–1648), of Bradfield Hall, Essex" by Andrew Thrush, accessed July 17, 2020.

144 *History of Parliament Online*, s.v. "Deane, Sir John (1583–1626), of Dynes Hall, Great Maplestead, Essex" by Andrew Thrush, accessed July 17, 2020; "A Letter to the High Sheriffe and Deputy Lieutenantes of the county of Essex," December 20, 1622, in *Acts of the Privy Council of England, 1621–1623* (London: His Majesty's Stationery Office, 1932), 371–72, in HathiTrust Digital Library; Robert C. Winthrop, *Evidences of the Winthrops of Groton* (Boston, MA: privately printed, 1894–96), 150–51, 154; Bremer, *John Winthrop*, 112–14.

145 "Justices of the Peace for the hundred of Lexden and half hundreds...to Sir Thomas Bendishe, Sheriff," December 21, 1630, in Gale Cengage State Papers Online; Peile,

Biographical Register of Christ's College, 426; Browne Willis, *Notitia Parliamentaria* (London: for the author, 1750), 259–61, 272–74, in Google Books; Christopher Durston, *Cromwell's Major-Generals: Godly Government during the English Revolution* (Manchester, UK: Manchester University Press, 2001), 78–79.
146 Sir Thomas Barrington to Secretary Dorchester, December 21, 1630, in Gale Cengage State Papers Online.
147 Justices of the Peace for Essex to the Council, April 19, 1631, in Gale Cengage State Papers Online; *History of Parliament Online*, s.v. "Mildmay, Sir Henry (c. 1594–1668), of Wanstead, Essex and Twyford, Hants." by Andrew Thrush, accessed July 17, 2020; *History of Parliament Online*, s.v. "Cheke, Sir Thomas (1570–1659), of St. Martin-in-the-Fields, Westminster and Pyrgo, Havering, Essex" by Andrew Thrush, accessed July 17, 2020; *History of Parliament Online*, s.v. "Masham, Sir William, 1st Bt. (1591–1646), of Otes, High Laver, Essex" by Andrew Thrush, accessed July 17, 2020; Bremer, *John Winthrop*, 72; Winthrop, *Evidences of the Winthrops*, 47; Hunt, *Puritan Moment*, 167, 187, 249; Searle, *Barrington Family Letters*, 77, 91, 237, and Table 3. The document also bears the signature of Sir John Tyrell, who has been described as "equally hostile to Popery and puritanism" (*History of Parliament Online*, s.v. "Tyrell, Sir John (1597–1676), of Heron, East Horndon, Essex" by Gillian Hampson, accessed July 17, 2020) as well as the names of three men about whom I have been unable to uncover any information: Henry Gent, William Luckyn and one illegible signature.
148 Sharp, *In Contempt of All Authority*, 55.
149 Slack, "Books of Orders," 16.
150 Keith Wrightson and David Levine, *Poverty and Piety in an English Village: Terling, 1525–1700* (New York: Academic Press, 1979), 12, 17, 140 [quote], 143–45, 149, 159. On confessionalization, see especially R. Po-chia Hsia, *Social Discipline in the Reformation: Central Europe 1550–1750* (London: Routledge, 1989); Philip S. Gorski, *The Disciplinary Revolution: Calvinism and the Rise of the Early Modern State* (Chicago: University of Chicago Press, 2003); Heinz Schilling, "Confessional Europe," in *Handbook of European History 1400–1600: Late Middle Ages, Renaissance and Reformation*, vol. 2, ed. Thomas A Brady Jr., Heiko A. Oberman, and James D. Tracy (Leiden: E. J. Brill, 1995), 641–82.
151 Martin Ingram, "Religion, Communities and Moral Discipline in Late Sixteenth- and Early Seventeenth-Century England: Case Studies," in *Religion and Society in Early Modern Europe, 1500–1800*, ed. Kaspar von Greyerz (London: George Allen & Unwin, 1984), 182–83, 187–89.
152 Margaret Spufford, "Puritanism and Social Control?," in *Order and Disorder in Early Modern England*, ed. Anthony Fletcher and John Stevenson (Cambridge: Cambridge University Press, 1985), 43–44.
153 Samuel Collins to Arthur Duck, May 20, 1629, in Gale Cengage State Papers Online; John Rogers, *A Godly & Fruitful Exposition Upon all the First Epistle of Peter* (London: by John Field, 1650), 485–86, in Early English Books Online.
154 Hunt, *Puritan Moment*, 275; Pennie, "Evolution of Puritan Mentality," 95.
155 "Dr. Henry Sampson's Day-Books," *The Christian Reformer; or, Unitarian Magazine and Review*, n.s., 18, no. 2018 (April 1862), 240, in Google Books; Emmanuel Downing to John Winthrop, March 6, 1636/37, in *Winthrop Papers* 3:370.
156 William Prynne, *Canterburies Doome* (London: by John Macock for Michael Spark, 1646), 361, in Early English Books Online.
157 Shipps, "Lay Patronage," 257; Frank Grace, "'Schismaticall and Factious Humours': Opposition in Ipswich to Laudian Church Government in the 1630s," in *Religious Dissent in East Anglia III: Proceedings of the Third Symposium*, ed. David Chadd (Norwich: Centre of East Anglian Studies, University of East Anglia, 1996), 108.
158 Grace, "Schismaticall," 106, 99, 100, 108, 101 [quote]; Shipps, "Lay Patronage," 259–60, 262–63, 260n50, 265–66; Christopher Wren, *Parentalia: or, Memoirs of the Family of the Wrens*

(London: for T. Osborn and R. Dodsley, 1750), 100, in Eighteenth Century Collections Online; Bremer, *Puritans and Puritanism*, s.v. "Ward, Samuel (of Ipswich)" by John Craig, 1:266; Patrick Collinson, *The Religion of Protestants: The Church in English Society 1559–1625* (Oxford: Clarendon Press, 1982), 178.

159 Karen O. Kupperman, *Providence Island, 1630–1641: The Other Puritan Colony* (Cambridge: Cambridge University Press, 1993), 4.

Chapter Two The Puritan Ideology of Mobility

1 Steve Hindle, "Hierarchy and Community in the Elizabethan Parish: The Swallowfield Articles of 1596," *Historical Journal* 42, no. 3 (September 1999): 838.
2 Sidney and Beatrice Webb, *English Local Government from the Revolution to the Municipal Corporations Act*, vol. 1: *The Parish and the County* (London: Longmans, Green, 1906), in Internet Archive. Other responsibilities, such as the surveying of local roads and providing weapons for the militia, were delegated to the parish as well beginning in the mid-1500s; see Hindle, *State and Social Change*, 216.
3 Hindle, "Hierarchy and Community," 848–51.
4 Hindle, *State and Social Change*, 207–8; Webb, *English Local Government* vol. 1, 217; Hindle, "Hierarchy and Community," 837.
5 Rosser also documents the "broad range of representation" of diverse trades among the chief pledges of medieval Westminster. Gervase Rosser, *Medieval Westminster* (Oxford: Clarendon Press, 1989), 236, 235.
6 Henry S. Turner, *The Corporate Commonwealth: Pluralism and Political Fictions in England, 1516–1651* (Chicago: University of Chicago Press, 2016), xii; see also Pierre Michaud-Quantin, *Universitas: Expressions du Mouvement Communitaire dans le Moyen-age Latin* (Paris: Librarie Philosophique J. Vrin, 1970).
7 Kantorowicz, *King's Two Bodies*; Turner, *Corporate Commonwealth*, 11.
8 Michaud-Quantin, *Universitas*; Kenneth Pennington, *The Prince and the Law, 1200–1600* (Berkeley: University of California Press, 1993); Gaines Post, *Studies in Medieval Legal Thought: Public Law and the State, 1100–1322* (Princeton, NJ: Princeton University Press, 1964); Gianluca Raccagni, "Il Diritto Publico, la Pace di Costanza e i Libri Iurium dei Comuni," *Gli Inizi del Diritto Publico*, 2: *Da Federico I a Federico II* (Bologna: Il Mulino, 2008): 309–39. I am indebted to Prof. Damian Smith for assistance with the latter text. See also my unpublished 2009 paper "The Lombard League, the Glossators, and the Transformation of Roman Private Law into Public Rights" on Academia.edu.
9 John Najemy, "Guild Republicanism in Trecento Florence: The Successes and Ultimate Failure of Corporate Politics," *American Historical Review* 84, no. 1 (February 1979): 53–71. Gervase Rosser offers several English examples of "the guild as surrogate town council" in Rosser, *Medieval Westminster*, 289. Chris Wickham unaccountably and totally ignores the role of religious guilds and confraternities in the formation of urban communes, but makes the important point that Pisa's "wide areas of common land" helped promote communal cooperation, since "common land and collective organisation go together": Wickham, *Sleepwalking into a New World: The Emergence of Italian City Communes in the Twelfth Century* (Princeton, NJ: Princeton University Press, 2015), 96.
10 Hwa-Yong Lee, *Political Representation in the Later Middle Ages: Marsilius in Context* (New York: Peter Lang, 2008), 40–41; on the *maior et sanior pars*, see also Brian Tierney, *The Idea of Natural Rights* (Atlanta, GA: Scholars Press, 1997), 23.
11 For a more detailed treatment of this issue, see my unpublished 2009 paper "Special Pleading: The Suppression of 'Romanism' in English Legal History" on Academia.edu.
12 "Vt per multa corpora in uno loco congregata sequatur et vnica voluntas et vna eorumdem in relacione vnius ad alterum firma et sincera dilectio," my trans. "Statuta Gilde," in *The Acts of*

the Parliament of Scotland, vol. I (Edinburgh: By command of H. M. Queen Victoria, 1844), 431 [quote], 436, in HathiTrust Digital Library.

13 John Scott, *Berwick-upon-Tweed: The History of the Town and Guild* (London: Elliot Stock, 1888), 246, 256, 259.

14 Stella Kramer, "The English Craft Gilds and the Government" (PhD diss., Columbia University, 1905), 14–18, 28, 31–32, 36–37, in Internet Archive; Gervase Rosser, "Crafts, Guilds and the Negotiation of Work in the Medieval Town," *Past & Present* 154 (February 1997): 5–7, 9–11, 13, 29–30. On the close links between craft gilds and borough governments, see also Ian Anders Gadd and Patrick Wallis, "Reaching beyond the City Wall: London Guilds and National Regulation, 1500–1700," in *Guilds, Innovation, and the European Economy, 1400–1800*, ed. S. R. Epstein and Maarten Prak (Cambridge: Cambridge University Press, 2008): 292.

15 Samuel L. Thomas, *Creating Communities in Restoration England: Parish and Congregation in Oliver Heywood's Halifax* (Leiden, the Netherlands: Brill, 2012), 4–5; Turner, *Corporate Commonwealth*, xiii–xiv [quote], 25.

16 David Thomas Konig, *Law and Society in Puritan Massachusetts: Essex County, 1629–1692* (Chapel Hill: University of North Carolina Press, 1978), 22, 25.

17 William Sheppard, *Of Corporations, Fraternities, and Guilds* (London: for H. Twyford, T. Dring, and J. Place, 1659), 9, 12 [quote], in Early English Books Online.

18 J. Malet Lambert, *Two Thousand Years of Gild Life* (Hull, UK: A. Brown & Sons, 1891), 240–41, in Internet Archive; similar language was used in York—see D. M. Palliser, "The Trade Gilds of Tudor York," in *Crisis and Order in English Towns 1500–1700*, ed. Peter Clark and Paul Slack (London: Routledge, 2007), 88.

19 Sheppard, *Of Corporations*, 7–8; Nancy L. Matthews, *William Sheppard, Cromwell's Law Reformer* (Cambridge: Cambridge University Press, 1984), 4, 8, 16–17, 19; on the self-creation of associations in England, see Turner, *Corporate Commonwealth*, 21.

20 See Shaw Livermore, *Early American Land Companies: Their Influence on Corporate Development* (1939; repr., New York: Octagon Books, 1966), ix–x, xviii–xix, 12–15.

21 Ward, *Sermon Preached*, 9.

22 Eamon Duffy, *The Stripping of the Altars: Traditional Religion in England c.1400–c.1580*, 2nd ed. (New Haven, CT: Yale University Press, 2005). Augustine Thompson explored this theme for Italy in *Cities of God: The Religion of the Italian Communes, 1125–1325* (University Park, PA: Pennsylvania State University Press, 2005).

23 Bacon, *Annalls of Ipswche*, 102; M. Lyle Spencer, *Corpus Christi Pageants in England* (New York: Baker & Taylor, 1911), 11; Geoffrey Martin, "The Governance of Ipswich: From Its Origins to c. 1550," in *Ipswich Borough Archives 1255–1835: A Catalogue*, ed. David Allen (Woodbridge, UK: Boydell Press, 2000), xxv.

24 Mervyn James, "Ritual, Drama and Social Body in the Late Medieval English Town," *Past & Present* 98 (February 1983): 3–29; Natalie Zemon Davis, "The Sacred and the Body Social in Sixteenth-Century Lyon," *Past & Present* 90 (February 1981): 40–70; Turner, *Corporate Commonwealth*, xx, 24; David J. F. Crouch, "Piety, Fraternity and Power: Religious Gilds in Late Medieval Yorkshire 1389–1547" (PhD diss., University of York, 1995), 227 [quote], 167–68, 225–26, 285, in ETHOS; Gail McMurray Gibson, "Bury St. Edmunds, Lydgate, and the N-Town Cycle," *Speculum* 56, no. 1 (January 1981): 60–61; Ben R. McRee, "Traditional Religion," in *A Companion to Tudor Britain*, ed. Robert Tittler and Norman L. Jones (Malden, MA: Blackwell, 2004), 216. Sarah Beckwith, while highly critical of James's article, did not dispute his fundamental thesis but objected that in James's view the ideology of Corpus Christi was imposed entirely from above, leaving no space for agency or contestation. Sarah Beckwith, "Ritual, Theater, and Social Space in the York Corpus Christi Cycle," in *Bodies and Disciplines: Intersections of Literature and History in Fifteenth-Century England*, ed. Barbara A. Hanawalt and David Wallace (Minneapolis: University of Minnesota Press, 1996), 63–86.

25 Gervase Rosser, "Going to the Fraternity Feast," *Journal of British Studies* 33, no. 4 (October 1994): 433–35.
26 Muriel C. McClendon, "'Against God's Word': Government, Religion and the Crisis of Authority in Early Reformation Norwich," *Sixteenth Century Journal* 25, no. 2 (Summer 1994): 355; Muriel C. McClendon, *The Quiet Reformation: Magistrates and the Emergence of Protestantism in Tudor Norwich* (Stanford, CA: Stanford University Press, 1999), 118–19; Robert H. Skaife, *The Register of the Guild of Corpus Christi in the City of York* (Edinburgh: Surtees Society, 1872), xii–xiv, 317–20; Alan Kreider, *English Chantries: The Road to Dissolution* (Cambridge, MA: Harvard University Press, 1979), 158–59, 192–95; Gibson, "Bury St. Edmunds," 59, 66. The Candlemas Guild in Bury rose to prominence in part because it secured control of lands left by a wealthy benefactor for the use of the town; after the confiscation of Abbey properties and the dissolution of the religious guilds, Bury's Guildhall was surrendered by Queen Elizabeth to a group of feoffees including a number of former guild members and Sir Nicholas Bacon, Francis Bacon's father. This group was the de facto town government prior to incorporation. See Margaret Statham, "The Guildhall, Bury St. Edmunds," *Proceedings of the Suffolk Institute of Archaeology* 31, part 2 (1968): 138–42, 145–46; Margaret Statham, "Introduction" to Margaret Statham, ed., *Accounts of the Feoffees of the Town Lands of Bury St Edmunds, 1569–1622* (Woodbridge, UK: Boydell Press, 2003), xviii–xxxii, xliii–xlvi.
27 Arie van Steensel, "Identifying Contextual Factors: Religious Confraternities in Norwich and Leiden, c. 1300–1550," in *Space, Place, and Motion: Locating Confraternities in the Late Medieval and Early Modern City*, ed. Diana Bullen Presciutti (Leiden: Brill, 2017), 51–52; McClendon, "'Against God's Word,'" 359, 363–64; McClendon, *Quiet Reformation*, 101–3, 121–23, 200; Ben R. McRee, "The Mayor and the Saint: Remaking Norwich's Gild of St. George, 1548–1549," *Huntington Library Quarterly* 79, no. 1 (Spring 2016): 1–20.
28 Charles Phythian-Adams, "Ceremony and the Citizen: The Communal Year at Coventry 1450–1550," in *The Early Modern Town: A Reader*, ed. Peter Clark (New York: Longman, 1976), 106–28; Phythian-Adams, *Desolation of a City: Coventry and the Urban Crisis of the Late Middle Ages* (Cambridge: Cambridge University Press, 1979); Craig Muldrew, "The Culture of Reconciliation: Community and the Settlement of Economic Disputes in Early Modern England," *Historical Journal* 39, no. 4 (December 1996): 915–42; Marjorie Keniston McIntosh, *Controlling Misbehavior in England, 1370–1600* (Cambridge: Cambridge University Press, 1998), 189–90; Jürgen Habermas, "The Public Sphere: An Encyclopedia Article," *New German Critique*, no. 3 (Autumn 1974): 49–55; Michael Berlin, "Guilds in Decline? London Livery Companies and the Rise of a Liberal Economy, 1600–1800," in *Guilds, Innovation, and the European Economy*, ed. Epstein and Prak, 316, 321.
29 Philip Knowles, "Continuity and Change in Urban Culture: A Case Study of Two Provincial Towns, Chester and Coventry c. 1600–c. 1750" (PhD diss., University of Leicester, 2001), in ETHOS; Geoff Eley, "Nations, Publics, and Political Culture: Placing Habermas in the Nineteenth Century," in *Habermas and the Public Sphere*, ed. Craig J. Calhoun (Boston, MA: MIT Press, 1992), 301–6, 325–26; Palliser, "Trade Gilds," 86, 111–12; Phil Withington, "Public Discourse, Corporate Citizenship, and State Formation in Early Modern England," *American Historical Review* 112, no. 4 (October 2007): 1016–38; Gadd and Wallis, "Reaching beyond the City Wall," 290; Berlin, "Guilds in Decline," 324–26.
30 Avril Leach, "Being One Body: Everyday Institutional Culture in Canterbury and Maidstone Corporations, 1600–1660" (PhD diss., University of Kent, 2019), 118–20, in ETHOS; Hankins, "Crown, County, and Corporation," 34.
31 Phil Withington, "Company and Sociability in Early Modern England," *Social History* 32, no. 3 (August 2007): 291–307.
32 Palliser, "Trade Gilds," 89; F. J. Fisher, "Some Experiments in Company Organization in the Early Seventeenth Century," *Economic History Review* 4, no. 2 (April 1933): 191–94; Underdown,

Fire from Heaven, 15–16; see also Robert Tittler, "The End of the Middle Ages in the English Country Town," *Sixteenth Century Journal* 18, no. 4 (Winter 1987): 479.

33 Ben R. McRee, "Religious Gilds and Regulation of Behavior in Late Medieval Towns," in *People, Politics and Community in the Later Middle Ages*, ed. Joel Rosenthal and Colin Richmond (New York: St. Martin's Press, 1987), 108–22; Marjorie K. McIntosh, "Local Change and Community Control in England, 1465–1500," *Huntington Library Quarterly* 49, no. 3 (Summer 1986): 228–33; McIntosh, *Controlling Misbehavior in England*, 2–3, 7, 10, 12, 57–58, 87–89, 93–95, 204–8. In the latter work, McIntosh suggests that although Puritans did not cause the early modern reformation of manners, strictly speaking, their exuberant zeal for it proved disruptive to local communities. However, I would question whether her truly extraordinary dataset really supports this point of view.

34 Isabel M. Calder, "A Seventeenth Century Attempt to Purify the Anglican Church," *American Historical Review* 53, no. 4 (July 1948): 760–75; Seaver, *Puritan Lectureships*, 88, 236–37; French, "Chief Inhabitants," 140, 165–66. A group similar to the Feoffees for Impropriations operated in Norfolk, calling itself the "trustees for the religion in Norwich and Norfolk"; see Clive Holmes, *The Eastern Association in the English Civil War* (Cambridge: Cambridge University Press, 1974), 17.

35 Marjorie Keniston McIntosh, *Poor Relief and Community in Hadleigh, Suffolk, 1547–1600* (Hatfield, UK: University of Hertfordshire Press, 2013), 1, 5–6, 9, 11–12, 36 [quote], 37, 50, 57, 130–31, 141, 147.

36 Sheppard, *Of Corporations*, 13–15.

37 Emmison, *Early Essex Town Meetings*, v–vi, viii, 1, 4, 16; Philip Morant, *The History and Antiquities of the County of Essex*, vol. 2 (London: for T. Osborne, 1768), 398–99; Webb and Webb, *English Local Government* 1:222–23; French, "Chief Inhabitants," 150–51.

38 Churchwardens' account book for Clare, FL501/5/1/1, Suffolk Record Office, Bury St. Edmunds branch, UK; Clare glebe terrier, 1794, FL501/5/20, Suffolk Record Office, Bury St. Edmunds branch, UK; Gladys A. Thornton, *A History of Clare, Suffolk* (Cambridge: W. Heffer & Sons, 1928), 49, 51, 60–61, 62 [quote], 66–67, 121–22, 193–96, 202; Bailey, *Medieval Suffolk*, 269; Alan Everitt, *Suffolk and the Great Rebellion 1640–1660* (Ipswich, UK: Suffolk Records Society, 1960), 18–19; Sir Nathaniel Barnardiston to John Winthrop Jr., April 5, 1636, *Winthrop Papers* 3:245; Shipps, "Lay Patronage," 72–73, 96; Waters, *Genealogical Gleanings*, 2:887; *Oxford Dictionary of National Biography Online*, s.v. "Fairclough, Samuel" by Barbara Donagan, accessed February 19, 2013; Samuel Clark, *The Lives of Sundry Eminent Persons in This Later Age* (London: for Thomas Simmons, 1683), part 1, 153–54, in Google Books; McIntosh, *Poor Relief and Community*, 137.

39 Peter Clark and Paul Slack, *English Towns in Transition, 1500–1700* (Oxford: Oxford University Press, 1976), 25, 29; Martin, "Governance of Ipswich," in Allen, *Ipswich Borough Archives*, xxviii; Frank Grace, "The Governance of Ipswich c. 1550–1835," in Allen, *Ipswich Borough Archives*, xxix–xxx; Michael Reed, "Economic Structure and Change in Seventeenth-Century Ipswich," in *Country Towns in Pre-Industrial England*, ed. Peter Clark (Leicester, UK: Leicester University Press, 1981), 89, 127–28; Beier, *Masterless Men*, 164; Braddick, *State Formation*, 112.

40 Rosser, *Medieval Westminster*, 281.

41 Paul D. Halliday, *Dismembering the Body Politic: Partisan Politics in England's Towns, 1650–1730* (Cambridge: Cambridge University Press, 1998), 5 [quote], 39; Sheppard, "To His Dear Country-men," in *Of Corporations*, n.p.

42 Nathaniel Ward, "Epistle Dedicatory" and "To My Loving Brother Mr. Samuel Ward," in Ward, *Iethro's Iustice*, [1–4], 71–72, in Early English Books Online; *Oxford Dictionary of National Biography Online*, s.v. "Bacon, Sir Francis" by Markku Peltonen, accessed May 7, 2013.

43 Ward, *Iethro's Iustice*, 53; William Rawley, "Life of the Right Honourable Francis Bacon, Baron of Verulam," in *The Works of Francis Bacon*, vol. I, ed. James Spedding, Robert Leslie Ellis and Douglas Denon Heath (London: Longman, 1858), 4.

44 Francis Bacon, *Advancement of Learning, Novum Organum, New Atlantis* (Chicago, IL: Encyclopaedia Britannica, 1952), 12, 11, 14, 13, 4, 30.
45 Ward, *Iethro's Iustice*, 63; Webster, *Great Instauration*.
46 Harrison, *Fall of Man*, 119; Statham, "Introduction" to *Accounts of the Feoffees*, xxix, xliii.
47 Bacon, *Advancement of Learning, Novum Organum, New Atlantis*, 203, 206.
48 Ward, *Iethro's Iustice*, 4. The classic work on *prisca theologia* is D. P. Walker, *The Ancient Theology: Studies in Christian Platonism from the Fifteenth to the Eighteenth Century* (Ithaca, NY: Cornell University Press, 1972); see also Jean Seznec, *The Survival of the Pagan Gods: The Mythological Tradition and Its Place in Renaissance Humanism and Art* (New York: Pantheon, 1953) and Harrison, *Fall of Man*. For a fuller treatment than I have space for here, see my unpublished paper on Academia.edu, "Edwards and the Noachide Covenant: A Calvinist Theological Revolution," 1–6.
49 Harrison, *Fall of Man*, 188–90.
50 John Amos Comenius, *The Way of Light*, trans. E. T. Campagnac (Liverpool, UK: The University Press, 1938), 141; Ward, *Simple Cobler*, 10. One of Ward's successors in the Ipswich ministry, John Norton, would later support Dury's irenical efforts in "A Copy of the Letter … to Mr. John Dury about His Pacification," in John Norton, *Three Choice and Profitable Sermons upon Severall Texts of Scripture…* (Cambridge, MA: S. G. and M. I. for Hezekiah Usher, 1664), 1–12, in Early English Books Online.
51 Harrison, *Fall of Man*, 186; Donald R. Dickson, *The Tessera of Antilia: Utopian Brotherhoods & Secret Societies in the Early Seventeenth Century* (Leiden: Brill, 1998), 118, 114–15, 124–25; Michal Jan Rozbicki, "Between East-Central Europe and Britain: Reformation and Science as Vehicles of Intellectual Communication in the Mid-Seventeenth Century," *East European Quarterly* 30 (Winter 1996), 402–3.
52 "de propagando ad gentes orbis evangelio occasione tum in Anglia Nova feliciter factae sementis." Robert Fitzgibbon Young, *Comenius in England* (New York: Arno Press, 1971), 60; see my unpublished paper "God's Instruments: Praying Indians and Transatlantic Scholarship, 1646–1698" and my unpublished conference presentation "The New England Praying Indians As Participants in Transatlantic Religious and Scientific Dialogue" on academia.edu.
53 Samuel Hartlib to John Winthrop Jr., March 16, 1660, in G. H. Turnbull, ed. "Some Correspondence of John Winthrop, Jr., and Samuel Hartlib," *Proceedings of the Massachusetts Historical Society*, 3rd series, 72 (October 1957–December 1960), 36–40, 40–49. In 1661, Hartlib wrote to Winthrop about Antilia, reporting that "the designed Society, wch I sent you, is not put in practise, ye Principal Leaders judging Europe no ways worthy of it. They intend to erect the said foundation in some other part of the World." Samuel Hartlib to John Winthrop Jr., September 3, 1661, in Robert C. Winthrop, ed. *Correspondence of Hartlib, Haak, Oldenburg, and Others of the Founders of the Royal Society, with Governor Winthrop of Connecticut, 1661–1672* (Boston, MA: John Wilson and Son, 1878), in Google Books. On John Winthrop Jr. and colonial alchemy, see Walter W. Woodward, *Prospero's America: John Winthrop, Jr., Alchemy, and the Creation of New England Culture, 1606–1676* (Chapel Hill: University of North Carolina Press, 2010); William R. Newman, *Gehennical Fire: The Lives of George Starkey, an American Alchemist in the Scientific Revolution* (Cambridge, MA: Harvard University Press, 1994); William R. Newman and Lawrence M. Principe, *Alchemy Tried in the Fire: Starkey, Boyle, and the Fate of Helmontian Chemistry* (Chicago: University of Chicago Press, 2002).
54 Zachary McLeod Hutchins, "Building Bensalem at Massachusetts Bay: Francis Bacon and the Wisdom of Eden in Early Modern England," *New England Quarterly* 83, no. 4 (December 2010): 581–82, 584–87, 588 [quote]; Robert Cushman, "Reasons & considerations touching the lawfulnesse of remouing out of *England* into the parts of *America*," in *A Relation or Iournall of the Beginning and Proceedings of the English Plantation setled at Plimoth …* (London: for Iohn Bellamie, 1622), 67; John Cotton, *Gods Promise to His Plantations* (London: by William Jones for John Bellamy, 1634), 8.

55 Anne Bradstreet, *The Works of Anne Bradstreet*, ed. Jeannine Hensley (Cambridge, MA: Harvard University Press, 2010), 235–37; Zachary Hutchins, "The Wisdom of Anne Bradstreet: Eschewing Eve and Emulating Elizabeth," *Modern Language Studies* 40, no. 1 (Summer 2010): 50–52.
56 Bradstreet, *Works*, 24; Adrienne Rich, "Anne Bradstreet and Her Poetry," in Bradstreet, *Works*, xii–xiii; Harrison, *Fall of Man*, 113; William Andrews Pew, "The Worshipful Simon Bradstreet, Governor of Massachusetts," *Historical Collections of the Essex Institute*, 64, no. 4 (October 1928): 306; Charlotte Gordon, *Mistress Bradstreet: The Untold Life of America's First Poet* (New York: Little, Brown, 2005), 226–29; Elizabeth Wade White, *Anne Bradstreet: "The Tenth Muse"* (New York: Oxford University Press, 1971), 130–31.
57 Ward, *Iethro's Iustice*, 1.
58 Michael P. Clark, ed., *The Eliot Tracts* (Westport, CT: Praeger, 2003), 226–27; Richard W. Cogley, *John Eliot's Mission to the Indians before King Philip's War* (Cambridge, MA: Harvard University Press, 1999), 80.
59 Morris, *Frankpledge System*, 26–27.
60 Emmison, *Early Essex Town Meetings*, 14, 67, 68; see also McIntosh, *Poor Relief and Community*, 5. Gervase Rosser explicitly links the emergence of "headboroughs" to the earlier "chief pledges" appointed as part of the frankpledge system in Rosser, *Medieval Westminster*, 233–34.
61 Nathaniel B. Shurtleff, ed., *Records of the Governor and Company of the Massachusetts Bay in New England*, 5 vols. in 6 (Boston: W. White, 1853–1854), 5:154–55, in Internet Archive; see also 5:448, 5:452.
62 Ward, *Iethro's Iustice*, 54–55, 53–54, 56.
63 On popular participation in legal processes, see John Walter, "Grain Riots and Popular Attitudes to the Law," in *An Ungovernable People: The English and Their Law in the Seventeenth and Eighteenth Centuries*, ed. John Brewer and John Styles (New Brunswick, NJ: Rutgers University Press, 1980), 81; Andy Wood, *Riot, Rebellion and Popular Politics in Early Modern England* (New York: Palgrave, 2002), 30; Richard Cust and Peter G. Lake, "Sir Richard Grosvenor and the Rhetoric of Magistracy," *Bulletin of the Institute of Historical Research* 54 (1981): 44–45; Alison Wall, *Power and Protest in England 1525–1640* (New York: Oxford University Press, 2000), 70; Hindle, *State and Social Change*, 12, 16, 24–25; Cynthia B. Herrup, *The Common Peace: Participation and the Criminal Law in Seventeenth-Century England* (Cambridge: Cambridge University Press, 1987), 68, 70.
64 Ward, *Iethro's Iustice*, 15, 19.
65 Ward, *Iethro's Iustice*, 10, 3, 13; Wendel, "Introduction" to Martin Bucer, *De Regno Christi*, ed. François Wendel, Martini Buceri Opera Latina, vol. 15 (Paris: Presses Universitaires de France, 1955), xviii–xxiii.
66 Nathaniel Rogers, *A Letter, Discovering the Cause*, 9.
67 Bucer, *De Regno Christi*, e.g., 207, 269, 345–46, 361, 376.
68 Bucer, *De Regno Christi*, e.g., 258, 297, 364–65.
69 Bernd Moeller, *Imperial Cities and the Reformation: Three Essays* (Philadelphia, PA: Fortress Press, 1972), 83, 89, 103, 79, 47, 64, 69, 89. On this point, see also Black, *Guilds and Civil Society*, 111–13; Thomas A. Brady, *Ruling Class, Regime and Reformation at Strasbourg, 1520–1555* (Leiden: E. J. Brill, 1978), 17.
70 Bucer, *De Regno Christi*, 267, 362, 367.
71 Bucer, *De Regno Christi*, 368, 338, 363, 382–83.
72 Bucer, *De Regno Christi*, 257, 306–7, 315.
73 Bucer, *De Regno Christi*, 240–41.
74 Winthrop, *Journal*, 126.
75 Fletcher, *Gender, Sex and Subordination*, 16, 19.
76 Ezekiel Rogers to Lady Joan Barrington, February 2, 1629/30, November 1, 1630 and July 26, 1631, in Searle, ed., *Barrington Family Letters*, 128–30 [quote], 167–68, 198–99.
77 Rogers, *Treatise of Love*, 73–74, 77, 90–91, 62.

78 Rogers, *Commentarie vpon ... Iudges*, 3, 12–14, 48 [quote], 73.
79 Rogers, *Commentarie vpon ... Iudges*, 243.
80 Rogers, *Commentarie vpon ... Iudges*, 49, 50, 212; Dane, *Declaration of Remarkable Providences*, 12.
81 Hooker, *Survey of the Summe*, I:49–50.
82 John Winthrop to Simonds d'Ewes, July 20, 1635, in *Winthrop Papers*, 3:199–200.
83 For a full account of this conflict see McDermott, "Body of Liberties."
84 Winthrop, *Journal*, 103–4.
85 Winthrop, *Journal*, 166–67.
86 "Thomas Shepard's Election Sermon, in 1638," in *Election Day Sermons: Massachusetts*, vol. 1 of *A Library of American Puritan Writings: The Seventeenth Century*, ed. Sacvan Bercovitch (New York: AMS Press, ca. 1984), 361–66.
87 Shurtleff, *Records of the Governor and Company*, 1:222.
88 Shurtleff, *Records of the Governor and Company*, 1:170.
89 John Winthrop to John Winthrop Jr., April 26, 1636, in *Winthrop Papers*, 3:255–56.
90 "John Winthrop's Summary of His Letter to Thomas Hooker," in *Winthrop Papers*, 4: 53–54; Thomas Hooker to John Winthrop, ca. December 1638, *Winthrop Papers* 4:80–82; see also Perry Miller, "Thomas Hooker and the Democracy of Early Connecticut," *New England Quarterly* 4 (1931): 663–712. The sermon notes of Henry Wolcott, a founder of Windsor, Connecticut, reveal that even in his Hartford church, Hooker remained surprisingly preoccupied with political matters. In Wolcott's rendering, Hooker told his congregation on May 31, 1638, that "the choice of public magistrates belongs unto the people by Gods own allowance," and that the people who appoint magistrates can also limit the power of magistrates, because "the foundation of authority is laid 1stly in the free consent of people." Douglas Shepard, *The Wolcott Shorthand Notebook Transcribed* (PhD diss., University of Iowa, 1957), 57, ProQuest Dissertations & Theses Global.
91 To my knowledge the first scholar to apply this term to colonial New England was Robert Blair St. George, who praised the architectural historian Anthony N. B. Garvan for having "initiated work on the politics of place in early America." St. George, *Conversing By Signs: Poetics of Implication in Colonial New England Culture* (Chapel Hill: University of North Carolina Press, 1998), 27.
92 Edward Johnson, *Wonder-Working Providence of Sions Saviour in New England* (1654; repr., Andover, MA: Warren F. Draper, 1867), 61, Internet Archive. The Woburn town covenant, adopted in 1640 at the same meeting that elected Johnson town clerk, copied Article I of Ward's Body of Liberties almost verbatim before the law code was ratified. David A. Weir, *Early New England: A Covenanted Society* (Grand Rapids, MI: William B. Eerdmans, 2005), 103; Whitmore, *Bibliographical Sketch*, 33.
93 Or sometimes Johnson spoke of the "wandering race of Jacobites" or "this wandering people." Johnson, *Wonder-Working Providence*, 46, 61, 62, 67, 113, 175, 196, 200, 216.
94 Johnson, *Wonder-Working Providence*, 2–3.
95 Building on the anthropological work of Mary Douglas, numerous scholars have documented concern for the boundaries and health of the social body in both old and New England in the early modern period; see Mary Douglas, *Natural Symbols: Explorations in Cosmology* (New York: Pantheon Books, 1970), viii–ix, 70; Mary Douglas, *Purity and Danger: An Analysis of the Concepts of Pollution and Taboo* (1966; repr., London: Routledge, 1984), 116, 122–23, 125; Margaret Healy, *Fictions of Disease in Early Modern England: Bodies, Plagues and Politics* (Basingstoke, UK: Palgrave, 2001), 3, 16, 71; Heather Miyano Kopelson, *Faithful Bodies: Performing Religion and Race in the Puritan Atlantic* (New York: New York University Press, 2014), 111–12; Martha L. Finch, *Dissenting Bodies: Corporealities in Early New England* (New York: Columbia University Press, 2010), 80, 106, 139, 143, 164–65.
96 John Winthrop, "Objections Answered: First Draft," in *Winthrop Papers*, 2:135.

97 Thomas Weld, "Preface" to John Winthrop, *Short Story of the Rise, reign, and ruine of the Antinomians, Familists & Libertines*, in David D. Hall, ed., *The Antinomian Controversy, 1636–1638: A Documentary History*, 2nd ed. (Durham, NC: Duke University Press, 1990), 201–2.
98 Thomas Shepard, "Autobiography," in Michael McGiffert, *God's Plot: Puritan Spirituality in Thomas Shepard's Cambridge*, rev. ed. (Amherst: University of Massachusetts Press, 1994), 70.
99 John Winthrop, "A Declaration in Defense of an Order of Court Made in May, 1637," in *Winthrop Papers*, 3:422–23.
100 "John Winthrop's Discourse on Arbitrary Government," in *Winthrop Papers*, 4:468, 4:483–84.
101 Edward Elmer to John Winthrop Jr., August 29, 1649, in *Winthrop Papers*, 5:361; J. Hammond Trumbull, *The Memorial History of Hartford County, Connecticut, 1633–1884*, 2 vols. (Boston, MA: Edward L. Osgood, 1886), 1:237–38, in Internet Archive; Anderson, *Great Migration Begins*, 634–38.
102 Thomas Dudley to Countess of Lincoln, March 12, 1630/31–March 28, 1631, in *Chronicles of the First Planters*, ed. Young, 329.
103 "The Company's Humble Request," April 7, 1630, in *Chronicles of the First Planters*, ed. Young, 296.
104 Shurtleff, *Records of the Governor and Company*, 1:42, 1:1:58–59, 1:63 [quote], 1:64, 1:401.
105 "Iubet igitur replere terram, non solum generatione & habitatione, sed cum primis potestate cultu & usu," my trans. John White, *The Planters Plea* (London: William Jones, 1630), 2.
106 White, *Planters Plea*, 11, 13–14, 4–5, 20–21, 35, 34.
107 White, *Planters Plea*, 81, 66.
108 Shurtleff, *Records of the Governor and Company*, 1:43, 1:64, 1:363–64, 1:387–88, 1:391, 1:399; Nathaniel Ward, *Discolliminium* (London, 1650), 50–52, in Early English Books Online.

Chapter Three Land Distribution in Colonial Ipswich

1 Sumner Chilton Powell, *Puritan Village: The Formation of a New England Town* (Middletown, CT: Wesleyan University Press, 197), 7; Kenneth Lockridge, *A New England Town, The First Hundred Years: Dedham, Massachusetts, 1636–1736* (New York: W. W. Norton, 1970), 20; T. H. Breen, "Persistent Localism: English Social Change and the Shaping of New England Institutions" and "Transfer of Culture: Chance and Design in Shaping Massachusetts Bay, 1630–1660," in *Puritans and Adventurers: Change and Persistence in Early America* (New York: Oxford University Press, 1980), 3–23 and 68–80. "America was really a kind of intellectual Australia," wrote Stephen Foster, "where ideas long extinct elsewhere lived on far beyond their allotted time, sheltered in their isolation from the cataclysms that transformed the same species on the mainland into completely new forms." Foster, *Their Solitary Way: The Puritan Social Ethic in the First Century of Settlement in New England* (New Haven, CT: Yale University Press, 1971), 162.
2 John Frederick Martin, *Profits in the Wilderness: Entrepreneurship and the Founding of New England Towns in the Seventeenth Century* (Chapel Hill: University of North Carolina Press, 1991); Stephen Innes, *Labor in a New Land: Economy and Society in Seventeenth-Century Springfield* (Princeton, NJ: Princeton University Press, 1983).
3 David Grayson Allen, *In English Ways: The Movement of Societies and the Transferral of English Local Law and Custom to Massachusetts Bay in the Seventeenth Century* (Chapel Hill: University of North Carolina Press, 1981), 121–23, 129–31.
4 William Cronon, *Changes in the Land: Indians, Colonists, and the Ecology of New England*, 2nd ed. (New York: Hill and Wang, 1983), 138, 74; Martin, *Profits*, 2; Edward T. Price, *Dividing the Land: Early American Beginnings of Our Private Property Mosaic* (Chicago: University of Chicago Press, 1995), 33; Gloria L. Main, *Peoples of a Spacious Land: Families and Cultures in Colonial New England* (Cambridge, MA: Harvard University Press, 2001), 56–57, 252n14, 266n84; Robert Friedeburg, "Social and Geographical Mobility in the Old World and New World Communities: Earls Colne, Ipswich and Springfield, 1636–1685," *Journal of Social History* 29,

no. 2 (Winter 1995): 376. In addition, Allen's work helped inform Joseph S. Wood's idiosyncratic theory that New England towns were originally composed of dispersed farmsteads and that the nucleated village form was a creation of the nineteenth century; Joseph S. Wood, "'Build, Therefore, Your Own World': The New England Village as Settlement Ideal," *Annals of the Association of American Geographers* 81, no. 1 (March 1991): 48; Joseph S. Wood, *The New England Village* (Baltimore, MD: Johns Hopkins University Press, 1997), 41.

5 Allen, *In English Ways*, 269–79.
6 Here I am following the similar line of reasoning suggested by Garrett Hardin in "The Tragedy of the Commons," *Science*, n.s., 162, no. 3859 (December 13, 1968): 1244.
7 Douglas R. McManis, *Colonial New England: A Historical Geography* (London: Oxford University Press, 1975), 28.
8 Shurtleff, *Records of the Governor and Company*, 1:103.
9 Ipswich Land and Grants and Town Meetings, 1634, FamilySearch database (Church of Jesus Christ of Latter-Day Saints), film 476736, images 4–8 [hereinafter Ipswich Land and Grants]. Note: I consulted the town records in the custody of Pam Carakatsane, Ipswich Town Clerk, but I have chosen to cite the Ipswich town records based on the digitized versions available through FamilySearch, for three reasons: first, preservation efforts in 2002 appear to have placed some of the pages of the original records out of order; second, the digitized records are far more accessible to scholars and readers; finally, the originals of some records which are available through FamilySearch, thanks to microfilming efforts by the LDS Church, seem to have disappeared.
10 Ipswich Land and Grants, image 5.
11 "Focus on Ipswich," *Great Migration Newsletter* 3 (1992): 19–20, in AmericanAncestors.org; Johnson, *Wonder-Working Providence*, 66; Harold Field Worthley, *An Inventory of the Records of the Particular (Congregational) Churches of Massachusetts Gathered 1620–1805* (Cambridge, MA: Harvard University Press, 1970), 303; Shurtleff, *Records of the Governor*, 1:136.
12 Joseph J. Muskett, *Suffolk Manorial Families*, vol. I (Exeter: William Pollard, 1900), 25–26, Google Books.
13 B. A. Holderness, "East Anglia and the Fens," in *AHEW* V.I, 198; Joan Thirsk, "The Farming Regions of England," in *AHEW* IV, 13; Bailey, *Medieval Suffolk*, 273.
14 Allen, *In English Ways*, 149–53; MacCulloch, *Suffolk and the Tudors*, 28; Anderson, *New England's Generation*, 30.
15 Holderness, "East Anglia," 205–6. It should also be noted that farmers in south-central Suffolk derived more of their livelihood from marketing their crops, and less from their livestock, than did the farmers of "High Suffolk" to the east. As Robert Reyce put it in his 1618 *Breviary of Suffolk*, "those parts inclining to the east commonly called high Suffolk, do especially and cheifely consist upon pasture and feeding, contenting themselves onely, with so much tillage as will sattisfie their owne expences. The midle parts although enjoying much meddow and pasture, yett far more tillage doe from thence raise their cheifest maintenance." Reyce, *Suffolk in the XVIIth Century*, 29.
16 Robert C. Black, *The Younger John Winthrop* (New York: Columbia University Press, 1966), 68; *American National Biography Online*, s.v. "Winthrop, John, Jr.," by Francis J. Bremer, accessed February 16, 2013; Lauric Henneton, "Le Moment Atlantique de la Dynastie des Winthrop au XVIIe Siècle," *Les Cahiers de Framespa* 9 (2012): 5, in Academia.edu.
17 This analysis applies also to his various attempts to create colonial ironworks, as described in McManis, *Colonial New England*, 125–29.
18 Ipswich Land and Grants, image 5; Thomas Franklin Waters, *Ipswich in the Massachusetts Bay Colony* (Ipswich, MA: Ipswich Historical Society, 1905), 16, 19; Petition of the Inhabitants of Ipswich, June 21, 1637, in *Winthrop Papers* (Boston: Massachusetts Historical Society, 1943), 3:432; Nathaniel Ward to John Winthrop Jr., December 24, 1635, in *Winthrop Papers*, 3:215–17; Ipswich Land and Grants, image 48; Ipswich Town Records and Land Grants, 1634–1757, FamilySearch database (Church of Jesus Christ of Latter-Day Saints), film 476737,

image 192 [hereinafter Ipswich Town Records]; Samuel Symonds to John Winthrop Jr., ca. February 1637/38, in *Winthrop Papers* (Boston: Massachusetts Historical Society, 1944), 4:11–13. On the infrequency of absentee landholding in colonial Ipswich, see Edward S. Perzel, "The First Generation of Settlement in Colonial Ipswich, Massachusetts: 1633–1660" (PhD diss., Rutgers University, 1967), 67–68, accessed April 26, 2012, ProQuest Dissertations & Theses FullText.

19 Evidence of only one other land grant to Winthrop in Ipswich has survived: six acres near Ipswich River on its south side [Ipswich Town Records, image 164]. The historian of Ipswich, Thomas F. Waters, starting from a record of April 8, 1686 [Ipswich Town Records, image 116] documented that the smaller tract was conveyed to the family of Rev. Nathaniel Rogers. In his meticulous quest to reconstruct Ipswich colonial land-holding, Waters was unable to locate Winthrop's houselot because "no deed of sale has been preserved." Waters, *Ipswich in the Massachusetts Bay Colony*, 463–64, 398.

20 John Winthrop to John Winthrop Jr., August 31, 1622, in *Winthrop Papers*, 1:272; see also Richard Calis et al., "Passing the Book: Cultures of Reading in the Winthrop Family, 1580–1730," *Past & Present*, 241 (November 2018): 75.

21 "Catalogue of the Winthrop Library," in *Alphabetical and Analytical Catalogue of the New York Society Library* (New York: R. Craighead, 1850), 497, 499, 501, 502, 498. The Rogers book is listed under the title "Practical Catechisme," but as Samuel Eliot Morison pointed out, the titles in the list are often inaccurate. Morison, *The Puritan Pronaos* (New York: New York University Press, 1936), 131. On Johannes Magirus, see Charles B. Schmitt et al., eds., *The Cambridge History of Renaissance Philosophy* (Cambridge: Cambridge University Press, 1988), 825; on Goslicius, see Wienczyslaw J. Wagner et al., "Laurentius Grimaldus Goslicius and His Age—Modern Constitutional Law Ideas in the XVI Century," *Polish Review* 3, nos. 1–2 (Winter–Spring, 1958), 37–57. On Mornay's authorship of the *Vindiciae contra* tyrannos, see Julian H. Franklin, "Editor's Note" in *Constitutionalism and Resistance in the Sixteenth Century: Three Treatises by Hotman, Beza, and Mornay*, ed. and trans. Julian H. Franklin (New York: Pegasus, 1969), 138–40; David P. Henreckson, *The Immortal Commonwealth: Covenant, Community, and Political Resistance in Early Reformed Thought* (Cambridge: Cambridge University Press, 2019), 96n69. On Rogers, see Davids, *Annals of Evangelical Nonconformity*, 147; Tom Webster, "Introduction" to *Diary of Samuel Rogers*, xvi–xix; Bremer and Webster, *Puritans and Puritanism*, s.v. "Rogers, Daniel" by Tom Webster, 1:216–17. Note that while some works in this collection (now owned by the New York Society Library) belonged to descendants of John Winthrop Jr., rather than Winthrop himself, the five works I have cited are listed in the library's catalogue as belonging to Winthrop Jr. New York Society Library, https://www.nysoclib.org.

22 Thomas Pickering, "Epistle Dedicatorie" to William Perkins, *Christian Oeconomie* (London: Felix Kyngston, 1609), [3–5], in Early English Books Online.

23 "non solum ex nostra persona aestimanda[m] esse, vt sc[ilicet]. existimemus, tum nos beatos esse quando pro nobis ipsis solum satis habemus […] alios vero negligunt, sed sub nostra persona ait etiam co[m]prehendos esse, eos, qui ad nos pertine[n]t, quibus vel lege naturae, vel ratione officii tenemur benefacere: vt sunt parentes, liberi, propinqui, amici, domestici, & nostra ciues" (my trans.) Johannes Magirus, *Corona Virtutum moralium* (Frankfurt: in Collegio Musarum Paltheniano, 1601), 61, in Google Books.

24 "propria actio est, recte distribuere bona vel mala externa pro conditione, merito, dignitateq[ue]. […] Iustitiae autem commutatiuae propria actio est, iuste & recte res commutate, ita vt post factam permutationem vtraque pars aequalem habeat portionem"; "ad domesticum rerum administrationem […] economica nominatur." Magirus, *Corona Virtutum moralium*, 447, 468.

25 Magirus, *Corona Virtutum moralium*, 450–51, 453, 458–59, 468; quotes are from Aristotle, *Nicomachean Ethics*, 119.

26 [Laurentius Grimaldus Goslicius,] *A Common-wealth of Good Counsaile* (London: by R. B. for N. Lyng, 1607), 76, 102–3, in Google Books.

27 Stephanus Junius Brutus [Philippe du Plessis-Mornay], *Vindiciae contra tyrannos* (Frankfurt: Sumpt. Haered. Lazari Zetzneri, 1622), 37, 39–40, my trans., in Google Books. "vt licet vniuerso populo repugnare, ita & Principibus Regni, qui vniuersum repraesentant, non secus ac decurioniubus pro corporis vtilitate, contrahere. Vt vero refertur ad vniuersos, quod publice per maiorum parte[m] geritur, ita q[ue] maior pars Principum seu optimatum fecerit, omnes; quod omnes vniuersus populus fecisse dicetur."
28 Mornay, *Vindiciae*, 69. "quod de vniuerso populo dicimus [...] dictu[m] volumus qui populum vniuersum in omni Regno vrbeue legitime repr[a]esentant."
29 Mornay, *Vindiciae*, 125–26. "*Si legem meam obseruaris* [...] *Si ius unicuiq[ue] suum tribueris.*"
30 Mornay, *Vindiciae*, 82. "etsi moriuntur reges, populus interim, vt neq[ue] vulla alia Vniversitas, nunqua[m] moritur." On other early connections between corporatism and covenant among Puritans, see Livermore, *Early American Land Companies*, xi–xiv.
31 Henreckson, *Immortal Commonwealth*, 1–11, 98–107, 108 [quote].
32 Mornay, *Vindiciae*, 26. "Hinc animaduertimus, vniversum populum obligatum esse legi Dei curandae, Ecclesiaeq[ue] tuendae, vt e contrario idolis Gentium exterminandas e terra Chanaan, qu[a]e stipulatio ad singulos pertinere non potest, sed vniuersos tantum."
33 Ward, *Simple Cobler*, 32.
34 Allen, *In English Ways*, 271; James Savage, *Genealogical Dictionary of the First Settlers of New England* (Boston, MA: Little, Brown, 1860), 2:220; Arthur Gage, "Descendants of John Gage of Ipswich, Mass.," *New England Historical and Genealogical Register* 62 (July 1908): 254. Charles Edward Banks's works simply present his attributions with minimal or no documentation or supporting evidence; see, e.g., Banks, *Topographical Dictionary of 2885 English Emigrants to New England, 1620–1650*, 3rd ed., ed. Elijah Brownell (Baltimore, MD: Genealogical Publishing, 1963); Banks, *Winthrop Fleet of 1630*.
35 Thirsk, "Farming Regions," 7.
36 Anderson, *Great Migration Begins*, 719.
37 Anderson, *Great Migration*, 6:313, 6:316–18.
38 Anderson, *Great Migration* Begins, 1431–33; Gray, *English Field Systems*, 85–87, Internet Archive; Joan Thirsk, "The South-West Midlands," in *AHEW* V.I, 159, 161, 163–65; B. K. Roberts, "Field Systems of the West Midlands," in Baker and Butlin, *Studies of Field Systems*, 195–98; Hall, *Open Fields of England*, 3.
39 Allen, *In English Ways*, 273; Hall, *Open Fields*, 264–66; William Page, ed., *The Victoria History of Hampshire and the Isle of Wight*, vol. 5 (London: Constable, 1912), 498; W. E. Tate, "Field Systems and Enclosures in Hampshire," *Proceedings of the Hampshire Field Club & Archaeological Society* 16, no. 3 (1947): 257–59; Anderson, *Great Migration*, 5:206; Anderson, *Great Migration Begins*, 435, 1630.
40 Allen, *In English Ways*, 270; Savage, *Genealogical Dictionary*, 1:402; Anderson, *Great Migration*, 2:86, 2:89–95; G. Andrews Moriarty, "Clarke—Cooke (alias Carewe)—Kerrich," *New England Historical and Genealogical Register* 75 (January 1921): 273–76.
41 Allen, *In English Ways*, 272; Anderson, *Great Migration Begins*, 1024, 858; "Suffolk Historic Landscape Characterisation Map," Suffolk Heritage Explorer; Edward Martin, "Regionality in East Anglian Field Systems," in *Wheare most inclosures be*, ed. Martin and Satchell, 194, 197.
42 Tate, "Handlist of Suffolk Enclosure Acts," 253. Writing before HLC data was available, Nesta Evans perhaps underestimated the amount of open field left in South Elmham, but correctly emphasized the ongoing importance of greens and commons in the area: Nesta Evans, "Farming and Land-Holding in Wood-Pasture East Anglia 1550–1650," *Proceedings of the Suffolk Institute of Archaeology and History* 35, part 4 (1984): 303–5. Evans's refusal to notice the ongoing existence of open fields in this area seems to have been driven by the traditional definition of this region as a "wood-pasture" region; here Mark Overton's point that agricultural regions, like historical eras, have been constructed by historians, is relevant. Overton demonstrated that the distribution of enclosed dairy farms assarted from woodland in the supposedly

"wood-pasture" areas of Suffolk and Norfolk during our period did not, in fact, differ significantly from random distribution, suggesting the area was far from homogeneous. Overton, "Agricultural Change," 91–94. Diarmaid MacCulloch also contests the stark dichotomy of "wood-pasture" and "sheep-corn regions": MacCulloch, *Suffolk and the Tudors*, 19. Edward Martin suggests that common fields did exist in South Elmham but that they were of an irregular type, not conforming to the traditional two- or three-field systems of the Midlands and thus less "communal" in their organization. Martin, "Regionality," in *Wheare most inclosures be*, ed. Martin and Satchell, 197, 200.

43 Anderson, *Great Migration Begins*, 639; Francis J. Bremer, *First Founders: American Puritans and Puritanism in an Atlantic World* (Durham: University of New Hampshire Press, 2012), n.p., in ProQuest Ebook Central.

44 [Daniel Defoe,] *A Tour Thro' the Whole Island of Great Britain*, vol. 1 (London: for J. Osborn et al., 1742), 295; William Marshall, *Rural Economy of the West of England* vol. II (London: for G. Nicol, 1796), 131; Giles V. Harrison, "The South-West," in *AHEW* V.I, 358–61; J. H. Bettey, *Dorset* (Newton Abbot, UK: David & Charles, 1974), 47–49, 54–55; Frank Thistlethwaite, *Dorset Pilgrims: The Story of West Country Pilgrims Who Went to New England in the 17th Century* (London: Barrie & Jenkins, 1989), 19–20; J. H. Hexter, *The Reign of King Pym* (Cambridge, MA: Harvard University Press, 1941), 86–87.

45 For a full account see McDermott, "Body of Liberties," 138–47, 153.

46 Pew, "Worshipful Simon Bradstreet," 301–2; Dennis R. Mills, "Enclosure in Kesteven," *Agricultural History Review* 7, no. 2 (1959): 83, 91; John Lord and Alastair MacIntosh with contributions from Adam Partington, "The Historic Landscape Characterisation Project for Lincolnshire: The Historic Landscape Character Zones," September 2011, Archaeology Data Service, accessed July 20, 2019, 73–78; Thirsk, *Rural Economy of England*, 132–33; Joan Thirsk, *English Peasant Farming: The Agrarian History of Lincolnshire from Tudor to Recent Times* (London: Routledge & Kegan Paul, 1957), 182–84; Joan Thirsk, "Field Systems of the East Midlands," in *Studies of Field Systems*, ed. Baker and Butlin, 250; T. W. Beastall, *The Agricultural Revolution in Lincolnshire* (Lincoln: History of Lincolnshire Committee, 1978), 2, 9, 23.

47 Horbling Town Book, Horbling PAR/7/10; Extracts and Exchanges (Horbling enclosure), Horbling PAR 17/1; Award and Plan, 1765, Kesteven Award 42; and Horbling, Enclosure Act and Minutes, Smith 5/ENC/Horbling, Lincolnshire Archives, Lincoln, UK.

48 W. H. Hosford, "Some Lincolnshire Enclosure Documents," *Economic History Review*, n.s., 2, no. 1 (1949): 73, 77.

49 John Leland, *The Itinerary of John Leland the Antiquary*, 2nd ed. (Oxford: at the Theatre, 1745), 1:27.

50 Hall, *Open Fields of England*, 3; Hall, *Open Fields of Northamptonshire*; Bremer and Webster, *Puritans and Puritanism*, s.v. "Dudley, Thomas" by Francis J. Bremer, 1:78–79.

51 Leland, *Itinerary*, 8.

52 J. Charles Cox, ed., *The Records of the Borough of Northampton*, vol. 2 (Northampton: Borough of Northampton, 1898), 215–29; Helen M. Cam, "Northampton Borough," in *Victoria History of the County of Northampton*, ed. William Page (London: St. Catherine Press, 1930), 21.

53 Winthrop, *Journal*, 118.

54 Mather, *Magnalia*, 1:481; "Focus on Newbury," *Great Migration Newsletter* 20 (January–March, 2011), 6, in AmericanAncestors.org; Anderson, *Great Migration* 5:367; Benjamin Brook, *Lives of the Puritans*, 3 vols. (London: James Black, 1813), 3:469–70; Walter Money, *The History of the Ancient Town and Borough of Newbury*, 191–94, 251, 564–65, Internet Archive.

55 J. R. Wordie, "The South," in *AHEW* V.I, 318; Money, *History of…Newbury*, 252–59, 282–83; Anne B. Wallis Chapman, "Borough of Newbury," in *Victoria History of the County of Berkshire*, vol. 4 (London: St. Catherine Press, 1924), 134, 143 [quote].

56 William Dunn Macray, *A Register of the Members of St. Mary Magdalen College, Oxford, Fellows: 1576–1648*, n.s., vol. 3 (London: Henry Frowde, 1901), 90–91; Brook, *Lives of the Puritans*, 2:237–40; Wordie, "The South," 318; A. P. Baggs, D. A. Crowley, Ralph B. Pugh, Janet H. Stevenson,

and Margaret Tomlinson, "Parishes: Stanton St. Bernard," in *A History of the County of Wiltshire: Volume 10*, ed. Elizabeth Crittall (London: Victoria County History, 1975), 146–55, in British History Online, accessed August 9, 2019.

57 Bennett, "Historic Landscape Characterisation Report for Essex," 1:18–19; W. G. Hoskins, *The Making of the English Landscape* (1955; repr. Harmondsworth, UK: Penguin Books, 1986), 60–64; Thirsk, "Farming Regions," 8–9; W. R. Powell, ed., *A History of the County of Essex* vol. 4, Victoria History of the Counties of England (London: Oxford University Press, 1956), 241–42.

58 Among the numerous references in the town records to the two common fields and the common fences surrounding them, see, e.g., Ipswich Land and Grants, images 36–37, 48, 53; Ipswich Town Records, image 42. See also Alison I. Vannah, "Crotchets of Division: Ipswich in New England, 1633–1679" (PhD diss., Brandeis University, 1999), in ProQuest Dissertations & Theses FullText, 22–23 and 76, note 45.

59 Ipswich Land and Grants, image 5; Perzel, "First Generation of Settlement," 53, 57; Shurtleff, *Records of the Governor*, 1:344.

60 Ipswich Land and Grants, images 17, 6, 13, 7; Colin R. Chapman, *How Heavy, How Much and How Long?* (Dursley, UK: Lochin, 1996), 20–21.

61 Ipswich Town Records, image 16. A fragmentary record of 1643 may refer to the building of a common fence around the common field south of the river: Ipswich Land and Grants, image 56.

62 Ipswich Land and Grants, image 34; Shurtleff, *Records of the Governor*, 2:39. Alison Vannah's account of these discussions is somewhat confused because she believes the vote on particular fencing also took place in 1637/38, following a scribal error by Town Clerk Robert Lord when he re-copied the vote into the town records decades later. Vannah, "Crotchets of Division," 165–66.

63 Thomas Franklin Waters, "Ipswich Village and the Old Rowley Road," *Publications of the Ipswich Historical Society* 19 (1914): 3; Waters, "Jeffrey's Neck," *Publications of the Ipswich Historical Society* 18 (1912): 2.

64 Ipswich Land and Grants, image 55; for another example, see an order ca. 1640/41, image 37. See also Vannah, "Crotchets of Division," 164.

65 Donahue, *Great Meadow*, 89.

66 This was especially true after the colonists moved away from hoe agriculture and began cross-plowing their corn fields. In a communication to the Royal Society of London in 1677, John Winthrop Jr. reported that "the Fields thus Ploughed for this [Indian] Corne, after the Crop is off, are almost as well fitted for *English* Corn, especially Summer Grain, as Peason or Summer Wheat; as if lying fallow, they had had a very good Summer Tilth [dunging during fallow time]." John Winthrop Jr., "The Description, Culture, and Use of Maiz," *Philosophical Transactions* 12 (1677–78): 1067. In 1760, Jared Eliot praised the combination of plowing and hoeing in raising maize, likening it to the most advanced techniques of the English agricultural revolution and claiming that the New England method of corn tillage restored the soil instead of exhausting it. Eliot, *Essays upon Field-Husbandry in New-England* (Boston, MA: Edes and Gill, 1760), 113–14, in Internet Archive. That fish was used as fertilizer for corn in Ipswich is shown by the selectmen's order of May 11, 1644, that all dogs should have one leg tied up for the ensuing three weeks to prevent them from "scrapinge up fish" in the fields. Ipswich Land and Grants, image 65; see also Howard S. Russell, *A Long, Deep Furrow: Three Centuries of Farming in New England* (Hanover, NH: University Press of New England, 1976), 43. That the Indian corn, which is (as the author of the 1775 tract *American Husbandry* realized) "a very exhausting crop," did not usually ruin the soil quickly is probably due to the failure of winter wheat in New England, so that the fields did generally lie fallow in winter. The same author recorded that "they raise small quantities of common wheat" in New England and that "all their corn here is in general sowen in spring, from the common idea that the climate will not admit of an

autumnal sowing." *American Husbandry* (London: J. Bew, 1775), 52–53, in Internet Archive. See also McManis, *Colonial New England*, 89, 101.

67 Ipswich Land and Grants, image 36; Robert R. Walcott, "Husbandry in Colonial New England," *New England Quarterly* 9, no. 2 (June 1936): 227; see also McManis, *Colonial New England*, 90. As Alison Vannah pointed out, there is no evidence that crop rotation was carried out in Ipswich (Vannah, "Crotchets of Division," 163). See also Cronon, *Changes in the Land*, 150.

68 Winthrop Jr., "Description…of Maiz," 1067. On this practice, see also Russell, *Long, Deep Furrow*, 43–44.

69 This would especially be true if the Ipswich farmers' experiments with winter wheat proved short-lived, and indeed there is no other reference to winter wheat in the early town records. Percy Bidwell and John Falconer argued that winter wheat was rarely grown until 1660 when a "blast" or fungus "disastrously affected the summer grain," and that in general outside the Connecticut River Valley "wheat was generally regarded as a failure" in New England. Bidwell and Falconer, *History of Agriculture in the Northern United States, 1620–1860* (Washington, DC: Carnegie Institution, 1925), 13, 236. Jared Eliot wrote of a "Scarcity of Wheat" in New England as late as 1760. Eliot, *Essays*, 23.

70 Donahue, *Great Meadow*, 87–88; Russell, *Long, Deep Furrow*, 21, 65; McManis, *Colonial New England*, 113–14; Amy D. Schwartz, "Colonial New England Agriculture: New Visions, Old Directions," *Agricultural History* 69, no. 3 (Summer 1995): 457.

71 Francis Higginson, *New-Englands Plantation* (1630; repr. Salem, MA: Essex Book and Print Club, 1908), 91. This is probably what William Wood meant when he said that "*Agowamme* [the Algonquian name for the area that later became Ipswich] is nine miles to the north from *Salem*, which is one of the most spatious places for a plantation." Wood, *New Englands Prospect* (London: by Tho. Cotes, 1634), 44.

72 Cronon, *Changes in the Land*, 120. See also Main, *Peoples of a Spacious Land*, 57, on the desire to avoid fencing as a motivation for establishing open fields during early settlement.

73 Waters, "Jeffrey's Neck," 54; see Ipswich Land and Grants, 74, for an order to make a gate at Jeffrey's Neck. See also McManis, *Colonial New England*, 94.

74 Ipswich Land and Grants, images 9, 56, 61, 64, 65, 74, 88; Ipswich Town Meetings, images 23 [quote], 26, 38, 56. Offenders were regularly prosecuted for violating timber ordinances: see, e.g., Ipswich Land and Grants, images 65, 79; Ipswich Town Meetings, images 31, 37, 47. See also [Thomas F. Waters], "The Development of Our Town Government," *Publications of the Ipswich Historical Society* 8 (1900): 10–11.

75 Ipswich Town Meetings, image 14; Ipswich Land and Grants, image 82; see also Russell, *Long, Deep Furrow*, 66, on New England regulations against cutting timber to make fences. In issuing licenses to fell timber the selectmen were taking over a responsibility of the lord of the manor in the old country; see, for example, the License by Thomas Cole, lord of the manor of Haverhill, September 4, 1637, in Papers mainly involving the Cole family, D/DWv/B5, Essex Record Office, Chelmsford, UK.

76 For orders to repair common fences, see, e.g., Ipswich Land and Grants, images 36, 37, 68; Ipswich Town Meetings, images 17, 19, 35. Anyone familiar with the present-day New England landscape may wonder whether the colonists might have built stone walls around their individual planting lots. This was truly backbreaking and labor-intensive work which the first settlers would have had neither time nor manpower to do. As Susan Allport put it, "most of New England's stone walls are relative latecomers on the landscape." Allport, *Sermons in Stone: The Stone Walls of New England and New York* (New York: W. W. Norton, 1990), 23. Robert Walcott argues that particular lots were usually demarcated using stakes (Walcott, "Husbandry," 227); for an example of this in a division of marshland in 1669, see Ipswich Town Meetings, image 36; see also Rowley Freeholders' Records, 1643–1830 [hereinafter Rowley Freeholders' Records], image 851, FamilySearch database (Church of Jesus Christ of Latter-Day Saints), film 887760, items 5–6. However, in a unique reference from the Ipswich town records for

February 1670/71, "Ned Yndian" was granted a parcel of land and ordered to build a stone wall around it, presumably because he was not granted commonage and thus could not fell any timber at all—though one wonders if his ethnicity had something to do with this onerous requirement. Ipswich Town Meetings, image 42.

77 Dane, *Declaration of Remarkable Providences*, 13. Similarly, an order of February 20, 1665/66, required that firewood be taken from trees that were already felled or located in the swamps. Ipswich Town Meetings, image 23.
78 Ipswich Land and Grants, image 63.
79 Ipswich Town Meetings, images 46–47.
80 "Essay on the Ordering of Towns," ca. 1635, *Winthrop Papers* 3:181–85.
81 John Stilgoe, *Common Landscape of America, 1580 to 1845* (New Haven, CT: Yale University Press, 1982), 44. Alison Vannah emphasized the importance of "due proportion" in Ipswich land distribution; see Vannah, "Crotchets of Division," 141.
82 "Essay on the Ordering of Towns," 183; Vannah, "Crotchets of Division," 25; Samuel Symonds to John Winthrop, January 6, 1646/47, in *Winthrop Papers* 5:126.
83 Nathaniel Ward to John Winthrop, ca. April 1640, in *Winthrop Papers* 4:222.
84 Shurtleff, *Records of the Governor*, 1:136; John Henry Sears, *The Physical Geography, Geology, Mineralogy and Paleontology of Essex County, Massachusetts* (Salem, MA: Essex Institute, 1905), appendix A, 393.
85 Winthrop, *Journal*, 615.
86 Ward, *Simple Cobler*, 47; Aristotle, *Nicomachean Ethics*, 117–23; see also Fleischacker, *Short History of Distributive Justice*, 19–22.
87 Ward, *Discolliminium*, 12.
88 Whitmore, *Bibliographical Sketch*, 33.
89 Ipswich Town Meetings, images 46 [quote], 22; Ipswich Land and Grants, images 5, 51, 56, 63, 65, 70–71, 101, 111.
90 Ward, *Iethro's Iustice*, 38, 44–45.
91 Samuel Symonds to John Winthrop Jr., October 6, 1647, in Waters, *Ipswich in the Massachusetts Bay Colony*, 516–18; George Francis Dow, ed., *Records and Files of the Quarterly Courts of Essex County, Massachusetts*, 8 vols. (Salem, MA: Essex Institute, 1911–21), 1:124–25; Ipswich Town Records Copy, 1634–1864, FamilySearch database (Church of Jesus Christ of Latter-Day Saints), film 878652, items 2–4, images 139, 141. I have used this later copy of the records only when the original records have disappeared or are no longer legible.
92 Ipswich Land and Grants, image 104; "Copy of the Case of George Giddings and others of Ipswich, referring to Mr. Cobbet," in *The Hutchinson Papers*, ed. Thomas Hutchinson, 2 vols. (1769; repr., Albany, NY: Prince Society, 1865), 2:1–25; Perzel, *First Generation*, 109–12; Worthley, *Inventory*, 303. Cobbet's social teaching was very much in keeping with the Ipswich ethos of distributive justice and identical to the view expressed by Thomas Pickering in his foreword to Perkins's *Christian Oeconomie*. In the "Epistle to the Reader" in his *Fruitfull and Usefull Discourse Touching the Honour due from Children to Parents* (London: by S. G. for John Rothwell, 1656), Cobbet wrote that "the subject of this discourse [...] it is, in the nature thereof, Oeconomicall, respecting the Family, specially; but in the consequences and concernments thereof, it may not be unfitly termed, Politicall, yea Ecclesiasticall," since God chose "to lay the foundations both of State and Church, in a family" [3–4, in Google Books]. Similarly, in a lecture-day sermon of 1668, Cobbet argued that believers must obey godly magistrates even in matters of religion, based on the fifth Commandment, "Honour thy father, & thy mother"; the alternative was "Anarchy." Invoking corporatism, Cobbet insisted that all authority springs from "Christ as ye head of ye Church, & Saviour of ye body"; thus, Christians should oppose the "levelling spirit" of those who "undermine ye order in Civill & Church respect." Thomas Cobbet, Sermon, April 16, 1668, Miscellaneous Manuscripts, Misc. 1668 April 16, Massachusetts Historical Society, Boston, MA.

93 *Giddings v. Brown* (1657), in Mark DeWolfe Howe, ed., *Readings in American Legal History* (Cambridge: Harvard University Press, 1949), 232–40. On the role played by equity in Essex County, Massachusetts and New England in general, see Konig, *Law and Society*, 56–59; Edwin H. Woodruff, "Chancery in Massachusetts," *Boston University Law Review* 9, no. 3 (June 1929): 168–92; T. H. Breen, *The Character of the Good Ruler: Puritan Political Ideas in New England, 1630–1730* (New York: W. W. Norton, 1974), 12–13.
94 Ipswich Land and Grants, image 52.
95 Ipswich Land and Grants, images 36 and 55; for a similar record circa 1644, see image 63.
96 Ipswich Land and Grants, image 71.
97 Ward, *Simple Cobler*, 46.
98 On the "natural wisdom," which Puritans believed that God made available to men to carry out their various callings, see Breen, *Character*, 10.
99 Allen, *In English Ways*, 128, 143. On the uniqueness of Watertown in immediately dividing up its entire land grant to settlers who owned the land privately, see McManis, *Colonial New England*, 59.
100 Karen Ordahl Kupperman, ed., *Captain John Smith: A Select Edition of His Writings* (Chapel Hill: University of North Carolina Press, 1988), 275.
101 Wood, *New Englands Prospect*, 44; see McManis, *Colonial New England*, 37. In his *History of New England*, William Hubbard, minister of Ipswich throughout the second half of the seventeenth century, said that Ipswich was "one of the most commodious places in the country for cattle and tillage." William Hubbard, *General History of New England* (Boston, MA: Charles Little and James Brown, 1848), 161, in Internet Archive; *Concise History of the First Church of Christ, in Ipswich* (Boston, MA: Wright & Potter, 1862), 5, in Internet Archive. Hubbard's history was finished by 1682 but remained unpublished until the nineteenth century. John Langdon Sibley, *Biographical Sketches of Graduates of Harvard University, in Cambridge, Massachusetts*, 3 vols. (1873–85; repr., New York: Johnson Reprint, 1967), 1:54–55.
102 Ipswich Land and Grants, 7; George A. Schofield, *Ancient Records of the Town of Ipswich* (Ipswich: Chronicle Motor Press, 1899), n.p. [page image 15 in Internet Archive version]; Waters, "Jeffrey's Neck," 1. "Great Neck": Vannah, "Crotchets of Division," 18.
103 Ipswich Land and Grants, image 7 [quote], 8, 14, 19.
104 Ipswich Land and Grants, image 37; in another example from 1649, the selectmen permitted the lotlayers to "laye out to […] John Whipple a p[ar]sell of vpland being by his meddow in excange of so much in another place," but only "if […] they see it conveinant," image 86; Perzel, *First Generation*, 52. On those occasions when the town seemed to accede to attempts to build contiguous farms, it usually hedged its grants with qualifications designed to protect the town's interests. For example, when John Perkins the younger received 70 acres of land near a small island he had been granted previously, the town stipulated that Perkins had to surrender it if the land was given to "any new plantation," and, furthermore, if he hunted the cattle and pigs from the nearby common with his dogs, even if they trampled his crops, he was liable to damages. Similarly, Rev. Thomas Cobbet received Diamond Island but was forbidden to build a house on it, and if he decided to sell it, he had to give the town the right of first refusal. Ipswich Land and Grants, image 62; Ipswich Town Records, image 13.
105 Ipswich Town Records Copy, image 193; Ipswich Land and Grants, images 83 [quote], 33, 37, 41, 48, 50–51, 54, 70, 55; Vannah, "Crotchets of Division," 22.
106 Ipswich Land and Grants, images 54, 56, 74–75, 98, 66 [quote], 41, 35; Russell, *Long, Deep Furrow*, 31; Walcott, "Husbandry," 240–42; Bidwell and Falconer, *History of Agriculture*, 21; Burt Feintuch and David H. Watters, eds., *The Encyclopedia of New England* (New Haven, CT: Yale University Press, 2005), s.v. "Oxen" by Drew Conroy, 51.
107 Dow, *Records…of the Quarterly Courts of Essex County*, 3:151–52, 1:39; Ipswich Land and Grants, image 59 [quote].
108 Ipswich Town Records, images 22, 31; for a 1674 example, see image 53.

109 Ipswich Land and Grants, images 52 [quote], 37.
110 Ipswich Land and Grants, image 45; Ipswich Town Records, image 39.
111 "The humble petition of the select men of Ipswich," 1667, Massachusetts Archives 112:181, Boston, MA.
112 Ipswich Land and Grants, image 103; Ipswich Town Records, image 32.
113 Ipswich Land and Grants, image 35. The word "stinting" is now illegible in the original record; I have taken it from Ipswich Town Records Copy, image 125.
114 Ipswich Land and Grants, image 47; Martin, *Profits*, 257–80.
115 Joseph B. Felt, *History of Ipswich, Essex, and Hamilton* (Cambridge, MA: Charles Folsom, 1834), 37, in Internet Archive.
116 Ipswich Land and Grants, images 80, 83. A record of December 24, 1658, probably refers to this episode since it uses similar language: "Voted that the liberty granted to the select men to sell or exchange small p[ar]sells of Land is now repealed." Ipswich Land and Grants, image 104.
117 In 1670, Ipswich resident Roger Lancton made a deposition in a land dispute in which he referred to the time "at the beginning of the town before any particular order was made about commonage." Lancton was a politically active citizen, having served as constable in 1646. Dow, *Records...of the Quarterly Courts of Essex County*, 4:260; Ipswich Town Records Copy, images 136–37.
118 A record of ca. 1639 suggests that even the owners of houselots could be denied commonage if they failed to improve their land; the town granted commonage "for the two house lotts granted formerly for Mr Norton two friends in Case there be houses Biult on them." Ipswich Town Records, image 193.
119 Ipswich Land and Grants, images 46, 16, 64, 32 [quote]; "Early Ipswich Families," *New England Historical and Genealogical Register* 2 (1848): 176; "Autobiography of Major-General Daniel Denison," *New England Historical and Genealogical Register* 46 (1892): 127–33; Ipswich Deeds, Mortgages, Wills, 1639–95, FamilySearch database (Church of Jesus Christ of Latter-Day Saints), film 873018, image 169 [hereinafter Ipswich Deeds]; Vannah, "Crotchets of Division," 173–75.
120 Ipswich Land and Grants, image 111; for another copy, see Ipswich Town Records, image 15. Shurtleff, *Records of the Governor*, 4, part 1:417; Vannah, "Crotchets of Division," 524–26, 538, 572–74, 590; Konig, *Law and Society*, 50–52. How best to satisfy the demands of farmers for commonage proved an ongoing and intractable problem; a committee appointed by the town meeting in February 1669/70 to study the issue came back in March with a statement that "we haue not yett seene reason to grattifie all, nor found a satisfactory way to accomadate any for the present and desire that the matter may be suspended till some meanes be found out of more gen^{er}all satisfaction than any that is yett propounded." Ipswich Town Records, image 38.
121 Nathaniel Ward to John Winthrop Jr., December 24, 1635, in *Winthrop Papers*, 3:215–17.
122 Ipswich Town Records, image 34.
123 Ipswich Town Records, images 50 and 54; Levy, *Town Born*, 2–4, 103–10; Benton, *Warning Out*.
124 Daniel Vickers, "Working the Fields in a Developing Economy: Essex County, Massachusetts, 1630–1675," in *Work and Labor in Early America*, ed. Stephen Innes (Chapel Hill: University of North Carolina Press, 1988), 66; Vickers, *Farmers & Fishermen: Two Centuries of Work in Essex County, Massachusetts, 1630–1850* (Chapel Hill: University of North Carolina Press, 1994), 78; Cronon, *Changes in the Land*, 74. A rare mention of tenants in the Ipswich records occurs in the context of regulation of the commons: in 1650, having just granted a cow common to Topsfield, the town forbade "the Dwellers vppon the land of Mr Simonds" from using the Ipswich cow common. Ipswich Town Records, image 173. For evidence of Scottish and Irish tenants who arrived after the initial wave of settlement in Ipswich and Topsfield, see Marsha

L. Hamilton, *Social and Economic Networks in Early Massachusetts: Atlantic Connections* (University Park: Pennsylvania State University Press, 2009), 58–59.

125 Ipswich Town Records, image 51.
126 Ipswich Land and Grants, images 111 [quote], 112–14; Ipswich Town Records, images 8, 11.
127 Waters, "Jeffrey's Neck," 55; Donahue, *Great Meadow*, 171; Bidwell and Falconer, *History of Agriculture*, 19; Main, *Peoples of a Spacious Land*, 38; Ipswich Town Records, image 24; Walcott, "Husbandry," 238. In a letter to Simonds d'Ewes, Rev. Edmund Browne noted that "the ground graseth not so well as O: E:, for wee have not brought it into a way of baring English grasse [...] yet it feedeth cattle very well." "Report of Edmund Browne," in *Publications of the Colonial Society of Massachusetts* 7 (1905): 77, in Google Books.
128 Ipswich Town Records, images 7, 13.
129 Ipswich Town Records, images 24, 25.
130 Ipswich Town Records, images 17, 18.
131 Ipswich Town Records, image 19; Felt, *History of Ipswich*, 37; Sears, *Physical Geography...of Essex County*, appendix A, 393; see Vannah, "Crotchets of Division," 558–59.
132 See Vannah, "Crotchets of Division," 141; Perzel, "First Generation," 78.
133 Ipswich Town Records, images 58, 63, 92. This provision probably refers to the sort of enclosure described by Douglas McManis: "The distances separating fields from village could be considerable, and, in order to cut down on the time spent traveling among the fields, a farmer might put up a shed for tools, animals, or crop storage at a convenient point along one of the paths." However, it cannot be construed as favorable to enclosure in general. McManis, *Colonial New England*, 60.
134 Allen, *In English Ways*, 129–30.
135 Perzel, "First Generation," 77; Ipswich Land and Grants, image 46; *The Probate Records of Essex County, Massachusetts*, vol. 1 (Salem, MA: Essex Institute, 1916), 28–30; Anderson, *Great Migration*, 5:206–9; Arlin I. Ginsburg, "The Franchise in Seventeenth-Century Massachusetts: Ipswich," *William and Mary Quarterly* 34, no. 3 (July 1977): 446–52; Susan L. Norton, "Population Growth in Colonial America: A Study of Ipswich, Massachusetts," *Population Studies* 25, no. 3 (November 1971): 433–52.
136 Ipswich Deeds, images 343, 308, 310, 342, 269–71, 406, 338, 303; Anderson, *Great Migration*, 2:137–40.
137 *Essex Probate Records* 1:62–64; Ipswich Deeds, images 339, 243–44, 271–72, 209–10, 229–30, 395–96, 429–30, 447, 472–73; Anderson, *Great Migration*, 1:399.
138 Ipswich Deeds, image 382; *Essex Probate Records* 1:105, 107, 126, 268, 272, 278. Perzel, "First Generation," 343, has Payne moving to Boston, but in his data on Ipswich emigrants Perzel appears to follow the not-always-reliable attributions in Felt, *History of Ipswich*, 71–81; I have found no corroboration that Payne relocated.
139 Edward Perzel, "Landholding in Ipswich," *Essex Institute Historical Collections* 104, no. 4 (October 1968): 314; Perzel, "First Generation," 62–64. I reached this conclusion while using the modern genealogical resource AmericanAncestors.org (the New England Historic Genealogical Society's database) in an effort to correct Perzel's sometimes faulty conclusions as to who emigrated. Attempting to cite each individual resource I consulted within the NEHGR's website for each individual land seller would make this footnote longer than feasible.
140 Although Robert Friedeburg's premises were questionable, his conclusions are convincing:

  Nearly half of the 435 heads of households living some time in Ipswich (208, i.e. 47.8%) were members of the lower ownership group. Yet among those who decided to stay in Ipswich and eventually died there, less then [*sic*] 20% (27, i.e. 19.9%) were members of this lower group...both factors, the amount of land granted and the amount of local influence available, or rather the lack of both, encouraged the less well-off Ipswich residents to settle in another place.

Friedeburg, "Social and Geographical Mobility," 383–84.
141 Allen, *In English Ways*, 130; Dow, *Records...of the Quarterly Courts of Essex County*, 1:262.
142 Benjamin Mighill and George Blodgette, eds., *Early Records of the Town of Rowley, Massachusetts, 1639–1672* (Rowley, MA: Mighill and Blodgette, 1894), 1–51, in Internet Archive; see also "Focus on Rowley," *Great Migration Newsletter* 10 (October–December 2001): 27–30, in AmericanAncestors.org.
143 Shurtleff, *Records of the Governor*, 1:306–7; Max Farrand, ed., *The Laws and Liberties of Massachusetts: Reprinted from the Copy of the 1648 Edition in the Henry E. Huntington Library* (Cambridge, MA: Harvard University Press, 1929), 13–14; David Thomas Konig, "Community Custom and the Common Law: Social Change and the Development of Land Law in Seventeenth-Century Massachusetts," *American Journal of Legal History* 18, no. 2 (April 1974): 147; see also Konig, *Law and Society*, 40–42; Perzel, "First Generation," 242.
144 Sarah Irving, "Beyond Dominion and Stewardship: Humanity and Nature in Puritan Theology," *American Theological Inquiry* 8, no. 1 (2015): 50–53.
145 On spiritualizing the creatures, see, e.g., Robert Middlekauff, *The Mathers: Three Generations of Puritan Intellectuals, 1596–1728* (1971; repr., Berkeley: University of California Press, 1999), 206, 280, 310–12.
146 John Norden, *John Norden's* The Surveyor's Dialogue *(1618): A Critical Edition*, ed. Mark Netzloff (2010; repr, Abingdon, UK: Routledge, 2016), 34.

Chapter Four Town-Founding in Essex County: The Communities around Ipswich

1 *Thomas Shepard's Confessions*, ed. George Selement and Bruce C. Woolley (Boston: Colonial Society of Massachusetts, 1981); Edward Winslow, *Hypocrisie Unmasked*, in *Chronicles of the Pilgrim Fathers of the Colony of Plymouth*, ed. Alexander Young, 2nd ed. (Boston, MA: Charles C. Little and James Brown, 1844), 402–4; Paul T. McClurkin, "Presbyterianism in New England Congregationalism," *Journal of the Presbyterian Historical Society* 31, no. 4 (December 1953): 248–50; Thomas Parker, *The True Copy of a Letter Written By Mr. Thomas Parker...unto a member of the Assembly of Divines now at Westminster* (London: by Richard Cotes, for Ralph Smith, 1643), 3–4, in Early English Books Online.
2 Allen, *In English Ways*, 94–95; Newbury Town Records, 1635–1860, FamilySearch database (Church of Jesus Christ of Latter-Day Saints), film 886194, item 4, image 293. This is a copy of the original records in a later hand.
3 Allen, *In English Ways*, 110–11, 89; Allen uses the chart of the "Stint of the ox & Cow Com[m]on" in the volume of Newbury Proprietors' Records from 1635, 2–3, Newbury Town Clerk's Office, Newbury, MA.
4 Mather, *Magnalia*, 1:480–81.
5 Macray, *Register of the Members*, 90–91; *Alumni Dublinenses*, ed. George Burtchaell and Thomas Sadleir (Dublin: A. Thom, 1935), 653, 890.
6 Mather, *Magnalia*, 1:484; *Brasenose College Register, 1509–1909* (Oxford: Clarendon Press, 1909), 1:154, in Internet Archive; James Noyes, *The Temple Measured* (London: for Edmund Paxton, 1646), 1–2, in Early English Books Online; James Noyes, *Moses and Aaron* (London: by T. R. for Edmund Paxton, 1661), 3, 5, 7–8, in Early English Books Online.
7 Thomas Gage, *The History of Rowley, Anciently Including Bradford, Boxford, and Georgetown, from the Year 1639 to the Present Time* (Boston: Ferdinand Andrews, 1840), 13, 122, in Internet Archive; Allen, *In English Ways*, 19–54; Patricia Trainor O'Malley, "Rowley, Massachusetts, 1639–1730: Dissent, Division and Delimitation in a Colonial Town" (PhD diss., Boston College 1975), 4–5, 7, 11, 21, 41, in ProQuest Dissertations & Theses Global. However, Amos Jewett and Emily Adams Jewett deserve credit for debunking the myth that all property in early Rowley was communally owned: Amos Everett Jewett and Emily Mabel Adams Jewett, *Rowley,*

Massachusetts: "Mr Ezechi Rogers Plantation," 1639–1850 (Rowley, MA: Jewett Family of America, 1946), 19.

8 Allen, *In English Ways*, 19–54; K. J. Allison, ed., *A History of the County of York: East Riding* vol. 4 (Oxford: Oxford University Press, 1979), 140, 142; Alan Harris, "The Agriculture of the East Riding of Yorkshire before the Parliamentary Enclosures," *Yorkshire Archaeological Journal* 40 (1962): 119–28; Brodie Waddell, *Landscape and Society in the Vale of York, c. 1500–1800* (York, UK: Borthwick Institute, 2011), 15; Tate, *Domesday*, 289; K. J. Allison, *The East Riding of Yorkshire Landscape* (London: Hodder & Stoughton, 1976), 114–15, 120, 131; David Hey, "Yorkshire and Lancashire," in *AHEW* V.1, 75–76; M. W. Beresford, "Glebe Terriers and Open Field, Yorkshire," *Yorkshire Archaeological Journal* 37 (1951): 348–49, 357.

9 Comparing David Grayson Allen's table of "English Origins of the Original Landholders of Rowley, Massachusetts" (Allen, *In English Ways*, 245–49) with more recent research reveals only a few suspect attributions. Patricia Law Hatcher, "Focus on Rowley and Ezekiel Rogers' Company," *Great Migration Newsletter* 18 (2009): 19–30; Waddell, *Landscape and Society*, 28.

10 George Brainard Blodgette and Amos Everett Jewett, *Early Settlers of Rowley, Massachusetts* (1933; repr. Somersworth: New England History Press, 1981), 23, 168–69, 186–87; Hatcher, "Ezekiel Rogers' Company," 20; Shurtleff, *Records of the Governor and Company*, e.g., 1:318, 2:1, 2:22; Ezekiel Rogers to William Sykes, December 2, 1646, in "Letters Written by Rev. Ezekiel Rogers of Rowley, Rev. Daniel Rogers of Wethersfield, and Samuel Shepard of Cambridge, 1626–1647," *Essex Institute Historical Collections* 53 (1917): 219–21.

11 Shurtleff, *Records of the Governor and Company*, 1:319; Mighill and Blodgette, *Early Records of… Rowley*, 80–82.

12 "West Yorkshire Historic Landscape Characterisation Project: Bradford, Themed Results," 2017, in Archaeology Data Service, accessed July 20, 2019, 140–41; Hey, "Yorkshire and Lancashire," 82–84; Thirsk, "Farming Regions of England," 28–29, 31–32; John Crabtree, *Concise History of the Parish and Vicarage of Halifax* (Halifax: Hartley and Walker, 1836), 6, 13–14, 17–18; John James, *History and Topography of Bradford* (London: Longman, Brown, Green, and Longmans, 1841), 116, in Internet Archive; John James, *Continuation and Additions to the History of Bradford* (London: Longmans, Green, Reader, and Dyer, 1866), 304, in Internet Archive.

13 [Defoe], *Tour*, 3:111; Hey, "Yorkshire and Lancashire," 84; Martha J. Ellis, "A Study in the Manorial History of Halifax Parish in the Sixteenth and Early Seventeenth Centuries, Part II," *Yorkshire Archaeological Journal* 40 (1962): 425–27.

14 St. Peter Parish Records, Register of Baptisms, Marriages and Burials, 1653–1708, PE 62/2, East Riding (Yorkshire) Archives, Beverley, UK; A. N. Cooper, "How Rowley in Yorkshire Lost Its Population in the 17th Century, and How Rowley in Massachusetts Was Founded," *Transactions of the East Riding Antiquarian Society* 15 (1908): 86; Allison, *History of… York: East Riding*, 4:149. See also Dow, *Records… of the Quarterly Courts of Essex County*, 2:397.

15 M. W. Beresford, "The Lost Villages of Yorkshire, Part I," *Yorkshire Archaeological Journal* 37 (1951): 474–91; Allison, *East Riding of Yorkshire Landscape*, 114.

16 Rogers to Sykes, December 2, 1646, in "Letters Written by Rev. Ezekiel Rogers," 219–21; Deposition of Richard Bellingham in Dow, *Records… of the Quarterly Courts of Essex County*, 2:400–401; Tracy Elliot Hazen, "The English Ancestry of Edward Carlton of Rowley, Mass.," *New England Historical and Genealogical Register* 93 (January 1939): 32–33.

17 Samuel Maverick, "Briefe Discription of New England," *Proceedings of the Massachusetts Historical Society*, 2nd ser., 1 (1884–85): 231–48.

18 Ezekiel Rogers to John Winthrop, November 3, 1639, in *Winthrop Papers*, 4:151.

19 Ezekiel Rogers to John Winthrop, December 8, 1639, in *Winthrop Papers*, 4:159–60.

20 Winthrop, *Journal*, 430–31. In addition to his family ties to Ward, the leader of the opposition to Winthrop, Rogers also had close links to Ward's ally Thomas Shepard. After Bishop Laud barred Shepard from preaching in the London diocese, Rogers helped Shepard find a post with Sir Richard Darley in Buttercrambe, Yorkshire. In 1665, after Rogers's death, Shepard's

son Samuel would become the teacher of Rowley. Jewett and Jewett, *Rowley, Massachusetts*, 95; "Thomas Shepard's Memoir of His Own Life," in Young, *Chronicles of the First Planters*, 518–19, 522–23.

21 Peter N. Carroll, *Puritanism and the Wilderness: The Intellectual Significance of the New England Frontier, 1629–1700* (New York: Columbia University Press, 1969), 156–57; see also Foster, *Long Argument*, 28–29, 93, 158; Susan Hardman Moore, "Popery, Purity and Providence: Deciphering the New England Experiment," in *Religion, Culture and Society in Early Modern Britain: Essays in Honour of Patrick Collinson*, ed. Anthony Fletcher and Peter Roberts (Cambridge: Cambridge University Press, 1994), 267–68; Emmanuel Downing to John Winthrop, March 2, 1638/39, in *Winthrop Papers*, 4:102–3.

22 Winthrop, *Journal*, 287; Cotton Mather makes the same point in *Magnalia*, 1:411.

23 Shurtleff, *Records of the Governor and Company*, 253; Winthrop, *Journal*, 288.

24 Ezekiel Rogers to John Winthrop, November 3, 1639, in *Winthrop* Papers, 4:151; Shurtleff, *Records of the Governor and Company*, 1:289.

25 Ezekiel Rogers to John Winthrop, March 4, 1639/40, in *Winthrop Papers*, 4:215–16.

26 Ezekiel Rogers to John Winthrop, October 5, 1640, in *Winthrop Papers*, 289–91; Nathaniel Ward to John Winthrop, ca. April 1640, in *Winthrop Papers*, 4:221–22.

27 Shurtleff, *Records of the Governor and Company*, 292, 305; Winthrop, *Journal*, 338–39. This was not the only time that the Court showed its wariness of the ministerial cachet of the Ward/Rogers family. In 1642, John Rogers of Dedham's son Nathaniel Rogers, who was ministering in Ipswich, opposed Simon Bradstreet in a dispute between Bradstreet and the town. Bradstreet's father-in-law Thomas Dudley demanded of Rogers, "Do you think to come with your eldership here to carry matters[?]" By this time, thanks to the Antinomian Controversy, Dudley had reconciled with Winthrop and had moved from Ipswich to Roxbury. Winthrop, *Journal*, 452–53; McDermott, "Body of Liberties," 162–63.

28 John Woodbridge to John Winthrop, March 22, 1640/41, in *Winthrop Papers*, 4:327–28; Winthrop, *Journal*, 614; see also Jewett and Jewett, *Rowley, Massachusetts*, 13–15. During the controversy with Andover, Rogers had the nerve to muse in a letter to Winthrop, "Touching the businesse of the Bounds, which we haue now in agitation; I haue thought, that a good fence helpeth to keepe peace betweene neighbours; but let vs take heede that we make not a high stone wall, to keepe vs from meeting." Ezekiel Rogers to John Winthrop, August 31, 1640, in *Winthrop Papers*, 4:282.

29 The General Court records suggest that Rogers did gain the disputed land, temporarily. In 1652, the Court ruled that "five or six hundred acres" on the border of Andover and Rowley, which had been laid out to Rowley, had to be returned to Andover; however, Rowley was granted the same amount of land on the Ipswich River in compensation. Shurtleff, *Records of the Governor and Company* 4 pt. 1, 96; Gage, *History of Rowley*, 135.

30 Winthrop, *Journal*, 615; Rogers to Winthrop, October 5, 1640, in *Winthrop Papers*, 4:290.

31 Rowley Town Records No. 1, 1660–1712 [hereinafter Rowley Town Records], 16, Rowley Town Clerk's Office, Rowley, MA; see also Mighill and Blodgette, *Early Records of...Rowley*, 189, and the petition of Boxford inhabitants dated May 27, 1685, reprinted in Sidney Perley, *History of Boxford, Essex County, Massachusetts* (Boxford, MA: by the author, 1880), 83–84, in Internet Archive.

32 Petition dated May 7, 1673, reprinted in Perley, *History of Boxford*, 64–65.

33 Rowley Freeholders' Records, image 840.

34 Rowley Town Meetings, 1648–71 [hereinafter Rowley Town Meetings], 17r, Rowley Town Clerk's Office, Rowley, MA. There is some potential confusion here in that Boxford was first known as "Rowley Village," but in its early days Bradford was also called "Rowley Village, on the Merrimack," and the date makes it clear that this record refers to the area later called Bradford. See J. D. Kingsbury, *Memorial History of Bradford, Mass.* (Haverhill, MA: C. C. Morse

& Son, 1883), 14. For the land swap that made the separate existence of both villages possible, see Rowley Freeholders' Records, image 835; Rowley Town Meetings, 11v.
35 Shurtleff, *Records of the Governor and Company* 4, part 2, 380.
36 Rowley Town Records, 2. Similarly, the town was divided into "Circuits" for warning residents to come to town meetings. Rowley Town Meetings, 3v.
37 Rowley Town Records, 5; Rowley Town Meetings, 10r, 8r [quote], 9r, 32v.
38 Rowley Town Records, 1.
39 Rowley Town Meetings, 24r; Rowley Freeholders' Records, image 822.
40 Rowley Town Records, 6, 14; Rowley Town Meetings, 23r.
41 Rowley Town Records, 18–19; Rowley Town meetings, 10r, 17r.
42 Martin, *Profits in the Wilderness*; Deposition of Richard Bellingham, 1662, in Dow, *Records…of the Quarterly Courts of Essex County*, 2:400.
43 Rowley Town Records, 1.
44 Rowley Town Meetings, 10r.
45 Rowley Town Records, 1.
46 Rowley Town Records, 3, 5, 13, 16 [quote]; Rowley Town Meetings, 24v, 33r, 33v.
47 Rowley Town Records, 8, 14, 16; Rowley Town Meetings, 12v, 21v.
48 Rowley Town Records, 4. The Haverhill town records confirm what it meant for a law to be "crossed": a provision concerning the ox common was crossed out, with the notation, "This was by voate consented to by ye towne to be crost." And a vote about allotting land proportionably was also crossed out, but a note was added in the margins: "Notwithstanding this order was crossed by Thomas Hall through a mistake yet it standeth in force." Haverhill Town Meetings, 1643–60 [hereinafter Haverhill Town Meetings], Haverhill City Clerk's Office, Haverhill, MA, 131, 3.
49 Rowley Town Meetings, 34v.
50 Rowley Freeholders' Records, image 822, image 847; Rowley Town Meetings, 28r, 29r.
51 Rowley Freeholders' Records, image 859; Rowley Town Meetings, 22v; "Map of Rowley, Surveyed and Drawn by Philander Anderson," 1830, in Historic Ipswich.
52 Rowley Freeholders' Records, image 847.
53 Rowley Town Records, 24.
54 Plan of Rowley surveyed by Joseph Chapin, December, 1794, from Massachusetts Archives, in Digital Commonwealth.
55 Mather, *Magnalia*, 1:413.
56 Andover Town Meetings, 1660–1808 [hereinafter Andover Town Meetings], FamilySearch database (Church of Jesus Christ of Latter-Day Saints), film 878785, items 2–3, image 76.
57 Nathaniel Ward to John Winthrop, December 22, 1639, and Giles Firmin to John Winthrop, December 26, 1639, in *Winthrop Papers*, 4:162–64; Johnson, *Wonder-Working Providence*, 88; John Ward Dean, *A Brief Memoir of Rev. Giles Firmin* (Boston, MA: David Clapp and Son, 1866), 8, in Internet Archive; Anderson, *Great Migration*, 7:231.
58 Nathaniel Ward to John Winthrop, ca. April 1640, in *Winthrop Papers*, 4:221–22; Elinor Abbot, "Transformations: The Reconstruction of Social Hierarchy in Early Colonial Andover, Massachusetts" (PhD diss, Brandeis University, 1990), 55, in ProQuest Dissertations & Theses Global.
59 See Ward's reference to "the confluence of many ill and doubtfull persons" in Ipswich "and […] their behauiour since they came in drinking and pilferinge" in Nathaniel Ward to John Winthrop Jr., December 24, 1635, in *Winthrop Papers*, 3:215–17.
60 Firmin to Winthrop, December 26, 1639, in *Winthrop Papers*, 4:163–64; Ward to Winthrop Jr., December 24, 1635, in *Winthrop Papers*, 3:215–17.
61 Shurtleff, *Records of the Governor and Company*, 1:344, 2:38; Perzel, "First Generation of Settlement," 57; *American National Biography Online*, s.v. "Norton, John" by Janice Durbin-Dodd,

accessed December 14, 2013; Abbot, "Transformations," 87–89, 99; see also Shurtleff, *Records of the Governor and Company*, 1:290, for reference to "Newberry men" involved in Ward's project.

62 Shurtleff, *Records of the Governor and Company*, 2:38; Abiel Abbot, *History of Andover from Its Settlement to 1829* (Andover, MA: Flagg and Gould, 1829), 10–12; Hubbard, *General History*, 416.

63 Mary K. Talcott, "Genealogy of the Woodbridge Family," *New England Historical and Genealogical Review* 32 (1878): 292; Anderson, *Great Migration*, 7: 500–510; Philip J. Greven Jr., *Four Generations: Population, Land, and Family in Colonial Andover, Massachusetts* (Ithaca, NY: Cornell University Press, 1970), 42–44, 73–99; see also Greven, "Old Patterns in the New World: The Distribution of Land in 17th Century Andover," in *New England Rediscovered: Selected Articles on New England Colonial History, 1965 to 1973*, ed. Peter Charles Hoffer (New York: Garland Publishing, 1988), 42–57.

64 "The Declaration and agreement of ye Inhabitants of Andover att a Generall Towne Meeting ye 18th of January 1663," in Dow, *Records…of the Quarterly Courts of Essex County*, 8:81–82.

65 Johnson, *Wonder-Working Providence*, 210. Johnson incorrectly names the town as "Haverhil."

66 Greven, *Four Generations*, 45, 49 [quote]; Andover Town Meetings, images 74–75; O'Malley, "Rowley, Massachusetts," Appendix 1; Gage, *History of Rowley*, 130–32. The larger size of Andover houselots begs the question of why anyone would want a houselot of 20 acres, unless the land within the town were unusually rich, which does not seem to have been the case. However, not all of the larger houselots were contiguous: see the records for John Osgood, whose 20-acre houselot consisted of 6 acres next to his house and 14 "adioyning to his meadow," in Andover Ancient Records, [2r,] Andover Town Clerk's Office, Andover, MA.

67 Greven, *Four Generations*, 52–57; Andover Town Meetings, image 98; see also image 82: "it is ordered that all that haue any rite or interest in any meddow: for the conveniency of fencing of it shall haue libertie to fence such corners of necks of Land adioyning to it: for the running of this fence straight," and image 93, which requires those with "vpland: Lying in common or unfenced" to make sure their bounds are marked by trees, holes, or stones.

68 Andover Town Meetings, images 93, 96, 102, 103 [quote].

69 Pew, "Worshipful Simon Bradstreet," 308; Sarah Loring Bailey, *Historical Sketches of Andover* (Boston, MA: Houghton Mifflin, 1880), 14. Interestingly, Bailey also suggested that Andover's layout was influenced by the Essay on the Ordering of Towns; Bailey, *Historical Sketches*, 28.

70 McDermott, "Body of Liberties," 137, 153, 156, 200–201, 207, 209–10; Shurtleff, *Records of the Governor and Company* 1:277–78; George L. Kittredge, "Dr. Robert Child the Remonstrant," *Publications of the Colonial Society of Massachusetts* 21 (1920): 1–146; Hamilton, *Social and Economic Networks*, 9.

71 Anderson, *Great Migration*, 7:500; Gordon, *Mistress Bradstreet*, 227, 239–40; Mather, *Magnalia*, 1:595.

72 Anderson, *Great Migration*, 7:505–7; Talcott, "Genealogy of the Woodbridge Family," 293, 295; George Adlard, *The Sutton-Dudleys of England and the Dudleys of Massachusetts in New England* (New York: for George Adlard, 1862), 106, in Internet Archive. These connections provide an example of the "'social web'" described by Marsha L. Hamilton, which she defines as "the many ties that settlers had within and among their communities. The 'social cohesion' discovered by T. H. Breen and Stephen Foster was not simply the result of homogeneity, but came from the extensive communities and multiple identities that tied colonists together across social and economic boundaries." Hamilton, *Social and Economic Networks*, 23.

73 *Works of Anne Bradstreet*, ed. Hensley, 2.

74 *Works of Anne Bradstreet*, ed. Hensley, 3; on the friendship between Ward and Bradstreet, see Gordon, *Mistress Bradstreet*, 182, 236–37.

75 *Works of Anne Bradstreet*, ed. Hensley, 53.

76 *Works of Anne Bradstreet*, ed. Hensley, 159, 198.

77 *Works of Anne Bradstreet*, ed. Hensley, 265–66; Thomas Aquinas, *Summa Theologica* 1.2.3, in Anton C. Pegis, ed., *Introduction to Saint Thomas Aquinas* (New York: Modern Library, 1948), 27.

NOTES

78 See Martin, *Profits in the Wilderness*, 171, 218–21.
79 Andover Town Meetings, image 77.
80 Andover Town Meetings, images 125–26.
81 Andover Town Meetings, images 85–86; Greven, *Four Generations*, 62.
82 Robert E. Moody, ed., "Records of the Magistrates' Court at Haverhill, Massachusetts, Kept by Nathaniel Saltonstall, 1682–1685," *Proceedings of the Massachusetts Historical Society* 3rd ser., 79 (1967): 151; "An Historical Sketch of Haverhill, in the County of Essex," *Collections of the Massachusetts Historical Society* 2nd ser., 4 (1816; repr., 1846): 127, in Google Books.
83 John B. D. Cogswell, "Haverhill," in D. Hamilton Hurd, ed., *History of Essex County, Massachusetts* (Philadelphia: J. W. Lewis, 1888), 2:1902, in Internet Archive; Sears, *Physical Geography…of Essex County*, 393; "Historical Sketch of Haverhill," 121.
84 Shurtleff, *Records of the Governor and Company*, 3:186, 3:189, 3:246, 3:349, 3:365, 4 pt. 1:209; Johnson, *Wonder-Working Providence*, 197.
85 John Ward Dean, "A Brief Memoir of Rev. Giles Firmin," *New England Historical and Genealogical Register* 20 (1866): 50; Jonathan Edward Warren, "Polity, Piety, and Polemic: Giles Firmin and the Transatlantic Puritan Tradition" (PhD diss., Vanderbilt University, 2014), 14, in ProQuest Dissertations & Theses Global; Mather, *Magnalia*, 1:521–24; Venn, *Alumni Cantabrigienses…Part I*, 4:332–333; ECA CHA.1.4(c), 136r.
86 Haverhill Town Records, Nos. 2–3 [hereinafter Haverhill Town Records], 1643–1724, 151, 152, 153, 155, 163, 164, 165, 167, 168, 175, 176, 177, 194, Haverhill City Clerk's Office, Haverhill, MA. This is a transcription in a later hand, but I have been forced to rely upon it because of the deteriorated state of the original records in the volume of Haverhill Town Meetings, 1643–60.
87 Johnson, *Wonder-Working Providence*, 197.
88 Haverhill Town Records, 151; the damaged original is in Haverhill Town Meetings, 3.
89 Haverhill Town Records, 164.
90 Haverhill Town Records, 164; Haverhill Town Meeting Records No. 1, 1667–74 [hereinafter Haverhill Town Meeting Records], 49, Haverhill City Clerk's Office, Haverhill, MA. This book too is a later transcription of early records. As Edward T. Price described New England land allocation, "In dividing the land […] tracts were seldom divided equally, but rather were allocated on formulas determined by the proprietors and taking into account such matters as standing in the community, wealth, occupation, size of family, number of cattle, residence or birth in the town, and participation in the purchase of the land." Price, *Dividing the Land*, 31. John Stilgoe calls this approach to land distribution "eunomic"; John Robert Stilgoe, "Pattern on the Land: The Making of a Colonial Landscape, 1633–1800" (PhD diss., Harvard University, 1976), 4.
91 Haverhill Town Records, 152, 164; Haverhill Town Meetings, 77; B. L. Mirick, *The History of Haverhill, Massachusetts* (Haverhill, MA: A. W. Thayer, 1832), 24, in Internet Archive; George Wingate Chase, *The History of Haverhill, from Its First Settlement, in 1640, to the Year 1860* (Haverhill, MA: By the author, 1861), 69, in Internet Archive.
92 Haverhill Town Records, 166, 167, 168, 174, 175, 179.
93 Cogswell, "Haverhill," in Hurd, *History of Essex County*, 2:1912–13; Haverhill Town Meeting Records, e.g., 46–47.
94 Perhaps this was deemed worthy of mention only because fencing the parcels of meadowland, which were more scattered than individual plots of planting ground, might have required enough timber to cause concern. Haverhill Town Records, 180.
95 Haverhill Town Records, 170; Haverhill Town Meeting Records, 51.
96 Haverhill Town Records, 196.
97 Haverhill Town Records, 157, 187.

Epilogue: The Future of Corporatism and the Ideology of Mobility in America

1 On the repatriation, see Moore, *Pilgrims*; Andrew Delbanco, "Looking Homeward, Going Home: The Lure of England for the Founders of New England," *New England Quarterly* 59, no. 3 (September 1986): 358–86; Norman Pettit, "God's Englishman in New England: His Enduring Ties to the Motherland," *Proceedings of the Massachusetts Historical Society* 3rd ser., 101 (1989): 56–70; William L. Sachse, "The Migration of New Englanders to England, 1640–1660," *American Historical Review* 53, no. 2 (January 1948): 251–78.
2 Harry S. Stout, "The Morphology of Remigration: New England University Men and Their Return to England, 1640–1660," *Journal of American Studies* 10, no. 2 (August 1976): 151–72; Richard S. Dunn, *Puritans and Yankees: The Winthrop Dynasty of New England, 1630–1717* (Princeton, NJ: Princeton University Press, 1962), 37.
3 Mather, *Magnalia Christi Americana*, 1:522; David Hugh Farmer, *The Oxford Dictionary of Saints*, 3rd ed. (Oxford: Oxford University Press, 1992), 229–30; Oxford English Dictionary, accessed May 16, 2013. On Ward's humor, see Bruce C. Daniels, *Puritans at Play: Leisure and Recreation in Colonial New England* (New York: St. Martin's Griffin, 1995), 37.
4 Ward, *Simple Cobler*, 71, 22–23.
5 Ward, *Simple Cobler*, 78–79.
6 Ward, *Sermon Preached*, 16.
7 Ward, *Sermon Preached*, 18, 22.
8 Ward, *Simple Cobler*, 48; Juhani Norri, *Dictionary of Medical Vocabulary in English, 1375–1550: Body Parts, Sicknesses, Instruments, and Medicinal Preparations, Part I and II* (Abingdon, UK: Routledge, 2016), 798.
9 *Mercurius Anti-mechanicus* (London: for John Walker, 1648), 49, in Early English Books Online.
10 Ward, *Simple Cobler*, 3, 6.
11 Hall, *Puritans*, 282; Ward, *Simple Cobler*, 38; Thomas Edwards, *Gangraena* (London: for Ralph Smith, 1646), in Internet Archive; Ann Hughes, *Gangraena and the Struggle for the English Revolution* (Oxford: Oxford University Press, 2004).
12 Ralph F. Young, "Breathing the 'Free Aire of the New World': The Influence of the New England Way on the Gathering of Congregational Churches in Old England, 1640–1660," *New England Quarterly* 83, no. 1 (March 2010): 39–43; Francis J. Bremer, "Communications: The English Context of New England's Seventeenth-Century History," *New England Quarterly* 60, no. 2 (June 1987): 330.
13 Ward, *Discolliminium*, 49; J. H. Hexter, "The Problem of the Presbyterian Independents," *American Historical Review* 44, no. 1 (October 1938): 29–49; George Yule, *The Independents in the English Civil War* (Cambridge: Cambridge University Press, 1958); David Underdown, "The Independents Reconsidered," *Journal of British Studies* 3, no. 2 (May 1964): 57–84; George Yule, "Independents and Revolutionaries," *Journal of British Studies* 7, no. 2 (May 1968): 11–32; Stephen Foster, "The Presbyterian Independents Exorcized. A Ghost Story for Historians," *Past & Present* 44 (August 1969): 52–75.
14 Stephen Winthrop to John Winthrop, July 29, 1647, in *Winthrop Papers*, 5:175; Francis J. Bremer, "Stephen Winthrop: Soldier of the Lord," in Bremer, *First Founders*.
15 Ward, *Discolliminium*; Venn, *Alumni Cantabrigienses...Part 1*, 4:333.
16 Alexis de Tocqueville, *Democracy in America*, trans. Arthur Goldhammer (New York: Library of America, 2004), 625–27.
17 Whitney R. Cross, *The Burned-Over District: The Social and Intellectual History of Enthusiastic Religion in Western New York, 1800–1850* (1950; repr., Ithaca, NY: Cornell University Press, 2015); James E. Davis, *Frontier Illinois* (Bloomington: Indiana University Press, 1998), 202, 225, 253, 255, 276; Amy DeRogatis, "Models of Piety: Plan of Union Missionaries on the Western Reserve, 1800–1806," *Journal of Presbyterian History* 79, no. 4 (Winter 2001): 257–75;

Stephen Kissel, "'The Best of Bonds': How Methodist Circuit Riders Created Community in Antebellum Illinois, 1800–1850," *Ohio Valley History* 15, no. 2 (Summer 2015): 3–27; Allen P. Tankersley, "Midway District: A Study of Puritanism in Colonial Georgia," *Georgia Historical Quarterly* 32, no. 3 (September 1948): 149–57; Giles Firmin, *A Sober Reply to the Sober Answer of Reverend Mr. Cawdrey* (London: by J.G., 1653), 28, in Google Books. See also my unpublished paper "Elijah P. Lovejoy and the Demise of Evangelical Union," 2010, in Academia.edu.

18 Henry F. Brownson, ed., *The Works of Orestes A. Brownson* (1885; repr., New York: AMS Press, 1966), 18:209, 17:501, 18, 115; R. A. Herrera, *Orestes Brownson: Sign of Contradiction* (Wilmington, DE: ISI Books, 1999); Scott McDermott, "Orestes Brownson and the Contract of Government," *Catholic Social Science Review* 14 (2009): 245–69.

19 Max Weber, *The Protestant Ethic and the Spirit of Capitalism*, trans. Talcott Parsons (New York: Charles Scribner's Sons, 1958), 104–5, 108–9, 111–12, 120–21, 126, 157, 163.

20 For one famous exemplar of the Weber syndrome, see Ron Chernow, *Titan: The Life of John D. Rockefeller, Sr.* (New York: Random House, 1998).

21 Alfred D. Chandler Jr., *The Visible Hand: The Managerial Revolution in American Business* (Cambridge, MA: Harvard University Press, 1977), 32, 34; Edward S. Mason, "Introduction" to Edward S. Mason, ed., *The Corporation in Modern Society* (Cambridge, MA: Harvard University Press, 1966), 5; Abram Chayes, "The Modern Corporation and the Rule of Law," in Mason, *Corporation in Modern Society*, 35–36; Robert E. Wright, *Corporation Nation* (Philadelphia: University of Pennsylvania Press, 2014), 5; Thomas K. McCraw, "American Capitalism," in Thomas K. McCraw, ed., *Creating Modern Capitalism: How Entrepreneurs, Companies, and Countries Triumphed in Three Industrial Revolutions* (Cambridge, MA: Harvard University Press, 1997), 315, 317; Livermore, *Early American Land Companies*, 273, 296.

22 Chandler, *Visible Hand*; Mason, "Introduction," 8–9, 15; Chayes, "Modern Corporation," 25, 37; Earl Latham, "The Body Politic of the Corporation," in Mason, *Corporation in Modern Society*, 223–25; McCraw, "American Capitalism," 322, 325; Wright, *Corporation Nation*; Robert H. Wiebe, *The Search for Order, 1877–1920* (New York: Hill and Wang, 1967), 186–87.

23 Chandler, *Visible Hand*, 316; Nelson Lichtenstein, ed., *Wal-Mart: The Face of Twenty-First-Century Capitalism* (New York: New Press, 2006); Chayes, "Modern Corporation," 28; Norton Long, "The Corporation, Its Satellites, and the Local Community," in Mason, *Corporation in Modern Society*, 202; John Urry, *Offshoring* (Cambridge: Polity Press, 2014); McCraw, "American Capitalism," 323; R. H. Coase, "The Nature of the Firm," *Economica* 4, no. 16 (November 1937): 395.

24 Latham, "Body Politic of the Corporation," 219–20, 227; Peter F. Drucker, *Concept of the Corporation* (1946; repr., London: Transaction, 2007), 12, 20, 21; Wright, *Corporation Nation*, 198, 224; Otto von Gierke, *Political Theories of the Middle Age*, trans. Frederic W. Maitland (1900; repr., Boston: Beacon Press, 1958), 68.

25 Chayes, "Modern Corporation," 34; Charles H. McIlwain, "The Transfer of the Charter to New England, and Its Significance in American Constitutional History," *Proceedings of the Massachusetts Historical Society*, 3rd ser., 63 (October 1929–June 1930): 53–64; Whitmore, *Bibliographical Sketch*, 35.

26 Donahue, *Great Meadow*; Martin, *Profits in the Wilderness*, 259–80.

27 Drucker, *Concept of the Corporation*, xi; Weber, *Protestant Ethic*, 182; Charles Taylor, *A Secular Age* (Cambridge, MA: Harvard University Press, 2007); Brad S. Gregory, *The Unintended Reformation: How a Religious Revolution Secularized Society* (Cambridge, MA: Harvard University Press, 2012); McCraw, "American Capitalism," 327; Leo Panitch, "Recent Theorizations of Corporatism: Reflections on a Growth Industry," *British Journal of Sociology* 31, no. 2 (June 1980): 160, 173–74; J. T. Winkler, "The Coming Corporatism," in Robert Skidelsky, ed., *The End of the Keynesian Era: Essays on the Disintegration of the Keynesian Political Economy* (New York: Holmes & Meier, 1977), 82; Michael J. Hogan, "Corporatism," *Journal of American History* 77, no. 1

(June 1990): 153–60; Larry G. Gerber, "Corporatism and State Theory: A Review Essay for Historians," *Social Science History* 19, no. 3 (Autumn 1995): 317.

28 Wright, *Corporation Nation*, 217–20; Ellis W. Hawley, "The Discovery and Study of a 'Corporate Liberalism,'" *Business History Review* 52, no. 3 (Autumn 1978): 309–20; Gerard Colby Zilg, *DuPont: Behind the Nylon Curtain* (Englewood Cliffs, NJ: Prentice-Hall, 1974); Tocqueville, *Democracy in America*, 220–23, 595–99.

WORKS CITED

Note: URLs for Internet resources, and for more information on databases mentioned in the citations below, will be found in a separate section of "Electronic Resources" at the end.

Primary Sources

The Acts of the Parliament of Scotland. Vol. 1. Edinburgh: By command of H. M. Queen Victoria, 1844.
Acts of the Privy Council of England, 1621–23. London: His Majesty's Stationery Office, 1932. In HathiTrust Digital Library.
Add. Mss. 39245, f. 70. British Library, London, UK.
Alsted, J. H. *A Neglected Educator: Johann Heinrich Alsted. Translation, &c. from the Latin of His Encyclopaedia*. Translated by Percival R. Cole. Sydney: Government Printer, 1910. In Internet Archive.
American Husbandry. London: J. Bew, 1775. In Internet Archive.
Ames, William. *Conscience with the Power and Cases Thereof*. London: n.p., 1639.
Andover Ancient Records. Andover Town Clerk's Office, Andover, MA.
Andover Town Meetings, 1660–1808. In FamilySearch database (Church of Jesus Christ of Latter-Day Saints), film 878785, items 2–3.
Aristotle. *Nicomachean Ethics*. Translated by Martin Ostwald. Englewood Cliffs, NJ: Prentice Hall, 1962.
Award and Plan, 1765, Kesteven Award 42. Lincolnshire Archives, Lincoln, UK.
Bacon, Francis. *Advancement of Learning, Novum Organum, New Atlantis*. Chicago: Encyclopaedia Britannica, 1952.
———. *The Works of Francis Bacon*. Edited by James Spedding, Robert Leslie Ellis and Douglas Denon Heath. Vol. 1. London: Longman, 1858.
Bacon, Nathaniel. *Annalls of Ipswche* [sic]. Edited by William H. Richardson. 1654. Reprint, Ipswich: for the subscribers by S. H. Cowell, 1884. In Internet Archive.
Bacon, Nicholas. *The Recreations of His Age*. Oxford: Clarendon Press, 1919. In Internet Archive.
Baker Mss. B., Mm.2.23. Cambridge University Library, Department of Manuscripts and University Archives, Cambridge, UK.
Election Day Sermons: Massachusetts. Vol. 1 of *A Library of American Puritan Writings: The Seventeenth Century*. Edited by Sacvan Bercovitch. New York: AMS Press, ca. 1984.
Birch, Thomas, ed. *The Court and Times of Charles I*. Vol. 1. London: Henry Colburn, 1849. In Internet Archive.
Blome, Richard. *Britannia*. London: by Thomas Roycroft, 1673. In Google Books.
Bradstreet, Anne. *The Works of Anne Bradstreet*. Edited by Jeannine Hensley. Cambridge, MA: Harvard University Press, 2010.
Brownson, Henry F., ed. *The Works of Orestes A. Brownson*. 20 vols. 1885. Reprint, New York: AMS Press, 1966.
Bucer, Martin. *De Regno Christi*. In *Melanchthon and Bucer*, edited and translated by Wilhelm Pauck, 174–394. Philadelphia, PA: Westminster Press, 1969.
Calendar of State Papers, Domestic Series, of the Reign of Charles I: 1637–1638. London: Longmans, Green, 1869. In Google Books.
Churchwardens' account book for Clare, FL501/5/1/1. Suffolk Record Office, Bury St. Edmunds branch, UK.

Cicero. *The Academica of Cicero*. Edited by James S. Reid. London: Macmillan, 1874. In Google Books.
———. *Ciceronis selectae quaedam epistolae*. Edited by M. L. Hurlbut. Philadelphia, PA: H. Perkins, 1836. In Google Books.
———. *De Officiis*. Translated by Walter Miller. London: William Heinemann, 1921. In Google Books.
———. *M.T. Ciceronis pars secunda sive orationes omnes ad optimos codices*. Edited by N. E. Lemaire. Vol. 6. Paris: Nicolaus Eligius Lemaire, 1830. In Google Books.
———. *M. Tulli Ciceronis orationes ex editione Jo. Aug. Ernesti* .... Edited by A. J. Valpy. Vol. 1. London: A. J. Valpy, 1830. In Google Books.
———. *M. Tulli Ciceronis pro T. Annio Milone ad iudices oratio*. Edited by James S. Reid. Cambridge: Cambridge University Press, 1895. In Google Books.
———. *Orationes quaedam selectae in usum Delphini* .... Edited by Alexander J. Taylor. Philadelphia, PA: Towar and Hogan, 1826. In Google Books.
———. *Orationes, with a Commentary by George Long*. Edited by George Long and A. J. Macleane. Vol. 2. London: Whitaker, 1855. In Google Books.
———. *Selected Orations and Letters of Cicero*. Edited by Harold W. Johnston. Chicago: Albert, Scott, 1892. In Google Books.
Clare glebe terrier, 1794, FL501/5/20. Suffolk Record Office, Bury St. Edmunds branch, UK.
Clark, Michael P., ed. *The Eliot Tracts*. Westport, CT: Praeger, 2003.
Clark, Samuel. *The Lives of Sundry Eminent Persons in This Later Age*. Part 1. London: for Thomas Simmons, 1683. In Google Books.
Cobbet, Thomas. *Fruitfull and Usefull Discourse Touching the Honour Due from Children to Parents*. London: by S. G. for John Rothwell, 1656.
Cobbet, Thomas. Sermon, April 16, 1668, Miscellaneous Manuscripts, Misc. Apr. 16, 1668. Massachusetts Historical Society, Boston, MA.
Cogswell, T. S., ed. "Reasons agst a General Sending of Corne to ye Marketts in ye Champion parte of Norfolke." *Norfolk Archaeology* 20, no. 1 (1917): 10–21. In Archaeology Data Service.
Comenius, John Amos. *The Way of Light*. Translated by E. T. Campagnac. Liverpool, UK: University Press, 1938.
Cotton, John. *Gods Promise to His Plantations*. London: by William Jones for John Bellamy, 1634.
Court book of manor of Dedham Hall, f. 312, D/DU 457/1/2. Essex Record Office, Chelmsford, UK.
Court roll of Haverhill and Horsham with Helions, 1648–57, E7/26/2. Suffolk Record Office, Bury St. Edmunds Branch, UK.
Cox, J. Charles, ed. *The Records of the Borough of Northampton*. Vol. 2. Northampton: Borough of Northampton, 1898.
Dane, John. *A Declaration of Remarkable Providences in the Course of My Life*. Boston, MA: Samuel G. Drake, 1854. In Google Books.
[Defoe, Daniel]. *A Tour Thro' the Whole Island of Great Britain*. Vol. I. London: for J. Osborn, S. Birt, D. Browne, J. Hodges, A. Millar, J. Whiston, and J. Robinson, 1742.
d'Ewes, Simonds. *The Autobiography and Correspondence of Sir Simonds d'Ewes, Bart*. Edited by James Orchard Halliwell. Vol. 1. London: Richard Bentley, 1845. In Google Books.
"Dr. Henry Sampson's Day-Books." *The Christian Reformer; or, Unitarian Magazine and Review*, n.s., 18, no. 2018 (April 1862): 235–47. In Google Books.
Dow, George Francis, ed. *Records and Files of the Quarterly Courts of Essex County, Massachusetts*. 8 vols. Salem, MA: Essex Institute, 1911–21. In Internet Archive.
ECA CHA.1.4(c), Recepta ab Ingredientibus (Register of Admissions, 1584–1713). Emmanuel College Archives, Cambridge, UK.
Edwards, Thomas. *Gangraena*. London: for Ralph Smith, 1646. In Internet Archive.
Egan, Mary-Millicent. "Laudians, Puritans and the Laity in Essex c. 1630–1642." PhD diss., University College, London, 2001. In ETHOS.

Eliot, Jared. *Essays upon Field-Husbandry in New-England*. Boston, MA: Edes and Gill, 1760.
Emmison, F. G. ed. *Early Essex Town Meetings: Braintree, 1619–1636: Finchingfield, 1626–1634*. London: Phillimore, 1970.
Extracts and Exchanges (Horbling enclosure), Horbling PAR 17/1. Lincolnshire Archives, Lincoln, UK.
Farrand, Max, ed. *The Laws and Liberties of Massachusetts: Reprinted from the Copy of the 1648 Edition in the Henry E. Huntington Library*. Cambridge, MA: Harvard University Press, 1929.
Firmin, Giles. *The Real Christian*. London: for Dorman Newman, 1670. In Early English Books Online.
———. *A Sober Reply to the Sober Answer of Reverend Mr. Cawdrey*. London: by J. G., 1653. In Google Books.
Foedera, Conventiones, Literae. 2nd ed. Vol. 17. London: J. Tonson, 1727–28.
Fourth Report of the Royal Commission on Historical Manuscripts, Part I: Report and Appendix. London: George Edward Eyre and William Spottiswoode, 1874. In Google Books.
Gooch, William. *General View of the Agriculture in the County of Cambridge*. London: for Richard Phillips, 1811. In Internet Archive.
Gorton, Samuel. *Simplicities Defence against Seven-Headed Policy*. London: by John Macock, 1646. In Early English Books Online.
[Goslicius, Laurentius Grimaldus]. *A Common-wealth of Good Counsaile*. London: by R. B. for N. Lyng, 1607. In Google Books.
David D. Hall, ed. *The Antinomian Controversy, 1636–1638: A Documentary History*. 2nd ed. Durham, NC: Duke University Press, 1990.
Harley Mss. 389 and 3783. British Library, London, UK.
Haverhill Town Meeting Records, No. 1, 1667–74. Haverhill City Clerk's Office, Haverhill, MA.
Haverhill Town Meetings, 1643–60. Haverhill City Clerk's Office, Haverhill, MA.
Haverhill Town Records, Nos. 2–3, 1643–724. Haverhill City Clerk's Office, Haverhill, MA.
Heimert, Alan, and Andrew Delbanco, eds. *The Puritans in America: A Narrative Anthology*. Cambridge, MA: Harvard University Press, 1985.
Higginson, Francis. *New-Englands Plantation*. 1630. Reprint, Salem, MA: Essex Book and Print Club, 1908.
Holdsworth, Richard. "Directions for a Student in the Universitie." In vol. 2 of *The Intellectual Development of John Milton* by Harris Francis Fletcher, 623–64. Urbana: University of Illinois Press, 1961.
Hooker, Thomas. *The Danger of Desertion: Or a Farwell Sermon ....* London: by G. M. for George Edwards, 1641. In Early English Books Online.
———. *The Faithful Covenanter*. London: for Christopher Meredith, 1644. In Early English Books Online.
———. *A Survey of the Summe of Church-Discipline*. London: by A. M. for John Bellamy, 1648. In Internet Archive.
———. *Thomas Hooker: Writings in England and Holland, 1626–1633*. Edited by George H. Williams, Norman Pettit, Winfried Herget, and Sargent Bush Jr. Cambridge, MA: Harvard University Press, 1975.
———. *The Vnbeleevers Preparing for Christ*. London: by Thomas Cotes for Andrew Crooke, 1638. In Early English Books Online.
Horbling, Enclosure Act and Minutes, Smith 5/ENC/Horbling. Lincolnshire Archives, Lincoln, UK.
Horbling Town Book, Horbling PAR/7/10. Lincolnshire Archives, Lincoln, UK.
Howe, Mark DeWolfe, ed. *Readings in American Legal History*. Cambridge: Harvard University Press, 1949.
Hubbard, William. *General History of New England*. Boston, MA: Charles Little and James Brown, 1848. In Internet Archive.

"The humble petition of the select men of Ipswich." 1667. Massachusetts Archives 112: 181, Boston, MA.

Hutchinson, Thomas, ed. *The Hutchinson Papers*. 2 vols. 1769. Reprint, Albany, NY: Prince Society, 1865. In Internet Archive.

Ipswich Deeds, Mortgages, Wills, 1639–95. In FamilySearch database (Church of Jesus Christ of Latter-Day Saints), film 873018.

Ipswich Land and Grants and Town Meetings, 1634. In FamilySearch database (Church of Jesus Christ of Latter-Day Saints), film 476736.

Ipswich Town Records and Land Grants, 1634–1757. In FamilySearch database (Church of Jesus Christ of Latter-Day Saints), film 476737.

Ipswich Town Records Copy, 1634–1864. In FamilySearch database (Church of Jesus Christ of Latter-Day Saints), film 878652, items 2–4.

James I. *The Political Works of James I*. Edited by Charles H. McIlwain. Cambridge, MA: Harvard University Press, 1918.

Johnson, Edward. *Wonder-Working Providence of Sions Saviour in New England*. 1654. Reprint, Andover, MA: Warren F. Draper, 1867. In Internet Archive.

Judges, A. V., ed. *The Elizabethan Underworld*. 1930. Reprint, London: Routledge & Kegan Paul, 1965.

Kupperman, Karen Ordahl, ed., *Captain John Smith: A Select Edition of His Writings*. Chapel Hill: University of North Carolina Press, 1988.

Leigh, Edward. *A Systeme or Body of Divinity*. London: by A. M. for William Lee, 1654. In Google Books.

Leland, John. *The Itinerary of John Leland the Antiquary*. 2nd ed. Oxford: at the Theatre, 1745.

"Letters Written by Rev. Ezekiel Rogers of Rowley, Rev. Daniel Rogers of Wethersfield, and Samuel Shepard of Cambridge, 1626–1647." *Essex Institute Historical Collections* 53 (1917): 215–27.

Lewis, Thomas, Taylor, ed. *Letters of the Lady Brilliana Harley*. London: Camden Society, 1854.

Liber Gratiarum Epsilon, 1589–1620. Cambridge University Archives, Cambridge, UK.

License by John Winthrop, September 1, 1616, FL 506/11/8. Suffolk Record Office, Bury St. Edmunds, UK.

License by Thomas Cole, September 4, 1637. In Papers mainly involving the Cole family, D/DWv/B5. In Essex Record Office, Chelmsford, UK.

Magirus, Johannes. *Corona Virtutum moralium*. Frankfurt: in Collegio Musarum Paltheniano, 1601. In Google Books.

Manor of Dedham Hall, Parliamentary Survey, 1650, E 317 Essex/12. National Archives, Kew.

Map of Haverhill, 1825, M547/16. Suffolk Record Office, Bury St. Edmunds branch, UK.

Map of Haverhill, 1855, M547/17. Suffolk Record Office, Bury St. Edmunds branch, UK.

"Map of Rowley, Surveyed and Drawn by Philander Anderson," 1830. In Historic Ipswich.

Map of West Field Common, Haverhill, 1733, FL 595/13/12. Suffolk Record Office, Bury St. Edmunds Branch, UK.

Marshall, William. *Rural Economy of the West of England*. Vol. 2I. London: for G. Nicol, 1796.

Mather, Cotton. *Dr. Cotton Mather's Student and Preacher*. London: for Charles Dilly, 1781. In Google Books.

———. *Magnalia Christi Americana*. 2 vols. Hartford, CT: Silas Andrus & Son, 1853–55.

Maverick, Samuel. "Briefe Discription of New England." *Proceedings of the Massachusetts Historical Society*, 2nd ser., 1 (1884–85): 231–49.

Mercurius Anti-mechanicus. London: for John Walker, 1648. In Early English Books Online.

Mighill, Benjamin, and George Blodgette, eds. *Early Records of the Town of Rowley, Massachusetts, 1639–1672*. Rowley, MA: Mighill and Blodgette, 1894. In Internet Archive.

Milton, John. *Political Writings*. Edited by Martin Dzelzainis, translated by Claire Gruzelier. Cambridge: Cambridge University Press, 1991.

Mornay, Philippe du Plessis [Stephanus Junius Brutus]. *Vindiciae contra tyrannos*. Frankfurt: Sumpt. Haered. Lazari Zetzneri, 1622. In Google Books.

Newbury Proprietors' Records from 1635, 2–3. Newbury Town Clerk's Office, Newbury, MA.

Newbury Town Records, 1635–1860. In FamilySearch database (Church of Jesus Christ of Latter-Day Saints), film 886194, item 4.

Norden, John. *John Norden's* The Surveyor's Dialogue *(1618): A Critical Edition.* Edited by Mark Netzloff. 2010. Reprint, Abingdon, UK: Routledge, 2016.

Norton, John. *Three Choice and Profitable Sermons upon Severall Texts of Scripture* .... Cambridge, MA: S. G. and M. I. for Hezekiah Usher, 1664. In Early English Books Online.

Noyes, James. *Moses and Aaron.* London: by T. R. for Edmund Paxton, 1661. In Early English Books Online.

———. *The Temple Measured.* London: for Edmund Paxton, 1646. In Early English Books Online.

Parker, Thomas. *The True Copy of a Letter Written By Mr. Thomas Parker ... unto a member of the Assembly of Divines now at Westminster.* London: by Richard Cotes, for Ralph Smith, 1643. In Early English Books Online.

Perkins, William. *The Arte of Prophecying.* London: by Felix Kyngston for E. E., 1607. In Early English Books Online.

———. *Christian Oeconomie.* London: Felix Kyngston, 1609. In Early English Books Online.

———. *Epieikeia: Or, a Treatise of Christian Equitie and Moderation.* Cambridge: by Iohn Legat, 1604.

———. *The Whole Treatise of the Cases of Conscience.* Cambridge: by Iohn Legat, 1608. In Early English Books Online.

———. *The Works of that Famous and Worthie Minister of Christ ... M. W. Perkins ... Gathered into one volume.* Cambridge: by Iohn Legat, 1605. In Early English Books Online.

Plan of Rowley surveyed by Joseph Chapin, December, 1794. From Massachusetts Archives; in Digital Commonwealth.

Preston, John. *The Breast-Plate of Faith and Love.* London: by W. I. for Nicolas Bourne, 1630. In Internet Archive.

The Probate Records of Essex County, Massachusetts. Vol. 1. Salem, MA: Essex Institute, 1916.

Prynne, William. *Canterburies Doome.* London: by John Macock for Michael Spark, 1646. In Early English Books Online.

A Relation or Iournall of the Beginning and Proceedings of the English Plantation setled at Plimoth .... London: for Iohn Bellamie, 1622.

"Report of Edmund Browne." *Publications of the Colonial Society of Massachusetts* 7 (1905): 76–80. In Google Books.

Reyce, Robert. *Suffolk in the XVIIth Century. The Breviary of Suffolk.* London: John Murray, 1902. In Google Books.

Rogers, John. *The Doctrine of Faith.* London: by I. D. for Nathanael Newbery and Henry Overton, 1633.

———. *A Godly & Fruitful Exposition Upon all the First Epistle of Peter.* London: by John Field, 1650. In Early English Books Online.

———. *A Treatise of Love.* 2nd ed. London: by Iohn Dawson for Nathanael Newbery, 1632. In Google Books.

Rogers, Nathaniel. *A Letter, Discovering The Cause of Gods continuing wrath against the Nation* .... London: by G. M. for Christopher Meredith, 1644. In Early English Books Online.

Rogers, Richard. *Commentary vpon the Whole Booke of Iudges.* London: by Felix Kyngston for Thomas Man, 1615. In Early English Books Online.

———. *Seauen Treatises.* London: by Felix Kingston, for Thomas Man, 1610. In Internet Archive.

Rogers, Samuel. *The Diary of Samuel Rogers, 1634–1638.* Edited by Tom Webster and Kenneth Shipps. Woodbridge, UK: Boydell Press, 2004.

Rowley Freeholders' Records, 1643–1830. In FamilySearch database (Church of Jesus Christ of Latter-Day Saints), film 887760.

Rowley Town Meetings, 1648–71. Rowley Town Clerk's Office, Rowley, MA.

Rowley Town Records No. 1, 1660–1712. Rowley Town Clerk's Office, Rowley, MA.

Rufus, Quintus Curtius. *Q. Curti Rufi historiarum Alexandri Magni Macedonis*. Edited by Theodor Vogel. Leipzig: B. G. Teubner, 1875. In Google Books.
St. Peter Parish Records, Register of Baptisms, Marriages and Burials, 1653–1708, PE 62/2. East Riding (Yorkshire) Archives, Beverley, UK.
Saunders, H. W. ed., *The Official Papers of Sir Nathaniel Bacon of Stiffkey, Norfolk, as Justice of the Peace, 1580–1620*. London: Royal Historical Society, 1915. In Internet Archive.
Schofield, George A., ed. *Ancient Records of the Town of Ipswich*. Ipswich: Chronicle Motor Press, 1899. In Internet Archive.
Searle, Arthur, ed. *Barrington Family Letters, 1628–1632*. London: Offices of the Royal Historical Society, 1983.
Shepard, Douglas. "The Wolcott Shorthand Notebook Transcribed." PhD diss., University of Iowa, 1957. In ProQuest Dissertations & Theses Global.
Sheppard, William. *The Court-Keepers Guide*. London: by James Flesher, 1650. In Google Books.
———. *Of Corporations, Fraternities, and Guilds*. London: for H. Twyford, T. Dring, and J. Place, 1659. In Early English Books Online.
Shurtleff, Nathaniel B., ed. *Records of the Governor and Company of the Massachusetts Bay in New England*. 5 vols. in 6. Boston: W. White, 1853–54. In Internet Archive.
Skaife, Robert H., ed. *The Register of the Guild of Corpus Christi in the City of York*. Edinburgh: Surtees Society, 1872.
Spedding, James, ed. *The Letters and the Life of Francis Bacon*. Vol. 4. London: Longmans, Green, Reader, and Dyer, 1868. In Internet Archive.
The Statutes of Sir Walter Mildmay Kt Chancellor of the Exchequer .... Edited and translated by Frank Stubbings. Cambridge: Cambridge University Press, 1983.
Stewards' papers [original surrenders and presentments] for Haverhill, 1659, D/DWv M142. Essex Record Office, Chelmsford, UK.
Tacitus. *The Histories of Tacitus, Books I and II*. Edited by Frank Gardner Moore. New York: Macmillan, 1910. In Google Books.
Terence. *Terence's Comedies*. Translated by S. Patrick. Vol. 2. Dublin: Gilbert and Hodges, M. Keene, J. Fleming, J. Parry, and B. Smith, 1810. In Google Books.
Thomas Aquinas. *Saint Thomas Aquinas, the Treatise on Law*. Edited by R. J. Henle. Notre Dame, IN: University of Notre Dame Press, 1993.
Thomas Shepard's "Confessions." Edited by George Selement and Bruce C. Woolley. Publications of the Colonial Society of Massachusetts 58. Boston: Colonial Society of Massachusetts, 1981.
Turnbull, G. H., ed. "Some Correspondence of John Winthrop, Jr., and Samuel Hartlib." *Proceedings of the Massachusetts Historical Society*, 3rd series, 72 (October 1957–December 1960): 36–67.
Usher, Roland G., ed., *The Presbyterian Movement in the Reign of Queen Elizabeth As Illustrated by the Minute Book of the Dedham Classis, 1582–1589*. London: Royal Historical Society, 1905. In Internet Archive.
Vancouver, Charles. *General View of the Agriculture in the County of Essex*. London: by W. Smith, 1795. In Internet Archive.
Ward, John. *God iudging among the gods*. London: by I. L. for Christopher Meredith, 1645. In Early English Books Online.
Ward, Nathaniel. *Discolliminium*. London, 1650. In Early English Books Online.
———. *A Religious Retreat Sounded to a Religious Army*. London: for Stephen Bowtell, 1647. In Early English Books Online.
———. *A Sermon Preached before the Honourable House of Commons ....* London: Printed by R. I. for Stephen Bowtell, 1647. In Early English Books Online.
———. *The Simple Cobler of Aggawam in America*. 1647. Reprint, New York: Scholars' Facsimiles and Reprints, 1937.
Ward, Samuel. *Iethro's Iustice of Peace ....* London: Edw. Griffin for Iohn Marriot, 1618. In Early English Books Online.

———. *The Papists Powder Treason*. London: P. Stent, 1680? In Early English Books Online.
White, John. *The Planters Plea*. London: William Jones, 1630.
Whitmore, William H., ed. *A Bibliographical Sketch of the Laws of the Massachusetts Colony from 1630 to 1686*. Boston: Rockwell and Churchill, 1890. In Internet Archive.
Winthrop, John. *The Journal of John Winthrop, 1630–1649*. Edited by Richard S. Dunn, James Savage and Laetitia Yeandle. Cambridge, MA: Harvard University Press, 1996.
Winthrop Jr., John. "The Description, Culture, and Use of Maiz." *Philosophical Transactions* 12 (1677–78): 1065–69.
The Winthrop Papers. 6 vols. Boston: Massachusetts Historical Society, 1929–.
Winthrop, Robert C., ed. *Correspondence of Hartlib, Haak, Oldenburg, and Others of the Founders of the Royal Society, with Governor Winthrop of Connecticut, 1661–1672*. Boston, MA: John Wilson and Son, 1878. In Google Books.
Wood, William. *New Englands Prospect*. London: by Tho. Cotes, 1634.
Wren, Christopher. *Parentalia: or, Memoirs of the Family of the Wrens*. London: for T. Osborn and R. Dodsley, 1750. In Eighteenth Century Collections Online.
Yates, John. *A Modell of Divinitie, Catechistically Composed*. London: by Iohn Dawson for Fulke Clifton, 1622. In Early English Books Online.
Young, Alexander, ed. *Chronicles of the First Planters of the Colony of Massachusetts Bay, from 1623 to 1636*. 1846. Reprint, Williamstown, MA: Corner House Publishers, 1978.
———, ed. *Chronicles of the Pilgrim Fathers of the Colony of Plymouth*. 2nd ed. Boston, MA: Charles C. Little and James Brown, 1844.
Young, Arthur. *General View of the Agriculture of the County of Suffolk*. London: by B. Macmillan, 1797. In Internet Archive.

Secondary Sources

Abbot, Abiel. *History of Andover from Its Settlement to 1829*. Andover, MA: Flagg and Gould, 1829.
Abbot, Eleanor. "Transformations: The Reconstruction of Social Hierarchy in Early Colonial Andover, Massachusetts." PhD diss., Brandeis University, 1990. In ProQuest Dissertations & Theses Global.
Adlard, George. *The Sutton-Dudleys of England and the Dudleys of Massachusetts in New England*. New York: for George Adlard, 1862. In Internet Archive.
Aldred, Oscar, and Graham Fairclough. "Historic Landscape Characterisation: Taking Stock of the Method." 2003. In Archaeology Data Service.
Allen, David, ed. *Ipswich Borough Archives 1255–1835: A Catalogue*. Woodbridge, UK: Boydell Press, 2000.
Allen, David Grayson. *In English Ways: The Movement of Societies and the Transferal of English Local Law and Custom to Massachusetts Bay in the Seventeenth Century*. Chapel Hill: University of North Carolina Press, 1981.
Allison, K. J. *The East Riding of Yorkshire Landscape*. London: Hodder & Stoughton, 1976.
Allison, K. J., ed. *A History of the County of York: East Riding*. Vol. 4. Victoria History of the Counties of England. Oxford: Oxford University Press, 1979.
———. "The Sheep-Corn Husbandry of Norfolk in the Sixteenth and Seventeenth Centuries." *Agricultural History Review* 5, no. 1 (1957): 12–30.
Allport, Susan. *Sermons in Stone: The Stone Walls of New England and New York*. New York: W. W. Norton, 1990.
Alphabetical and Analytical Catalogue of the New York Society Library. New York: R. Craighead, 1850.
Anderson, James F. *The Bond of Being: An Essay on Analogy and Existence*. St. Louis, MO: B. Herder, 1949.
Anderson, Robert Charles, ed. *The Great Migration: Immigrants to New England, 1634–1635*. 7 vols. Boston, MA: New England Historic Genealogical Society, 1999–2011.
———, ed. *The Great Migration Begins: Immigrants to New England, 1620–1633*. 3 vols. Boston, MA: New England Historic Genealogical Society, 1995.

———. *Puritan Pedigrees: The Deep Roots of the Great Migration to New England*. Boston, MA: New England Historic Genealogical Society, 2018.

Anderson, Virginia DeJohn. *New England's Generation: The Great Migration and the Formation of Society and Culture in the Seventeenth Century*. Cambridge: Cambridge University Press, 1991.

Ault, Warren O. "Open-Field Husbandry and the Village Community: A Study of Agrarian By-Laws in Medieval England." *Transactions of the American Philosophical Society* 55, no. 7 (1965): 1–102.

———. "Village By-Laws by Common Consent." *Speculum* 29, no. 2, part 2 (April 1954): 378–94.

Bailey, Mark. *Medieval Suffolk: An Economic and Social History, 1200–1500*. Woodbridge, UK: Boydell Press, 2007.

Bailey, Sarah Loring. *Historical Sketches of Andover*. Boston: Houghton Mifflin, 1880.

Baker, Alan R. H. ed. *Explorations in Historical Geography*. Cambridge: Cambridge University Press, 1984.

Baker, Alan R. H., and Robin A. Butlin, eds. *Studies of Field Systems in the British Isles*. Cambridge: Cambridge University Press, 1973.

Banks, Charles Edward. *Topographical Dictionary of 2885 English Emigrants to New England, 1620–1650*. 3rd ed. Edited by Elijah Brownell. Baltimore, MD: Genealogical Publishing, 1963.

Banks, Charles Edward. *The Winthrop Fleet of 1630*. 1930. Reprint, Westminster, MD: Heritage Books, 2008.

Barnes, Thomas G. "Thomas Lechford and the Earliest Lawyering in Massachusetts, 1638–1641." In *Law in Colonial Massachusetts, 1630–1800: A Conference Held 6 and 7 November 1981 by The Colonial Society of Massachusetts*, 3–38. Boston: Colonial Society of Massachusetts, 1984.

Barton, David. *The Myth of Separation: What Is the Correct Relationship between Church and State? A Revealing Look at What Founders and Early Courts Really Said*. Aledo, TX: WallBuilder Press, 1989.

Beastall, T. W. *The Agricultural Revolution in Lincolnshire*. Lincoln: History of Lincolnshire Committee, 1978.

Beaumont, George Frederick. *A History of Coggeshall, in Essex*. London: Marshall Brothers, 1890.

Beier, A. L. *Masterless Men: The Vagrancy Problem in England, 1560–1640*. London: Methuen, 1985.

Bendall, Sarah, Christopher Brooke, and Patrick Collinson. *A History of Emmanuel College, Cambridge*. Woodbridge, UK: Boydell Press, 1999.

Bennett, Alison. "Historic Landscape Characterisation Report for Essex, Volumes 1 and 2." In Archaeology Data Service.

Benton, Josiah Henry. *Warning Out in New England, 1656–1817*. Boston: W. B. Clarke, 1911. In Internet Archive.

Béranger, Jean. *Nathaniel Ward (ca. 1578–1652)*. Études et Recherches Anglaises et Anglo-Américaines 1. Bordeaux, France: SOBODI, 1969.

Beresford, Maurice W., and John G. Hurst. *Deserted Medieval Villages: Studies*. 1971. Reprint, Gloucester: Sutton, 1989.

Beresford, Maurice W. "Glebe Terriers and Open Field, Yorkshire." *Yorkshire Archaeological Journal* 37 (1951): 325–68.

———. *The Lost Villages of England*. London: Lutterworth Press, 1954.

———. "The Lost Villages of Yorkshire, Part I." *Yorkshire Archaeological Journal* 37 (1951): 474–91.

Bettey, J. H. *Dorset*. Newton Abbot, UK: David & Charles, 1974.

Bidwell, Percy, and John Falconer. *History of Agriculture in the Northern United States, 1620–1860*. Washington, DC: Carnegie Institution, 1925.

Black, Robert C. *The Younger John Winthrop*. New York: Columbia University Press, 1966.

Blodgette, George Brainard, and Amos Everett Jewett. *Early Settlers of Rowley, Massachusetts*. 1933. Reprint, Somersworth: New England History Press, 1981.

Blythe, James M. "'Civic Humanism' and Medieval Political Thought." In *Renaissance Civic Humanism: Reappraisals and Reflections*, edited by James Hankins, 30–74. Cambridge: Cambridge University Press, 2000.

Bohi, Mary Janette. "Nathaniel Ward, Pastor Ingeniosus: 1580?–1652." PhD diss., University of Illinois at Urbana-Champaign, 1959. In ProQuest Dissertations & Theses.
Bohstedt, John. *The Politics of Provisions: Food Riots, Moral Economy, and Market Transition in England, c. 1550–1850*. 2010. Reprint, London: Routledge, 2016.
Booth, Ted. *A Body Politic to Govern: The Political Humanism of Elizabeth I*. Newcastle-upon-Tyne: Cambridge Scholars, 2013.
Braddick, Michael J. *State Formation in Early Modern England, c. 1550–1700*. Cambridge: Cambridge University Press, 2000.
Brady Jr., Thomas A., Heiko A. Oberman, and James D. Tracy, eds. *Handbook of European History 1400–1600: Late Middle Ages, Renaissance and Reformation*. Vol. 2. Leiden: E. J. Brill, 1995.
Brasenose College Register, 1509–1909. Oxford: Clarendon Press, 1909. In Internet Archive.
Breen, T. H. *The Character of the Good Ruler: A Study of Puritan Political Ideas in New England, 1630–1730*. New Haven, CT: Yale University Press, 1970.
Breen, T. H., and Stephen Foster. "Moving to the New World: The Character of Early Massachusetts Immigration." *William and Mary Quarterly* 30, no. 2 (April 1973): 189–222.
Breen, T. H. *Puritans and Adventurers: Change and Persistence in Early America*. New York: Oxford University Press, 1980.
Bremer, Francis J. "Communications: The English Context of New England's Seventeenth-Century History." *New England Quarterly* 60, no. 2 (June 1987): 323–35.
———. *Congregational Communion: Clerical Friendship in the Anglo-American Puritan Community, 1610–1692*. Boston, MA: Northeastern University Press, 1994.
———. *First Founders: American Puritans and Puritanism in an Atlantic World*. Durham: University of New Hampshire Press, 2012. In ProQuest Ebook Central.
———. *John Winthrop: America's Forgotten Founding Father*. Oxford: Oxford University Press, 2003.
Bremer, Francis J., and Tom Webster, eds. *Puritans and Puritanism in Europe and America: A Comprehensive Encyclopedia*. 2 vols. Santa Barbara, CA: ABC–CLIO, 2006.
Brewer, John, and John Styles, eds. *An Ungovernable People: The English and Their Law in the Seventeenth and Eighteenth Centuries*. New Brunswick, NJ: Rutgers University Press, 1980.
Brook, Benjamin. *Lives of the Puritans*. 3 vols. London: James Black, 1813.
Bruce, John. "The Caricatures of Samuel Ward of Ipswich." *Notes and Queries*, 4th ser., 1 (January–June 1868): 1–2. In Internet Archive.
Burch, Dinah, and Katy Hooper, eds. *The Concise Oxford Companion to English Literature*. 4th ed. Oxford: Oxford University Press, 2012.
Burchill, Christopher J. "Girolamo Zanchi: Portrait of a Reformed Theologian and His Work." *Sixteenth Century Journal* 15, no. 2 (Summer 1984): 185–207.
Burtchaell, George, and Thomas Sadleir. *Alumni Dublinenses*. Dublin: A. Thom, 1935.
Butterfield, Herbert. *The Whig Interpretation of History*. London: G. Bell & Sons, 1959.
Calder, Isabel M. "A Seventeenth Century Attempt to Purify the Anglican Church." *American Historical Review* 53, no. 4 (July 1948): 760–75.
Calhoun, Craig J., ed. *Habermas and the Public Sphere*. Boston, MA: MIT Press, 1992.
Calis, Richard, Frederic Clark, Christian Flow, Anthony Grafton, Madeline McMahon, and Jennifer M. Rampling. "Passing the Book: Cultures of Reading in the Winthrop Family, 1580–1730." *Past & Present* 241 (November 2018): 69–141.
Campbell, Bruce M. S. *Field Systems and Farming Systems in Late Medieval England*. Farnham, UK: Ashgate, 2008.
Carroll, Peter N. *Puritanism and the Wilderness: The Intellectual Significance of the New England Frontier, 1629–1700*. New York: Columbia University Press, 1969.
Chadd, David, ed. *Religious Dissent in East Anglia III: Proceedings of the Third Symposium*. Norwich: Centre of East Anglian Studies, University of East Anglia, 1996.
Chandler, Alfred D., Jr. *The Visible Hand: The Managerial Revolution in American Business*. Cambridge, MA: Harvard University Press, 1977.

Chaplin, Joyce E. *Subject Matter: Technology, the Body, and Science on the Anglo-American Frontier, 1500–1676*. Cambridge, MA: Harvard University Press, 2001.
Chapman, Colin R. *How Heavy, How Much and How Long?* Dursley, UK: Lochin, 1996.
Chapman, John. "The Chronology of English Enclosure." *Economic History Review* 37, no. 4 (November 1984): 557–59.
Chase, George Wingate. *The History of Haverhill, from Its First Settlement, in 1640, to the Year 1860*. Haverhill, MA: by the author, 1861. In Internet Archive.
Chernow, Ron. *Titan: The Life of John D. Rockefeller, Sr.* New York: Random House, 1998.
Chester, Joseph Lemuel. "Herbert Pelham, His Ancestors and Descendants." *New England Historical and Genealogical Register* 33 (July 1879): 285–95.
Clark, Jo, John Darlington, and Graham Fairclough. "Using Historic Landscape Characterisation." In Archaeology Data Service.
Clark, Peter, and Paul Slack. *Crisis and Order in English Towns 1500–1700: Essays in Urban History*. London: Routledge, 2007.
Clark, Peter, ed. *Country Towns in Pre-Industrial England*. Leicester, UK: Leicester University Press, 1981.
Clark, Peter. "Migration in England." *Past & Present* 83 (May 1979): 57–90.
———, ed. *The Early Modern Town: A Reader*. New York: Longman, 1976.
Clark, Peter, and Paul Slack. *English Towns in Transition, 1500–1700*. Oxford: Oxford University Press, 1976.
Clark, Peter, and David Souden. *Migration and Society in Early Modern England*. Totowa, NJ: Barnes & Noble, 1988.
Clouse, Robert G. "The Influence of John Henry Alsted on English Millenarian Thought in the Seventeenth Century." PhD diss., State University of Iowa, 1963.
Coase, R. H. "The Nature of the Firm." *Economica* 4, no. 16 (November 1937): 386–405.
Cogley, Richard W. *John Eliot's Mission to the Indians before King Philip's War* Cambridge, MA: Harvard University Press, 1999.
Coleman, D. C. "An Innovation and Its Diffusion: The 'New Draperies.'" *Economic History Review* 22, no. 3 (December 1969): 417–29.
Collingwood, Deryck. *Thomas Hooker, 1586–1647: Father of American Democracy*. Interlaken, NY: Heart of the Lakes, 1995.
Collinson, Patrick. "De Republica Anglorum: Or, History with the Politics Put Back." In *Elizabethan Essays*, 1–30. London: Hambledon Press, 1994.
———. *The Elizabethan Puritan Movement*. Berkeley: University of California Press, 1967.
———. *The Religion of Protestants: The Church in English Society 1559–1625*. Oxford: Clarendon Press, 1982.
Concise History of the First Church of Christ, in Ipswich. Boston, MA: Wright & Potter, 1862. In Internet Archive.
Cooper, A. N. "How Rowley in Yorkshire Lost Its Population in the 17th Century, and How Rowley in Massachusetts Was Founded." *Transactions of the East Riding Antiquarian Society* 15 (1908): 85–100.
Cooper, Janet, ed. *A History of the County of Essex*. Vol. 10. Victoria History of the Counties of England. Oxford: Oxford University Press, 2001.
Costello, William T., SJ. *The Scholastic Curriculum at Early Seventeenth-Century Cambridge*. Cambridge, MA: Harvard University Press, 1958.
Crabtree, John. *Concise History of the Parish and Vicarage of Halifax*. Halifax: Hartley and Walker, 1836.
Cronon, William. *Changes in the Land: Indians, Colonists, and the Ecology of New England*. 2nd ed. New York: Hill and Wang, 1983.
Cross, Whitney R. *The Burned-over District: The Social and Intellectual History of Enthusiastic Religion in Western New York, 1800–1850*. 1950. Reprint, Ithaca, NY: Cornell University Press, 2015.

Crouch, David J. F. "Piety, Fraternity and Power: Religious Gilds in Late Medieval Yorkshire 1389–1547." PhD diss., University of York, 1995. In ETHOS.
Curtis, Mark. *Oxford and Cambridge in Transition, 1558–1642: An Essay on Changing Relations between the English Universities and English Society.* Oxford: Clarendon Press, 1959.
Cust, Richard. *The Forced Loan and English Politics, 1626–1628.* Oxford: Clarendon Press, 1987.
Cust, Richard, and Peter G. Lake. "Sir Richard Grosvenor and the Rhetoric of Magistracy." *Bulletin of the Institute of Historical Research* 54 (1981): 40–53.
Daly, James. "Cosmic Harmony and Political Thinking in Early Stuart England." *Transactions of the American Philosophical Society* 69, no. 7 (1979): 1–41.
Daniels, Bruce C. *Puritans at Play: Leisure and Recreation in Colonial New England.* New York: St. Martin's Griffin, 1995.
Davids, T. W. *Annals of Evangelical Nonconformity in the County of Essex.* London: Jackson, Walford and Hodder, 1863. In Google Books.
Davis, James E. *Frontier Illinois.* Bloomington: Indiana University Press, 1998.
Davis, Natalie Zemon. "The Sacred and the Body Social in Sixteenth-Century Lyon." *Past & Present*, no. 90 (February 1981): 40–70.
Dawson, Jane. *Scotland Re-formed, 1488–1587.* Edinburgh: Edinburgh University Press, 2007.
Dean, John Ward. *A Brief Memoir of Rev. Giles Firmin.* Boston, MA: David Clapp and Son, 1866. In Internet Archive.
———. "A Brief Memoir of Rev. Giles Firmin." *New England Historical and Genealogical Review* 20 (1866): 47–58.
———. *A Memoir of the Rev. Nathaniel Ward, A.M ....* Albany, NY: J. Munsell, 1868. In Google Books.
Delbanco, Andrew. "Looking Homeward, Going Home: The Lure of England for the Founders of New England." *New England Quarterly* 59, no. 3 (September 1986): 358–86.
Denholm, Andrew. "Thomas Hooker: Puritan Preacher, 1586–1647." PhD diss., Hartford Seminary Foundation, 1961. In ProQuest Dissertations and Theses FullText.
DeRogatis, Amy. "Models of Piety: Plan of Union Missionaries on the Western Reserve, 1800–1806." *Journal of Presbyterian History* 79, no. 4 (Winter 2001): 257–75.
de Tocqueville, Alexis. *Democracy in America.* Translated by Arthur Goldhammer. New York: Library of America, 2004.
Dickson, Donald R. *The Tessera of Antilia: Utopian Brotherhoods & Secret Societies in the Early Seventeenth Century.* Leiden: Brill, 1998.
Donagan, Barbara. "The Clerical Patronage of Robert Rich, Second Earl of Warwick, 1619–1642." *Proceedings of the American Philosophical Society* 120, no. 5 (October 15, 1976): 388–419.
———. "Godly Choice: Puritan Decision-Making in Seventeenth-Century England." *Harvard Theological Review* 76, no. 3 (July 1983): 307–34.
Donahue, Brian. *The Great Meadow: Farmers and the Land in Colonial Concord.* New Haven, CT: Yale University Press, 2007.
Douglas, Mary. *Natural Symbols: Explorations in Cosmology.* New York: Pantheon Books, 1970.
———. *Purity and Danger: An Analysis of the Concepts of Pollution and Taboo.* 1966. Reprint, London: Routledge, 1984.
Drucker, Peter F. *Concept of the Corporation.* 1946. Reprint, London: Transaction Publishers, 2007.
Duffy, Eamon. *The Stripping of the Altars: Traditional Religion in England c.1400–c.1580.* 2nd ed. New Haven, CT: Yale University Press, 2005.
Dunn, Richard S. *Puritans and Yankees: The Winthrop Dynasty of New England, 1630–1717.* Princeton, NJ: Princeton University Press, 1962.
Durston, Christopher. *Cromwell's Major-Generals: Godly Government during the English Revolution.* Manchester, UK: Manchester University Press, 2001.
Dyson-Bruce, Lynn, and Alison Bennett. "Essex Historic Landscape Characterisation Project." 2013. In Archaeology Data Service.
"Early Ipswich Families." *New England Historical and Genealogical Register* 2 (1848): 176.

Eccleshall, Robert. *Order and Reason in Politics: Theories of Absolute and Limited Monarchy in Early Modern England.* Oxford: Oxford University Press, 1978.

Elcoat, Geoffrey. "Richard Holdsworth, Fourth Master of Emmanuel, Vice-Chancellor of the University of Cambridge." *Emmanuel College Magazine* 75 (1992–93): 73–76.

Ellis, Martha J. "A Study in the Manorial History of Halifax Parish in the Sixteenth and Early Seventeenth Centuries, Part II." *Yorkshire Archaeological Journal* 40 (1962): 420–42.

Epstein, S. R., and Maarten Prak, eds. *Guilds, Innovation, and the European Economy, 1400–1800.* Cambridge: Cambridge University Press, 2008.

Evans, Nesta. "Farming and Land-Holding in Wood-Pasture East Anglia 1550–1650." *Proceedings of the Suffolk Institute of Archaeology and History* 35, part 4 (1984): 303–15.

Everitt, Alan. *Suffolk and the Great Rebellion 1640–1660.* Ipswich, UK: Suffolk Records Society, 1960.

Farmer, David Hugh. *The Oxford Dictionary of Saints.* 3rd ed. Oxford: Oxford University Press, 1992.

Feingold, Mordecai. "The Ultimate Pedagogue: Franco Petri Burgersdijk and the English Speaking Academic Learning." In *Franco Burgersdijk (1590–1635): Neo-Aristotelianism in Leiden,* edited by E. P. Bos and H. A. Krop, 151–65. Amsterdam: Rodopi, 1993.

Feintuch, Burt, and David H. Watters, eds. *The Encyclopedia of New England.* New Haven, CT: Yale University Press, 2005.

Felt, Joseph B. *History of Ipswich, Essex, and Hamilton.* Cambridge: Charles Folsom, 1834. In Internet Archive.

Figgis, John Neville. *The Divine Right of Kings.* 1914. Reprint, Gloucester, MA: Peter Smith, 1970.

Finch, Martha L. *Dissenting Bodies: Corporealities in Early New England.* New York: Columbia University Press, 2010.

Fincham, Kenneth, ed. *The Early Stuart Church, 1603–1642.* Basingstoke, UK: Macmillan Press, 1993.

Fisher, F. J. "Some Experiments in Company Organization in the Early Seventeenth Century." *Economic History Review* 4, no. 2 (April 1933): 177–94.

Fleischacker, Samuel. *A Short History of Distributive Justice.* Cambridge: Harvard University Press, 2004.

Fletcher, Anthony. *Gender, Sex and Subordination in England 1500–1800.* New Haven, CT: Yale University Press, 1995.

Fletcher, Anthony, and John Stevenson, eds. *Order and Disorder in Early Modern England.* Cambridge: Cambridge University Press, 1985.

Fletcher, Anthony, and Peter Roberts, eds. *Religion, Culture and Society in Early Modern Britain: Essays in Honour of Patrick Collinson.* Cambridge: Cambridge University Press, 1994.

"Focus on Ipswich." *Great Migration Newsletter* 3 (1992): 19–22. In AmericanAncestors.org.

"Focus on Newbury." *Great Migration Newsletter* 20 (January–March 2011): 3–6. In AmericanAncestors.org.

"Focus on Rowley." *Great Migration Newsletter* 10 (October–December 2001): 27–30. In AmericanAncestors.org.

Foster, Joseph. *The Register of Admissions to Gray's Inn, 1521–1889.* London: Hansard Publishing Union, 1889. In Internet Archive.

Foster, Stephen. *The Long Argument: English Puritanism and the Shaping of New England Culture, 1570–1700.* Chapel Hill: University of North Carolina Press, 1996.

———. "The Presbyterian Independents Exorcized. A Ghost Story for Historians." *Past & Present,* no. 44 (August 1969): 52–75.

———. *Their Solitary Way: The Puritan Social Ethic in the First Century of Settlement in New England.* New Haven, CT: Yale University Press, 1971.

Franklin, Julian H. "Editor's Note." In *Constitutionalism and Resistance in the Sixteenth Century: Three Treatises by Hotman, Beza, and Mornay,* ed. and trans. Julian H. Franklin, 138–40. New York: Pegasus, 1969.

French, H. R. "Chief Inhabitants and Their Areas of Influence: Local Ruling Groups in Essex and Suffolk Parishes 1630–1720." PhD diss., Cambridge University, 1993.

———. *The Middle Sort of People in Provincial England, 1600–1750*. Oxford: Oxford University Press, 2007.

Friedeburg, Robert. "Social and Geographical Mobility in the Old World and New World Communities: Earls Colne, Ipswich and Springfield, 1636–1685." *Journal of Social History* 29, no. 2 (Winter 1995): 375–400.

Fuller, Thomas. *History of the Worthies of England*. 3 vols. London: for Thomas Tegg, 1840. In Internet Archive.

Fumerton, Patricia. *Unsettled: The Culture of Mobility and the Working Poor in Early Modern England*. Chicago: University of Chicago Press, 2006.

Gage, Arthur. "Descendants of John Gage of Ipswich, Mass." *New England Historical and Genealogical Register* 62 (July 1908): 254–63.

Gage, Thomas. *The History of Rowley, Anciently Including Bradford, Boxford, and Georgetown, from the Year 1639 to the Present Time*. Boston, MA: Ferdinand Andrews, 1840. In Internet Archive.

Games, Alison. *Migration and the Origins of the English Atlantic World*. Cambridge, MA: Harvard University Press, 1999.

———. "Venturers, Vagrants and Vessels of Glory: Migration from England to the Colonies under Charles I." PhD diss., University of Pennsylvania, 1992. In ProQuest Dissertations and Theses Global.

Gardiner, Samuel R. *History of England from the Accession of James I to the Outbreak of the Civil War, 1603–1642*. 10 vols. London: Longmans, Green, 1883.

Gavitt, Philip. *Gender, Honor, and Charity in Late Renaissance Florence*. Cambridge: Cambridge University Press, 2011.

Gay, Edwin F. "The Midland Revolt and the Inquisitions of Depopulation of 1607." *Transactions of the Royal Historical Society*, n.s., 18 (1904): 195–244.

George, M. Dorothy. *English Political Caricature to 1792: A Study of Opinion and Propaganda*. Oxford: Clarendon Press, 1959.

Gerber, Larry G. "Corporatism and State Theory: A Review Essay for Historians." *Social Science History* 19, no. 3 (Autumn 1995): 313–32.

Gibson, Gail McMurray. "Bury St. Edmunds, Lydgate, and the N-Town Cycle." *Speculum* 56, no. 1 (January 1981): 56–90.

von Gierke, Otto. *Political Theories of the Middle Age*. Translated by Frederic W. Maitland. 1900. Reprint, Boston, MA: Beacon Press, 1958.

Ginsburg, Arlin I. "The Franchise in Seventeenth-Century Massachusetts: Ipswich." *William and Mary Quarterly* 34, no. 3 (July 1977): 446–52.

Gonner, E. C. K. *Common Land and Inclosure*. London: Macmillan, 1912. In Internet Archive.

Gordon, Charlotte. *Mistress Bradstreet: The Untold Life of America's First Poet*. New York: Little, Brown, 2005.

Gorski, Philip S. *The Disciplinary Revolution: Calvinism and the Rise of the State in Early Modern Europe*. Chicago: University of Chicago Press, 2003.

Grabill, Stephen J. Introduction to "On the Law in General" by Jerome Zanchi. *Journal of Markets and Morality* 6, no. 1 (Spring 2003): 309–16.

Grabill, Stephen J. *Rediscovering the Natural Law in Reformed Theological Ethics*. Grand Rapids, MI: William B. Eerdmans, 2006.

Gray, Howard L. *English Field Systems*. Cambridge: Harvard University Press, 1915. In Internet Archive.

Green, V. H. H. *Religion at Oxford and Cambridge*. London: SCM Press, 1964.

Gregory, Brad S. *The Unintended Reformation: How a Religous Revolution Secularized Society*. Cambridge, MA: Harvard University Press, 2012.

Greven Jr., Philip J. *Four Generations: Population, Land, and Family in Colonial Andover, Massachusetts*. Ithaca, NY: Cornell University Press, 1970.

Habermas, Jürgen. "The Public Sphere: An Encyclopedia Article." *New German Critique*, no. 3 (Autumn 1974): 49–55.
Hall, David. *The Open Fields of England*. Oxford: Oxford University Press, 2014.
———. *The Open Fields of Northamptonshire*. Northampton, UK: Northamptonshire Record Society, 1995.
Hall, David D. *The Puritans: A Transatlantic History*. Princeton, NJ: Princeton University Press, 2019.
Halliday, Paul D. *Dismembering the Body Politic: Partisan Politics in England's Towns, 1650–1730*. Cambridge: Cambridge University Press, 1998.
Hamilton, Marsha L. *Social and Economic Networks in Early Massachusetts: Atlantic Connections*. University Park: Pennsylvania State University Press, 2009.
Hanawalt, Barbara A., and David Wallace. *Bodies and Disciplines: Intersections of Literature and History in Fifteenth-Century England*. Minneapolis: University of Minnesota Press, 1996.
Hankins, Jeffery R. "Crown, County, and Corporation in Early Seventeenth-Century Essex." *Sixteenth Century Journal* 38, no. 1 (Spring 2007): 27–47.
———. "Papists, Power, and Puritans: Catholic Officeholding and the Rise of the 'Puritan Faction' in Early Seventeenth-Century Essex." *Catholic Historical Review* 95, no. 4 (October 2009): 689–717.
Hardin, Garrett. "The Tragedy of the Commons." *Science*, n.s., 162, no. 3859 (December 13, 1968): 1243–48.
Harris, Alan. "The Agriculture of the East Riding of Yorkshire before the Parliamentary Enclosures." *Yorkshire Archaeological Journal* 40 (1962): 119–28.
Harrison, Peter. *The Fall of Man and the Foundations of Science*. Cambridge: Cambridge University Press, 2007.
Harrison, Sarah. "Open Fields and Earlier Landscapes: Six Parishes in South-East Cambridgeshire." *Landscapes* 3, no. 1 (2002): 35–54.
Harvey, Shirley Wilcox. "Nathaniel Ward: His Life and Works." PhD diss., Boston University, 1936.
Hatcher, Patricia Law. "Focus on Rowley and Ezekiel Rogers' Company." *Great Migration Newsletter* 18 (2009): 19–30.
"Haverhill." *Proceedings of the Suffolk Institute of Archaeology and Natural History* 4 (1874): 99–106.
Hawley, Ellis W. "The Discovery and Study of a 'Corporate Liberalism.'" *Business History Review* 52, no. 3 (Autumn 1978): 309–20.
Hazen, Tracy Elliot. "The English Ancestry of Edward Carlton of Rowley, Mass." *New England Historical and Genealogical Register* 93 (January 1939): 3–46.
Healy, Margaret. *Fictions of Disease in Early Modern England: Bodies, Plagues and Politics*. Basingstoke, UK: Palgrave, 2001.
Henneton, Lauric. "Le Moment Atlantique de la Dynastie des Winthrop au XVIIe Siècle." *Les Cahiers de Framespa* 9 (2012): 2–20. In Academia.edu.
Henreckson, David P. *The Immortal Commonwealth: Covenant, Community, and Political Resistance in Early Reformed Thought*. Cambridge: Cambridge University Press, 2019.
Herrera, R. A. *Orestes Brownson: Sign of Contradiction*. Wilmington, DE: ISI Books, 1999.
Herrup, Cynthia B. *The Common Peace: Participation and the Criminal Law in Seventeenth-Century England*. Cambridge: Cambridge University Press, 1987.
Hexter, J. H. "The Education of the Aristocracy in the Renaissance." *Journal of Modern History* 22, no. 1 (March 1950): 1–20.
———. "The Problem of the Presbyterian Independents." *American Historical Review* 44, no. 1 (October 1938): 29–49.
———. *The Reign of King Pym*. Cambridge, MA: Harvard University Press, 1941.
Hindle, Steve. "Hierarchy and Community in the Elizabethan Parish: The Swallowfield Articles of 1596." *Historical Journal* 42, no. 3 (September 1999): 835–51.
———. "Imagining Insurrection in Seventeenth-Century England: Representations of the Midland Rising of 1607." *History Workshop Journal* 66 (Autumn 2008): 21–61.

———. *The State and Social Change in Early Modern England, 1550–1640*. Basingstoke, UK: Palgrave, 2002.
"An Historical Sketch of Haverhill, in the County of Essex." *Collections of the Massachusetts Historical Society* 2nd ser., 4 (1816; repr., 1846): 121–76. In Google Books.
Hoffer, Peter Charles. *New England Rediscovered: Selected Articles on New England Colonial History, 1965 to 1973*. New York: Garland, 1988.
Hogan, Michael J. "Corporatism." *Journal of American History* 77, no. 1 (June 1990): 153–60.
Holmes, Clive. *The Eastern Association in the English Civil War*. Cambridge: Cambridge University Press, 1974.
———. *Seventeenth-Century Lincolnshire*. Lincoln, UK: History of Lincolnshire Committee for the Society for Lincolnshire History and Archaeology, 1980.
Horrox, Rosemary, and Sarah Rees Jones, eds. *Pragmatic Utopias: Ideals and Communities, 1200–1630*. Cambridge: Cambridge University Press, 2001.
Hosford, W. H. "Some Lincolnshire Enclosure Documents." *Economic History Review*, n.s., 2, no. 1 (1949): 73–79.
Hoskins, W. G. *The Making of the English Landscape*. 1955. Reprint, Harmondsworth, UK: Penguin Books, 1986.
Hotson, Howard. *Johann Heinrich Alsted, 1588–1638: Between Renaissance, Reformation, and Universal Reform*. Oxford: Clarendon Press, 2000.
Howell, Wilbur Samuel. *Logic and Rhetoric in England, 1500–1700*. New York: Russell & Russell, 1961.
Hoyle, Richard W., ed. *Custom, Improvement and the Landscape in Early Modern Britain*. London: Routledge, 2016.
Hsia, R. Po-chia. *Social Discipline in the Reformation: Central Europe 1550–1750*. London: Routledge, 1989.
Hughes, Ann. *Gangraena and the Struggle for the English Revolution*. Oxford: Oxford University Press, 2004.
Hull, Felix. "Agriculture and Rural Society in Essex, 1560–1640." PhD diss., University of London, 1950.
Hunt, William. *The Puritan Moment: The Coming of Revolution in an English County*. Cambridge, MA: Harvard University Press, 1983.
Hurd, D. Hamilton, ed. *History of Essex County, Massachusetts*. Philadelphia, PA: J. W. Lewis, 1888. In Internet Archive.
Hutchins, Zachary. "Building Bensalem at Massachusetts Bay: Francis Bacon and the Wisdom of Eden in Early Modern England." *New England Quarterly* 83, no. 4 (December 2010): 577–606.
———. "The Wisdom of Anne Bradstreet: Eschewing Eve and Emulating Elizabeth." *Modern Language Studies* 40, no. 1 (Summer 2010): 38–59.
Ibish, Joan Schenck. "Emmanuel College: The Founding Generation, with a Biographical Register of Members of the College, 1584–1604." PhD diss., Harvard University, 1985. In ProQuest Dissertations & Theses FullText.
Ingram, Martin. "Religion, Communities and Moral Discipline in Late Sixteenth- and Early Seventeenth-Century England: Case Studies." In *Religion and Society in Early Modern Europe, 1500–1800*, edited by Kaspar von Greyerz, 177–93. London: George Allen & Unwin, 1984.
Innes, Stephen. *Labor in a New Land: Economy and Society in Seventeenth-Century Springfield*. Princeton, NJ: Princeton University Press, 1983.
———, ed. *Work and Labor in Early America*. Chapel Hill: University of North Carolina Press, 1988.
Irving, Sarah. "Beyond Dominion and Stewardship: Humanity and Nature in Puritan Theology." *American Theological Inquiry* 8, no. 1 (2015): 49–59.
James, John. *Continuation and Additions to the History of Bradford*. London: Longmans, Green, Reader, and Dyer, 1866. In Internet Archive.
———. *History and Topography of Bradford*. London: Longman, Brown, Green, and Longmans, 1841. In Internet Archive.

James, Mervyn. "Ritual, Drama and Social Body in the Late Medieval English Town." *Past & Present*, no. 98 (February 1983): 3–29.

Jardine, Lisa, and Alan Stewart. *Hostage to Fortune: The Troubled Life of Francis Bacon*. New York: Hill and Wang, 1999.

Jardine, Lisa. "The Place of Dialectic Teaching in Sixteenth-Century Cambridge." *Studies in the Renaissance* 21 (1974): 31–62.

Jewett, Amos Everett, and Emily Mabel Adams Jewett. *Rowley, Massachusetts: "Mr Ezechi Rogers Plantation," 1639–1850*. Rowley, MA: Jewett Family of America, 1946.

Johnson, Arthur H. *The Disappearance of the Small Landowner*. Oxford: Clarendon Press, 1909. In Internet Archive.

Kantorowicz, Ernst H. *The King's Two Bodies: A Study in Mediaeval Political Theology*. Princeton, NJ: Princeton University Press, 1957.

Kendall, R. T. *Calvin and English Calvinism to 1649*. Oxford: Oxford University Press, 1979.

Kent, Joan R. "Population Mobility and Alms: Poor Migrants in the Midlands during the Early Seventeenth Century." *Local Population Studies* 27 (Autumn 1981): 35–51.

Kerridge, Eric. *The Agricultural Revolution*. London: George Allen & Unwin, 1967.

———. *The Common Fields of England*. Manchester: Manchester University Press, 1992.

Kingsbury, J. D. *Memorial History of Bradford, Mass*. Haverhill, MA: C. C. Morse & Son, 1883.

Kirk, James. "'The Polities of the Best Reformed Kirks': Scottish Achievements and English Aspirations in Church Government after the Reformation." *Scottish Historical Review* 159 no. 167, pt. 1 (April 1980): 22–53.

Kissel, Stephen. "'The Best of Bonds': How Methodist Circuit Riders Created Community in Antebellum Illinois, 1800–1850." *Ohio Valley History* 15, no. 2 (Summer 2015): 3–27.

Kittredge, George L. "Dr. Robert Child the Remonstrant." *Publications of the Colonial Society of Massachusetts* 21 (1920): 1–146.

Knappen, M. M., ed., *Two Elizabethan Puritan Diaries by Richard Rogers and Samuel Ward*. Chicago: American Society of Church History, 1933.

Knowles, Philip. "Continuity and Change in Urban Culture: A Case Study of Two Provincial Towns, Chester and Coventry c. 1600–c. 1750." PhD diss., University of Leicester, 2001. In ETHOS.

Konig, David Thomas. "Community Custom and the Common Law: Social Change and the Development of Land Law in Seventeenth-Century Massachusetts." *American Journal of Legal History* 18, no. 2 (April 1974): 137–77.

———. *Law and Society in Puritan Massachusetts: Essex County, 1629–1692*. Chapel Hill: University of North Carolina Press, 1978.

Kopelson, Heather Miyano. *Faithful Bodies: Performing Religion and Race in the Puritan Atlantic*. New York: New York University Press, 2014.

Kramer, Stella. "The English Craft Gilds and the Government." PhD diss., Columbia University, 1905.

Kreider, Alan. *English Chantries: The Road to Dissolution*. Cambridge, MA: Harvard University Press, 1979.

Kupperman, Karen Ordahl. *Providence Island, 1630–1641: The Other Puritan Colony*. Cambridge: Cambridge University Press, 1993.

Lambert, J. Malet. *Two Thousand Years of Gild Life*. Hull, UK: A. Brown & Sons, 1891. In Internet Archive.

Leach, Avril. "Being One Body: Everyday Institutional Culture in Canterbury and Maidstone Corporations, 1600–1660." PhD diss., University of Kent, 2019. In ETHOS.

Lee, Hwa-Yong. *Political Representation in the Later Middle Ages: Marsilius in Context*. New York: Peter Lang, 2008.

Lee, Sidney, ed. *Dictionary of National Biography*. Vol. 44. New York: Macmillan, 1895. In Google Books.

Levy, Barry. *Town Born: The Political Economy of New England from Its Founding to the Revolution.* Philadelphia: University of Pennsylvania Press, 2009.
Lewis, C. S. *The Discarded Image: An Introduction to Medieval and Renaissance Literature.* Cambridge: Cambridge University Press, 1964.
Lichtenstein, Nelson, ed. *Wal-Mart: The Face of Twenty-First-Century Capitalism.* New York: New Press, 2006.
Livermore, Shaw. *Early American Land Companies: Their Influence on Corporate Development.* 1939. Reprint, New York: Octagon Books, 1966.
Lindman, Janet Moore, and Michelle Lise Tarter, eds. *A Centre of Wonders: The Body in Early America.* Ithaca, NY: Cornell University Press, 2001.
Lockridge, Kenneth. *A New England Town, the First Hundred Years: Dedham, Massachusetts, 1636–1736.* New York: W. W. Norton, 1970.
Long, Steven A. *Analogia Entis: On the Analogy of Being, Metaphysics, and the Act of Faith.* Notre Dame, IN: University of Notre Dame Press, 2011.
Lord, John, and Alastair MacIntosh with contributions from Adam Partington. "The Historic Landscape Characterisation Project for Lincolnshire: The Historic Landscape Character Zones." September 2011. In Archaeology Data Service.
Lovejoy, Arthur O. *The Great Chain of Being: A Study of the History of an Idea; the William James Lectures Delivered at Harvard University, 1933.* Cambridge, MA: Harvard University Press, 1957.
Lynch, William F. *Christ and Apollo: The Dimensions of the Literary Imagination.* 1960. Reprint, Wilmington, DE: ISI Books, 2004.
MacCulloch, Diarmaid. *The Reformation.* London: Penguin Books, 2004.
———. *Suffolk and the Tudors: Politics and Religion in an English County 1500–1600.* Oxford: Clarendon Press, 1986.
Macray, William Dunn. *A Register of the Members of St. Mary Magdalen College, Oxford, Fellows: 1576–1648.*, n.s., vol. III. London: Henry Frowde, 1901.
Main, Gloria L. *Peoples of a Spacious Land: Families and Cultures in Colonial New England.* Cambridge, MA: Harvard University Press, 2001.
Maitland, Frederic W. *Township and Borough.* Cambridge: Cambridge University Press, 1898.
Mannheim, Karl. *Ideology and Utopia: An Introduction to the Sociology of Knowledge.* Translated by Louis Wirth and Edward Shils. New York: Harcourt, Brace & World, 1936.
Martin, Edward, and Max Satchell, eds. *Wheare most inclosures be: East Anglian Fields: History, Morphology and Management.* Ipswich, UK: Archaeological Service, Suffolk County Council, 2008.
Martin, John Frederick. *Profits in the Wilderness: Entrepreneurship and the Founding of New England Towns in the Seventeenth Century.* Chapel Hill: University of North Carolina Press, 1991.
Martin, Julian. *Francis Bacon, the State, and the Reform of Natural Philosophy.* Cambridge: Cambridge University Press, 1992.
Mason, Edward S., ed. *The Corporation in Modern Society.* Cambridge, MA: Harvard University Press, 1966.
Matthews, Nancy L. *William Sheppard, Cromwell's Law Reformer.* Cambridge: Cambridge University Press, 1984.
McClendon, Muriel C. "'Against God's Word': Government, Religion and the Crisis of Authority in Early Reformation Norwich." *Sixteenth Century Journal* 25, no. 2 (Summer 1994): 353–69.
———. *The Quiet Reformation: Magistrates and the Emergence of Protestantism in Tudor Norwich.* Stanford, CA: Stanford University Press, 1999.
McClurkin, Paul T. "Presbyterianism in New England Congregationalism." *Journal of the Presbyterian Historical Society* 31, no. 4 (December 1953): 245–56.
McClymond, Michael. "Analogy: A Neglected Theme in Jonathan Edwards and Its Pertinence to Contemporary Theological Debates." *Jonathan Edwards Studies* 6, no. 2 (2016): 153–75.
McCraw, Thomas K., ed. *Creating Modern Capitalism: How Entrepreneurs, Companies, and Countries Triumphed in Three Industrial Revolutions.* Cambridge, MA: Harvard University Press, 1997.

McDermott, Scott A. "Body of Liberties: Godly Constitutionalism and the Origin of Written Fundamental Law in Massachusetts, 1634–1666." PhD diss., Saint Louis University, 2014. In ProQuest Dissertations & Theses.

———. "Edwards and the Noachide Covenant: A Calvinist Theological Revolution." In Academia.edu.

———. "Elijah P. Lovejoy and the Demise of Evangelical Union." In Academia.edu.

———. "God's Instruments: Praying Indians and Transatlantic Scholarship, 1646–1698." In Academia.edu.

———. "The Lombard League, the Glossators, and the Transformation of Roman Private Law into Public Rights." In Academia.edu.

———. "The New England Praying Indians as Participants in Transatlantic Religious and Scientific Dialogue." In Academia.edu.

———. "The Opening of the American Mind: Protestant Scholasticism at Harvard, 1636–1700." In *Catholicism and Historical Narrative: A Catholic Engagement with Historical Scholarship*, edited by Kevin Schmiesing, 19–46. Lanham, MD: Rowman & Littlefield, 2014.

———. "Orestes Brownson and the Contract of Government." *Catholic Social Science Review* 14 (2009): 245–69.

———. "Special Pleading: The Suppression of 'Romanism' in English Legal History." In Academia.edu.

McGiffert, Michael. *God's Plot: Puritan Spirituality in Thomas Shepard's Cambridge*. Rev. ed. Amherst: University of Massachusetts Press, 1994.

McIlwain, Charles H. "The Transfer of the Charter to New England, and Its Significance in American Constitutional History." *Proceedings of the Massachusetts Historical Society*, 3rd ser., 63 (October 1929–June 1930): 53–64.

McIntosh, Marjorie Keniston. *Controlling Misbehavior in England, 1370–1600*. Cambridge: Cambridge University Press, 1998.

———. "Local Change and Community Control in England, 1465–1500." *Huntington Library Quarterly* 49, no. 3 (Summer 1986): 219–42.

———. *Poor Relief and Community in Hadleigh, Suffolk, 1547–1600*. Hatfield, UK: University of Hertfordshire Press, 2013.

McManis, Douglas. *Colonial New England: A Historical Geography*. London: Oxford University Press, 1975.

McRee, Ben R. "The Mayor and the Saint: Remaking Norwich's Gild of St. George, 1548–1549." *Huntington Library Quarterly* 79, no. 1 (Spring 2016): 1–20.

Michaud-Quantin, Pierre. *Universitas: Expressions du Mouvement Communitaire dans le Moyen-age Latin*. Paris: Librarie Philosophique J. Vrin, 1970.

Middlekauff, Robert. *The Mathers: Three Generations of Puritan Intellectuals, 1596–1728*. 1971. Reprint, Berkeley: University of California Press, 1999.

Miller, Perry. *Nature's Nation*. Cambridge: Harvard University Press, 1967.

———. *The New England Mind: The Seventeenth Century*. 1939. Reprint, Boston, MA: Beacon Press, 1961.

———. *The Responsibility of Mind in a Civilization of Machines*. Edited by John Crowell and Sanford J. Searl Jr. Amherst: University of Massachusetts Press, 1979.

———. "Thomas Hooker and the Democracy of Early Connecticut." *New England Quarterly* 4 (1931): 663–712.

Mills, Dennis R. "Enclosure in Kesteven." *Agricultural History Review* 7, no. 2 (1959): 82–97.

Mirick, B. L. *The History of Haverhill, Massachusetts*. Haverhill, MA: A. W. Thayer, 1832. In Internet Archive.

Mitchison, Rosalind. *A History of Scotland*. 3rd ed. London: Taylor & Francis, 2002.

Moch, Leslie Page. *Moving Europeans: Migration in Western Europe since 1650*. Bloomington: Indiana University Press, 1992.

Money, Walter. *The History of the Ancient Town and Borough of Newbury*. In Internet Archive.
Moody, Robert E., ed., "Records of the Magistrates' Court at Haverhill, Massachusetts, Kept by Nathaniel Saltonstall, 1682–1685." *Proceedings of the Massachusetts Historical Society* 3rd ser., 79 (1967): 151–86.
Moore, Jonathan D. *English Hypothetical Universalism: John Preston and the Softening of Reformed Theology*. Grand Rapids, MI: William B. Eerdmans, 2007.
Moore, Susan Hardman. *Pilgrims: New World Settlers & the Call of Home*. New Haven, CT: Yale University Press, 2007.
Morant, Philip. *The History and Antiquities of the County of Essex*. Vol. 2. London: for T. Osborne, 1768.
Morgan, Victor. *A History of the University of Cambridge, 1546–1750*. Vol. 2 of *A History of the University of Cambridge*, edited by Christopher Brooke. Cambridge: Cambridge University Press, 2004.
Moriarty, G. Andrews. "Clarke—Cooke (alias Carewe)—Kerrich." *New England Historical and Genealogical Register* 75 (January 1921): 273–301.
Morison, Samuel Eliot. *The Founding of Harvard College*. Cambridge, MA: Harvard University Press, 1935.
———. *The Puritan Pronaos*. New York: New York University Press, 1936.
Morris, William Alfred. *The Frankpledge System*. London: Longmans, Green, 1910. In Internet Archive.
Muldrew, Craig. "The Culture of Reconciliation: Community and the Settlement of Economic Disputes in Early Modern England." *Historical Journal* 39, no. 4 (December 1996): 915–42.
Muller, Richard A. *After Calvin: Studies in the Development of a Theological Tradition*. Oxford: Oxford University Press, 2003.
———. *Grace and Freedom: William Perkins and the Early Modern Reformed Understanding of Free Choice and Divine Grace*. Oxford: Oxford University Press, 2020.
Muskett, Joseph J. *Suffolk Manorial Families*. Vol. I. Exeter: William Pollard, 1900. In Google Books.
Najemy, John. "Guild Republicanism in Trecento Florence: The Successes and Ultimate Failure of Corporate Politics." *American Historical Review* 84, no. 1 (February 1979): 53–71.
Newman, William R. *Gehennical Fire: The Lives of George Starkey, an American Alchemist in the Scientific Revolution*. Cambridge, MA: Harvard University Press, 1994.
Newman, William R., and Lawrence M. Principe. *Alchemy Tried in the Fire: Starkey, Boyle, and the Fate of Helmontian Chemistry*. Chicago: University of Chicago Press, 2002.
Norri, Juhani. *Dictionary of Medical Vocabulary in English, 1375–1550: Body Parts, Sicknesses, Instruments, and Medicinal Preparations, Part I and II*. Abingdon, UK: Routledge, 2016.
Norton, Susan L. "Population Growth in Colonial America: A Study of Ipswich, Massachusetts." *Population Studies* 25, no. 3 (November 1971): 433–52.
O'Malley, Patricia Trainor. "Rowley, Massachusetts, 1639–1730: Dissent, Division and Delimitation in a Colonial Town." PhD diss., Boston College, 1975. In ProQuest Dissertations & Theses Global.
Ong, Walter J., SJ. *Ramus, Method, and the Decay of Dialogue: From the Art of Discourse to the Art of Reason*. Chicago Press ed. Chicago: University of Chicago Press, 2004.
Orwin, C. S., and C. S. Lowry Orwin. *The Open Fields*. Oxford: Clarendon Press, 1938.
Overton, Mark. "Agricultural Change in Norfolk and Suffolk, 1580–1740." PhD diss., Cambridge University, 1980.
Page, William, ed., *The Victoria History of Hampshire and the Isle of Wight*. Vol. 5. Victoria History of the Counties of England. London: Constable, 1912.
———, ed. *Victoria History of the County of Northampton*. Victoria History of the Counties of England. London: St. Catherine Press, 1930.
Panitch, Leo. "Recent Theorizations of Corporatism: Reflections on a Growth Industry." *British Journal of Sociology* 31, no. 2 (June 1980): 159–87.
Patterson, W. B. *William Perkins and the Making of a Protestant England*. Oxford: Oxford University Press, 2014.

Pegis, Anton C., ed. *Introduction to Saint Thomas Aquinas.* New York: Modern Library, 1948.
Peltonen, Markku. *Classical Humanism and Republicanism in English Political Thought, 1570–1640.* Cambridge: Cambridge University Press, 1995.
Peile, John. *Biographical Register of Christ's College, 1505–1905.* Vol. 1. Cambridge: Cambridge University Press, 1910.
Pennie, A. R. "Evolution of Puritan Mentality in an Essex Cloth Town: Dedham and the Stour Valley, 1560–1640." PhD diss., University of Sheffield, 1989. In ETHOS.
Pennington, Kenneth. *The Prince and the Law, 1200–1600.* Berkeley: University of California Press, 1993.
Perley, Sidney. *History of Boxford, Essex County, Massachusetts.* Boxford, MA: by the author, 1880.
Perzel, Edward S. "The First Generation of Settlement in Colonial Ipswich, Massachusetts: 1633–1660." PhD diss., Rutgers University, 1967. In ProQuest Dissertations & Theses FullText.
———. "Landholding in Ipswich." *Essex Institute Historical Collections* 104, no. 4 (October 1968): 303–28.
Pettegree, Andrew, ed. *The Reformation World.* London: Taylor & Francis, 2000.
Pettit, Norman. "God's Englishman in New England: His Enduring Ties to the Motherland." *Proceedings of the Massachusetts Historical Society* 3rd ser., 101 (1989): 56–70.
Pew, William Andrews. "The Worshipful Simon Bradstreet, Governor of Massachusetts." *Historical Collections of the Essex Institute* 64, no. 4 (October 1928): 301–28.
Phythian-Adams, Charles. *Desolation of a City: Coventry and the Urban Crisis of the Late Middle Ages.* Cambridge: Cambridge University Press, 1979.
Pocock, J. G. A. *The Machiavellian Moment: Florentine Political Thought and the Atlantic Republican Tradition.* Princeton, NJ: Princeton University Press, 1975.
Porter, H. C. *Reformation and Reaction in Tudor Cambridge.* Cambridge: Cambridge University Press, 1958.
Post, Gaines. *Studies in Medieval Legal Thought: Public Law and the State, 1100–1322.* Princeton, NJ: Princeton University Press, 1964.
Postgate, M. R. "The Field Systems of Breckland." *Agricultural History Review* 10, no. 2 (1962): 80–101.
Powell, Sumner Chilton. *Puritan Village: The Formation of a New England Town.* Middletown, CT: Wesleyan University Press, 1963.
Powell, W. R., ed., *A History of the County of Essex.* Vol. 4. Victoria History of the Counties of England. London: Oxford University Press, 1956.
———, ed., *A History of the County of Essex.* Vol. 8. Victoria History of the Counties of England Oxford: Oxford University Press, 1983.
Presciutti, Diana Bullen, ed. *Space, Place, and Motion: Locating Confraternities in the Late Medieval and Early Modern City.* Leiden: Brill, 2017.
Price, Edward T. *Dividing the Land: Early American Beginnings of Our Private Property Mosaic.* Chicago: University of Chicago Press, 1995.
Quintrell, B. W. "The Government of the County of Essex, 1603–1642." PhD diss., University of London, 1965.
Raccagni, Gianluca. "Il Diritto Publico, la Pace di Costanza e i Libri Iurium dei Comuni." In *Gli Inizi del Diritto Publico,* 2: *Da Federico I a Federico II,* 309–339. Bologna: Il Mulino, 2008.
Randall, David. "Joseph Mead, Novellante: News, Sociability, and Credibility in Early Stuart England." *Journal of British Studies* 45, no. 2 (April 2006): 293–312.
Reynolds, Matthew. *Godly Reformers and Their Opponents in Early Modern England: Religion in Norwich, c. 1560–1643.* Woodbridge, UK: Boydell Press, 2005.
Rippon, Stephen. *Making Sense of an Historic Landscape.* Oxford: Oxford University Press, 2012.
Roberts, Brian K., and Stuart Wrathmell. *Region and Place: A Study of English Rural Settlement.* London: English Heritage, 2002.
Rosenthal, Joel, and Colin Richmond, eds. *People, Politics and Community in the Later Middle Ages.* New York: St. Martin's Press, 1987.

Rose-Troup, Frances. *The Massachusetts Bay Company and Its Predecessors*. New York: Grafton Press, 1930.
Rosser, Gervase. "Crafts, Guilds and the Negotiation of Work in the Medieval Town." *Past & Present*, no. 154 (February 1997): 3–31.
———. "Going to the Fraternity Feast." *Journal of British Studies* 33, no. 4 (October 1994): 430–46.
———. *Medieval Westminster*. Oxford: Clarendon Press, 1989.
Rozbicki, Michal Jan. "Between East-Central Europe and Britain: Reformation and Science as Vehicles of Intellectual Communication in the Mid-Seventeenth Century." *East European Quarterly* 30 (Winter 1996): 401–20.
Runciman, W. G. "Ideology and Social Science." In *Knowledge and Belief in Politics: The Problem of Ideology*, edited by Robert Benewick, R. N. Berki, and Bhikhu Parekh, 13–35. New York: St. Martin's Press, 1973.
Russell, Howard S. *A Long, Deep Furrow: Three Centuries of Farming in New England*. Hanover, NH: University Press of New England, 1976.
Sachse, William L. "The Migration of New Englanders to England, 1640–1660." *American Historical Review* 53, no. 2 (January 1948): 251–78.
St. George, Robert Blair. *Conversing By Signs: Poetics of Implication in Colonial New England Culture*. Chapel Hill: University of North Carolina Press, 1998.
Salerno, Anthony. "The Social Background of Seventeenth-Century Emigration to America." *Journal of British Studies* 19, no. 1 (Autumn 1979): 31–52.
Salzman, L. F., ed. *Victoria History of the County of Cambridge and the Isle of Ely*. Vol. 2. Victoria History of the Counties of England. London: Oxford University Press, 1948.
Savage, James. *A Genealogical Dictionary of the First Settlers of New England* .... 4 vols. Boston, MA: Little, Brown, 1860. In Internet Archive.
Schmitt, Charles B., Quentin Skinner, Eckhard Kessler, and Jill Kraye, eds. *The Cambridge History of Renaissance Philosophy*. Cambridge: Cambridge University Press, 1988.
Schwartz, Amy D. "Colonial New England Agriculture: New Visions, Old Directions." *Agricultural History* 69, no. 3 (Summer 1995): 454–81.
Scott, John. *Berwick-upon-Tweed: The History of the Town and Guild*. London: Elliot Stock, 1888.
Sears, John Henry. *The Physical Geography, Geology, Mineralogy and Paleontology of Essex County, Massachusetts*. Salem, MA: Essex Institute, 1905.
Seaver, Paul S. *The Puritan Lectureships: The Politics of Religious Dissent, 1560–1662*. Stanford, CA: Stanford University Press, 1970.
Seznec, Jean. *The Survival of the Pagan Gods: The Mythological Tradition and Its Place in Renaissance Humanism and Art*. New York: Pantheon, 1953.
Shagan, Ethan. *The Rule of Moderation: Violence, Religion, and the Politics of Restraint in Early Modern England*. Cambridge: Cambridge University Press, 2011.
Sharp, Buchanan. *In Contempt of All Authority: Rural Artisans and Riot in the West of England, 1586–1660*. Berkeley: University of California Press, 1980.
Sharpe, Kevin. *Remapping Early Modern England: The Culture of Seventeenth-Century Politics*. Cambridge: Cambridge University Press, 2000.
Shuckburgh, E. S. *Emmanuel College*. London: F. E. Robinson, 1904. In Google Books.
Shipps, Kenneth. "Lay Patronage of East Anglian Puritan Clerics in Pre-Revolutionary England." PhD diss., Yale University, 1971. In ProQuest Dissertations & Theses.
———. "The Puritan Emigration to New England: A New Source on Motivation." *New England Historical and Genealogical Register* 135 (1981): 83–97.
Sibley, John Langdon. *Biographical Sketches of Graduates of Harvard University, in Cambridge, Massachusetts*. 3 vols. 1873–85. Reprint, New York: Johnson Reprint, 1967.
Simpson, Alan. "The East Anglian Foldcourse: Some Queries." *Agricultural History Review* 6, no. 2 (1958): 87–96.

Slack, Paul. "Books of Orders: The Making of English Social Policy, 1577–1631." *Transactions of the Royal Historical Society* 30 (1980): 1–22.

———. "Vagrants and Vagrancy in England, 1598–1664." *Economic History Review* 27, no. 3 (August 1974): 360–79.

Slade, Daniel Denison. "Autobiography of Major-General Daniel Denison." *New England Historical and Genealogical Register* 46 (1892): 127–33.

Slater, Gilbert. *The English Peasantry and the Enclosure of the Common Fields*. London: Archibald Constable, 1907. In Internet Archive.

Smith, Richard M., ed. *Land, Kinship and Life-Cycle*. Cambridge: Cambridge University Press, 1984.

Spencer, M. Lyle. *Corpus Christi Pageants in England*. New York: Baker & Taylor, 1911.

Spufford, Margaret. "General View of the Rural Economy of the County of Cambridge." *Proceedings of the Cambridge Antiquarian Society* 89 (2000): 69–85.

Statham, Margaret, ed. *Accounts of the Feoffees of the Town Lands of Bury St Edmunds, 1569–1622*. Woodbridge, UK: Boydell Press, 2003.

———. "The Guildhall, Bury St. Edmunds." *Proceedings of the Suffolk Institute of Archaeology* 31, part 2 (1968): 117–57.

Stilgoe, John. *Common Landscape of America, 1580 to 1845*. New Haven, CT: Yale University Press, 1982.

———. "Pattern on the Land: The Making of a Colonial Landscape, 1633–1800." PhD diss., Harvard University, 1976.

Stoll, Abraham. *Conscience in Early Modern English Literature*. Cambridge: Cambridge University Press, 2017.

Stone, Lawrence. "The Educational Revolution in England, 1560–1640." *Past & Present*, no. 28 (July 1964): 41–80.

Stout, Harry S. "The Morphology of Remigration: New England University Men and Their Return to England, 1640–1660." *Journal of American Studies* 10, no. 2 (August 1976): 151–72.

Stuart, Denis. *Manorial Records: An Introduction to Their Transcription and Translation*. Chichester, UK: Phillimore, 1992.

Talcott, Mary K. "Genealogy of the Woodbridge Family." *New England Historical and Genealogical Review* 32 (1878): 292–96.

Tankersley, Allen P. "Midway District: A Study of Puritanism in Colonial Georgia." *Georgia Historical Quarterly* 32, no. 3 (September 1948): 149–57.

Tate, W. E. "Cambridgeshire Field Systems, with a Hand-list of Cambridgeshire Enclosure Acts and Awards." *Proceedings of the Cambridge Antiquarian Society* 40 (July 1939–December 1942): 56–88.

———. *A Domesday of English Enclosure Acts and Awards*. Edited by M. E. Turner. Reading: Library, University of Reading, 1978.

———. "Field Systems and Enclosures in Hampshire." *Proceedings of the Hampshire Field Club & Archaeological Society* 16, no. 3 (1947): 257–79.

———. "A Handlist of Suffolk Enclosure Acts and Awards." *Proceedings of the Suffolk Institute of Archaeology and Natural History* 25, part 3 (1952): 225–63.

Tawney, R. H. *The Agrarian Problem in the Sixteenth Century*. London: Longmans, Green, 1912. In Internet Archive.

Tawney, R. H., and Eileen Power, eds. *Tudor Economic Documents*. Vol. 2. London: Longmans, 1963.

Taylor, Charles. *A Secular Age*. Cambridge, MA: Harvard University Press, 2007.

Thirsk, Joan, ed. *The Agrarian History of England and Wales, Volume IV, 1500–1640*. Cambridge: Cambridge University Press, 1967.

———, ed. *The Agrarian History of England and Wales, Volume V, 1640–1750; Part I, Regional Farming Systems*. Cambridge: Cambridge University Press, 1984.

———. "The Common Fields." *Past & Present* 29 (December 1964): 3–25.

———. *English Peasant Farming: The Agrarian History of Lincolnshire from Tudor to Recent Times*. London: Routledge & Kegan Paul, 1957.

———, ed. *The Rural Economy of England: Collected Essays*. London: Hambledon Press, 1984.
Thirsk, Joan, and J. P. Cooper, eds. *Seventeenth-Century Economic Documents*. Oxford: Clarendon Press, 1972.
Thistlethwaite, Frank. *Dorset Pilgrims: The Story of West Country Pilgrims Who Went to New England in the 17th Century*. London: Barrie & Jenkins, 1989.
Thomas, Samuel L. *Creating Communities in Restoration England: Parish and Congregation in Oliver Heywood's Halifax*. Leiden, the Netherlands: Brill, 2012.
Thompson, Augustine. *Cities of God: The Religion of the Italian Communes, 1125–1325*. University Park: Pennsylvania State University Press, 2005.
Thompson, Roger. "Early Modern Migration." *Journal of American Studies* 25, no. 1 (April 1991): 59–69.
———. *Mobility and Migration: East Anglian Founders of New England, 1629–1640*. Amherst: University of Massachusetts Press, 1994.
———. "*The Uprooted* or 'Worlds in Motion': East Anglian Founders of New England 1629–1640." *Parergon*, n.s., 11, no. 2 (December 1993): 1–15.
Thornton, Gladys A. *A History of Clare, Suffolk*. Cambridge: W. Heffer & Sons, 1928.
Tierney, Brian. *The Idea of Natural Rights*. Atlanta: Scholars Press, 1997.
Tillyard, E. M. W. *The Elizabethan World Picture*. 1944. Reprint, New York: Vintage Books, 1960s.
Tipson, Baird. *Hartford Puritanism: Thomas Hooker, Samuel Stone, and Their Terrifying God*. Oxford: Oxford University Press, 2015.
Tittler, Robert, and Norman L. Jones, eds. *A Companion to Tudor Britain*. Malden, MA: Blackwell, 2004.
Tittler, Robert. "The End of the Middle Ages in the English Country Town." *Sixteenth Century Journal* 18, no. 4 (Winter 1987): 471–87.
Todd, Margo. *Christian Humanism and the Puritan Social Order*. Cambridge: Cambridge University Press, 1987.
———. *The Culture of Protestantism in Early Modern Scotland*. New Haven, CT: Yale University Press, 2002.
Trumbull, J. Hammond. *The Memorial History of Hartford County, Connecticut, 1633–1884*. 2 vols. Boston, MA: Edward L. Osgood, 1886. In Internet Archive.
Turner, Henry S. *The Corporate Commonwealth: Pluralism and Political Fictions in England, 1516–1651*. Chicago: University of Chicago Press, 2016.
Tyack, N. C. P. "Migration from East Anglia to New England before 1660." 2 vols. PhD diss., Cambridge University, 1951.
Tyacke, Nicholas. *Anti-Calvinists: The Rise of English Arminianism c. 1590–1640*. Oxford: Oxford University Press, 1990.
Tyler, Richard. "The Children of Disobedience: The Social Composition of Emmanuel College, Cambridge, 1596–1645." PhD diss., University of California at Berkeley, 1976. In ProQuest Dissertations & Theses.
Underdown, David. *Fire from Heaven: Life in an English Town in the Seventeenth Century*. New Haven, CT: Yale University Press, 1992.
———. "The Independents Reconsidered." *Journal of British Studies* 3, no. 2 (May 1964): 57–84.
———. *Revel, Riot, and Rebellion: Popular Politics and Culture in England, 1603–1660*. Oxford: Oxford University Press, 1987.
Urry, John. *Offshoring*. Cambridge, UK: Polity Press, 2014.
Vainio, Olli-Pekka. "The Curious Case of *Analogia entis*: How Metaphysics Affects Ecumenics?" *Studia Theologica* 69, no. 2 (2015): 171–89.
VanDrunen, David. *Natural Law and the Two Kingdoms: A Study in the Development of Reformed Social Thought*. Grand Rapids, MI: William B. Eerdmans Publishing, 2010.
van Engen, Abram C. *Sympathetic Puritans: Calvinist Fellow Feeling in Early New England*. Oxford: Oxford University Press, 2015.

Vannah, Alison I. "Crotchets of Division: Ipswich in New England, 1633–1679." PhD diss., Brandeis University, 1999. In ProQuest Dissertations & Theses FullText.
Venn, J. A. *Alumni Cantabrigienses ... Part I: From the Earliest Times to 1751*. 4 vols. Cambridge: Cambridge University Press, 1922–27.
Vickers, Daniel. *Farmers & Fishermen: Two Centuries of Work in Essex County, Massachusetts, 1630–1850*. Chapel Hill: University of North Carolina Press, 1994.
Victoria History of the County of Berkshire. Vol. 4. London: St. Catherine Press, 1924.
Waddell, Brodie. "Governing England through the Manor Courts, 1550–1850." *Historical Journal* 55, no. 2 (June 2012): 279–315.
———. *Landscape and Society in the Vale of York, c. 1500–1800*. York, UK: Borthwick Institute, 2011.
Wagner, Wienczyslaw J., Arthur P. Coleman, and Charles S. Haight. "Laurentius Grimaldus Goslicius and His Age–Modern Constitutional Law Ideas in the XVI Century." *Polish Review* 3, nos. 1–2 (Winter–Spring 1958): 37–57.
Walcott, Robert R. "Husbandry in Colonial New England." *New England Quarterly* 9, no. 2 (June 1936): 218–52.
Walker, D. P. *The Ancient Theology: Studies in Christian Platonism from the Fifteenth to the Eighteenth Century*. Ithaca, NY: Cornell University Press, 1972.
Wall, Alison. *Power and Protest in England 1525–1640*. New York: Oxford University Press, 2000.
Warren, Jonathan Edward. "Polity, Piety, and Polemic: Giles Firmin and the Transatlantic Puritan Tradition." PhD diss., Vanderbilt University, 2014. In ProQuest Dissertations & Theses Global.
Waters, Henry F. *Genealogical Gleanings in England*. 2 vols. Boston, MA: New England Historic Genealogical Society, 1901.
[Waters, Thomas Franklin]. "The Development of Our Town Government." *Publications of the Ipswich Historical Society* 8 (1900): 10–11.
———. *Ipswich in the Massachusetts Bay Colony* .... 2 vols. Ipswich, MA: Ipswich Historical Society, 1905–17. In Internet Archive.
———. "Ipswich Village and the Old Rowley Road." *Publications of the Ipswich Historical Society* 19 (1914): 1–69.
———. "Jeffrey's Neck." *Publications of the Ipswich Historical Society* 18 (1912): 1–85.
Webb, Sidney, and Beatrice Webb. *English Local Government from the Revolution to the Municipal Corporations Act*, vol. 1: *The Parish and the County*. London: Longmans, Green, 1906. In Internet Archive.
Weber, Max. *The Protestant Ethic and the Spirit of Capitalism*. Translated by Talcott Parsons. New York: Charles Scribner's Sons, 1958.
Webster, Charles. *The Great Instauration: Science, Medicine and Reform, 1626–1660*. New York: Holmes & Meier, 1976.
Webster, Tom. *Godly Clergy in Early Stuart England: The Caroline Puritan Movement, c. 1620–1643*. Cambridge: Cambridge University Press, 1997.
Weir, David A. *Early New England: A Covenanted Society*. Grand Rapids, MI: William B. Eerdmans Publishing, 2005.
Weis, Frederick Lewis. *Ancestral Roots of Certain American Colonists Who Came to America before 1700*. 8th ed. Edited by William R. Beall and Kaleen E. Beall. Baltimore, MD: Genealogical Publishing, 2004.
Wendel, François. "Introduction" to Martin Bucer, *De Regno Christi*. Edited by François Wendel. Martini Buceri Opera Latina. Vol. 15. Paris: Presses Universitaires de France, 1955.
"West Yorkshire Historic Landscape Characterisation Project: Bradford, Themed Results." 2017. In Archaeology Data Service.
White, Elizabeth Wade. *Anne Bradstreet: "The Tenth Muse."* New York: Oxford University Press, 1971.
Whiting, George W. "Pareus, the Stuarts, Laud, and Milton." *Studies in Philology* 50, no. 2 (April 1953): 215–29.
Wickham, Chris. *Sleepwalking into a New World: The Emergence of Italian City Communes in the Twelfth Century*. Princeton, NJ: Princeton University Press, 2015.

Wiebe, Robert H. *The Search for Order, 1877–1920*. New York: Hill and Wang, 1967.
Willey, Basil. *The Seventeenth Century Background*. New York: Columbia University Press, 1958.
Williamson, Tom. "Understanding Enclosure." *Landscapes* 1, no. 1 (2000): 56–79.
Willis, Browne. *Notitia Parliamentaria*. London: for the author, 1750. In Google Books.
Winchester, Angus J. L. *The Harvest of the Hills: Rural Life in Northern England and the Scottish Borders, 1400–1700*. Edinburgh: Edinburgh University Press, 2000.
Winkler, J. T. "The Coming Corporatism." In *The End of the Keynesian Era: Essays on the Disintegration of the Keynesian Political Economy*, ed. Robert Skidelsky, 78–87. New York: Holmes & Meier, 1977.
Winthrop, Robert C. *Evidences of the Winthrops of Groton*. Boston, MA: privately printed, 1894–96.
Withington, Phil. "Company and Sociability in Early Modern England." *Social History* 32, no. 3 (August 2007): 291–307.
———. "Public Discourse, Corporate Citizenship, and State Formation in Early Modern England." *American Historical Review* 112, no. 4 (October 2007): 1016–38.
Wodderspoon, John. *Memorials of the Ancient Town of Ipswich*. Ipswich, UK: Pawsey, 1850. In Google Books.
Wood, Andy. *Riot, Rebellion and Popular Politics in Early Modern England*. New York: Palgrave, 2002.
Wood, Joseph S. "'Build, Therefore, Your Own World': The New England Village as Settlement Ideal." *Annals of the Association of American Geographers* 81, no. 1 (March 1991): 32–50.
———. *The New England Village*. Baltimore, MD: Johns Hopkins University Press, 1997.
Woodruff, Edwin H. "Chancery in Massachusetts." *Boston University Law Review* 9, no. 3 (June 1929): 168–92.
Woodward, Walter W. *Prospero's America: John Winthrop, Jr., Alchemy, and the Creation of New England Culture, 1606–1676*. Chapel Hill: University of North Carolina Press, 2010.
Wordie, J. R. "The Chronology of English Enclosure, 1500–1914." *Economic History Review* 36, no. 4 (November 1983): 483–505.
Wormald, Jenny. *Court, Kirk, and Community: Scotland, 1470–1625*. Edinburgh: Edinburgh University Press, 2018.
Worthley, Harold Field. *An Inventory of the Records of the Particular (Congregational) Churches of Massachusetts Gathered 1620–1805*. Cambridge, MA: Harvard University Press, 1970.
Wright, Robert E. *Corporation Nation*. Philadelphia: University of Pennsylvania Press, 2014.
Wrightson, Keith. *English Society 1580–1680*. 1982. Reprint, London: Routledge, 2003.
Wrightson, Keith, and David Levine. *Poverty and Piety in an English Village: Terling, 1525–1700*. New York: Academic Press, 1979.
Yelling, J. A. *Common Field and Enclosure in England 1450–1850*. London: Macmillan Press, 1977.
Young, Ralph F. "Breathing the 'Free Aire of the New World': The Influence of the New England Way on the Gathering of Congregational Churches in Old England, 1640–1660." *New England Quarterly* 83, no. 1 (March 2010): 5–46.
Young, Robert Fitzgibbon. *Comenius in England*. New York: Arno Press, 1971.
Yule, George. *The Independents in the English Civil War*. Cambridge: Cambridge University Press, 1958.
———. "Independents and Revolutionaries." *Journal of British Studies* 7, no. 2 (May 1968), 11–32.
Zilg, Gerard Colby. *DuPont: Behind the Nylon Curtain*. Englewood Cliffs, NJ: Prentice-Hall, 1974.

Electronic Resources

Academia.edu, https://www.academia.edu.
AmericanAncestors.org, https://www.americanancestors.org.
American National Biography Online, https://www.anb.org.
Archaeology Data Service, https://archaeologydataservice.ac.uk.
British History Online, https://www.british-history.ac.uk.
Digital Commonwealth, https://www.digitalcommonwealth.org.
Early English Books Online, https://about.proquest.com/products-services/databases/eebo.html.

Eighteenth Century Collections Online, https://www.gale.com/primary-sources/eighteenth-century-collections-online.
ETHOS, https://ethos.bl.uk.
FamilySearch, https://www.familysearch.org.
Gale Cengage State Papers Online, https://www.gale.com/primary-sources/state-papers-online.
Google Books, https://books.google.com.
HathiTrust Digital Library, https://www.hathitrust.org.
Historic Ipswich, https://historicipswich.org.
History of Parliament Online, https://www.historyofparliamentonline.org.
Internet Archive, https://archive.org.
New York Society Library, https://www.nysoclib.org.
Oxford Dictionary of National Biography Online, https://www.oxforddnb.com.
Oxford English Dictionary, http://www.oed.com.
ProQuest Dissertations & Theses Global, https://about.proquest.com/products-services/pqdtglobal.html.
ProQuest Ebook Central, https://about.proquest.com/products-services/ebooks/ebooks-main.html.
Suffolk Heritage Explorer, https://heritage.suffolk.gov.uk/hlc.

INDEX

A Common-wealth of Good Counsaile 58, 131n26
Advancement of Learning, The 41
Advertisements for the Unexperienced Planters of New England 70
Agricultural Revolution 8, 74
Alison Games 2, 3
Allen, David Grayson 53, 79
  analysis of Ipswich 53
  list of Ipswich residents 54
  study of surviving land deeds of early Ipswich 76
  theory of the commodification of land 53
Andover settlers 91
Anglian cloth industry, depression in 27
Anglo-American democratic institutions 3
Annalls of Ipswche 5
Antinomian Controversy 60
Arbella 51
Aristotelian distributive justice 45, 46, 57, 86
Aristotelian concept of natural sociability 38
A Survey of the Summe of Church-Discipline 23

"betterment migrants," 12
"body politique," 41
Bacon, Francis 13, 26, 41, 43
Bacon, Nicholas 5, 26, 42
Baconian Instauration 44
Barnardiston, Nathaniel 40
Berwick-upon-Tweed 35
Black, Robert C. 55
Book of Orders 27, 30
Boston congregation 94
Boxford 80, 84, 85, 88
Bradford 80, 81, 84, 85, 88
Bradstreet, Anne 44, 61, 92
Bradstreet, Simon 61, 71, 84, 88, 89, 92
Braintree 13, 19, 22, 24, 27, 28, 30, 39, 40, 45
Breviary of Suffolk 8

"Christs Academy," 42
"College of the Six Day's Works," 42
"Company of the Four and Twenty," 24, 39

"Companyes," 85
"Cow pasture," 71
Chantries Act of 1547 37, 38
Christian Oeconomie 57
Church of England 18, 22, 23, 24, 31, 51
Clare 40
cloth trade depression (1622–23) 29
Collins, Samuel 13, 24, 39
Collinson, Patrick 18, 33
commercial sheep farming 61
commons 8, 9, 66, 71, 72–75, 87
confraternities 34, 36–38
Corona virtutum moralium 57
corporate boroughs 36
corporatism 33, 35, 41, 46, 47, 50, 51, 57, 59, 82, 91, 97, 99–101, 104
  future of 97–104
  idiom of 50
Corpus Christi 36, 37, 41
crisis of 1629–31 28
Crouch, David 37

Danger of Desertion, The 22, 23, 48
De optimo Senatore, English translation of 57
De Regno Christi 25, 46
Dedham 6, 10, 11, 12, 14–16, 18–20, 22, 23, 31, 38, 40, 47
Digest 34, 46
Discolliminium 52
Dividing the Land 54
Doctrine of Faith 22
Dorchester Corporation 38
Dudley, Thomas 1, 2, 44, 48, 49, 51, 61
Duffy, Eamon 36

"English corn," 65
"Epistle Dedicatorie," 57
Elizabethan poor laws 14, 28, 33, 39
Essex Justices 26, 28, 29

"Feoffees for the Purchase of Impropriations," 38
"Forced Loan," 11

INDEX

Faithful Covenanter, The 22, 23
Farmers and Fishermen 74
fiue Raile fence 86, 87
food riots between 1586 and 1631 28

"Gods ordinances," 24, 48
"good Ynglish hay," 75
Giddings v. Brown case 69
Great Instauration 13, 42
Great Migration 1, 3, 11, 33, 97
Gunpowder Plot 5

"Humble Request," 51
Hadleigh 39
Hankins, Jeffrey 38
Harrison, Peter 42, 44
Hatfield Broad Oak priory 8
Haverhill's settlement 96
Henreckson, David P. 59
Hindle, Steve 28, 33
historic landscape 9, 61, 81
Hooker, Thomas 1, 2, 47, 48
Hosford, W. H. 61
House of Commons 36, 41, 98
Hypocrisie Unmasked 79

Iethro's Iustice of Peace 41, 68
In English Ways 53, 54
Interregnum 36
Ipswich
  Daniel Denison in 73
  founder of 65
  land distribution in 64
  land patterns of 53
  records of 63
  Thomas Clark in 60
  Thomas Dudley in 44

James, Mervyn 37
Jethro scheme 45, 46
John Rogers of Dedham 1, 14, 15, 22, 31, 47

King, John 39
Konig, David Thomas 36, 77
Kramer, Stella 35

"lammas lands," 7, 10
land use 6, 10, 53, 54, 61, 62, 64, 66, 70, 77, 79, 85, 91, 96
Laws and Liberties of Massachusetts 77
Leach, Avril 38

Lee, Hwa-Yong 35
Lombard League 35

Magnalia Christi Americana 88
maior et sanior pars 35, 49, 58
Massachusetts Bay Company 36, 47, 51, 52, 102
Massachusetts General Court 45, 47, 54, 64, 81
McIntosh, Marjorie Keniston 38
McRee, Ben 38
mixed farming 3, 53, 103

New Atlantis 42
New England 1–6, 10, 21, 22, 25, 33, 34, 36, 40, 41, 44, 45, 49, 50, 52–55, 63, 65, 67, 70–76, 79, 82, 86, 92, 93, 95–103
Newbury 3, 60, 62, 76, 77, 79, 82, 85, 89, 95, 96
Nicomachean Ethics 57
Noyes, James 79, 80

"Oeconomicall subiection," 57
Of Corporations, Fraternities, and Guilds 36
Old Testament 42
Owen, John 36

"paraliturgical" dimension 37
"patriarchalism," 91
"Practical Catechisme," 57
"proborum hominum," 35
Parker, Thomas 54, 55, 62, 63, 79, 80
Peace of Constance 35
Peoples of a Spacious Land 54
Pickering, Thomas 57
Planters Plea, The 51
Powell, Sumner 53
Protestant scholasticism 4, 5, 10, 38, 41, 58, 66, 70, 79, 94, 96
Presbyterian movement 17, 19
prisca theologia 42, 44
Profits in the Wilderness 55, 86
Protestant scholasticism 4, 5, 10, 38, 66, 70, 79, 96
Puritan
  settlers of New England 49
  villages of the Stour Valley 11

Reformation Parliament 17
Rogers, Ezekiel 1, 4, 6, 47, 80, 84–88, 92
Rogers, Nathaniel 2, 6, 25, 28, 46, 87, 92
Rogers, Richard 1, 4, 6, 9, 16, 19, 20, 24, 26, 47
Roman civil law 46, 177

Roman law of corporations 34, 35, 46
Rosser, Gervase 34, 35, 37, 40
Rowley 3, 6, 76, 77, 80–94

"sacral corporatism of the Reformation era," 46
"Society of Salomon's House," 42
"subsistence migrants," 12–14
Salomon 43
Saybrook Colony 55
Seauen Treatises 24
Sheppard, William 36, 39
Short Story of the Rise, reign, and ruine of the Antinomians, Familists & Libertines 50
Simple Cobler of Aggawam, The 4, 59, 70, 97, 98
social hierarchy 25, 39, 57, 67, 69, 70, 79, 86
Spanish Armada in 1588, destruction of 5
St. George, religious gild of 37
Surveyor's Dialogue 77
sustainability 63, 70, 99
Swallowfield 33, 34, 35

"town studies," 53, 70
The Immortal Commonwealth 59

Thomas, Samuel L. 35
Treatise of Love 14, 20
Turner, Henry S. 34, 37
two kingdoms theory 17, 19

"The Vanity of All Worldly Things," 44
Via Lucis 42, 44
Vindiciae contra tyrannos 57, 58

wandering Jacobites 49
Ward, Nathaniel 1–6, 9, 10, 14, 22, 28, 40, 42, 48, 49, 51, 52, 54–57, 59, 62, 63, 67, 68, 70, 73, 80, 83, 84, 86, 88, 90, 92, 97, 102
Ward, Samuel 5, 25, 31, 32, 37, 40, 41, 45, 46, 68
White, John 13, 51, 61
Whole Treatise of the Cases of Conscience 25
Winthrop, John 2, 14, 22, 29, 31, 40, 44, 47, 50, 54, 55, 56, 57, 60, 61, 62, 64, 67–69, 73, 79, 82, 88, 92, 99
theory of discretion 48
Withington, Phil 38
Wonder-Working Providence 49

www.ingramcontent.com/pod-product-compliance
Lightning Source LLC
Chambersburg PA
CBHW021142230426
43667CB00005B/220